Telling Time

STUART SHERMAN

Telling Time

CLOCKS,

DIARIES,

AND ENGLISH

DIURNAL FORM,

1660–1785

The University of Chicago Press   Chicago & London

STUART SHERMAN is associate professor of English at Washington University, St. Louis.

The University of Chicago Press, Chicago 60637
The University of Chicago Press, Ltd., London
© 1996 by The University of Chicago
All rights reserved. Published 1996
Printed in the United States of America
05 04 03 02 01 00 99 98 97 96   1 2 3 4 5

ISBN (cloth): 0-226-75276-3
ISBN (paper): 0-226-75277-1

Library of Congress Cataloging-in-Publication Data

Stuart, Sherman, 1953–
    Telling time : clocks, diaries, and English diurnal form,
    1660–1785 / Stuart Sherman.
        p.   cm.
    Includes index.
    ISBN 0-226-75276-3 (alk. paper). — ISBN 0-226-75277-1 (pbk. :
alk. paper)
    1. English prose literature—Early modern, 1500–1700—History and
criticism.   2. English prose literature—18th century—History and
criticism.   3. Travelers' writings, English—History and criticism.
4. Literature and technology—England—History.   5. Literature and
society—England—History.   6. English diaries—History and
criticism.   7. Clocks and watches—England—History.   8. Journalism—
England—History.   9. Time measurements—History.   10. Time in
literature.   11. Literary form.   I. Title.
PR769.S78   1996
828'.08—dc20   96-8533
                                                                CIP

Photograph of the John Shaw, Holborn, circa 1705 watch courtesy Camerer
Cuss, *The Camerer Cuss Book of Antique Watches,* Antique Collectors' Club, Ltd.

∞ The paper used in this publication meets the minimum requirements of
the American National Standard for Information Sciences—Permanence of
Paper for Printed Library Materials, ANSI Z39.48-1984.

for

Gordon   *Corinne*

Sharman

Benjamin Gordon   *Corin Mischa*

Contents

P r e f a c e

Clocks tell time, narratives tell what transpires in time. *Telling Time* traces the relations between the two in a place and period critical to the development of both clocks and narrative, England from the mid-seventeenth through the late eighteenth centuries.

Clocks tell time in ways more various than the familiar phrase might at first suggest, ways embedded in its etymologies. First, clocks *count* time (OE *tellan*, to narrate, is cognate with Middle Low German *tellen*, to count, reckon), or rather, they make it available for human counting by translating duration into number according to the system of timekeeping current in the culture. The earliest mechanical clocks did so audibly, striking the hour on a bell. The instruments then most familiar, sundial and astrolabe, addressed the eye rather than the ear, and the English name for the new timekeepers, from Flemish *klok*, bell, made a point of the distinction; such clocks, without dials, hands, or numerals, told time solely by sounding it—in fact, by tolling it. The two verbs, similarly formed but etymologically distinct (*toll* derives from an obscure OE root, *tyllan*, "to pull"—in this application, the bell-rope), converged by the fifteenth century to represent the new experience of time's report, one denoting the physical actions and sensations involved (the pulling of the rope and, by association, the ringing of the bell) and the other the acts of intelligence (of counting, of informing) on the part of the human agents: clockmaker, ringer, auditor.[1] While the bell tolled time, both clock and listener told it.

Clocks, like all chronometers, tell time another way as well. They articulate its meanings in and for the culture that produces them. By virtue of its impalpability, time is peculiarly susceptible of cultural construction. Every report—every means of making time present—will also entail an interpretation. Every clock proposes a temporality—a way of conceiving time, using it, inhabiting it— by its look and sound, its modes of motion and of definition, its placement and its purpose, within a culture composed of multiple temporalities operating separately and simultaneously. As a historian of chronometry has recently remarked, it makes sense to speak not of a culture's "time" but only of its several "times," precisely distinguished and carefully related, in their conflicts, their alignments, their convergences.[2]

Narratives tell time too, but with a difference. The fusion of "counting" and "narrating" in the etymology of *tell* apparently derives from the importance of sequence in both processes; OE *tellen* signified particularly "to *tell in order*." In order to make themselves intelligible, narratives specify sequence almost always; durations often; dates, hours, and other "numbers of time" more selectively. Where clocks count time, narratives *re*count it, and the repetition may take place at many removes, and over many spans. Given the gulf between language and experience, the duration of story will rarely (if ever) match the duration of event. Narrative possesses a temporal elasticity, a freedom from concurrency with "real" time, and even from chronological sequence, that runs counter to the whole purpose of chronometry. A story will not, by and large, work well as a clock. Yet narratives, like clocks, tell time in the larger sense of articulating its local forms and meanings, making them available to eye, ear, and mind. A given narrative will inevitably, by the particulars of its form, absorb and register some of the temporalities at work in the world that surrounds its making, and having configured them in language and in structure, will offer its temporality back as a new or newly combined enactment of current time-consciousness. What Bakhtin argues specifically for the novel holds true with respect to time for all kinds of narrative. Time in narrative is *always* "dialogic." The telling will always entail an encounter between at least two temporalities: between narrative's deployment of its special temporal properties and privileges (elasticities of language) on the one hand, and on the other the time (duration, sequence) of the events narrated. But usually it will orchestrate something far more complex. It will offer by its form a reading of, and a contribution to, the workings of time in the culture.

In *Telling Time* I track such readings, contributions, and workings in what I argue was a culturally critical encounter between a chronometry and a prose structure both new in the mid-seventeenth century. In England during the 1660s, a new technology for counting time on clocks emerged simultaneously with a new paradigm for recounting it in prose. In both timekeepers and texts, the new temporality dealt in small durations closely tracked. The new kind of clock could, for the first time, count minutes reliably. The new pattern of prose numbered the days. It represented itself as accumulating by consecutively dated daily installments. In England this diurnal design appears first in the manuscript diary and then, four decades later, in the daily newspaper. Over the ensuing century and a half, closely calibrated clocks and calendrically successive texts gradually came to govern time consciousness and social practice. By the end of the eighteenth century the data of the minute hand had grown both familiar and effectual, structuring work and days. Diurnal form too had established something like omnipresence; it structured some of the most innovative, widely implemented prose genres that the period produced: not only diary and newspaper, but also periodical essay, journal-letter, and travel book. All these genres, I argue, deployed diurnal form as a means of enabling authors to write the time the new clocks told, and enabling readers to recognize, interpret, and inhabit the temporality by which the whole culture was learning to live and work. Writers in these genres, however diverse their other purposes and designs, were deeply concerned with the figuration of—and response to—a new kind of time.

My book takes up many texts, but structures itself around four: Samuel Pepys's diary, Joseph Addison's and Richard Steele's *Spectator*, Samuel Johnson's *Journey to the Western Islands of Scotland*, and James Boswell's *Journal of a Tour to the Hebrides*. This sequence, I suggest, maps the main route by which the new-timed texts approach cultural dominion. Pepys, I argue, devised a new diurnal template in manuscript for the tracking of time and self; Addison and Steele were the first to take the template into print; and at the end of the century in which diurnal form had taken hold amid considerable wariness and opposition, Johnson and Boswell debated its uses and implications, in ways that manifested not only their own ambivalence but also that of the culture they inhabited.

The list announces limits as well as scope. These works are non-fiction written by men who for long stretches of their lives occupied positions near centers of power, Pepys as naval administrator, Steele as Gazetteer, Addison as high placed Secretary, Johnson as Great Cham, Boswell as lawyer and laird. For the purposes of my argument, their canonicity—their literary power—matters too. Pepys's proximity to power enables him both to apprehend important implications of the new chronometry very early and to work out a corresponding structure in text; his canonicity is in part a re-sponse to his temporal innovation. Steele's access to breaking news and Ad-dison's political-literary eminence facilitated careers that (in the pages of the *Spectator*) established diurnal form as an unprecedented public attraction and a permanent feature of the century's social and temporal consciousness. Johnson's position as arbiter of letters, and Boswell's as his assiduous (some said frantic) amanuensis and portrayer, rendered their policies and practices of textual temporality particularly consequential among readers.

The two earlier texts have long awaited close critical scrutiny of any kind. By bringing them into conjunction with each other and with questions of chronometry and temporality, I have hoped to make strong sense of them, and to show how they make new sense of the two more-canvassed later texts as well.

In my attention to these tasks I have scanted others. Two crucial stories go untold here: of women and diurnal form, and of the novel's temporality. In a concluding chapter on Defoe and Burney I try to pursue the issues I have raised into these two adjacent territories. But in the making of this book I have discovered that these stories need books of their own.

A c k n o w l e d g m e n t s

This book on time has taken time, and profited from many kindnesses. I wish to thank three organizations, each for the gift of a year in which to do the work: the Mrs. Giles B. Whiting Foundation; the American Council of Learned Societies; the Chicago Humanities Institute.

At Columbia, John H. Middendorf ushered me into eighteenth-century studies in a memorable seminar; by his example and his friendship, he showed me the satisfactions to be gained from inhabiting that world. Michael Seidel kept me there entranced, guiding me through the dissertation and into the profession with the mix of vast knowledge, shrewd sense, and antic spirit that continues to delight and instruct me whenever we re-meet.

Friends and colleagues read and reread part or all of the manuscript, with a keen eye to the welfare of the work and its author: Wayne Booth, Margaret Anne Doody, Stephen Collins, Joanna Gondris, Janice Knight, Gwin Kolb, Christopher Looby, Janel Mueller, Matt Neuburg, Julie Stone Peters, Christina Root, Edward Rosenheim, Larry Rothfield, Lisa Ruddick, Edward Tayler, Cynthia Wall, Howard Weinbrot, and Robert Zimmer. John Bender's and Patricia Meyer Spacks's readings for the Press proved critical in two senses of the word, acute and crucial; they deftly launched the project into its second phase. J. Paul Hunter and Joshua Scodel worked through the entire text at several stages, enhancing my sense of direction and possibility with every reading. Richard Strier and William Veeder, cherished teachers long ago and colleagues now, willingly became my teachers again, to the benefit of the book and the pleasure of their pupil.

From the students in my courses on diaries and on documentary prose I learned as much as I taught; they made both activities a pleasure. The assembling and verifying of corroborative detail became easier through the inspired assistance of Conrad Curtis, Paula Schiller, Will Pritchard, and Paige Reynolds. I am grateful to them not only for the information they gathered, but for the cheerfulness with which they secured and delivered it; they made the work exhilaratingly communal.

Bruce Redford and David Damrosch brought this sense of shared endeavor to its highest perfection. Over the years they performed a series of remarkable rescue missions, reading new matter at a moment's notice, providing needed counsel at just the right juncture. All these interventions took generosity and intelligence; some took bravery too. From both friends I learned more about crafting a book than I'd known there was to know. I shall treasure the knowledge, and the memory of its acquisition, all my life.

The University of Chicago Press provided me with the help of extraordinarily talented people. Randy Petilos and Carol Saller oversaw logistics and Gayle Ormand Boyer performed the copy-editing, all with a mesmeric combination of patience and precision. I used to think that it was the author who made the book, but my editor Alan Thomas's wholehearted and creative involvement with this one has convinced me otherwise; by the brilliance of his tactics and the bounty of his tact, he brings the elusive epithet "only begetter" irresistibly to mind. "What Is an Editor?" asks the title of a book about one of the great ones (Saxe Commins). I may no longer need that book; for me the title's answer is compacted in a luminous proper name.

Others made the work possible without reading a word of it, simply by helping me to be happy as it progressed: Leslie Adelstein, Robert Alpert, Albert Berenberg, John Gedo, Ingrid Goodman, Mary, Jack, and Roberta Jaffe, Fred Levin, Jamie Little Ruhl, Bette Lou Seidner, Bernard, Lillian, and Sheldon Stein, Sarita Warshawsky; and my brothers Loren, Jeremy, and Robert Sherman.

For the five named in the dedication, the sweetness is too much to speak. My parents took pleasure in the book's beginnings, my children surrounded its completion with voluble distraction and delight, but the dates of deaths and births prevented the generations from ever meeting and embracing. At times the book-work itself seemed to serve as precarious surrogate for disrupted continuities. My wife Sharman has built for us a better bridge. From our first meeting (5 : 30 p.m. EDT, 19 June 1984) I date the start of many things, in work as well as love; by her bright advent, she showed me how the two might mesh. She has eased me through loss and guided me to gain with strength and tenderness; in her I find the blessings of the other four combined. Darlings all, you've taught me what time is for.

Christiaan Huygens's pendulum regulator, in one of the earliest clocks to incorporate the technology (1657). The numbers along the dial's outer ring register the instrument's new precision. The spring that powers this small clock, from the cylinder at the panel's center, makes possible a certain miniaturization. The more conventional weight-driven timepieces—dubbed "grandfather clocks" two centuries later—stood six to eight feet tall. In 1675, by using springs to regulate as well as drive the clockwork, and hence to fulfill the pendulum's function in a very small space, Huygens and others produced the first timekeepers to combine precision, privacy, and easy portability: pocket watches capable of counting the minutes. Photograph courtesy of the Time Museum, Rockford, Illinois.

Telling Time

Tick, Tick, Tick:

Chronometric Innovation and Prose Form

*I*n his well-known essay on "Time, Work-Discipline and Industrial Capitalism," E. P. Thompson coins a telling phrase to pinpoint his elusive topic. He says he writes to trace "changes in the inward notation of time."[1] He knows that he can recover these experiential phenomena only by looking at outward notations, in clocks and documents. In the first section of this chapter I identify important seventeenth-century changes in outward notation, in the mechanisms of clocks and on their dials, in English vocabulary and prose structure. In the second section I suggest why the modes of temporal notation embodied in diurnal form have been overlooked, and how a study of them can be useful.

CLOCK SOUNDS

In 1680 John Aubrey, writing up his "Minutes" for the life of the astrologer and mathematician Thomas Allen (1542–1632), set down a story about Allen's watch:

> One time being at Hom Lacy in Herefordshire, at Mr. John Scudamore's, he happened to leave his watch in the chamber windowe—(watches were then rarities)—The maydes came in to make the bed, and hearing a thing in a case cry *Tick, Tick, Tick*, presently concluded that it was his Devill. . . .[2]

Tick, Tick, Tick: etymologically, the onomatopoeia qualifies as neologism; horologically, as anachronism. The *OED* cites this passage as the earliest known appearance of a usage now long familiar, one in which the mimicry of the watch's sound draws on an older, substantive sense. The noun "tick" had denoted, since at least 1440, "a light but distinct touch; a light quick stroke." In an act of retrospective narrative imagination, Aubrey hears such a sound in Allen's watch.

Or rather, he projects it. The maids at Holm Lacy more than fifty years earlier would almost certainly not have used Aubrey's means to represent the "cry" of the "thing in a case," even had they understood exactly what that thing was. Writers of the early seventeenth century put a very different construction on the clockwork's pulse, deeming it not a "tick" but a "jar"—a "harsh inharmonious sound." Early in *The Winter's Tale*, Shakespeare's Hermione avows that she loves her husband not "a jar o' th' clock behind / What lady she her lord," [3] and the word's association with clocks and watches lasts (in the written record) until just before the middle of the seventeenth century.[4]

The shift in wording parallels a real change in referent. In 1656 Christiaan Huygens, by the single, decisive innovation of attaching a pendulum regulator to the back of the clockwork, changed much in the precision with which clocks measured time, and in the signs by which they reported it to eye, ear, and intellect. It is impossible to ascertain exactly when *Tick, Tick, Tick* entered English, and so to collate precisely horological reality with linguistic representation. By the time Aubrey uses the phrase, though, it appears to register two linked but distinct constructions of the sound of Huygensian chronometry: as sensation and as pattern. The audible novelty in the pattern almost certainly preceded that in the sound by about two decades. Huygens's innovation could not at first have changed very much the individual sounds, produced one after another by the running clockwork, because it left the clock's escapement, the mechanism that made the sound, essentially intact. Later, the anchor escapement and the balance spring, refinements engineered by Huygens and by technicians in England working under his influence, did combine to produce the lighter, more distinct touch that "tick" (in contrast with "jar") suggests. These took place in the mid-1670s, just a few years before Aubrey wrote his notes on Allen.

Something else in Aubrey's phrasing, though, goes directly to the core of Huygens's initial accomplishment, and of everything in horology that followed from it. What is most telling about *Tick, Tick, Tick* is not so much the change in diction as the pattern of iteration. Here the language that mimics the timepiece conspicuously *takes* time, and patterns it in such a way as to insist that what is the most salient feature of the clock's report is not simply the single sound but the running sequence. Aubrey's phrase represents the clock's report not as a startlingly individuated instant ("a jar o' th' clock") but as a succession of small, identical impulses that define (by inference) a succession of small, identical intervals. The phrase performs compactly what was in fact newest about Huygensian time: its capacity to track and report newly small durations—minutes, seconds—in regular, perceptible, continuous succession. It proposes as language a temporality to match the one the pendulum clock propounds as sound: time as steady series.

In fact, *Tick, Tick, Tick* enacts in language the principle of physics by which Huygens revolutionized timekeeping: isochronicity. The mechanical clock depends on three essential components in order to translate time's impalpable passage into a succession of regular motions. First, it needs a source of energy to start and sustain movement; second, a brake-and-release mechanism to parcel out the energy into a succession of small motions by a rapidly repeated series of starts and stops; third, a regulating device to assure that the stops and starts occur at even intervals. Over the first four centuries of clockmaking these components most commonly took these forms: the energy was supplied from a slowly falling weight attached to a cord coiled around a drum; the weight turned the clockwork as it fell. Its descent was slowed and regulated by a "verge escapement," a stop-start device consisting of a toothed wheel alternately checked and released by a pair of small brakes, and a "foliot" regulator, an oscillating bar bearing weights at both ends, which controlled the motion and the impact of the brake pads and so ensured that the wheel moved and stopped (actually recoiled slightly, turning momentarily the other way) at small regular intervals.

At least that was the intention. In reality, the foliot regulator made its limitations conspicuous in every clock it governed. Technicians gradually recognized that the regulator ought ideally to possess an intrinsic constancy of motion in itself, ought to move isochronically, taking exactly the same time (Gr. *iso chronos*) to complete the same motion, time after time. Clockmakers understood isochronicity as a desideratum in theory, but did not know how to put it into practice. The weights suspended on the foliot regulator could be moved in such a way as to change the interval of the brakes' operation—and often had to be, because the device possessed no isochronicity of its own. Indeed the motion of the regulator was so enmeshed with that of the rest of the clockwork that, while it ostensibly dictated the tempo of the clockwork's pulse, it also took dictation from the movement it purported to govern. Such a design proved too reflexive to work well. Even the best-maintained clocks built on these principles could not track the hours reliably, gaining or losing fifteen minutes a day. According to one expert but hardly disinterested witness, such timepieces declared their limitations audibly over much smaller spans. "I never yet heard a clock or watch," wrote Robert Hooke, Fellow of the Royal Society, and Huygens's most emulous rival for horological attainment, "whose ballance [i.e., regulator] did not very sensibly beat very vnequally." [5]

In 1637, Galileo envisioned a solution to the problem. He discovered a source of isochronism governed and guaranteed by physical law: a pendulum of given length and weight, once set in motion, will complete every successive swing in precisely the same period, even if the arc of the swing should narrow or widen. Huygens, linking this intrinsically isochronous instrument to the clockwork (a project Galileo had envisioned but perhaps never actualized), immediately imparted to the machinery a new accuracy and a new auditory impact. The first clocks built to his designs lost only fifteen seconds a day, and rendered isochronism audible by a newly steady sound. Even Hooke grudgingly conceded that Huygens's pendulum "performes very much. . . . [A]s to sense [i.e., as far as sense can detect] his Pendulum seems to vibrate in equall time." [6] Under the regulation of the foliot, the clock's pulsation (the sound of the small brakes alternately stopping the wheelteeth) had come, in effect, singly: nothing but mechanical contingency made predictable the intervals at which the pulses would follow one another. The pendulum imported a regularity underwritten by a law of nature. Hence, perhaps, the shift in English wording, from a singular noun for the isolate sensation, to a serial, isochronous onomatopoeia.

The clock's new sound-series did more than announce an epochal innovation in technology. It made available to sense and thought a new experience of time as it passed; it proffered a new and concrete means for coming to grips with an old elusive mystery. Where church bells and clock towers had for centuries tolled time intermittently and at a distance, Huygens's clocks, ticking steadily, translated time into a sound both constant and contiguous. For the tiny, persistent increments that the ear could newly hear, the eye found numerous equivalents on the dial-plate. Before the advent of the pendulum, the vast majority of timepieces sported only a single hand, delegated to mark the hour. Their technology, too limited to deal in finer distinctions, was hard-pressed to keep pace even with this one. The earliest pendulum clocks, by contrast, bore an added hand to tell the minutes, now marked and numbered along the dial's outer edge. By 1670, a third hand had begun to appear on the most costly clocks; set within a small dial of its own, it tracked the seconds, spans so small as to elude all notice only a few years before. Such clocks delivered the data of passing time unceasingly to both sight and hearing at once: with every swing of the pendulum, the ear hears the clock click and the eye sees the hand move. Technically, Huygens accomplished simply a change in scale, a sixtyfold improvement in accuracy (precisely the proportion of the old hours to the new minutes, and of the newly measured minutes to the newly measured seconds). From the vantage of the senses, though, the change in scale amounted virtually to a change in kind: the new clocks were the first to make the *progress* of time available to the senses by way of a running report. As a form of language *Tick, Tick, Tick* provides an emblem for a new construction of time as series within series, concentric and cumulative, beginning with the small intervals clicked out at the clock's core, and radiating outward to the markings on the dial, to encompass a whole system of measurement and calibration: ticks, seconds, minutes, hours, and (on calendrical clocks) days and years as well.

Tick, Tick, Tick registers the impact of a new chronometry. If a phrase can do so much, then narrative can do more, and more intricately. For one thing, it can place chronometries and temporalities within a culture and a history, as Aubrey does compactly here in looking back over the century that had engineered the most emphatic changes in the whole history of time measurement. "Watches were then rarities" he remarks, parenthetically and accurately, by way of setting up and explaining the maids' misapprehension. The maids undoubtedly know the sounds of time on church bells and house clocks, but since they know of no chronometry more portable they find nothing familiar about the "thing in a case," and construe it under an entirely separate system of surmise: they already regard Allen as a black magician, and so reckon this instrument to be his "Devill." "In those darke times," Aubrey has explained by way of preamble, "astrologer, mathematician, and conjurer, were accounted the same things" (1.27). Aubrey expects his own audience to draw the implied distinctions, and so to recognize in the watch a sign of "darke times" past and of the present distance from them. Allen is intimate with time and numbers; he bears a seemingly animate instrument of their convergence on his very person. In a world where watches are rarities the maids don't know what to make of it; the reader (presumably) does. Times, with regard to timepieces, have certainly changed, and the watch offers a touchstone for a distribution of knowledge-as-power over meshed hierarchies of rank (impressive houseguest, comic servants), of gender (educated men, ignorant women), and even of historical time (horologically sophisticated readers, their more benighted forebears).

Since in Aubrey's manuscript *Tick, Tick, Tick* is also an anachronism, it provides a second kind of socio-horological datum as well. It gauges to some extent the capacity of the new chronometry, with its attendant experiences and language, to "naturalize" itself—to get itself taken for granted as something perpetual, to slip in below the radar of consciousness even in a knowing, careful scientist and historian. At the time that Aubrey wrote, the steadiness that the phrase figures was only two decades old on standing clocks and *very* new on watches (Huygens had succeeded in "miniaturizing" his technology only five years earlier). Yet Aubrey, though alert to the change in the *distribution* of timepieces ("watches were then rarities"), forgets for the moment the decisive change in their *operation*. He projects new time far backward across the Huygensian horological divide. Evidently the sound of the new clocks conveyed something so compelling, so capable of eclipsing earlier impressions, as to lead even an accomplished antiquarian into anachronism, to cause him to forget how clocks and language had made time sound for more than half his life.[7] Aubrey tells a story, in effect, of two watches, not of one; by transposing the newer temporality onto the older timepiece, he inadvertently indexes the new chronometry's increasing eminence.

It may be well here to clarify two terms already in play. The timepiece makes available a new *chronometry*, a means for measuring time. *Tick, Tick, Tick*, translating sound to language, encapsulates a *temporality*, a way of reckoning time that includes but goes beyond counting, a way of conceiving it and experiencing it. Chronometry inheres in the clock. Temporality may suffuse other components of the culture, notably its narratives. What happens in Aubrey as a slippage of fact will happen often in narrative as a condition of form: the form will absorb, manifest, and respond to local temporalities, contemporary shapes of time, without necessarily "knowing" that it does so.

Such absorption can occur in narrative theory too, and so limit the theory's capacity to contextualize temporalities produced in cultures other than its own. Something like this happens in Frank Kermode's graceful, influential series of narratological lectures, *The Sense of an Ending*. Seeking to understand the "sense-making paradigms, relative to time," that humans deploy in life and narrative, Kermode takes as "a very simple example" the sound of a clock—a sound notably different from the one "heard" by Aubrey and his century.

> We ask what [a clock] *says*: and we agree that it says *tick-tock*. By this fiction we humanize it, make it talk our language. Of course, it is we who provide the fictional difference between the two sounds; *tick* is our word for a physical beginning, *tock* our word for an end. We say they differ.[8]

Kermode rightly emphasizes the inherent fictiveness of the differentiation, but he quickly embraces it as a necessary or inevitable fiction, founded in automatic human response; our propensity to organize clock sound this way has been "shown by experiment," in the work of cognitive psychologists like Paul Fraisse. *Tock*, for Kermode, is the crucial term; it grounds his central narratological claim. Not only does it conveniently miniaturize the "sense of an ending," but it also suggests, as the means by which we make clocks "talk our language," that our need for that "sense" is intrinsic to us, and governs narratives:

> The fact that we call the second of the two related sounds *tock* is evidence that we use fictions to enable the end to confer organization and form on temporal structure. The interval between . . . *tick* and *tock* is . . . charged with significant duration. The clock's *tick-tock* I take to be a model of what we call a plot, an organization that humanizes time by giving it form; and the interval between *tock* and *tick* represents purely successive, disorganized time of the sort that we need to humanize. . . . *Tick* is a humble genesis, *tock* a feeble apocalypse. . . . (Kermode 45)

What is arresting in Kermode's argument is the consistency of the pattern, the neatness of the fit, among varied phenomena on different scales: an instantaneous cognitive response (*tick-tock*), a millennial scriptural paradigm (genesis/apocalypse), a pervasive human activity (shaping plots). In Kermode's reckoning, all these name ways—all name essentially the same way—in which "we humanize" time.

Yet for all the attractiveness of its conflations, the argument starts from a faulty assumption. Kermode takes *tick-tock* for granted as the way "we" make clocks "talk our language"; he does not take account of historical specificity of the phrasing.[9] The *OED* cites its earliest appearance in 1848 (in Thackeray's *Vanity Fair*). In English "we" have been hearing clock time in this way for only a hundred and fifty years. What Kermode says "can be shown by experiment" can be at least partly disproved by text. Aubrey and others attest that they and their contemporaries heard another structure of time in the sound of the clock.[10] *Tick, Tick, Tick*, responsive to a historical moment when the clock actually changed its way of operating, propounds not a "fictional difference" but a "fictional sameness" (fictional because no successive impulses of the clock's escapement will actually sound identical). Technology prompted and underwrote the fiction by enhancing the perceptible "sameness" of chronometric units many times over. The wider culture may initially have encouraged the fiction by a kind of indirection: in a world long suffused, through its sacred texts and its earlier clocks, with the broad, enclosed time of genesis and apocalypse, a temporality of smallness and sameness occurred as an arresting innovation. *Tick, Tick, Tick*, poised between "genesis/apocalypse" in one historical direction and "tick-tock" in the other, differs from both in roughly the same way. As Aubrey's "error" indicates, by 1680 this figuration of time had already begun a cultural ascent, a widespread concurrency of mind. A temporality so constructed, and so increasingly dominant, might plausibly open up the possibility for a narrative different in kind from Kermode's "plot," one in which durations regularly marked and transmuted into language accumulate in an unbroken, potentially open-ended series.

Over the century that follows the importation of Huygens's pendulum, England produces an unprecedented spate of texts that work this way in time. During the Restoration and after, the temporality of *Tick, Tick, Tick* recognizably presides over remarkable developments in both chronometry and narrative. London, not notable for its clockmaking before, had become by 1680 the horological center of Europe by virtue of its immediate adaptation and enhancement of Huygens's inventions.[11] By advancing the technology, it began to achieve that dominion over planetary timekeeping which still obtains in the institution of Greenwich Mean Time. In the eighteenth century the search for a chronometric navigational tool for reckoning longitude triggered a nationwide desire for a *Tick, Tick, Tick* ever lighter, more distinct, more uniform in both its pulse and its intervals. Concurrent with this quest, textual practices developed along parallel lines. The production of new installments at regular daily intervals became a common, even a determining feature in several genres: diaries, periodicals, daily newspapers, diurnal essays. This new, pervasive textual timing served (I shall argue) a particular purpose: a continuous self-construction, a running report on identities both shifting and fixed, private and public. The serial and closely calibrated temporality that became a widespread preoccupation on clocks and watches became concurrently a widespread practice in prose written, distributed, and read over steady, small increments of real time. The horologic and textual forms for which *Tick, Tick, Tick* figures a crucial principal of organization served as instruments not only of keeping time but of making and recognizing selves—what Raymond Williams might call a structure of feeling about time.

There were, of course, differences in scale: Huygens's clocks deal systematically in the artificial units of minute and second, which the instruments themselves in effect create (none before them had actually "produced" minutes at all); diaries and daily newspapers operate systematically in the apparently natural unit of the day. This seeming discrepancy points to others, notably the fundamental differences between the ways clocks and texts figure time in the first place: clocks pursue a constant, running correspondence between numerical index and passing moment, whereas texts virtually always move away from the momentary towards permanence. The striking historical coincidence whereby England, over the course of the late seventeenth and eighteenth centuries, engineered massive, celebrated developments in both Huygensian time and narrative time-forms suggests a linkage without specifying one. Without more mediation, the parallel between chronometry and chonography risks figuring as that *fata morgana* of the lesser New Historicism, the under-argued juxtaposition, shimmering, suggestive, insubstantial. The claims need better blueprints, sounder carpentry. Such construction is the task of the chapters to follow.

TICK, TICK, TICK AND TICK-TOCK: HOROLOGY, NARRATOLOGY, HISTORY, AND DIURNAL FORM

The story of clocks and culture has been told often, and often well;[12] the story of clocks, diurnal forms, and self-constructions has only been touched on.[13] This second story has much to offer the first by way of completion and complication. On the current map drawn by students of time, that space where new instruments, new literary structures, and new subjectivities first converge remains remarkably underexplored. Several modes of inquiry operate along its borders: horological, intellectual, literary, and social history, as well as narrative theory, genre history, and criticism; still the site stays comparatively unmapped. I mean to fill it in. I do not think the blank is there by accident. It is rather the side effect of a rightly powerful paradigm concerning time and culture, at work in all the fields named, that favors "emptiness." Frank Kermode, E. P. Thompson, Michel Foucault, Benedict Anderson, and others have all argued that early modern Europe witnessed— indeed was brought into being by—a shift from what Walter Benjamin calls "Messianic time" to a culture-wide acceptance of "homogeneous, empty time."[14] This view explains many things, and the signs that warrant it are everywhere. But it has tended to discourage attention to the workings of those diurnal forms that emerged with the new mode of time and textualized it most closely. *Tick, Tick, Tick* figures both emptiness and fullness at once: it fills previously uncalibrated durations with a new and constant definition. Emphasis on the new temporal emptiness has limited our understanding of the new forms of fullness—the new rules for filling, the new criteria for completeness— that *Tick, Tick, Tick* entailed.

In narratology, the argument from emptiness may be said to begin with Kermode's clock sound. *Tick-tock*, he concedes, is "not much of a plot," but he develops from the onomatopoeia the key terms and main structure of his argument; it helps him to define, in effect, what forms of narrative are most worth looking at. The whole purpose of plotting, by Kermode's reckoning, is to combat the threat of empty time. Plot works

> to defeat the tendency of the interval between *tick* and *tock* to empty itself. . . . To put it another way, the interval must be purged of simple chronicity, of the emptiness of . . . humanly uninteresting successiveness. It is required to be a significant season, *kairos* poised between beginning and end. [Through plotting,] that which was conceived as simply successive becomes charged with past and future: what was *chronos* becomes *kairos*. (46)

With the shift from English onomatopoeia to ancient Greek, Kermode finishes laying the foundation for his argument. Theologians have discerned in the New Testament uses of *kairos* and *chronos* an "antithesis" absent in earlier cultures, between on the one hand a "moment of crisis," "a point in time filled with significance," and on the other "passing time," "simple chronicity," "one damn thing after another." *Kairos* is "filled," *chronos* "empty," and for the remainder of the book Kermode deploys this binary opposition in order to discern how narrative has filled a void of a different order, the one left by history. In the New Testament "the divine plot is the pattern of *kairoi* in relation to the End," but as the cultural certainty of that apocalypse has subsided, writers have contrived "many more fictional devices" calculated to sustain, over the course of long narratives, "a lively expectation of *tock*" even though the actual conclusion may lie far off. These devices "will be of essentially the same kind as calling the second . . . sound *tock*," and they will produce the same effect: they will represent the time narrated as "filled," as "charged with significant duration" (45–47).

Aubrey's series of *Ticks* without *Tocks* ought, by Kermode's logic, to produce *chronos* without *kairos*, but the phrase proffers both a historical and a conceptual critique of Kermode's argument. On the one hand, *Tick, Tick,* like Kermode's "chronicity," is "simple" (monadic rather than dyadic); it proffers no "sense of an ending" (only of open-endedness); purely as a form of language it does a fair job of rendering "humanly uninteresting successiveness"; it is literally "one damn thing after another"—though strictly speaking neither damned nor blessed, but (again like Kermode's *chronos*) simply secularized (46–47). On the other hand, Aubrey's phrase, like Kermode's *kairos*, forestalls the void and figures order: identical syllables vouch for identical durations, and leave no "gap" of the kind Kermode and Fraisse posit between *tock* and *tick*. Furthermore, Aubrey's anecdote makes clear how deeply "interesting" seventeenth-century persons found this new figure of the "simply successive": interesting enough to warrant a neologism, to prompt mystification (on the part of the maids, who do deem the sounds "damned"), and to become a preoccupation for the likes of Allen, Aubrey, and a widening community of the chronometry-conscious and the timepiece-proud over the ensuing two hundred years. *Tick, Tick, Tick* fills what were hitherto emptier and more shapeless tracts of time (minutes, quarters, hours) with steady, sharp definition. The Huygensian act of measurement that *Tick, Tick, Tick* represents—sheer *chrono*metry—performs some of the functions that Kermode reserves for *tock* and *kairos*; it organizes intervals and fills them (and hence perhaps charges them also), but in terms that privilege successiveness and resist closure.

The primacy of *Tock* in *The Sense of an Ending* forestalls attention to narrative forms developed under the alternate sign of *Tick*. Kermode's distinction "between mere chronicity and times which are discordant and full" limits the range of his narratology. *Kairos* "is the time of the novelist" (46) as well as of the New Testament, and of the poet and the playwright too, but not of the annalist, chronicler, or diarist (so the whole thrust of the argument, as well as the distribution of examples, suggests). The practitioners of these and other forms in which sheer, numbered-and-measured "successiveness" is so conspicuous a feature find no place in the narratological reckoning; the supposed antithesis between *kairos* and *chronos* rules them out.

As with clocks, so with narratives: the new diurnal forms of the seventeenth and eighteenth centuries—diaries, newspapers and related writings—occupy a paradigm of time and form undreamt of (or at least unattended to) in Kermode's narratology. And in Gérard Genette's, and Paul Ricoeur's. Kermode's commitment to *kairos* as he defines it has found analogues and exerted influences in the work of subsequent theorists. In his comprehensive syntactic taxonomy for narrative, Genette provides a useful way of describing how diurnal form operates in time, but to the form itself he devotes only a scant footnote, uncharacteristically imprecise.[15] Ricoeur appears to speak for many of his fellow narratologists when he denies to "chronography" the privileged fullness of "narrativity": beginning, middle, and ending; "historicalization"; and the "deep temporality" where "within-timeness" confronts eternity. For Ricoeur, chronography attains the conditions of "narrativity"—primarily the power to symbolize "structures of temporality"—in only the most rudimentary, proto-narrative way. But he underestimates the potency of the practice (indeed he examines no particular "chronographer"). The new diurnalists of the seventeenth and eighteenth centuries work quite intricately to "emplot" (Ricoeur's key verb) "structures of temporality" from the midst of their lives and writing, even within the confines of a single day's entry, which has its own beginning, middle, and end beaded along a continuous strand of such sequences. Such structures refute Ricoeur's assertion, at the outset of *Time and Narrative*, that chronography is "the true contrary" of "temporality itself";[16] instead it mirrors current "structures of temporality" with unusual clarity.[17] Diurnalists began "humanizing" time on a new pattern at just that juncture when a new time was made available to be so engaged—a time at once recognizably more human (the new, smaller clocks and watches were more "personal" than the old bells and towers) and more abstract (figured as numbered spaces rather than pictorial and programmatic "forms"). Chronography is chameleonic; it will inevitably take on the temporal coloration of its cultural surroundings. Its operations within its contexts deserve a closer look than ahistorical approaches to narrative can provide.

Such scrutiny has begun in several fields, beginning with narratology itself. In his essay on "Narrativity in the Representation of Reality," Hayden White attempts to rescue chronography for narratology by reading it on its own temporal terms. He looks at examples of those chronographic forms, annals and chronicles, not in order to point up (as have Kermode and others) "what appear" by modern standards of historiography "to be gaps, discontinuities, and lack of causal connections," but to read these texts "rather as particular products of possible conceptions of historical reality, conceptions that are alternatives to . . . the fully realized historical discourse that the modern history form is supposed to embody."[18] Examining the *Annals of St. Gall*, which lists every *Annus Domini* from 702–1072 but identifies events (in short phrases) for only a few of them, White begins from the *kairos-chronos* antithesis, only to undermine it later on. The annalist's running calendar of years, White suggests, "locates events, not in the time of eternity, not in *kairotic* time, but in chronological time, in time as it is humanly experienced. This time has no high points or low points; it is, we might say, paratactical and endless" (8). But that very adjacency and continuity, White proceeds to argue, invests the written calendar with meaning, and hence with "fullness." "It has no gaps. The list of times is full even if the list of events is not" (8), and since the "times" are reckoned as years of the Lord, the *Annals*, despite the "blanks," proffer to their maker and readers a "possible gratification . . . implicitly present in the list of dates that make up the left-hand column. The fullness of this list attests to the fullness of time . . ." (11). At the end of this reading, the *Annals*, which White began by deeming "chronological," has by dint of its relentless successiveness achieved that "fullness" which Kermode deems *kairotic*, and denies to successiveness altogether.

Comparable acts of recovery, of forms of chronography more recent than the medieval, have taken place in literary criticism, particularly with its widening out into cultural studies. In diurnal form, the kinds of *kairoi* favored by formalists (e.g., irony) and by mythographers (e.g., archetypes) are hard to come by or to recognize, and it is a common characteristic of most of the genres I am dealing with—diaries, newspapers, periodical essays—that literary historians and critics have, until quite recently, not much known what to *do* with them. What can a critic do with a body of writing so large, so various, so sequestered, and so intractable?[19] For most of this century the answer for literary studies resided mainly in describing and classifying the texts, rather than in analyzing them. The career of William Matthews, perhaps the most important scholar of the diary in this century, offers an answer that is paradigmatic in several respects. Matthews, a linguist, came to diaries as many do, intent on "rifling [them] for . . . data"—in his case, on the history of pronunciation.[20] Unexpectedly intrigued, he stayed to catalogue the documents he had started out to plunder, and produced, in *British Diaries*, an annotated bibliography that, though now in need of expansion, still stands as the central reference work in the field; later he edited the diaries of Dudley Ryder and Samuel Pepys. For more than a century, much of the most useful work on diaries has been of Matthews's kind. Bibliographers catalogue new finds; textual scholars edit new texts, and re-edit old, enhancing at a rapid rate both the quantity and the quality of diaristic resources. But the question of what to do with them persists, and the extent of puzzlement tells in the fact that critics, faced with the fascination and challenge of interpreting diaries, have often fallen back on variants of Matthews's "cataloguing" response: they survey the field (or whatever large portion of the field they have marked off for study), either arranging diaries in ahistorical groupings according to design, purpose, or "character,"[21] or examining and describing them in chronological sequence.[22] Even the most critically astute surveys (many of them prompted by recent interest in female diaries as central texts for women's studies[23]) are encumbered by an imperative to be comprehensive, which is prompted by the comparative novelty of the subject matter. Such surveys depend more on a capacious, intelligent display of and guidance through the materials than on a rigorously developed thesis about them.[24] Initial exposure of the texts rather than close study is still largely the point.[25] The surveyors' copious quotations and discerning comments alter the proportions of Matthews's procedure but not its underlying intellectual structure. In perhaps no other field of literary study does most of the criticism replicate so closely—not only in its information but also in its design and approach—the workings of its central reference materials.

Recently, though, critics have found more fruitful methods for investigating diaries. Cultural historians, recognizing the diary as one practice among many, have been able to provide for it various contexts that the diaristic surveyors tend to set aside, in order to examine constructions of the self.[26] In literary studies this has primarily meant reckoning the diary's place among the textual practices surrounding it—letters, conduct manuals, household records, published genres, etc.; seventeenth- and eighteenth-century diaries have already benefited considerably from such situating. Patricia Meyer Spacks in *Imagining a Self* and Felicity A. Nussbaum in *The Autobiographical Subject* examine more numerous, more varied, and in several cases more "marginal" specimens of autobiography than had been assayed before, setting them in wider contexts of other kinds of writing, and attending more carefully to the complicated "conversation" among texts, and between texts and contexts, than had previous critics of autobiography.[27] These strategies have proven particularly useful in advancing that history of diaries that had previously found expression only in bibliographies and other surveys. First, both critics deal closely not with one diary but with several: Spacks with Burney's as well as Boswell's (and, among his, with the late journals as well as the early); Nussbaum with John Wesley's, Boswell's, and Hester Thrale's, as well as with the journals of many lesser-known Puritan and Methodist practitioners of the form. Less obviously, and more importantly, both critics, by the very variety of works they undertake to survey, discover for the diary those contexts, those continuities within the culture, that more monolithic surveys of the diary, which take the form's isolation at face value, usually overlook. Spacks, for example, juxtaposes Burney's private writings with her own novels and with those of earlier and later women writers (such as Lennox and Wollstonecraft) to gauge the distances and links between the self-suppressive keeper of diaries and the more assertive, openly though complicatedly rebellious maker of "selves" in fiction. Nussbaum arranges Boswell's and Thrale's private and published prose in various juxtapositions to show how Boswell resists, and Thrale ambivalently accepts then declines, the new cultural power women are attaining through published prose. In Spacks's and Nussbaum's accounts, the diary operates as part of—and as a force in—struggles transpiring within both the life of the diarist and the life of the culture.

Nussbaum's study, similar to Spacks's in its subject matter and in its strategies of mixed genders and genres, carries on a pointed conversation with its predecessor, one adumbrated in the alignments and differences of wording in the two books' full titles. Spacks subtitled her work "Autobiography and Novel in Eighteenth-Century England." She was writing at a time when such a juxtaposition of genres, such a perforating of boundaries between fiction and non-fiction, was comparatively new and when the procedure itself was much of the point, yielding as its first fruit the revelation of continuities hitherto unsuspected. Spacks works to show that eighteenth-century authors of autobiographies, diaries, and novels are all engaged in essentially the same task: the creation in writing of a coherent "self." Nussbaum sees in the word "self" an imprecision—the possibility of an essential, preexistent identity discovered rather than made by writing—that works against Spacks's own claim about "imagining." Nussbaum, avowedly Foucauldian, prefers the term "subject," with its connotations of inexorable construction and concomitant subjection; she supplants Spacks's subtitular pairing with "*Gender* and *Ideology* in Eighteenth-Century England," and by that shift commits herself to examining the play of cultural forces at work behind and within the proliferation of autobiographical forms. In Nuss-baum's argument the diary acquires a new preeminence, as chief exemplar of a significant, specifically eighteenth-century writing practice that she calls "serial autobiography."

Nussbaum, declaring for a "materialist feminism" continuously mindful of the cultural practices that surround writing and impinge upon it, reads in diaries the discourses of gender and of class current in the culture and pro-duced or reproduced on the page by diarists "complicit" (often uncon-sciously) with the workings of power around them. Nussbaum's method admirably fulfills the purposes for which she employs it. It enables her to be much more specific than Spacks about the "self"—about its many, highly differentiated formations in both the real world and the written word, about the sources on which it draws and the purposes it serves, about its cultur-ally dictated inconsistencies. For Nussbaum, eighteenth-century diarists (and critics who take their "versions of the self" at face value) participate in a naive humanism that sees the self as a given, essential mode of being, "au-tonomous and free," as recognizably different from others and recognizably the same, as the sole or central determinant of its own shaping (29). Reading diaries through what she calls (following Fredric Jameson) the "ideology of genre," Nussbaum analyzes the humanism to expose the naiveté.

Yet Nussbaum, deeply engaged with constructions of gender and class as they manifest themselves in the pages of diaries, overlooks a "construction" especially significant to the making of serial autobiography: the particular conceptions of narrative time that shape the series, and their relations to the instruments that made practices of timekeeping material—that is, both palpable and important—in eighteenth-century England as in no previous culture. When Nussbaum writes of time, her diction displays a telling lapse: diaries, she says, are remarkable for their "articulation of human chronol-ogy"; they "seem to question what tenet, other than human time, is pow-erful enough to connect events" (23, 18). These pronouncements, though accurate as to time's central importance in the making of diaries, are also striking in point of vocabulary. Nussbaum permits herself, in her account of time, that very adjective "human" whose de-historicizing, essentializing ten-dencies she works elsewhere to abjure.

The phrase "human time" unavoidably echoes the title of the work to which all subsequent investigations of time and literature owe a primary debt: George Poulet's *Studies in Human Time*.[28] Poulet, who is distinctly humanist, attempts in each of his "studies" to set forth by a method of close reading and impressionistic writing the temporal vision of a particular author: for Fontenelle "time is no more, in the final analysis, than an undulating texture that unites the thousands of forms of the real and the possible" (148); for Emerson "to destroy time . . . is to destroy what does not exist, to destroy a dream. Time has no spiritual reality" (323).[29] Poulet presents his writers chronologically, arranging them on a timeline he sketches in his introduction, where he presents the concise history of a single idea about time, by ascribing to each succeeding century from the fifteenth to the twentieth a different variant of, or deviation from, the medieval conception of "continuous creation." Yet he is more interested in defining their individual authorial essences than their interaction with their successive cultures. Material manifestations of time—clocks or calendars, for example—appear rarely and incidentally; they are not central to Poulet's purpose. Echoing Poulet's phrase, Nussbaum imports a tincture of his procedure. By and large, she does not account for where her timebound texts "get" their temporality, how they construct it, how they use it.[30] Dedicated to historicizing, Nussbaum neglects to historicize time.

The "ideology of genre" to which Nussbaum devotes her opening manifesto is by her own account deeply involved with time. The eighteenth-century diary, she writes, "does not fit into existing aesthetic categories" (of whole, polished, autobiography, for example) precisely because of its unique way of conceiving and representing the self in time (23): the diary's practitioners "measure their identity in its daily repetition but remark on the contradictory positionings of the self from moment to moment, day to day, year to year. [They collect] . . . notes or memoranda that, *in time*, were revised to produce new versions of selves" (22; italics mine). But when Nussbaum characterizes this self-presentation (as she does in her chapter title and often elsewhere) as "*the* ideology" of the diary genre, her singulative article occludes the complexities of time that are at work in the genre's making. Like all narratives, but in particularly pronounced ways, diaries deal in temporality, or rather in a mesh of temporalities, both narrative and "real," a complex at once analogous, related, and comparable in importance to the "conflictual discourses" of gender and class that Nussbaum so readily identifies in private journals. Reckoned one way, a single narrative "temporality" may serve different ideologies in different texts: by a long series of daily entries, the Puritan diarist Margaret Hoby commits herself to God,

Samuel Pepys to a very different, more secular network of powers and au-
tonomies. Conversely, kindred ideologies may engender different temporalities in actual diaries (the variety of time forms in Puritan journals is a
case in point). To write as Nussbaum does of "the" ideology of so timebound and various a genre, without reference to the many possible temporalities at work within the genre, is—uncharacteristically for Nussbaum—
to oversimplify, to eclipse differences under a rubric of similarity. If, as she
says, "diaries articulate human chronology," then Nussbaum, by leaving the
uninterrogated adjective in place, prevents herself from usefully following
suit: she cannot articulate the local, material chronologies and temporalities
that shape the texts and practices she investigates.

I hope to offer, with respect to Nussbaum's account, a filling in of the
picture, a shift of emphasis, and a consequent correction. On the one hand,
the new chronometry presented timeframes ideally designed for cultivating
that sense of autonomy Nussbaum considers illusory. The particular forms
of time proffered by the clocks, watches, and memorandum books so new
and conspicuous in the period seemed to many serial autobiographers to
limn a new temporality—of durations closely calibrated, newly and increasingly synchronized, and systematically numbered—durations that might
serve as "blanks" in which each person might inscribe a sequence of individual actions in an individual style. The actions and the style may, as the
diarists well know, resemble to some extent those of other diarists (diaries
accommodate the commonality of their practices more knowingly and comfortably than Nussbaum, in her eagerness to debunk what she deems their
illusion of individuality, admits); but each diarist tacitly surmises, what no
diarist can empirically prove, that the entry for this day, this public, numbered "blank," will be *identical* with no other.

On the other hand, Nussbaum overemphasizes the illusion here. What
seems to the diarists to be so—that time closely tracked offers a rigorous
grid of "sameness" in which to perform the self as a particular narrative
"difference"—turns out at one important level to *be* so: daily entries do
differ, in ways that Nussbaum's approach does not allow her sufficiently to
acknowledge and distinguish. Nussbaum chooses to focus on those texts that
will most readily demonstrate the prevalence of cultural norms rather than
individual assertion. Most of the writers she examines produced religious
diaries and autobiographies, and hence consciously "subjected" themselves
to an overtly prescriptive, highly articulated, and well-publicized system of
writing that defined what the narrative should contain and how it should

present it. For the seventeenth century, all Nussbaum's authors are religious. For example, she deals at length with Bunyan but barely at all with Pepys (or even with Evelyn), who would prove far less assimilable to her scheme.[31] To Nussbaum's persistent undermining of autonomy (a matter of tone as well as of evidence and argument) a study of temporality in secular diurnal forms offers a counterbalance and corrective.

In contrast to literary scholars, professional historians have always known what to do with diurnal forms. They harvest diaries, newspapers, periodical essays for data. And they have been alert to the ways in which chronometry has contributed to the "humanizing" of time. The story most commonly told about clocks and culture is notably teleological, shaped and governed by its familiar ending: clocks, by their increasing abundance, precision, and ubiquity, have over the past five centuries contributed decisively to the "making of the modern world" we now inhabit, the "metronomic society" whose every motion is closely measured and tightly meshed by the pulsing instruments visible everywhere on walls, tables, wrists.[32] E. P. Thompson and Michel Foucault, whose approaches to cultural time differ greatly in other respects, concur on this point: that by the early nineteenth century clocks (and their textual counterparts the time-table and the time-sheet) had made of time minutely measured a central tool of power, a device indispensable in the "discipline" of large multitudes (workers, students, soldiers, prisoners); that key noun appears both in the title of Thompson's seminal essay, "Time, Work-Discipline, and Industrial Capitalism" and in the English title of Foucault's influential book, *Discipline and Punish*.[33] Both studies tell useful truth, but their influence has produced a side effect somewhat at odds with their own practice: the partial eclipse, in subsequent scholarship, of that century and a half of socio-horological history separating the pendulum clock and the Industrial Revolution. Thompson's and Foucault's work almost inevitably pitches attention forward to the early nineteenth century, that moment when clock-time demonstrably and decisively assumes control, when, for example (as Foucault reports), the *Écoles mutuelles* devised a time-table calibrated to the minute: "8.52 the monitor's summons, 8.56 entrance of the children and prayer, 9.00 the children go to their benches . . ." (150). Thompson and Foucault profess interest in the processes, the gradual and often imperceptible developments over the previous hundred and fifty years, that produced such a result. Foucault describes the development of "discipline" as "a multiplicity of often minor processes, of different origin and scattered location, which overlap, repeat, or imitate one another, support one another, distinguish themselves from one another according to the domain of their application, converge and gradually produce the blueprint of a general method" (138); in practice, though, he often cites one historical instance from "before" the shift (for example, a fairly generalized directive about how soldiers should march, from the early seventeenth century) and another, demonstrably different, "after" (a late eighteenth-century directive, articulated down to durations smaller than a second) and interpolates from these the advent of "discipline" in between (151).[34] In *Discipline and Punish*, Foucault's interest in power focuses him on those moments when power is achieved.

Thompson, interested in resistance to power, commits himself more explicitly to investigating the "in between." Intent on chronicling the "*rebellious* traditional culture" of the eighteenth century (*Customs* 9), wherein laborers resist loud and long the imposition of a new "work-discipline" regularized by the clock, he is more alert than Foucault to the many tensions and gradations entailed in the shift, and more concerned to set the time-customs of the eighteenth century ("Saint Monday," for example) within their own proper context before documenting their dissolution in the factories of the nineteenth. Nonetheless, in Thompson's essay as in its title, the end-term "industrial capitalism" operates powerfully over the whole account, and this tendency becomes more pronounced in the work of those who follow him. Nigel Thrift, for example, a geographer of space-time who acknowledges his debt to both Thompson and Foucault, writes at one point that "the preconditions for capitalist time had been laid by 1750."[35] "Pre-" is perhaps a necessary but also a precarious prefix in historical accounting. It defines developments solely with respect to ends known to (often actually established by) the historian, but unrecognizable to the participants. The syllable allows at times for a premature escape from the complexities of local context. In English studies, for example, the term "pre-Romanticism," long ascendant and now long discredited, warranted a situation in which eighteenth-century writing was both reduced to and "rescued" for anthologies and survey courses as the forerunner of a more important cultural shift. For a long while, as J. Paul Hunter has remarked, teachers, textbooks, and sophisticated critics—"Northrop Frye, Frank Kermode, M. H. Abrams, and Stanley Fish, for example—[found] room between 1667 and 1787 only for Renaissance leftovers and anticipations of the High Romantics."[36] A comparable, though less drastic, elision still obtains in the history of English time and culture: in the mid-seventeenth century Huygens invents the precision timepiece, in the early nineteenth it fulfills its capitalistic, disciplinary purpose; only a single refinement, the marine chronometer (with its attendant, micro-technological innovations), comes between. In both socio-horological and literary history, the eighteenth-century story's seeming endpoint has come to shape—or to misshape, to compress in the rush to the finish—the reading of its middle.

Such teleological accounts sort oddly with the temporalities they chronicle. In the late seventeenth and eighteenth centuries clock-dials, minute hands, diaries, newspapers, and novels were new precisely in that they called attention away from endpoints and invested it in middles—of the current hour, of the ongoing life—that were sharply defined and indefinitely extended. A study of eighteenth-century narrative time, and particularly of diurnal form, can both correct the latent teleology and detail the history of time and cultural "discipline" by recovering the temporal textures and complexities of that middle period when precise clocks and watches, conspicuous but not yet ubiquitous, proffered to their owners a temporality closely calibrated, but not yet controlling: when the metaphorical societal "metronome" was audible but not yet dominant.[37] This approach entails a shift of focus up the social scale (from Thompson's laborers, Foucault's prisoners) as well as back along the timeline. The gentry and the merchants who could first afford clocks and watches in the late seventeenth and early eighteenth centuries were socially positioned to see in these instruments a figuration of personal time—and by extension of the private self in time—as a kind of liquid capital and portable property. If the timepieces, by their visible and audible precisions, suggested possibilities of discipline, they intertwined them with promises of autonomy, self-empowerment, and liberation.

Of this new conviction about time the private diary is a central document. Recording time in a secret book, like measuring it on a personal chronometer, is a way of owning it. The diary is of course a "time-discipline," in some respects the very model of those processes Foucault describes which, initially "scattered," gradually coalesce into a "general method"—in this case a method of reckoning and recording the self in time so general as to subsume (among other forms and practices) timepieces, memorandum books, essays, biographies, newspapers, and novels. But I think that, in its early stage at least, "discipline" is not the method's full and proper name. The diaristic promise to enact autonomy is not as illusory as Foucauldians like Nussbaum insist. The written creation of the "subject" in new time does not necessarily entail (to use Foucault's and Nussbaum's central pun) a fundamental subjection. "He who is subjected to a field of visibility, and who knows it, assumes responsibility for the constraints of power," Foucault writes of the Panopticon, that paradigm of "discipline" whose inhabitants are made to feel themselves always anonymously watched from a central point of observation. "He makes them play spontaneously upon himself; he inscribes in himself the power relation in which he simultaneously plays both roles; he becomes the principle of his own subjection" (202–203). This account may apply readily enough to some religious diarists, who monitor themselves, in effect, as God's deputies and judge their actions as they imagine He would; like the occupant of the Panopticon, the religious diarist knows of the punishments that may follow wrongdoings so observed. Foucault notes that "in England, it was private religious groups that carried out, for a long time, the functions of social discipline" (213), and Nussbaum shows that religious diarykeeping is often essentially a centralized and communal process (80–102). It is more difficult, though, to make the panoptic paradigm explain the whole of secular diaries produced under the sign of *Tick, Tick, Tick*—of the *quotidian* as series and structure, of time as measured but blank, as a field open for self-creation by self-inscription (at least for those with access to the timepieces, and with leisure for the writing). The model of subjectivity and subjection that Foucault derives from an unexecuted design for a penitentiary is complicated by the diurnal documents of the self (as opposed to the institutional documents he favors in *Discipline and Punish*) that were produced in the course of the century and a half whose disciplinary end-product he undertakes to depict.[38]

In *Imagined Communities* Benedict Anderson pays closer attention than either Thompson or Foucault to the ways in which cultural temporalities and texts shape each other. In his account, clocks, calendars, and print culture converge to produce a new sense of time:

> What has come to take the place of the mediaeval [i.e., "Messianic," typo-logical] conception of simultaneity-along-time is, to borrow again from Benjamin, an idea of 'homogeneous, empty time,' in which simultaneity is, as it were, transverse, cross-time, marked not by prefiguring and fulfillment, but by temporal coincidence, and measured by clock and calendar.[39]

For Anderson, the notion of "homogeneous, empty time" is of "fundamental importance" in understanding "the obscure genesis of nationalism," because it is the medium that fosters that sense of "simultaneity" whereby individuals too numerous to know each other imagine themselves into community (24). The argument counters Foucault's disciplinary paradigm with a certain measure of elasticity. The occupants of imagined communities understand themselves to be inhabiting an articulated and coordinated social structure while at the same time going about what they construe (perhaps rightly) to be their own business. For Anderson, one of the central figures for this sense of simultaneity is diurnal print. No "more vivid figure for the secular, historically clocked, imagined community can be envisioned," Anderson argues, than "the newspaper reader, observing exact replicas of his own paper being consumed by his subway, barbershop, or residential neighbours" (35). This is well seen and said; it suggests the possible usefulness of a study of how diurnal forms were written as well as read. Anderson reads adroitly the *reading* of newspapers, but he does not read an actual paper. The temporal textures of the prose within diurnal texts reveal much about their operation, and suggest lines of cultural continuity: the diary, as I have already suggested, is also a "vivid figure"—and an earlier one—for "simultaneity" as a means for structuring identity, and some of its strategies for coordinating community with autonomy play a crucial role (as I shall argue in my chapter on the *Spectator*) in the development of daily print. Intent on tracking the ways in which the construct of "homogeneous, empty time" fosters new nationalisms, Anderson focuses (like Thompson and Foucault) on the end of the eighteenth century; the scope of his project demands that he be more alert to the ways texts structure time in culture than to the ways writers structure time in texts. I want to look more closely at the internal syntax of the new diurnal forms, in order to discern how "homogeneous, empty time" was both constructed and filled by texts.

Benjamin's and Anderson's model of a cultural shift from Messianic to empty time maps fairly directly onto Kermode's narratological binary of *kairos* and *chronos*: the "Messianic" is for Kermode the central source of *kairos*, residual still in secular forms. Yet Kermode at one point concedes that (as the theologian James T. Barr has argued) the "antithesis" between *chronos* and *kairos* does not hold firmly even in the New Testament, its putative point of origin. Citing a text from Galatians (4.4) that has long served as a Biblical *locus classicus* for the idea of temporal plenitude, Kermode notes that "The words translated as 'the fulness of the time' are *pleroma tou chronou*"—nót *tou kairoi* (48). The evidence, then, that underwrites his theological categories proves as partial and problematic as that behind his horological onomatopoeia. According to the Greek, *chronos* (*Tick, Tick, Tick*) is as susceptible of fullness (*pleroma*) as is *kairos* (*tick-tock*). Diurnalists of the seventeenth and eighteenth centuries, filling the blank pages of diaries and blank sheets of newsprint with entries and items under successive dates, certainly proceeded as though this were so. The new emptiness of time creates a need, a means, and a structure for fullness in text.

As I have already suggested, "filling in" is my book's métier as well. I have not found it necessary to mount large counter-arguments against most of the critics I've named, or to try to demolish structures of argument that, grounded sturdily in the Renaissance on one side and in the late eighteenth and early nineteenth century on the other, actually accommodate my account rather comfortably. One advantage of a study of seventeenth- and eighteenth-century temporalities and narrative forms lies in the way it can inhabit, and in doing so slightly modify, standing structures well-built but under-tenanted: it can offer a means of tracing horological history further and more accurately into the fabric of the culture it transformed, of reading and historicizing diaries more precisely, and of testing and extending theories of literary time. The chief risk in merging the historian's story of clocks and culture with the critic's and the theorist's stories of time and narrative is that the newly melded account will come out slant: clocks and watches are not the sole arbiters of time in the period, and diaries and published diurnal forms do not constitute the sole means of rendering and responding to the time clocks tell. Seventeenth- and eighteenth-century English culture, with its newly heightened consciousness of time, was awash in models of temporality, some conflicting, some congruent: philosophical, social, theoretical, scientific, and psychological.

Yet for all of these, Huygensian chronometry offered a new and critical mode of definition. Clocks and watches, by rendering time palpable, audible, and visible, brought themselves to the center of temporal attention, established themselves as the new point of reference not only for measuring time but for talking and thinking about it. Concurrently, the time-meshed forms for self-narration that suffused both private and public practice became for the culture a circulating medium in which to write about time, locate the self within it, inhabit it fully and attentively. The site where the two discourses—one non-verbal, the other narrative—converge lies near the center of the culture. It needs new mapping.

•

Since temporalities operate everywhere, virtually any text can yield some clue to the textures of time in its culture, and different clusters of texts will yield differently focused accounts. But the particular story I propose to tell here—of the absorption into narrative form of the kinds of time propounded by the new chronometry, and of the emergence of new narrative time, at first (necessarily) in private writings and then in public performances—requires certain texts and strongly suggests the relevance of several others. The argument demands first of all that I deal in a number of narrative genres, partly because of the deep differences between private and public prose, and partly because the shaping—indeed the creation—of genres by the pressures of the new temporality is the core of what I wish to show. In that process, several texts (or clusters of texts) act as indispensable agents; they attempt and accomplish what other texts do not, and without them the history of eighteenth-century narrative time would be unimaginably different. Pepys's diary inscribes a private account of the new time earlier, more assiduously, and more attentively than does any of its extant contemporaries. The *Spectator* takes diurnal, "secret" time public, and establishes it as a social practice and cultural rhythm, so that readers as well as writers are encouraged to conceive and narrate their lives on this new template. The published travel journal extends and complicates this process. The first popular print genre to embody diurnal rhythm as book rather than periodical, it prompts a wide ambivalence as to the value of the diaristic paradigm as a structure for public narrative. Johnson's *Journey to the Western Islands* and Boswell's *Journal of a Tour to the Hebrides* play out with unprecedented complexity the tensions of time and form for which travel writing has provided a culturally central site.[40] The novel absorbs the diary template more equivocally, in ways perhaps most fully documented in the works of Defoe (the first writer to incorporate a journal within a larger fiction) and Burney, whose assiduous practice of serial forms (journals and journal letters) and complex recasting of them in fiction bear significant witness to the relations between novel and diary time.

For tracing these shifts in seventeenth- and eighteenth-century time-consciousness, Raymond Williams's concept of "changes in *structures of feeling*" has proven particularly useful, partly because its assertion of order ("structures") within the seemingly inchoate ("feeling") corresponds well with the way new clocks gave definition to the most impalpable dimension of experience, but more importantly because Williams's formulation of how such structures work precisely describes the situation of the diary as Pepys practices it in the 1660s, and accurately predicts how diurnal form will develop from there. Williams defines a "structure of feeling" as "a social experience which is still *in process*, often indeed not yet recognized as social but taken to be private, idiosyncratic, and even isolating, but which in analysis (though rarely otherwise) has its emergent, connecting, and dominant characteristics." At this initial phase of the process, Williams argues, the "forms and conventions" of current literary discourse may function "as the articulation (often the only fully available articulation) of structures of feeling which as living processes are much more widely experienced." The diary, written in solitude, conceiving itself as "private, idiosyncratic, and even isolating," but abounding in "forms and conventions" it draws from the culture, would seem on this reckoning to offer an especially responsive instrument for articulating *many* "emergent" structures of feeling, but particularly (given the formal commitment to temporality identified in its name) structures of feeling about time.[41]

This proves so. Williams's vocabulary for cultural change makes possible an analysis of new temporality, in which clock and diary—the measured minute, the narrated day—function as central, formative constituents, distinct in their operations, parallel in their development, and combinatory in their cultural consequences. Huygens's clocks structure a feeling about time, encompassing days as well as minutes. The core elements of this new structure—comprehensiveness, precision, and possession—are already "emergent" in other cultural constructions and practices (fiscal ledgers, news-books, pockets, and private rooms) but quickly coalesce around clocks and watches as these instruments become the preeminent signifiers, the central, palpable points of reference for time in the culture. Even at their earliest stage, Huygens's clocks perform as the agents by which (in Williams's phrasing) the "living process" of the new temporality becomes most "widely experienced," though (as a non-verbal discourse) little articulated. At this same stage too the new structure of feeling finds its first full (and "fully available") narrative articulation in Pepys's diary. It finds subsequently an even fuller, culturally pervasive and polymorphic account in the numerous published diurnal genres of the next century, which themselves enact the recognition of the social that Williams speaks of as a later stage of the structural shift.

These genres construe clock time and diurnal form as central components of the culture's time-consciousness, of its narrative practices, and of its self-reckoning. The *Spectator* constructs a print diurnal form as an instrument of social interaction, at just that juncture when the minute watch is beginning to coordinate the social motions of its readers. Later in the century, when precision chronometry has (partly through the quest for the longitude) become an even more dominant mode and concern in the culture, Boswell attempts to expand the dominion of diurnal form, while Johnson resists these new temporalities of clock and text precisely because he recognizes them as dominant.

My story needs these texts; these texts, I suggest, also need this story if they are to be more fully understood. "We have no books . . . on Pepys's diary," Lawrence Rosenwald writes, "or on Boswell's"[42]—or (with one admirable exception) on the *Spectator*.[43] I mean by my undertaking to begin to remedy these curious omissions, and to remedy a larger critical predicament as well: I argue that since these texts are new attempts to write in new time, a study of their "timings"—their movement in time, their articulations of time—provides the most fruitful means for attending to them, for making sense of their historical, cultural, and artistic importance. These texts are not mere witnesses to their culture; they are active embodiments of one of its newest, most important, and withal most elusive organizing principles: its temporality.

Finally, a word about method. I deal often in close, sometimes extensive readings of short passages in very long texts. This attention to stylistic detail has seemed important for several reasons. First, literary criticism has long bypassed these texts, particularly the diary and the periodical, viewing them as archival resources whose apparent artlessness made them particularly useful and reliable for documentary purposes but uninteresting as literary achievements; surmising no aesthetic, critics sought none. New Criticism particularly condoned this neglect;[44] it seems to me that New Historicism has in a curious way followed suit. New Historicists, deeply interested in data and impelled by methodology to assimilate a huge number and variety of texts, quote abundantly and move rapidly. But I think that the method will find more of what it is looking for—more about the intricate fabric of lives lived, more material for that "conversation with the dead" that Stephen Greenblatt announced early on as the purpose of the procedure—if it pays more attention to the verbal textures of the testimony.

This holds particularly true with respect to my impalpable topic, time.

Previous accounts of time and literature have focused primarily on passages in which the chosen authors write about clocks, and about time.[45] I think there is more to be gained by an investigation, carefully conducted, of what they wrote *in* time, which in the case of diaries, periodicals, and other eighteenth century forms constitutes a much larger and more intriguing field of possibility. I too shall deal of course with passages explicitly *about* time (their evidence is indispensable). But because I am interested in discovering not only a "thematics"—what people thought and wrote about time, clocks, and watches—but more importantly a cultural texture—how people measured, used, conceived, and placed themselves in time—I shall pay as much attention to the form of such passages as to their specific assertions, and shall in other instances take up temporally inexplicit passages where all the testimony about time inheres in the texture. The authors herein often write most effectively about time when they are not writing about it at all. Like St. Augustine, they often know best what time is—for themselves, for their culture—when they are not explicitly "asked" about it but are simply occupying it, working in it, deploying it, giving it (and hence giving themselves) form in narratives overtly concerned with other matters. The only way to get at the temporalities they absorb and encode is by careful attention to the ciphers in which they are encoded—to sequence, proportion, and syntax; to the placement of subjects, verbs, and modifiers; to the delay or rapidity of closure; and to the distribution of structures and rhythms through sequences of sentences, entries, periodical numbers, and narratives. By its impalpability time requires close attention to its artificial forms, as Augustine knows well: he finally tells time (that is, explains it conceptually) by closely analyzing his own recitation of a psalm. Only by so minute an attention to procedures—to countings, recountings, and recitations, on clocks, in narratives, in criticism literary and cultural—can one hope to tell time accurately at all.

2

"In the Fullness of Time"

*I*nto his diary's first dated entry, for Sunday, 1 January 1660, Samuel Pepys transcribes the touchstone text from Galatians on time and fullness. He gets it slightly wrong:

> Went to Mr. Gunnings church at Exeter-house, where he made a very good sermon upon these words: That in the fullness of time God sent his Son, made of a woman, &c., shewing that by "made under the law" is meant his circumcision, which is solemnised this day.[1]

Peter Gunning, the most defiant of Anglican ministers during the Commonwealth, doubtless cited the Authorized Version: "But when the fulness of the time was come, God sent forth his son, made of a woman, made under the law." In this sentence "the fulness of the time" (*to pleroma tou chronou*) identifies a particular occasion, *the* time *when* "God sent forth his son," the specific moment of Messianic arrival; it is, in Kermode's terms, the *tock* that concludes the long and charged duration between Old Testament prophecy and New Testament fulfillment, and the shorter one between Annunciation and Nativity. Pepys's rephrasing construes "the fullness of time" as ongoing process (without definite article), a medium *in* which the event transpires, with "fullness" persisting on either side of it. In both Pepys's version and King James's, time possesses fullness as its sole specified attribute, but it is a fullness differently set in syntax and hence differently "timed." Where Kermode's argument fudges the terminology of the Greek text, denying *pleroma* to *chronos*, Pepys's transcription muddles the arrangement of the Anglican, but in such a way as to approximate one key feature of the original Greek. In his rendition, plain time and not only *the* time—*chronos* as well as *kairos*—may lay a claim to plenitude.

Over the next two chapters I shall try to show that the difference between the words Pepys writes on New Year's Day and the words he hears—between *in* and *when*, between *time* and *the* time—encapsulates larger, interconnected differences at work in this text and this culture, in 1660 and beyond: between the temporality Pepys produces in his diary, and that which characterizes the writing of his predecessors and contemporaries in the chronography of the self; between Huygensian chronometry and the technologies it was just starting to supplant; between older templates for textualizing time and self, and the diurnal form that would acquire increasing sway in coming years. I shall argue also that what Pepys does with time and text is central to both his achievement as a diarist and his significance as a cultural figure. It makes him an initiatory architect and occupant of a structure of feeling about time and self that over the ensuing century many will inhabit, whether or not they write diaries themselves.

The novelty and nature of Pepys's diary have hitherto proven hard to pinpoint for two main reasons: first, because popular regard for the diary, ever since its first publication in 1825, has figured it as a paradigm of the genre and a classic dissevered from its original contexts; second, because scholars who consult the diary tend to use it as a resource rather than regard it as a performance, and this has forestalled the possibility of seeing it whole. William Matthews, in his annotated bibliography of *British Diaries*, dubs Pepys's "the nonpareil" (29); Robert Fothergill, in his aesthetic critique of what he deems the fifteen most "distinguished" English diaries, remarks near the outset that "on 1 January 1660, Samuel Pepys condemned all previous diary-keeping to be the pre-history of the genre" (13). Pepys's preeminence has influenced the writing as well as the scholarship of diaries. Innumerable diarists make clear in their entries that they have taken Pepys as their pattern. Following what they assume to be his precedent, they aim at (and reproach themselves for falling short of) a chronological narrative written at the end of every day into a secret book; a few of them even appropriate the famous tag line, "And so to bed." In the face of such fame, "pre-history" as well as post-history fall away: all diaries (so the impression goes) work Pepys's way, or ought to. In truth, though, Pepys himself did not work the way he is widely assumed to, and history (pre- and post-) is indispensable for setting the assumptions right. Pepys's timing, his secrecy, even his tag line are more intricate than is commonly recognized; in devising them he draws on antecedents in his culture, but works changes on them too (changes that, now familiar and misconstrued, have come to seem standard). The paradigm of diary-keeping that Pepys unintentionally constructed has obscured both what he actually did and how new it was within the traditions of self-recording current when he wrote.

A second kind of eminence has prevented Pepys's diary, and its ways of figuring time, from being more fully historicized: its nearly matchless utility for history. Scholars who value the diary one way tend to ignore it another: they work from it, not on it. Instead of full studies, we have on the one hand innumerable citations from the diary in books and articles on the topics Pepys takes up, and on the other "appreciations"—chapters, articles, prefaces, essays in *belles lettres* (articles more specific and scholarly are rare).[2] Many raid the diary as a database; fewer read it as a document with its own timings and textures, which inevitably get lost during the raids.

Raiders and readers value the text for essentially the same reason: its apparent omniprehensility. The diary gives the impression of grabbing hold of everything the diarist encounters; it seems to promise that whatever topic interests the researcher—theater, dress, gender, power, powder (face or gun)—Pepys will somewhere have written something about it. While the raiders make his range their resource, the appreciators make it their theme. Matthews, seeking "to explain why Pepys's diary is so much more interesting than others," uses all the terms of praise in which a long tradition of admirers have concurred. "In Pepys," Matthews writes in the introduction to his edition, the "diversity of his interests" proceeds "from one single comprehensive quality, vitality. . . . This zest and energy, this ready delight in things new as well as in old things, are vital in making Pepys the diarist he is. Of all English writers, perhaps the only one who is his equal in gusto is Chaucer. . . . Who else among English writers has Pepys's enthusiasm for everyday people, everyday life, or his habit of judging everything he liked the best that ever there was?" (1.cx–cxi). "Vitality," "enthusiasm," and above all "gusto": with these words Matthews joins Walter Scott, Robert Louis Stevenson, Virginia Woolf, Arthur Ponsonby, and V. S. Pritchett in explaining the phenomenon of the diary by the personality of the diarist. These lines appear near the end of perhaps the most important study of

Pepys ever written, in which Matthews has investigated, more exactly and revealingly than anyone before, the writing practices that produced the diary, and has in the process exploded many popular misimpressions by tracing long chains of mediation behind the diarist's apparent, oft-celebrated "immediacy." He has shown that Pepys did not write an entry every day (though he represents every day by an entry); that he may sometimes have put an entry through as many as five different stages of revision, at various temporal removes from the events recorded; that the famous force of personality is not merely filtered through, but actually formed by, the several cultures in which Pepys participates—the techniques demanded of the efficient administrator (bookkeeping, shorthand); the versatility and curiosity cultivated by the virtuoso; the impulse towards accumulation characteristic of the devout Baconian and the aspiring historian; the impulse towards self-regulation that makes Pepys "a sort" of puritan. Yet after so much well-traced mediation, Matthews revives a notion of transparency, as though diary and diarist were one and the same. In his peroration he both repeats this notion and resists it: "In his own bailiwick, and at his best, [Pepys] is as much a nonpareil as are Chaucer and Shakespeare. And in one matter he is unique. No one else has ever composed so brilliant and so full an account of an actual man as he actually was. And that must be because he was not only a great man but because he was also a great writer" (cxiii). The closing distinction between person and prose has about it something of lip service. Matthews still refers the accomplishment of the writing to the general character of the man, and treats it as an object fitter for encomium than for analysis (unmediated "actuality" counts for all). The accomplishments of Chaucer and of Shakespeare have long been reckoned in terms more intricate, through sustained attention to the textures of the text, and to its interplay with the culture.

In Pepys's text, I want to suggest, the omniprehensility that raiders cherish and the gusto that readers prize are both functions of a less apparent process: the diary's culturally specific prehensility as to time; the many strategies and the running engagement by which Pepys enacts as prose form the temporality figured in his early mistranscription, "in the fullness of time." In remarking on Pepys's "enthusiasm for everyday people and everyday life," Matthews obscures (though he repeats) a point more historically significant and textually demonstrable than the abstract attribute of enthusiasm: the simple choice Pepys makes to write up every day in turn, and the subtler

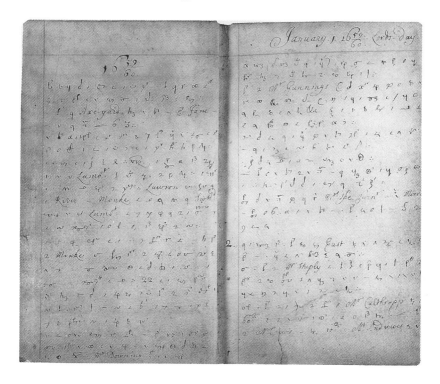

Figure 1. The opening pages of Pepys's diary. Courtesy of the Master and Fellows, Magdalene College, Cambridge.

designs he devises for doing so. The rudiments of Pepys's scheme can be discerned in the way *kairos* engages with *chronos* on the first page of dated entries (see Fig. 1, recto). "January 1, 1659/60 Lord's Day" is a date kairotically overdetermined by the reckonings of both Messianic and homogeneous time: a "Lord's Day" that is also (as Gunning reminds his congregation) the "solemnization" of a significant moment in Christ's life; the first day of a new week, month, year, and decade. This confluence of commencements plainly plays a role in Pepys's decision to start his diary from this date, but what he starts is a rigorously continuous and steady serial narrative—*Tick, Tick, Tick* as no one in English has quite written it before. The second of January ("2.") bears no special calendrical charge, nor does the third, fourth, fifth, or sixth, yet each day will be narrated in succession, as will every day thereafter (save for a single stretch of eleven missing from the record) through 31 May 1669, when Pepys ends the diary in the mistaken conviction that he is going blind. In the kinds of plot that engage Kermode, "*chronos* becomes *kairos*." In Pepys's plotting *kairos* becomes resubsumed in *chronos*; the day's narrative (however distinguished the event or date) is plotted on a continuous, calendrical grid. As the account of each date takes its place within the series, *the* time *when* becomes *a* time *in*. "Simple successiveness" is the form's controlling feature.

Pepys constructs continuity a second way as well, as he signals in the diary's most frequent and famous locutions. He undertakes to represent the whole of his waking day, from "Up" at the beginning of nearly every entry, to "bed" at the close. This second kind of continuity is fiction as the first is not. That Pepys writes up every day in succession is verifiable by collating his text with the numbers of the calendar; that he writes the "entirety" of any one day is impossible by limitations intrinsic to the textualization of time. "A full account [of any day] is impossible," notes Lawrence Rosenwald, and he quotes in this connection an essay by Stevenson: "There are not words enough in all Shakespeare to express the merest fraction of a man's experience in an hour." [3] Pepys accords far fewer words to any given day (twelve hundred at the most). He deploys all the privileged elasticities of narrative time—compression, selective emphasis, omission—in the act of turning the day to prose. Nonetheless he endeavors throughout to foster the textual illusion of temporal continuity; it is a critical (though tacit) stipulation of his narrative contract.

This narrative contract, stipulating continuity across all days and within each, construes the "homogeneity" of time straightforwardly—as a series of identical, numbered durations ("clocked," as in Benedict Anderson's chronometric synthesis, "by the calendar"). It figures the "emptiness" of time in more complicated ways. Both Benjamin and Anderson emphasize the "emptiness" of new (i.e., early modern) time, but both understand it as emptiness waiting to be filled: by "progress" in Benjamin's argument, by "nation" in Anderson's. Pepys fills "homogeneous, empty time" (as will the daily newspapers of the next century, in Anderson's account) by narrative portioned to the new time's terms, the openness of the calendar and the rigor of the clock. The uniform durations, provisionally blank, are seen by the diarist both to require filling (by experience in life, by inscription on the page) and also to facilitate it. They function as isochronic containers that in the uniformity, specificity, and seriality of their temporal dimensions make it possible to reckon fullness and hence to "realize" it: to embody it palpably on the page. The date makes fullness necessary and makes it possible. Pepys's diary figures homogeneous time as full rather than empty by a strategy of double containment: a plenum of narrative within each day, and a plenum of narrated days within the calendar. Measure defines narrative obligation; the fulfillment of the obligation produces temporal fullness in text. Each event recounted within the diary occupies a place "in the fullness of time" so constructed and contained.

If a daily design for a diary seems unsurprising, that may be partly because Pepys has done so much to set the paradigm. The day would seem to afford a natural unit of narrative, needing no particular cultural or horological imprimatur to valorize its use, and the very words "diary" and "journal" suggest that writers found it so well before Pepys set down his first entry. In practice, though, the day as unit differs greatly from "day by day" as mode. No English diary before Pepys's moves literally day by day over the entire course of the document.[4] Earlier diarists wrote on a temporal scheme considerably more sporadic, for several reasons grounded in several textual traditions. They accounted for certain moments and days of consequence, as well as for certain consecutive stretches of days, but not for all days in sequence (and no predecessor attempts the *double* fullness—within the day and across the days—that Pepys does). Earlier diarists figure the fullness of time by narratives of signal occasions, Pepys by one of serial measure. The temporal templates differ not in degree but in kind. Pepys constructs narrative fullness in accordance with a model of time different from that of his predecessors: one that is steady and continuous rather than intermittent.

Huygens had just produced such a model. In the 1660s, Huygensian chronometry and Pepysian narrative were new, and new in similar ways. They were not wholly new in conception: Galileo had thought of the pendulum, and clocks had borne minute hands, before Huygens's innovation; diarists had certainly *thought* to write in daily installments before Pepys. But both were new in execution: Huygens's clocks actually implemented new rules of engagement with passing time in order to measure the minutes; Pepys devised similar rules to track the days as (on the available evidence) no one writing English had done before. One of the chief characteristics of the new clock time was the comprehensiveness of its account: the minute and the second hand purport to tell time not intermittently (as did the hour bell and hour hand) but continuously, to provide a running tally.[5] In Pepys's diary and in the published diurnal forms of the next century (newspapers, essays, and books that appropriate the diaristic design of dated entries), the day enacts the role that the audible *tick* and the visible minute play in new modes of reckoning time: that of the small, integral unit, closely and individually tracked over an unbroken series, which gives detail and definition to larger tracts of time wherein such detailing was heretofore unavailable. The day in Pepys's narrative, like the minute on Huygens's clocks, is not just the index of measurement; it is the unit of innovation.

In order to establish the nature, degree, and significance of the shift, I would like in this chapter to set Pepysian temporalities against earlier traditions of timekeeping and time writing: the practices of bellringing in which the dialogue between measure and occasion was more conspicuous than anywhere else in the culture; and the texts of the self in time that were composed within their earshot. These texts align themselves in various ways with the older temporality of occasion rather than the newer one of measure. Two weeks into the diary, Pepys tries a small experiment in chronography, built around the sound of a bell outside his chamber window. In the first part of this chapter I shall juxtapose this passage against parallel moments in John Donne's *Devotions upon Emergent Occasions*. The *Devotions* and the diary display sufficient formal kinship to make them worth comparing for their salient temporal difference. Both Donne and Pepys perform a rigorous self-recording at close intervals, but Donne keys his to occasion (as his title foretells), while Pepys keys his to measure; the bell-moments in each offer an opportunity both to read their differences and to sketch the models of time that produce them. In the second part of the chapter I shall show how and why, in the first half of the seventeenth century, the paradigm of occasion rather than of measure governed even those practices of self-recording that deal (as Donne's does not) in the numbers of the calendar and the clock: popular almanacs (which were perhaps the most common venue of chronography in the period), fiscal account books, and diaries of all kinds. In the following chapter I shall turn to Pepys's first encounters with Huygens's new chronometry. He comes across it in the midst of his diary-keeping, and makes use of it in ways that establish fundamental affinities between his diary and the Huygensian watch as instruments of a new temporality.

BELLS AND OCCASIONS

Half a month into his diary, at the end of his entry for 16 January, Pepys momentarily breaks with his already established practice of narrating the day's events in retrospect. Here he writes down what is happening as he writes:

. . . thence home, where I found my wife and maid a-washing.

I sat up till the bell-man came by with his bell, just under my window as I was writing of this very line, and cried, "Past one of the clock, and a cold, frosty, windy morning." I then went to bed and left my wife and the maid a-washing still. (1.16.60; 1.19)

By its form the passage plays out in miniature some of the temporal possibilities limned in Pepys's scriptural mistranscription two weeks earlier. The governing figure here is *inclusio*: the same phrase, "my wife and maid a-washing," lightly altered, frames the account on both sides; the chronometric report (the time when) and its attendant circumstances appear enclosed inside a fullness that Pepys produces as self-centered experience, inscription, and form. What is distinctive in this move will come clearer after comparison with Donne, but it is worth pointing out in a preliminary way that the strategies of enclosure, indeed the *materials* of enclosure (shorthand script, sequestered book, "my window," "my wife") construe the moment and the bellman who announces it as things abducted and possessed. The passage enacts a pronounced prehensility as to passing time.

The sound Pepys records functions as adjunct to a much larger system of bell signals that had survived, in its general outlines and operations, all the efforts of Reformation and Commonwealth to reduce its instruments and instances (the Restoration would shortly bring a reflorescence).[6] In an England where few owned clocks and even fewer owned watches, bells rang everywhere, and every ringing signaled a time of one kind or another.[7] Hearers could differentiate not only between the bells of occasion and those of measure, but also between the signals for different kinds of occasion, for which the bells performed markedly different functions. Some bells exhorted the hearer to perform an action: to pray, to attend services, to retire for the night, to start work or to stop it. Some ringings were narrative rather than hortatory, in that they registered events or announced news, local or national: weddings and funerals, royal births, imminent dangers, military victories. Bells, that is, could realize "occasion" either as noun or as transitive verb: they might simply announce the occasion, or they might occasion an action by their ringing. In practice, the three categories of function— measure, hortatory occasion, and narrative occasion—often overlapped. The narrative and the hortatory converged often and easily: the alarm bell, while announcing an emergency, also mustered militia; the victory peal, while declaring triumph, also dictated celebration. Likewise the hortatory and the horological gradually become enmeshed. The bell that rang the hour could also, for large contingents among its auditors, dictate action.[8] Of the three categories of bellringing, only two are reciprocally exclusive: the narrative and the horological. The peals that announced extraordinary events— danger, death, victory—had to distinguish themselves by sound and timing from the ones that routinely rang the hour.

The bell that catches Pepys's attention is an ancilla of chronometry, the adjunct of the larger tower bell whose time the bellman is tracking. The bells that preoccupy John Donne on his sickbed in *Devotions upon Emergent Occasions*—the sickness bell, the passing bell, and the funeral bell—deal intensively in exhortation and narrative; they have nothing to do with chronometry. Taken together, the three ringings constituted perhaps the most overtly narrative sequence in the Anglican repertoire: three stages in a single story.[9] They combined information with imperative, announcing the condition of one mortal in the parish, and enjoining others to pray for the soul at its departing.[10] Donne intensifies the admonition traditionally ascribed to these bells by a melding of identities, expressed compactly in the heading for the eighteenth devotion—"The [passing] bell rings out, and tells me in him, that I am dead"—and explained more fully in the prayer that just precedes it: "O eternall and most gracious *God* . . . I humbly accept thy *voice*, in the sound of this sad and funerall *bell*. And first, I blesse thy glorious name, that in this *sound* and *voice*, I can heare thy *instructions*, in *another mans* to consider *mine owne condition.* . . ."[11] The formulation involves three fusions: of future with present ("I am dead"); of self with other ("me in him"); and of the bell's sound with God's voice and instructions.[12] With the ringing, eternity penetrates time, *kairos* intrudes on *chronos*. (Kermode's distinction works well for this text, wherein the fatal illness, with its attendant sense of an ending, governs all.) The engineering of such disruption is central to Donne's design. At one point he asks, in self-exasperation, "if I be entring now into *Eternitie*, where there shall bee no more distinction of *houres*, why is it al my business now *to tell Clocks?*" (78). The question expresses local weariness (Donne is telling clocks because he cannot fall asleep), but it also functions as rationale and prelude for the very next devotion, where Donne will cease counting the time of measure and begin telling that of occasion, which is sounded by a bell that is not a clock.[13]

The bells' significance, as instruments of a temporality operating both in the *Devotions* and beyond it, becomes apparent not only in the particular meditative applications Donne devises in the sections he devotes to them, but also from their place in the structure of the whole book. The text constructs the bells, as it does the symptoms of Donne's illness, as "emergent" (that is, arising, unexpected) "occasions": "opportunities," construed (in the Latin root *occasio*) as a "falling together or juncture of circumstances favorable . . . to an end or purpose" (*OED* sb. I.1.).[14] The *Devotions* deals in events beyond the author's control that nonetheless redound to his use when recognized as incitements to redemptive thought—meditation, expostulation, prayer. What "falls together," on this reckoning, is outward occurrence—symptom, bell—and the willingness of the writer to make the right inner sense of it: "[H]ow little of our *life* is *Occasion, opportunity* to receyve good in," Donne laments at one point, "and how little of that *occasion*, doe wee apprehend, and lay hold of?" (72).

The bells, if anything, compound this process. Their ringing enacts occasion doubly, as both noun and verb. They announce one event—what Donne in a pun calls "*his* [the dying man's] occasion" (his moment and his fall). They bring about another, *Donne's* "occasion," construed as thought rather than present death: "The *Bell* doth toll for him that *thinkes* it doth; and though it *intermit* againe, yet from that *minute*, that that occasion wrought upon him, hee is united to *God*" (86–87). To "thinke" this way is to "apprehend" the occasion and to "lay hold of" it, as Donne earlier desired. The bell sound, emergent, occasions devotion, as the title foretells. In the culture that encompasses the sickroom, the death bells routinely perform that very function—blunted, perhaps, through long familiarity—which the entire apparatus of the *Devotions* is designed to make strong and strange by new scrutiny: the conversion of narrative into exhortation, the "laying hold of" external occasion for purposes of self-reckoning and prayer. The bell devotions epitomize the book's general method, and they take it public by referring it not to the solitude of the sickroom but to the commonality of a signal audible and (so Donne's argument insists) usable by all. The death bells, that is, sound a temporality powerful in the culture, widely heard from towers and here written into text—a temporality that registers not measured spans but disparate events, and that seeks to maximize opportunity by identifying the divine instruction in the sublunary occasion.[15]

Of that other temporality, the chronometric, though also audible in bells, there is little in the *Devotions*. The time-term "minute" appears often, from the first lines ("this minute I was well, and am ill, this minute" [7]) to the last ("I durst deliver my selfe over to thee this *Minute*, If this *Minute* thou wouldst accept my *dissolution* . . ." [126]), but almost all contexts favor the meaning "point of time, instant" over "sixtieth part of an hour."[16] Donne is concerned throughout to identify "that *minute*" in which "occasion wrought upon him," but to define it circumstantially (the bell rings) and affectively (the hearer responds), not chronometrically. Indefinition touches larger durations as well. In the fourteenth devotion, on the "criticall dayes" of the illness, days and weeks become, via a scriptural allusion, counters of variable value in a sequence of temporal relativities, both between time and eternity, and within the psyche of the sick man. Quoting 2 Peter 3.8, Donne writes, "Since *a day is as a thousand yeres with thee*, Let, *O Lord*, a *day*, be as a *weeke* to me; and in this one, let me consider *seven daies*, seven *critical daies*, and *judge my selfe, that I be not judged by thee*" (74−75).

As temporal durations prove elastic, so temporal identifications prove elusive. Donne scholars have persuasively diagnosed as typhus the illness that prompted the *Devotions*, and have dated it to November and December 1623, the time of an epidemic in London.[17] Though they agree, working primarily from external evidence, on the general season of Donne's sickness, they differ as to its exact duration. Donne records his first symptoms in the book's first section, the passing of the crisis in the nineteenth. The book's most careful readers cannot agree as to how much time is covered by the tract of text between. For R. C. Bald these nineteen devotions recount a period of seven days, for Kate Frost approximately fourteen, for Clara Lander exactly twenty-three, at the rate of one Devotion "for each day or station of the sickness" (and incipient convalescence).[18] The disagreement arises because the text, so minutely circumstantial about the disease as to constitute virtually a case study, is silent on particulars of time.[19] Donne specifies no temporal linkup (such as Lander imagines) between devotions and days, no temporal span between occasion and occasion, and no dates. The *Devotions* dispenses with precisely those time signals that the calendrically minded biographer seeks out.

The omission is so systematic as to look like policy. At one point Donne argues in effect that text is incapable of pinpointing local time: "if we consider *Tyme* to be but the *Measure of Motion*, and howsoever it may seeme to have three *stations, past, present,* and *future,* yet the *first* and *last* of these *are* not (one is not, now, & the other is not yet) And that which you call *present,* is not *now* the same that it was, when you began to call it so in this *Line,* (before you sound that word, *present,* or that *Monosyllable, now,* the present,

& the *Now* is past,) if this *Imaginary halfe-nothing, Tyme*, be of the Essence of our *Happinesses*, how can they be thought *durable?*" (71). The argument looks back to the *locus classicus* on language and time in Augustine's *Confessions*, where the syllable lengths in the spoken words *Deus Creator omnium* enable Augustine to advance his argument as to how humans measure time. "Each of the long syllables [in these words] is a double quantity compared with each of the short ones. I can tell this because, by pronouncing them, I find it to be the case, in so far as I can rely upon the plain evidence of my own hearing. . . . What, then, is it that I measure? What has become of the short syllable . . . [and] the long one . . . ? The sound of both is finished and has been wafted into the past. They no longer exist. All the same I measure them . . . I say confidently that one is a single and the other a double quantity. . . . I must be measuring something which remains fixed in my memory."[20] Donne echoes Augustine, though, largely to confute him. Where Augustine "confidently" uses words as a means to measure time, to affirm its existence and explore its nature, Donne invokes language to call both into question. This "*Imaginary halfe-nothing, Tyme*" is so evanescent that it cannot endure even as long as the mere "*Monosyllable, now*" that denotes its only conceivable mode of existence, the present. It is time, not language, that falls short. The difference from Augustine is partly one of medium. The saint imagines language spoken and heard, the dean written and read: "you began to call it so in this *Line*," he writes, writing the line. The correspondence between the spoken "now" and the moment it designates is at least perceptible to the ear ("the plain evidence of my own hearing"). That between the written "now" and its moment is far less determinate. Writing both takes time and abides in time, so that in Donne's terms "the *Now* is past" even before the word is set down, and the inscription, though ostensibly designating the present, contains also the past of its own inception, and endures into what at that inception was the future. The written text can extend the reach of the *now* indefinitely, but in doing so it calls into question (by the logic Donne develops here) the substantiality of the time that it purports, unreliably, to represent.

Donne's text does all this with peculiar intentness and ingenuity. As Frost and other critics have observed, the *Devotions* cultivates an "overwhelming sense of metaphorical present time" in which the local moment—the time when, the immediate occasion—appears to absorb events both past and future with the relentlessness of a black hole (Frost 138). The process begins early, in the work's first sentence. "This minute I was well, and am ill, this

minute" (7). The first two words establish a seeming present that the ensuing clause (with its *was*) tugs into the immediate past (as if to say "*just* this
minute")—a moment immediately countered by the closure of the chias-
mus, which strongly argues that the minutes of "well" and "ill" (both
designated "*this* minute") are one and the same. The strategy, once begun,
sustains itself throughout the text by varied surprises of verb tense and sentence structure (the rubric already cited, "I am dead," being one of the
simplest). The *Devotions* takes its cue from the temporal (symptoms, bells)
but strives to develop from them a *now*, a *nunc stans*, situated outside time
and against it, highlighting its "half-nothingness" by calculated contrast.

The absence of chronometry abets this design. Amid so many devices of
immediacy, the data of dates and hours would mediate between moment and
reader in ways at odds with the argument of the book. The *Devotions* argues
for, and models, a capacity to "apprehend and lay hold of" occasions. Donne
contrives to write repeatedly "from that *minute*, that [the] occasion wrought
upon him." He implies throughout that such moments may arise—like the
bells that furnish the occasion in this phrase, and like the mortality that
prompts the bells—at any time. The occurrence of these minutes resists
location on a time grid as their duration and impact defy measurement. To
anchor such instants in the numbers of time would be to betray their efficacy
as occasions, and to distort the achronicity of death (its indifference to human scheduling) that the occasions limn. The bells Donne contemplates, and
the text in which he contemplates them, construe time as a medium in which
occasions for devotion unfold in sequence but not on schedule.

The text of the *Devotions* is so intricately made that it resists alignment
with any one genre or pious practice. In its time form, though, it displays
affinities with a peculiarly Anglican exercise, the "occasional meditation."
Pioneered in both theory and practice by Donne's acquaintance Joseph Hall
in the early 1600s, the form attained enormous popularity by mid-century.[21]
Robert Boyle, in his *Occasional Reflections* (1665), purveyed models that
many imitated, in print and manuscript.[22] Hall, in his *Arte of Divine Meditation*
(1606), defines the practice, for the first time, as "a bending of the mind
upon some spiritual object . . . occasioned by outward occurrences offered
to the mind" (72). To distinguish this mode from another (the "deliberate"
meditation, to which Hall devotes most of the book), he assigns it a telling
adjective: "extemporal." For Hall as for Donne, the value of devotion upon
emergent occasions derives in part from its independence of chronometry,
the sense that the "extemporal" meditation, arising "out of the moment,"

can for that very reason lead the meditator outside time, away from the "businesse" of "*tell[ing] Clocks*" and towards that of "entring . . . into *Eternitie*." What Hall calls "the suddenness of this act" warrants also its intensity, authenticity, and redemptive power (73).

The extemporality of the practice exerts, in the writings that model it, a curious pressure on images of timekeeping. Bells, clocks, and dials often appear, but usually in such a way as to call into question (without explicit denunciation) whether timekeeping is desirable or even feasible—to point away from measure and towards occasion. Hall meditates upon "a cracked bell," upon a celebratory (i.e., occasion-driven) "peal of bells," and "upon the tolling of a passing bell," but he does not muse on the bell that tells the hour. Boyle does, but listening, like Donne, from his sickbed, he finds the public bell stunningly erratic, and meditates "Upon telling the Strokes of an ill-going Clock in the Night." [23] The extemporal meditation seeks out the occasional even in the instruments of timekeeping; it picks up on those signals in which "distinction of houres" dissolves, where measure loosens its hold. [24] George Swinnock, a follower in Boyle's tradition, captures the essential temporality of the practice in a governing metaphor: for the maker of occasional meditations, he writes, "Every object is as a *Bell*, which if but turned, makes a report of the great Gods honour and renown." [25]

Like Donne, Hall, Boyle, and Swinnock, Pepys too seizes on the sound of a bell and transposes it into text. But he does so with a difference: he chooses a sound from a different sector of the time system, and he makes of it a different kind of occasion. Here is the text again:

> . . . thence home, where I found my wife and maid a-washing.
> I sat up till the bell-man came by with his bell, just under my window as I was writing of this very line, and cried, "Past one of the clock, and a cold, frosty, windy morning." I then went to bed and left my wife and the maid a-washing still.

Like the occasional meditators, Pepys writes (in Richardson's famous phrase) "to the moment": [26] his record is his response to a fresh stimulus, depicted as concurrent with the act of writing (compare Donne's "The *Bell* rings out" [91]). In his case, though, the occasion is constituted as an act of temporal measure: the bellman tells the time. The passage differs from occasional meditation in larger ways as well. Pepys "apprehends and lays hold of" the occasion (to adapt Donne's wording) not in order to discover its "Spiritual Uses" (to borrow a phrase of Boyle's [2.1]), but in order to experiment with its temporal transcription. This early sentence, like all others in the document to come, may have traveled through revisions to arrive at its final form;[27] unlike almost any that follow, it purports to narrate the precise moment of its creation. Pepys is testing the capacity of his new medium and its materials literally to tell time—and the timekeeper—as it passes.

The telling proves nuanced in ways worth noting; the pursuit of synchrony yields odd disjunctures. First, although "this *very* line" asserts that the actions it records are simultaneous with its own "making," Pepys narrates them (as he has narrated most of the day) in the past tense ("sat," "came," "cried"). Where Donne cultivates "an overwhelming sense of metaphorical present time," Pepys insists on an irreducible sense of the actual (albeit immediate) past. In writing, Pepys suggests by his choice of tense, true simultaneity is impossible. Text must move in the wake of the speech and actions it sets down. The discrepancy resonates (even in some details of the diction) with Donne's argument that time will always outpace prose: "that which you call *present*, is not *now* the same that it was, when you began to call it so in this *Line*, (before you sound that word, *present*, or that *Monosyllable*, *now*, the present, & the *Now* is past) . . ." (71). Pepys's echo of Donne (like Donne's of Augustine) amounts to opposition. Donne assumes in his addressee a delusion that "that which you call *present*" is stable and palpable enough to endure translation into text. Pepys, sidestepping the delusion, in effect reverses the line of argument, and the argument from "line." Whereas Donne invokes the act of writing in order to argue time's nullity, Pepys performs an act of writing that establishes time's practical, familiar presence, and (like Augustine's act of recitation) tracks the means by which, though impalpable, time makes itself accessible to mind and measure. Pepys's project is to make time almost palpable through multiple mediations. The "very line" of ink on paper, whose sense and syntax are shaped by the force of time, is the last in a quick sequence of embodiments. Time here has a sound (the bell's), a body and a voice (the bellman's), and finally a number, which the bellman represents (as Pepys represents the bellman) as a moment ("one o'clock") already "past" at the time of report. Time here is real and full enough to work interventions on street and sheet.

To the degree that time is palpable, it can also be possessed. The bellman functions as a medium through which his hearers may partly privatize time's report. He operates somewhere between the public clock (whose time he tells, naming only the hour) and the occupants of private rooms, where clocks and watches are as yet far from common.[28] To any given auditor the bellman will sound loudest when he is nearest; his constant movement makes of his repeated patter a sequence of addresses that successive hearers will construe, simply by virtue of the hearing, as specifically pitched at them.[29] Passing "just under *my* window," the bellman moves along the borderline between public and private space; his report of public circumstance (weather as well as time) will enter the room though he will not. Pepys, by writing the moment into his journal, pushes much further the privatization that the bellman has begun. Pepys transposes the data—the sound of the bell, the words of the man—from the realm of the audible and public to that of the visible but private in "this very line" composed for his eyes only. The transcription is attentive. An unwonted metric regularity (anapestic tetrameter) even hints at onomatopoeia—

˘ ˘ ´ | ˘ ˘ ´ | ˘ ˘ ´ | ˘ ˘ ´
I sat up till the bell-man came by with his bell

—and mimicry here is a mode of abduction. The sound, thus imitated, becomes subdued to the materials Pepys works in. His shorthand, legible only to the initiated, achieves as script what a whisper works as speech—a selective and sequestered address, the bellman's *modus operandi* writ small.

Pepys privatizes the occasion another way as well, not simply by the tools of his transcription, but also by its syntax. Amid the prevailing simple past tense ("sat," "came," "cried") the diarist allows a single deviation. He casts his own writing in the progressive past ("as I *was* writing of this very line"), which coupled with the pleonastic "of" suggests a process still in progress. The line he was "writing of" had not yet been completed when the bellman appeared and passed. This ongoing activity, so the slight verb shift suggests, encompasses the more transitory actions that presently accompany it. The bellman passes "under my window," only to be fixed in the phrase that "I was writing of"—to inhabit, that is, a subordinate construction in a sentence of whose main clause ("I sat up") Pepys himself is subject. The sentence miniaturizes and makes explicit the diary's technology for laying hold of fugitive phenomena and enclosing them within a fullness of time constructed by the act of serial writing.

The writing that compasses the bellman in "this very line" is itself compassed by the slightly larger frame Pepys builds around it: the *inclusio,* already mentioned, that Pepys performs with the phrase about "my wife and maid a-washing." *A*-washing, like "writing *of*," is a pleonasm that points to unlimited process. The closing variation, "with my wife and the maid a-washing *still*," enhances the impression of continuity—of time itself as an *inclusio* that encompasses endpoints ("I went to bed") within the ongoing. The particular subject matter of this inclusio sustains the sense of proprietorship as well as process. Pepys ends his day amid the activity of subordinates. "*My wife and maid*" within the house, like the bellman at "*my* window," serve the diarist himself as adjuncts in his life and items in his book—they index his control. In the passage's set of compound enclosures, Pepys's writing is in the middle and also at the edge: he compasses the bellman, is compassed by his own family, and compasses them in composition and conception. If Pepys possesses the bellman by situating him inside a frame that Pepys constructs as ownership (household) and prose (book), he enacts self-possession by similar means.

Like Pepys in this entry, Donne in the *Devotions* makes bell sound a harbinger of closure—but a misleading one. Donne invokes a last bellringing that is linked like Pepys's with the end of the day and the start of sleep. "It is not in *mans body*, as it is in the *Citie*, that when *the Bell* hath rung, to cover your *fire*, and rake up the *embers*, you may lie downe, and sleepe without feare. Though you have by *physicke* and *diet*, raked up the *embers* of your *disease*, stil there is a feare of a *relapse*" (121). In Donne's hands the curfew bell appears not as a present reality (like the passing bell) but as a metaphor, a figure that both contrasts and resonates with his predicament. Its name (*covre feu*) expresses an imperative that few now obeyed; its function had gradually shifted, since its institution in the middle ages, from the hortatory to the chronometric. It tolled a specific hour (generally eight o'clock in English cities), without strongly enforcing the specific behaviors for which it had been originally devised.[30] In contrast with the earlier death bells, and in concert with the metaphor Donne has developed over the previous section, of his disease as a fire, the curfew here operates as a figure of sublunary time, an arbitrary limit easily bypassed by continuity and contingency. The death bells, conduits out of time to eternity, ineluctably enforce the sense of an ending. The curfew does so more provisionally, and in this sense it resembles rather than differs from the precarious cure of "*physicke* and *diet*" of which Donne now writes. The illness threatened the end of life; the cure cannot promise the end of illness.

Placed at the beginning of the book's last Devotion, the curfew bell marks a shift from the kind of time the text has written into the kind of time it will not write. Donne titles this devotion *Metusque Relabi: They warne mee of the fearefull danger of relapsing*. In the course of it, the fear shifts its focus from one kind of relapse to another. "My *meditation*," Donne writes, "is feare-fully transferred from the *body* to the *minde*" (122). With the lifting of his bodily disease, Donne fears the return of the "*spirituall sicknesse*" of habitual sin and inattention to grace: "My *sicknesse* brought mee to *thee* in *repentance,* and my *relapse* [into health and into sin] hath cast mee farther from thee" (125). What alarms Donne most, his last expostulation and prayer make clear, is the withdrawal of that sense of imminent ending that has suffused his recent days and prompted his autobiographical text. With the recovery from crisis and the reentry into *chronos* the text of emergent occasions comes to an end, as though, with author trapped again in ordinary time, there is nothing in this kind to write about.

Donne's figure of the diurnal bell calls to mind how closely, in some respects, the temporality of the *Devotions* resembles that of the diary as Pepys constructs it. Both texts combine a chronologically sequential narrative with a highly wrought fiction of immediacy and a concomitantly provisional (and fictional) closure.[31] Both writers repeatedly manifest a structurally deter-mined uncertainty as to what will come next, Donne at the end of each devotion (and emphatically at the end of the last), Pepys at the end of every entry.

Between the two texts, though, the figuration of time's fullness differs sharply in ways that are made clear by each work's structural use of number. In both the *Devotions* and the diary each new tract of text (devotion, entry) is headed by a numeral. Donne numbers irregular crises in chronological sequence ("1. Insultus Morbi primus; 2. Actio Laesa. 3. Decubitus sequitur tandem"). Pepys numbers fixed durations; his numerals are dates. Donne's serial numbers figure a kind of optative fullness. They itemize, as his subtitle establishes, "severall steps in my Sicknes," but not necessarily every step: they represent the totality of occasions he has "apprehended" as text, which is not, he makes clear, the same thing as all the occasions God has proffered. Pepys's numbers track a completeness more schematic and (on its own terms) compulsory. The record is full only if the day-numbers introduce narratives in a calendrically unbroken series. Donne's criterion for textual fullness, like that which governs the bells that announce and exhort, depends on the unscheduled convergence of event and response; Pepys's, like that of the bells that ring the hours, depends on fixed measures of time.

What "emergent occasion" does for Donne, ordinary measure does for Pepys: it structures time in text, but to the opposite effect. The opposi-tion becomes clearest, perhaps, in the oddly aligned points of experience at which Donne ends his text and Pepys starts his. In a preamble that precedes his first dated entry, Pepys devotes his diary's first words to remarking the *absence* of a relapse: "Blessed be God, at the end of the last year I was without any sense of my old pain, except upon the taking of cold" (1.1). Pepys's "old pain" is that of a potentially fatal kidney stone that a surgeon had removed (in a potentially fatal operation) twenty-one months earlier; Pepys too is expressing, less directly than Donne, a *metus relabi*. As it happens, Donne mentions the affliction of the stone just after his figure of the curfew, in an argument as to how mortals make a kind of property out of experience: "Even in *pleasures*, and in *paines*, there is a *propriety*, a *Meum & Tuum*; and a man is most affected with that *pleasure* which is *his, his* by former enjoying and experience, and most intimidated with those *paines* which are *his, his* by a wofull sense of them, in former afflictions. . . . [I]n *bodily paines*, in a fit of the *stone*, the patient wonders why any man should call the *Gout* a *paine*" (121). Every textualization of time, perhaps, produces a kind of *Meum*, a degree of *propriety*, but Donne in the *Devotions* has selected those *kairoi* when his pain enables him to shed his own time (the telling of clocks) and approach the timeless, when he can be "united" (as the passing bell unites him) "with God." For two-thirds of each devotion (in the expostulations and the prayers) Donne makes God his addressee. In Pepys's opening sentence, God appears in a subjunctive clause; the main clause (like that encompassing the bellman) belongs to the diarist. Pepys pursues a propriety in time rather than a release from it. That is one reason why he can begin his text where Donne leaves off—at a point of re-entry into ordinary time through the portal of a recovery from illness, and in an explicit absence of *experiential* occasion ("I was without . . . pain"), coincident (on New Year's Day) with a plethora of calendrical commencements. It is the reason, too, that he structures the diary as he does. The *Meum*, which he enacted by *inclusio* in the bellman moment, he performs as steady, serial chronometry in the diaristic scheme; the proprietary method depends on a continuous temporal tracking, regardless of occasion. Pursuing such propriety, Pepys numbers his days as Donne does not.

OCCASION WITHIN MEASURE: LEDGERS, ALMANACS, JOURNALS

The theology of occasions does not necessarily militate against measure. Early in the *Devotions* Donne represents the abundance of God's grace in terms of ordinary, sublunary time, portioned by calendar and clock: "We are *Gods tenants* heere, and yet here, he, our *Land-lord* payes us *Rents*; not yearely, nor quarterly, but hourely, and quarterly; *Every minute he renewes his mercy . . .*" (9). The passage diverges somewhat from the text's larger patterns of resistance to "tell[ing] clocks," and of insistence on the rarity of occasions. Here occasions of a certain kind (God's "payments") are so copious that the measures of ordinary time offer a convenient framework: hours, quarters, and minutes abound with the opportunity for grace.

The kind of argument Donne here advances, combined with the pecuniary figure in which he couches it, had been pervasively invoked throughout the late sixteenth and seventeenth centuries to endorse a practice of self-chronicling that was temporally distinct from that of the *Devotions*, and to provide for it a governing trope. The practice was the daily "Diurnall," and the trope depicted it as a kind of narrative ledger book. John Fuller invoked the figure in his introduction to his brother minister John Beadle's treatise on *The Journal or Diary of a Thankful Christian*, the "one Puritan treatise on diary-keeping." [32] "Tradesmen keep their shop books. Merchants their Accompt books. . . . Some wary husbands have kept a Diary of dayly disbursements. Travellers a Journal of all they have seen, and hath befallen them in their way. A Christian that would be exact hath more need, and may reap much more good by such a Journall as this." [33] In the seventeenth century the precedent of the "Accompt book" lies behind many (perhaps most) diaries, Pepys's included, as a model of efficiency and a tool for steady self-reckoning. If "disbursements" (whether divine or human) take place "dayly," so should their setting down in text.

Over the hundred years preceding Pepys's first entry, the Puritan diarists and divines who developed the strongest and best-articulated traditions concerning the practice of journal-keeping insisted on the importance of a relentless continuity. In order to enjoy any hope of salvation, the believer must exercise a constant vigilance over thought and action, a ceaseless monitoring of the relation between self and God. Fuller in 1656 speaks effectively for the whole tradition: "There is a book of three leaves thou shouldest read dayly to make up this Diary; the black leaf of thy own and others sins with shame and sorrow; the white leaf of Gods goodnesse . . . ; the red leaf of Gods judgments felt, feared, threatned, with fear and trembling" (b4r). Fuller here construes journal-keeping as an act of transcription and interpretation: his disciples are first to "read dayly" the signs of sins, goodness, and judgment, in the soul and in the world, and then to write down their readings at the same diurnal rate. Since every thought, action, and event bears implications for the relation between the diarist and God, so pervasive a piece of prose ought theoretically to encompass every possible kind of occasion, and should narrate every waking hour of its author's day. Beadle, in the midst of the manual proper, restates this argument as a commandment and a question: "Remember, and for that end put into your Journal all deliverances from dangers, vouchsafed to you or yours. And indeed, what is our whole life, but a continued deliverance? We are daily delivered . . ." (55). Hence, the "whole life" requires recounting, and (by the logic Donne briefly limned), since the opportunities for grace and for deliverance are constantly "continued," the continuity can best be reckoned by fixed durations, in the steadfast time discipline of diurnal form.

Yet as I've already remarked, this is not the way diaries of the early seventeenth century, religious or secular, actually work. They do not treat the calendar as a cluster of contiguous measures of time, each to be consistently represented and filled by text, but rather as the arena of marked occasions, often thematically coherent but temporally scattered. I want, over the next few pages, to examine briefly and to explain in part the discontinuities of diary-keeping in the early seventeenth century, by pointing to possible sources for it in each of the three fields of practice that (often in combination) generated most of the diaries in the period: religious self-examination, astrology, and bookkeeping. First, the theory of religious diary-keeping contained contradictions inimical to the continuity it purportedly espoused: the purposes the diary was supposed to serve told against the time-form it was supposed to take. Second, astrology, while it entailed sharp attention to the calendar and clock, favored also a highlighting of occasions and significant junctures. The astrological almanac, which was the most popular book on sale, was also one of the most common repositories for diary-keeping; taking its template from astrology, it privileged occasion over continuum. Finally, fiscal accounting, which functions in some diaries as a governing metaphor and in some as a concurrent activity (with the diarist tracking expense and income among other things), produced similar results. It modeled an account of discrete transactions—and this pattern operated, courtesy of the bookkeeping precedent, in secular as well as religious journals.

It is striking that John Beadle, despite the diurnal pleonasm in the title of his treatise (*The Journal or Diary* . . .) addresses to his readers no specific injunction to write in the diary every day. He spends many pages telling them what to write and why, but gives no sentence specifying when and at what rate. Within Beadle's advocacy there lurks a running contradiction as to the possibility of continuity. On the one hand, all pious people will profit from keeping "a constant Diary by them of all Gods gracious dealings with them" (a1v). On the other, to tell "all" is impossible for mortals, however "constant": "Our deliverances are more then we can number, greater then we can value" (56); "Who can number the stars or sands; Gods blessings, or our sins?" (b4r). The avowed impossibility of full enumeration may help explain why many Puritan diarists, who display a marked propensity for self-reproach, do not reproach themselves for skipping days (often many days) in their journals.[34] Beadle and Fuller repeatedly set up Scripture as the model for the diarist: Moses, narrating the sojourn in the wilderness, kept "a Jour-nall of all Gods mercies" (13)—but that is not a daily record either.

Nonetheless, the Puritan propensity for "daily direction" and discipline was sufficient to give the etymologies of "journal" and "diary" the force of temporal directive for some self-chroniclers, who produced, for stretches at least, an entry for every day. The Puritan journal's commitment to occasion rather than measure is rooted more deeply, in the widespread concept of its proper content. The "black leaf of thy own . . . sins," which Fuller specifies as the diary's first text, will often produce in practice a catalog of disparate lapses, named but not narrated. Such is the case in the diary of Samuel Ward:

> *June 10, 1595.* Thy sin in not goyng to Mr. Newhouse prayers, with thy scandall to Mr. Huchinson and Sir Sharpes thereby.

> *June 11, 1595.* Thy sin of pride, beyng with Mr. Briggs in Burwell his shop. Thy sin of prid[e] comming thorow the court, the same day att night. Thy neglect in calling upon God that day. Thy bythoughtes att prayer in the sameevening.[35]

The entries, consecutive as to date, are fragmentary as to syntax: noun phrases without predication. In such constructions Ward's sins of omission ("not goyng," "neglect") come through more intelligibly than their opposites, perhaps because they mirror in their nature the diarist's elliptical method. For Ward the mere naming of sins suffices. In specifying what he did not do, he implies what he should have done, and so provides a much fuller account of such lapses than he does of his more active misdeeds, whose complex action he covers (and obscures) in succinct abstractions. He renders it impossible, for example, to reconstruct how he committed the "sin of prid[e]" in "comming thorow the court." He itemizes but does not explain.

Puritan diaristic practice endorsed narrative omissions, whatever the theory might propose to the contrary. Beadle argues that God supervises mortal actions at all times but, "all God's dealings" being impossible to track, he implicitly encourages his readers to recount in detail those occasions on which divine interventions proved most conspicuous, and to pass in silence over plainer parts of time. Richard Rogers, a near-contemporary of Ward's but a far more copious diarist, attempts in some of his early entries to narrate certain parts of his everyday experience once and for all, so that he can skip over them in future. As he writes on 22 December 1587,

> And here in these 2 months I have more particu[larly] set downe thinges—
> not to observe the same course throughout, for that were infinit—but where
> any part of my life hereafter shall agree with any of this, which I have here
> set downe, that I may mak relation of it to some of this and not allwaies sett
> downe the same thinges again. (71)

Rogers here dispenses with the very narrative task to which Pepys, seventy-two years later, will commit himself: that of setting down the same things—rising, dining, and (most famously) going "to bed"—again and again, in pursuit of temporal continuity by a design effectually "infinit" (there is no telling how many repetitions will follow).

Among diaries kept by Puritans, perhaps the one that comes closest to Pepys's in its way of moving through time is that of Lady Margaret Hoby. For nearly two and a half years, from August 1599 through December 1601, she writes a series of daily entries remarkably uniform in content, length, and phrasing, and remarkably unbroken save for two lacunae where she suspends the record because of illness (ten days in 1600, thirty-nine in 1601). Like Pepys, and unlike Rogers, Hoby is sufficiently interested in full coverage of the day to court it by repetition. In her diary's fullest years she, too, tracks her time between rising from bed and returning to it:

> [*March* 1599 *The Lordes day* :16:]
> After priuat praers I did eate, read, and then goe to the church: after, I
> praied, then I dined and, when I had talked a whill, I went to church againe :
> after, I went to visite a neighboure, then I walked : after, I vret notes in my
> bible and, after I had dressed my patients, I went to priuat praier, and so to
> supper : after, to publeck, and, when I had taken order for diner the next
> day and praied priuatly, I went to bed

> [*The next day the* :17:]
> After priuat praers I did eate, heare Mr Rhodes read, dressed my patients,
> praied, went to my workmen, and then dined : after, I wrought, walked

abroad, took a lector, reed of the testement, praied with Mr Rhodes and, before supper, examined my selfe and praied priuatly: after, went to supper, then to the lector, and lastly to bed:[36]

Still, despite the continuity of her syntax (full clauses rather than fragments) Hoby, like Ward and unlike Pepys, deals extensively in itemization, in naming rather than narrating; what she names most often are occasions of prayer. She rarely specifies what she ate, read, wrote, heard, wrought, or talked about—the kinds of particulars which (like the bellman's bell and words, Pepys's window, line, wife and maid) fill out the timeframe from the inside. Over the course of the diary, itemization becomes compounded by larger discontinuities. Beginning in 1601, the record becomes intermittent and, as Hoby's editor notes, "there are large gaps in the diary [through] the end of that portion which has survived" (283, n. 527). The gaps occasionally assume a significant pattern of their own: for some stretches Hoby writes only an entry for every Sunday ("the Lordes day"). The pattern confirms what the earlier, continuous portion also suggests: that Hoby is most interested in that portion of her time that belongs most explicitly to God. Throughout the document she reckons the date by a double scheme: first by the number of days since the previous "Lordes day" and only then by the date of the month: "*The first day after [Sunday]: the :14 [of April, 1600]*." Hoby hovers intriguingly, then, between a theocentric time, focused on acts of piety, and the more eclectic comprehensiveness of temporality in Pepys.

Leopold Damrosch, Jr., attributes the temporal discontinuities that Puritans produced in their life writings to "striking ambiguities in their conception of time." They "were keenly interested in temporality," he writes, yet "if in one sense they were peculiarly concerned with the possible significance of every moment, in another sense they sought constantly to raise the significant moment *out* of time and to interpret it in the light of eternity. . . . Confronting the mysteriousness of Providence, and deeply aware of the crucial importance of each of their actions, Puritans tended to stress temporal separateness rather than continuity. . . . [For them,] the moments of experience are separate and disjunct."[37] Puritan diaries share with Donne's *Devotions* a preoccupation with occasion, albeit differently construed: Donne values the bells for their ritualized stimulus, their "helpes to devotion"; Puritans, repudiating such helps, seek their occasions in moments of private prayer, signals of Providence, and shifts of affect. The sources and nature of the occasions partly differ, but the fundamental temporal structure is the same. Beadle gives it voice and warrant when he urges his readers to "Observe Gods goodness in the choice of time. As God doth all things well, so he doth all at the best time" (89). By way of illustration and assurance, Beadle, like Pepys, misquotes the touchstone text: "Christ is said to be sent at the fullnesse of time, or at the full time" (90). Once again diction dockets the temporal discourse. Beadle's double translation acknowledges the complexity of the concept, but both translations point the same way. "At" is not "in": it specifies a moment; it does not adumbrate a continuum.

Astrology makes much of moments also, and it too influenced enormously the ordinary time patterns for self-recording in the seventeenth century, sometimes separately from religious practices, sometimes in combination. Self-chronographers devoted to the discipline made astrology their document's *raison d'être* and arbiter of form. Samuel Jeake (1652–1699) wrote a "Diary of Actions & Accidents" consisting mostly of short (one or two lines) sporadic entries, each preceded by the date and the appropriate zodiacal sign. A nonconformist minister and obsessive astrologer, Jeake takes his temporal cues from both systems of belief, which occasionally produce, at their convergence, an unusually long and detailed entry:

> Jan. 9 About 5h p.m. As I went over London bridge to go to the posthouse then in Bishopsgate street; there being a great stop on the bridge, & I having gone as far as the uncovered place a little before the drawbridge; was thrust to the Eastside close to the stonewall; where a Cart passed so nigh to the wall, that I had scarce room left to stand between; & if I had not providentially lift up my Foot, & stept into a puddle of mud I believe the Cart had run over it & broke it.[38]

Here is Pepysian particularity in abundance, but stemming from a different source, and from a diametrically opposite conception of time. This detailed account sits surrounded by a narrative void: the previous entry dates from seventeen days earlier, and proffers in a half line the abbreviated title of a book Jeake read; the next entry, offering similar data with similar sparseness, occurs ten days later. This present story derives its fullness from the intersection, at one moment ("About 5h p.m.") and in one motion (the "lift[ing] up my Foot") of two immense time schemes: astrological and Providential. As his editors explain, Jeake appends the horoscopic diagram (as he does several times elsewhere in the diary) in order to demonstrate that "the astrological configuration indicated impending catastrophe which would inexorably have followed had God not providentially intervened" (12). Jeake narrates a conjunction of conjuncts, *kairoi* compounded.

As the opening phrase of his entry makes clear, the astrological paradigm encouraged textual precision about the clock time of events. Elias Ashmole took such precision further. Where Jeake occasionally inserted a horoscope into his narrative, Ashmole often wrapped his narrative inside a horoscope (the bracketed passages are explanations by Ashmole's editor, C. H. Josten):

22 *Jan.* 1653
[Inside a horoscope for 8.30 a.m.:]
The time when I returned from Bradfield and entered London / 15′ after [i.e., fifteen minutes later] I entered my house /

24 *Jan.* 1653
[An horary question, inside a horoscope for 1 p.m.:]
Whether the things that were stolen from Sir Thomas Leigh will be had again.
. . .

26 *Jan.* 1653
[An horary question, inside a horoscope for 6.20 a.m.:]
Whether it will be good for me if I join with my Brother Dudly in the patent for mines or not / [39]

Josten explains the phenomenon of the "horary question" and the necessity of precision to the minute: "Even the time at which a question first crossed the astrologer's mind, or at which such a question was put before him, was significant; its horoscope would point to the answer" (1.24). As with Jeake, precision in itself is not conducive to continuity; the texts above represent the complete written record for their days. Horoscopy, as the name implies, entails the sighting of particular, significant *horae*, not the representation of them in smooth succession.

Jeake records a past deliverance; Ashmole pinpoints the present conception of a question about the future. Astrology claimed to order the whole field of time, and practicing astrologers were not the only figures who produced texts within its framework. Anyone could buy into the temporality simply by acquiring an almanac, and an enormous number of people did. No other book in English circulated as widely. In the 1660s, Bernard Capp points out, "sales averaged about 400,000 copies annually, a figure which suggests that roughly one family in three bought an almanac each year." They were purchasing a reference work that ranged through time's three modes. It systematized the past—for example in tables of monarchs' reigns. It facilitated the present, by the *Kalendar* (one month per page) that usually began the book, and by useful tables and practical counsel that varied with the maker (more prosperous people bought a set of almanacs each year, in order to attain a wider range of reference). It predicted the future in the separate section labeled "Prognostication." For many families, the almanac and the Bible comprised the entire household library, and the almanac, like the family Bible, offered a venue for self-recording. People not only read it; they also wrote in it the data of their lives.[40]

The customary titles of the almanacs—*Almanack and Prognostication, Ephemeris and Prognostication*—convey a fair idea of the structures of time into which these inscriptions were entered. *Almanack* and *Ephemeris*, like *diary* and *journal*, have *day* at their root, and almanacs, unlike most manuscript diaries of the period, did take note of every day of the year by multiple systems of designation (dates, days of week, dominical letters, holidays); they prognosticated the days too, by methods ranging from the systematic (forecasting times of sunrise and sunset and charting phases of the moon) to improvisatory (foretelling weather, political events, signs and wonders, more often by month and season than by individual day). As with Puritan "diary theory," the almanac's built-in diurnality might be expected to have encouraged a corresponding daily practice in its inscribers, but (as with Puritan diary practice) this proves not to be the case. They too write only occasionally.

There are several reasons. The space provided for inscription varied from format to format. Many almanacs set aside no particular space. The astrologer and mathematician John Dee wrote his diary "in a very small illegible hand on the margins of old Almanacs," and spacing imposed selectivity, as a series of successive entries will suggest: "1592. March 6th, the Quene granted my sute to Dr. Awbrey. March 9th, the pryvy seale at night.

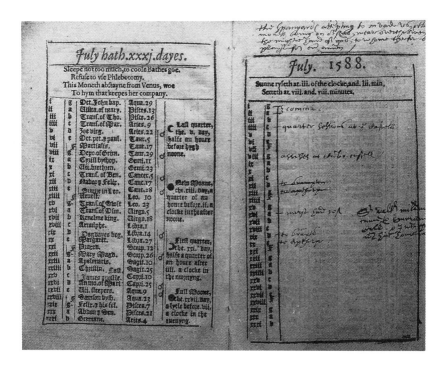

Figure 2. Two pages from a copy of Gabriel Frende's *Almanacke and Prognostication*, 1588, owned and inscribed by Thomas Byng, Master of Clare College Cambridge. Reproduced by permission of the Dean and Chapter of Canterbury.

March 16th, the great seale. March 18th, Arthur and Katharine were let blud at London by Doctor Dodding's cownsayle."[41] Some almanacs, called "blanks," alternated a page full of the month's printed data with a facing page open for inscription (though often calibrated to the datelines opposite; see Fig. 2). The scheme did not leave much room for narrative expatiation, and inscribers generally chose in any case to itemize memorable but disparate events rather than to perform each day as prose; Frank H. Stubbings points out that for the Cambridge Master's six-year almanac-diary represented in Fig. 2 "there are seldom more than half a dozen entries in one month, and they never constitute anything approaching a continuous journal."[42] John Aubrey's contentious colleague Anthony à Wood wrote perhaps the most sustained, copious, and best-known of almanac diaries, in interleaved almanacs over a 38-year period (1657–98), but they too run to form: short notes, some days.[43] It may be that the almanac fostered such occasionality not merely by the spatial limitations of its format but by the continuities of its own content. Inscribers could set down their autobiographical occasions with the knowledge that time was being tracked steadily elsewhere in the volume.

Time was not merely tracked, of course, but foretold as well. The almanac owner's inscriptions, retrospective and usually brief, punctuate pages amply occupied by proleptic print. This timing, too, abets intermittency of inscription; those days that the owner does not narrate in retrospect, the almanac has already charted in prospect. (Parodic almanacs, a concurrent and popular genre, made mirth on this point by including in their pages the kind of trivial memoranda that almanac diarists were assumed to write: "The red cow took bull"; "The black cat caught a mouse in the barn."[44] The public book thus "prophesied" private action.) The standard *Almanack and Prognostication* presented a time span already filled at the time of purchase, and copiously charted and narrated in the future tense; it figured the fullness of time to some extent as a *fait accompli*. Even the blanks prefabricated the year's time as space, allotting by their format just so much to each passing day, and most blanks retained as well the full prognostic apparatus. At the cultural moment when Pepys began his diary, the textual account of days most commonly purchased and possessed, read and inscribed, constructed a kind of time literally booked in advance.

Pepys read almanacs more for mirth than for instruction (there is no record of his writing in them). He found amusement in the published almanac parodies (1.288–89) and in the errors of the real thing: "We read and laughed at Lillys prophecies this month—in his almanac this year" (6.14.67; 8.270). For a naval administrator, the laugh was bitter. William Lilly had predicted English victory and peace with Holland; the Dutch warships were now in the Medway. Pepys's method of textualizing "this year" and "this month" is at once more circumspect and more supple: to narrate the days as or after they pass, and at the length that their events seem to him in retrospect to demand. Rather than insert experience into a time span prefigured as proleptic structure (as do the almanac diarists), Pepys renders experience as process, accumulating in tandem with time.

The bound volumes Pepys bought to write the diary in were wholly blank, and by the first marks he made in them—the red lines, top and left, that frame the entries—he associated his enterprise with another tradition of self-recording: this was the standard page format for the book of fiscal accounts. At the time that Pepys began the diary, he worked as Clerk of the Exchequer; he spent his days setting down financial transactions. "The diary," Matthews remarks, "is a concomitant of Pepys's delight in book-keeping. . . . [The] manuscript bears some of the marks of a book-keeper's hand, in its precise spacing and lining, its almost complete freedom from blots. . . . At the end of certain months, and more fully at the end of each year, Pepys presents a balance-sheet for himself and the nation, a concise statement that sets out the debits and credits in politics, morality and finance, particularly his own finance" (1.cvi–cvii). This procedure, Matthews admits, "loses distinctiveness in the body of the diary," nor is it quite as distinct as his wording may suggest even at the moments in question (Pepys never writes into the diary a formal balance sheet of any kind). Matthews is nonetheless right that "delight in bookkeeping" was a motive "that explains the origin of many diaries of [Pepys's] time and later" (1.cviii). Again, though, the temporality Pepys builds from this motive and this mode differs radically from that produced in other diaries of this time, both religious and secular, that start from the same paradigm.

Many of the reasons reside in the paradigm. The affinity between account making and journal writing is confirmed by language: "Journal" is the technical term for the middle stage of double-entry bookkeeping, which demands the maintenance of three separate documents. Transactions first set down and narrated in the memorandum book are then transferred to the journal, where they are translated into a concise, standardized language and format; subsequently they are recast once again into the more elaborately articulated symmetries of the double-entry ledger.[45] The initial transfer, from memoranda to journal, was to be conducted daily; hence the name "journal" for the second text. Yet the word no more ensures systematically diurnal form in accounting than it does in spiritual self-chronicling. For a day on which no transactions take place (a Sunday for example) nothing at all will be recorded. Bookkeeping entails its own sharply defined thematics. It demands completeness in recording a particular kind of occasion, and systematizes the "laying hold" (in Donne's phrase) of such occasions. But it is for that very reason emphatically "occasional" as text. Its purposes have nothing to do with the figuration of time as continuum.

From this model of methodical finance, many diarists developed a narrative of discontinuous incidents and instances. The general arc of development can be discerned in an expressively confused bit of textual genealogy set down by the diarist Sir Henry Slingsby, a Royalist country gentleman. Early in his self-chronicle, he names Montaigne as his model: "I do likewise take his advise in Registering my daily accidents which happens in my house. He saith his father observ'd this order, in his house. . . ."[46] Both the advice and its enactment here work in more complicated ways than Slingsby declares (or, perhaps, perceives). Here is the passage from the *Essais* that he has in mind:

> In his domestic administration my father had this system, which I can praise but not follow: besides the record of household affairs [*le registre des négoces*] kept by his steward, in which were entered petty accounts, payments, and transactions not requiring the notary's hand, he ordered the servant whom he used as his secretary to keep a journal [*un papier journal*] and insert in it all occurrences of any note, and the memorabilia of his family history day by day. A record very pleasant to look at when time begins to efface the memory of events, and very well suited to get us out of perplexity: When was such and such a thing begun? When completed? What retinues came? How long did they stay? Our trips, our absences; marriages; deaths; the receipt of happy or unhappy news; the change of principal servants; such matters. An ancient custom, which I think it would be good to revive, each man in each man's home. And I think I am a fool to have neglected it.[47]

Montaigne actually puts three models of self-documentation in play here: first the *registre des négoces*, detailing fiscal transactions; second the *papier journal*, kept "day by day," of "remarkable occurrences," which his father's secretary sustains parallel to the *registre* but on a higher plane; third, the avowedly less systematic approach Montaigne himself deploys: the essays themselves, in which Montaigne repeatedly declares his determination to avoid any schematics of order. Slingsby's write-up mingles the models: "I follow'd the advise of Michael de Montaigne to sett down in this Book such accidents as befall me, not that I make my study of it, but rather a recreation at vacant times, without observing any time, method, or order in my wrighting, or rather scribbling . . ." (55). Slingsby professed at first to follow Montaigne's ostensible advice and imitate the father ("He saith his father observ'd this order"); here he declares for the son. The final phrases echo the flourishes with which Montaigne often abjures "order." Slingsby proposes, in short, to follow more Montaigne's practice than his preaching. In fact, though, there is considerable common ground between the two. The *papier journal* as Montaigne describes it consists (like the *registre des négoces* with which he parallels it) of signal moments systematically recorded:

the times when "such and such a thing" was begun and when completed; "absences, marriages, deaths," etc. The *Essais* are intrinsically occasional too (though they reckon and write occasion another way). Slingsby produces something in between, less wide-ranging than the *Essais*, and less systematic than the *journal*. Writing during the Civil Wars, Slingsby tracks two topics: the building of his own estate and the struggles (political, military, and personal) of Charles I, which "when completed" (in Montaigne's phrase), end the book: "he end'd his good life upon the 30 of January 1648–9. I hear. . . . Thus I ended these commentaries or book of remembrance, beginning in the Year 1638 & ending in the year 1648" (184–5).[48] For Slingsby, the textual representation of serial, continuous, open-ended time is no more the point of the record, the object of narrative pursuit, than it is for the Montaignes *père et fils*.

Bookkeeping functions in many seventeenth-century diaries not only as a paradigm but also as a practice: prices appear amid the prose as the diarist tracks outlay and income. What Matthews says of Pepys holds true for many such diaries: the degree to which the paradigm is articulated and the practice deployed varies considerably both within journals and between them. The three kinds of account books that Fuller cites as precedents for the Christian journal—tradesmen's shop books, merchants' account books, and the household diary of daily disbursements—differ in sophistication, and hence in the kind of model they offer for the diarist. The merchant's account books, seeking systematically to track profit and show probity, usually deployed the double entry method, with its careful symmetry whereby every transaction figures as a credit to one account and a debit to another within the same system. The merchant's goal of maximally precise accounting governs the ideal of the Puritan diary that Fuller propounds: "Thou fearest not to be strict for [i.e., concerning] thy estate and outward concernments, why art thou lesse carefull for thy soul? many not exact in casting up their books, they have cast them[selves] up; thy Audit will be strict, so should thy accounts be" (b4v). Puritan diarists, in a phenomenon often remarked, devote considerable energy to reckoning up credit and debit in God's dealings with them, though their model is generally less intricate than the double entry. The most famous case is fictional. Robinson Crusoe recalls that early in his island life

> I drew up the State of my Affairs in Writing . . . and I stated it very impartially, like Debtor and Creditor, the Comforts I enjoy'd, against the Miseries I suffer'd, Thus,

EVIL	GOOD
I am cast upon a horrible	But I am alive, and not drown'd
desolate Island, void of all	as all my Ship's Company was.[49]
Hope of Recovery.	

Despite the double columns this is not quite double entry; Crusoe refers all circumstances to the single account of his own well-being. He will come closer to the double entry model later on when he learns to reckon every good to himself as a debit to God.

Such a reckoning suffuses both the fiscal and the spiritual account-keeping in the diary of Ralph Josselin (1616–1683), the methodical vicar of an Essex parish, who composed over the course of forty-two years one of the most substantial diaries of the century. As his editor Alan Macfarlane points out, Josselin "kept a detailed yearly account of his receipts, disbursements and debts, usually entered in the Diary at the beginning of the ecclesiastical year, 26 March."[50] It took the form of a literal balance sheet, with items and sums, which Josselin titled "the value of my outward estate which god hath given mee." In his ordinary entries (he wrote three or four a week), Josselin keeps a running record of "God's dealings," performed as narrative prose rather than two-column table. It governs the diary and supplies Josselin with his most frequent formulation: "This weeke past the lord was good and mercifull to mee and mine in many outward mercies," he begins many entries. He then proceeds (sometimes without pause or punctuation) to itemize his own sense of shortfall: "the lord knoweth my heart was in a very dead cold frame, for the Sabbath and I was very unprepared for it, carelesness eats up my spirit, and I doe not stirre up my heart within to goddes service, and yett my god (did not) faile mee. . . ."[51] The paradigm of credit and debit, coupled with the assumed innumerability of "God's blessings" and "our sins" (in Fuller's phrase), figured the diarists as always in debt, and helps account for the spiritual oscillation often remarked as a chief characteristic of seventeenth-century religious journals. When perceived merit diminishes the debt, the diarist rejoices; where "a very dead cold frame" deepens the debt, the diarist is threatened with despair.

In other diaries, particularly those not consecrated to the spiritual, the bookkeeping is simpler both in the practice and in the paradigm. It corresponds less to the merchant's account book than to the household diary of daily disbursements—a list of expenditures. Robert Hooke provides an example: "*Saturday, January 17th* [1673/4].—At home all the morn transcribing papers. Lord Brereton here. Dined with him at Levets and with him till 8 *p.p.* Mr. Haak swooned with the heat of the fire but recovered that night. Paid new shoemaker in Find Lane for 1 pair of shoos, 1 pair shoos and Goloshoos 11sh., for dancing puffs 2s.8d. At Garways till 10. Brother sent Goose 1s.6d. Received from Brother 51sh. by Harry from Hewet. Shomaker paid."[52] Here items enter the record because they cost money. It is sufficient for the diarist's purposes simply to name the items and their prices. What's more, the spare syntactic form that itemization takes— asyndetic, omitted subject, minimal predicate—encompasses activities as well as goods: Mr. Haak is the subject of the only full sentence, and of the closest thing to story, with cause, effect, and reversal. The entry limns some timespans ("till 8," "till 10") but it does not fill them with much more than a name ("Lord Brereton," "Garways"). The syntax in Hooke's secular diary, like that of Rogers's religious journal, moves the form away from narrative towards list.

In the mid-seventeenth century, the syntax and the temporality of itemization also structured many diaries in which fiscal bookkeeping was not conspicuously a paradigm or a practice, including some that by their length in years achieved near-record word counts. The parliamentarian Bulstrode Whitelocke (1605–1675) composed a diary for thirty years (1645–1675), while the royalist John Evelyn (1620–1706) composed one that extended (by means of some "retrospective" entries) throughout his life. Both men produce, for long stretches of their diaries, scattered occasions rendered as brief items. Here are consecutive entries by Whitelocke for June 1667 and by Evelyn for October 1657:

16. He [i.e., Whitelocke] wrote to Mr Barker about Greenland butt to no effect.

17. The Dog kennell begun to please the young men.

19. Visit att dinner by the Mayor of Marleborough & others.

21. Visits to neighbours.

22. Wh[itelocke] sent a messenger w[i]th letters to the L[ord] Lovelace to excuse his not sending a horse to the Musters.[53]

Octob: 4: Our *Viccar* proceedes. 10: I dind at *Lond:* with the *Dutch* Ambassador, now taking his leave, I return'd. 11: The *Viccar* on his former: see your notes: 18 he preached on: 1 *John:* 1.1. about *Christs* humane-nature. 21: Came Mr. *Henshaw* & Lady to visite us, with his Bro: in Law Mr. *Dorrell:* 25 The *Viccar* proceedes how our B: S. was the *Word:* 31: I was now 37 yeares of age: *Lord* so teach me to number my dayes, that I may apply my heart to Wisedome:[54]

In both passages, the occasion construed as worth noting (kennel, visits, sermon) draws the date into the record; days without such occasions go unrecorded. The date then introduces the occasion, rendered as a kind of line-item. Evelyn's criteria for inclusion demand that he write up Sundays; he records all four for the month, and from the vicar's "proceedings" he constructs the passage's sole simulacrum of continuity. As in the later portion of Hoby's diary, it links the calendrical *kairoi* of the Lord's Days, but leaves out days between. Evelyn's syntax is somewhat fuller than Whitelocke's and can grow fuller still; he often writes long narrative entries. Nonetheless the same temporal principle remains in play throughout. Evelyn selects for the day's "remarkable occurrences" not its full waking span. Like Whitelocke, Rogers, Slingsby, Montaigne, Ward, Josselin, Dee, Jeake, and Ashmole, he endeavors to record the occasions that count, but not to embed them within an account contrived both to fill the day and to link the dates (Hoby attempts the second continuity for a while, but not the first).

Pepys writes a text more continuous in time, but the manuscript evidence makes clear that most of his entries began where many of Evelyn's and Whitelocke's end—in itemization. In the diary's final volume Pepys inserted pages of rough notes for two stretches of days for which he never composed finished entries. These papers, Matthews observes, constitute "the best evidence we have about Pepys's method of composition" (9.160). They make clear how thoroughly the diarist's practice was engaged with the forms and practices of the account book.

> *Monday*
>
> [April] 1 3 spent at *Michells* ————————————   0-0-6
>
> ~~oyster~~ in the *Folly* ————————————   0-1-0
>
> oysters ————————————   0-1-0
>
> coach to *W C[oventry]* about Mr. *Pett* ———————   0-1-0 √
>
> Thence to Commissioners Treasury and so   ⎫   0-0-6 √
>
> to *W[estminste]r* hall by water ———————   ⎭   0-0-6 √
>
> with G M[ountagu] and *R P[epys]* and spoke   ⎫
>
> with *Vaughan* and *Birch* all in trouble about the
>
> prize business. And so to *Ld. Crews* (calling   0-1-0 √
>
> for a low pipe by the way where *Creed* and
>
> *G M[ountagu]* and *G C[artaret]* came ———————   ⎭

So with *Creed* to play Little Thief _____ 0-4-0

Thence ~~into the~~ towards the park by coach _____ 0-2-6 √

Came home met with order of Commissioners of

Accounts which put together with the rest vexed me

and so home to supper and to bed.

(4.13.68; 9.161—62)

In their general layout these notes correspond closely to the diary of daily disbursements that Fuller mentions. The right-hand column figures the day as a sequence of expenditures; the left-hand column accomplishes something slightly more complex: though linked (literally, by drawn lines) to the expense account, it plays out in miniature several different methods of adumbrating expenditure and experience in words, in a sequence of generally increasing narrativity. The flat itemizations of the first three lines are even sparer than Hooke's. Pepys specifies expenditures in broken phrases, and prices prevail so far over other particulars that in the first case Pepys records how much he spent but not what he spent it on. The next three lines manifest more continuity, in part because Pepys deploys the connectives that Hooke eschews: "thence"; "and so." By means of these he links three separate phases of motion (to William Coventry, to the Treasury, to Westminster). The numbers here still mirror the words in the manner of the line item: each line limns a motion and each motion (by coach) entails an expense. Next the proportions change. Pepys recounts not only where he went but with whom he talked (Mr. Pett), what he talked about ("the prize business," in which Pepys and his colleagues are being investigated on suspicion of having received illegitimate profits) and what he did "by the way" (stopped to pick up a "low pipe"—a bass recorder that will preoccupy him in the coming days). As the space of narrative expands, the numbers begin to wait upon the words. The brackets, framed to encompass the prose and relate it to the integers, make clear that Pepys is doing his verbal recounting first and his pecuniary accounting second. Narrative further asserts its primacy at the end of the entry, where Pepys tells of experiences which have (so far) cost him nothing in cash but much in emotion; here, indeed, the question of "Accounts" impinges upon the narrative (in connection with "the prize business") less as a listing of particular fiscal facts than as a source of general "vex[ation]." The day's notes read at their beginning like the itemizations of Pepys's diaristic contemporaries, and at their end more like his own finished entries. As the writing advances, the staccato of fiscal accounting modulates into the legato of personal narrative.[55]

It is worthwhile to track the modulation further, in order to see what other changes obtain between rough note and diary text. Since Pepys supplies no final version for the days he drafts in the surviving notes, no direct collation is possible. Here instead is a full entry from two days before the rough notes begin.

[8 April 1668] Up and at my office all the morning doing business; and then at noon home to dinner all alone. Then to White-hall with Sir J. Mennes in his coach to attend the Duke of York upon our usual business, which was this day but little; and thence with Lord Brouncker to the Duke of York's playhouse, where we saw *The Unfortunate Lovers*, no extraordinary play methinks; and thence I to Drumbleby's and there did talk a great deal about pipes and did buy a Recorder which I do intend to <learn to> play on, the sound of it being of all sounds in the world most pleasing to me. Thence home and to visit Mrs. Turner; where among other talk, Mr. Foly and her husband being there, she did tell me of young Captain Holmes's marrying of Pegg Lowther last Saturday by stealth; which I was sorry for, he being an idle rascal and proud, and worth little I doubt, and she a mighty pretty, well-disposed lady, and good fortune. Her mother and friends take on mightily; but the sport is, Sir Rob. Holmes [Capt. Holmes's brother] doth seem to be mad too with his brother and will disinherit him, saying that he hath ruined himself, marrying below himself and to his disadvantage; whereas, I said in this company that I had married a sister lately with little above half that portion that he should have kissed her breech before he should have had her—which, if R. Holmes should hear, would make a great quarrel; but it is true, and I am heartily sorry for the poor girl that is undone by it. So home to my chamber, to be fingering of my Recorder and getting of the scale of Musique without book, which I at last see is necessary, for a man that would understand music as it is now taught, to understand, though it be a ridiculous and troublesome way and I know I shall be able hereafter to show the world a simpler way. But like the old Hypotheses in philosophy, it must be learned, though a man knows a better. Then to supper and to bed. <This morning Mr. Chr. Pett's widow and daughter came to me to desire my help to the King and Duke of York, and I did promise, and do pity her.> (9.156−58)

Money is a preoccupation (in the talk about brides' portions and widows' pensions) but its signs and numbers have disappeared from the text. Pepys entered his expenditures from the rough notes into his account books, now lost (in keeping with his professional practice, he generally crossed out the price numbers in the notes as he entered them in the books); in the diary he sometimes preserves prices that strike him as exorbitant, or as indices of his own waxing powers of acquisition. Even in its absence, though, the daily record of disbursements contributes much to the diary's texture as a representation of space and time. Because coach and boat rides cost money, Pepys ended each day with a thorough written itemization of his major traversals of urban space, and this record gives the entries their kinetic specificity (akin to the effect that Joyce claimed to pursue in his narrative of Bloom's single day): a sense of many motions closely mapped. The geography of London acts as a checkpoint for one kind of narrative completeness. Pepys never gives the impression (as the itemizers often do) of having moved through hyperspace, materializing at one point on the map and then at another, without transition; there is always at least the minimal notation exemplified here by "Thence home and to visit Mrs. Turner." (When he has traveled by coach or boat Pepys almost always mentions his mode of transport; where he does not, he traveled on foot. This morning's ride in John Mennes's coach is distinctive because it does *not* cost money.)

The initial itemization abets continuity of space, and this in turn abets continuity of time: a sense, intrinsically fictitious in any verbal account of time but assiduously cultivated here, that no step has been skipped. Pepys pursues this effect by other means more purely temporal. First he persists, as I have already noted, in recording precisely the repeated actions that other diarists omit: rising, dining, returning home and to bed. Then there are the devices by which Pepys explicitly identifies the events he chooses to highlight as selections from the larger spans of time and activity that fill the day. The discussion of Captain Holmes's marriage occurred, Pepys takes pains to note, "among other talk"; Ann Pett's visit (narrated as afterthought in a marginal note) made part of the "business" that Pepys conducted "all the morning." "Among other talk" and "all the morning" aim at the kind of continuity in time that the place names and transport-transitions achieve in space; the accounts of Captain Holmes and Mrs. Pett supply detail for the spans denoted. Unlike the itemizers, Pepys does specify what was talked about at visits.[56]

Among the entry's instruments of continuity, the syntactic connectives are perhaps most important, and do the most to distinguish Pepys's temporality from that of his predecessors. After the initial "Up" every syntactic unit in the entire entry (with one exception) begins with some kind of connective to the phrase foregoing: an adverb of time ("Then to Whitehall") or place ("Thence home"); a coordinating conjunction ("but it is true, and I am heartily sorry for it"); a relative pronoun ("where we saw *The Unfortunate Lovers*"; "which, if R. Holmes should hear . . ."). If polysyndeton links the clauses, it also suffuses them: "he being an idle rascal and proud, and worth little I doubt, and she a mighty pretty, well-disposed lady, and good fortune." In Pepys, connectivity is conspicuously pleonastic. His favorite connectives appear to achieve that status because of their capacity to limn several kinds of connection at the same time: "and so," his most frequent choice (though underrepresented here) combines, in variable proportions, simple temporal sequence ("and then"), causal connection ("and therefore"), and adverbial context ("and in that manner") with several other shadings. "Thence" technically refers to space, but aurally and effectually conflates space with time (*then* I went from there). In the bellman passage, Pepys subsumes the moment (and thereby takes possession of it) by means of a more formal rhetoric (*inclusio*) and an uncharacteristic archaism ("a-washing"). In the diary as a whole, connectives pleonastically deployed are the instruments of temporal plenitude. By their means Pepys constructs a fullness of time without apparent gaps, and embeds within the fullness the kinds of individual instances that he itemizes (without embedding) on the rough notes. The point of daily bookkeeping is to use measures of time as a preliminary means for organizing and tracking the accumulation of property. This is precisely what Pepys does at the Exchequer and, in a more complicated way, in his rough notes. In remaking the rough notes into finished entries, though, he effectually reverses this process. He uses considerations of property—the scattered occasions of expenditure and acquisition—as a foundation on which to construct narrative continuity within even measures of time.

MEASURE AS OCCASION: THE DIARY'S FIRST PAGES

There are signs at the start of the diary that Pepys's entire project of laying hold of time by narrative, and all the strategies by which he executes it, arise from his concern about the prospects for two particular kinds of continuity: that of his own life and that of his progeny. Both of these come up as questions on the diary's first page. I have shown that for Pepys, measure takes the place that occasion occupied in earlier paradigms; it demands representation and structures narrative. I have also suggested that this holds true in a particular way at the beginning of the diary, which takes off from a cluster of calendrically determined beginnings and endings. Pepys does striking things with these in his initial sentences. He appears at first to insist on the value of these as sharply defined starts and stops, but quickly accords them an alternate temporal value: he figures them not as termini but as middle elements, moved into the midst of the chronistic narrative that they initially seemed to frame. By the time he has mistranscribed the text from Galatians, only 325 words into the diary, he has already demonstrated the strategies of syntax, structure, and inscription by which he will construct a fullness of time in whose midst he can locate *all* moments, even those conspicuous commencements and closures that the calendar, on New Year's Day, puts close to hand. He has also begun to adumbrate why the strategies matter, and what purposes they serve.

One of the strategies is simple and spatial. The entry for 1 January is actually the second unit of text in the book; Pepys prefaces it with a stretch of prose on the facing page (see Fig. 1). This he inscribes in accordance with rules that (as it turns out) will govern the representation of time in space throughout the diary. His editor spells them out: "the great majority of pages begin with a new entry and end with the last words of the same or another entry" (1.xliv); beginnings and endings in textual space are to correspond, whenever possible, to those of diurnal time. Matthews also remarks Pepys's rare scriptorial skill "in taking his lines [legibly] to the very edge of the page" (1.xliii). Just as continuity in time derives in part from continuity of space in the diary's prose (with Pepys carefully tracking his own motion), so in the diary's layout the fullness of time is figured as a fullness of space. The borderlines that Pepys inscribes on every page define an enclosure that, like the dates that run vertically along them, demands filling by text.

The first sentences of the first page evince a corresponding confidence that the boundary lines of the calendar can produce effectual enclosures, defining and separating past and present.

> Blessed be God, at the end of the last year I was in very good health, without any sense of my old pain but upon taking of cold.

I lived in Axe=yard, having my wife and servant Jane, and no more in family than us three.

The diction renders with curious emphasis the power of the calendrical cusp. The period that Pepys here describes as "the end of last year" came to a close only yesterday, and the conditions he locates there still obtain as he writes. The next sentence both reinforces the sense of temporal enclosure (of "last year" as a profoundly separate duration) by hinting at its rationale, and subverts it by a complication of verb tense.

My wife, after the absence of her terms for seven weeks, gave me hopes of her being with child, but on the last day of the year she hath them again.

Against the larger revolutions of year and decade Pepys counterpoints an odder measure of time: "seven weeks," the idiosyncratic physiological suspension of Elizabeth Pepys's "terms" and the corresponding psychological span (as the prose represents it) of her husband's "hopes." "Terms" contains its own counterpoint. Rooted in the Latin *terminum*, end or limit, it compasses in English several definitions: the publicly prescribed, calendrically determined timespans of legal and academic sessions, the duration of normal pregnancy, and the more variable rhythms of menstruation, wherein the woman's body declares its own calendar. "But on the last day of the year," as Pepys records, the counterpoint of private and public time concludes in cadence. Elizabeth Pepys's "terms" coincide with the calendar's, compounding its abstract endings with her own more palpable one. Body and calendar have here combined to perform that kind of doubled and coordinated ending that Pepys will engineer in the diary by aligning the entry's ending with the page's edge. In his wife's case, though, the doubled closure enacts not order but disappointment, and may account for the emphatic finality with which Pepys writes up "the end of last year," when (as today at the beginning of this year) there were "no more in family than us three."

At the same time, the sentence that announces that Elizabeth "hath her terms" partly dissolves the enclosure. The present-tense verb imports "last year" into the present moment—or would do so if we could be certain that that's the word Pepys wrote. The verb "to have" is the least stable term in the shorthand system Pepys deploys: a single symbol stands for all its forms. As a result, it permeates the boundary between past and present (the future will always be signaled by an auxiliary verb) by ambiguity rather than transgression: Pepys leaves unclear where he locates the occasion of his disappointment in relation to the date line that until now has so rigorously divided last year from this. The permeation corresponds with larger cultural uncertainties surrounding the date line itself. Pepys heads his page "1659./60." not because he is crossing between the two years but because he is technically inhabiting both. January 1 commenced the year in most countries on the continent, where the "New Style" Gregorian calendar had taken effect beginning in 1592. Protestant England will initiate another ninety-two years in the "Old Style," whereby the year-number changes on March 25, Lady Day, which was reckoned as the anniversary of the Annunciation (the Nativity is nine months after) and hence an appropriate date for inception. That date possesses particular significance for Pepys. It was on 26 March 1658 that he underwent his risky lithotomy, and he now celebrates the anniversary as a private festival with an annual feast. The English New Year may have prompted his resolution to face the operation, as the Gregorian New Year has now prompted him to begin the diary. In any case, both New Years are present in the diary's first markings. The doubled number was a standard device by which English writers manifested a doubled calendrical consciousness. Pepys's punctuation, with a period after each year and a line dividing them, maximizes their separation in one way while asserting their concurrence in another (the large "16" governs both). In the first sentence he writes under this ambiguous sign, Pepys alludes indirectly to the alternate New Year, which precedes by one day the date on which his "old pain" was alleviated at the risk of death, and in the third sentence he alludes to the present New Year, which follows by one day a new disappointment consequent on "hopes" of birth, and carried across the year's boundary line by the similarly ambiguous sign "hath/had," which will seed a certain measure of temporal ambiguity throughout the diary.

Prompted perhaps by the disappointment, Pepys abruptly changes subject and provides a more detailed display of the shifting time frames that the verb "hath" has hinted at:

> . . . but on the last day of the year she hath them again. The condition of the State was thus. *Viz.* the Rump, after being disturbed by my Lord Lambert, was lately returned to sit again.

The simple past tense, once resumed, proves again unstable; it yields immediately to a "neutral" tense that, by eliminating main and auxiliary verbs, makes itself available to several timeframes while committing itself to none:

> The officers of the army all forced to yield.

This temporal limbo next converts into the simple present:

> Lawson lie[s] still in the River and Monke is with his army in Scotland.

And the final sentence of the paragraph introduces the future tense in a subordinate clause:

> Only my Lord Lambert is not yet come in to the Parliament; nor is it expected that he will, without being forced to it.

Unlike the almanac makers (whose labors he will laugh at), Pepys here neither projects himself into the remote nor predicts the immediate future; he reports instead on present expectation.

Pepys's modulations of tense here forecast the mix that will contribute to the diary's temporal texture. As he does so conspicuously in the bellman episode, Pepys uses the past tense as a way of registering the motion of time; he recurs to the present or the verbless neutral tense in such a way as to complicate this registration with a strong sense of immediacy, of proximate concurrency between the event and its writing down; and he abjures the unfettered future tense (i.e., the future tense in a main clause) as outside the diary's temporal province. The result is almost always, as here, a sustained focus on what Shakespeare calls the "ignorant present." The diarist commits himself to rendering the moment's uncertainties even on those occasions when a few days' hindsight confers on him the advantage of subsequent knowledge. The present passage manifests present ignorance in a way that accords exactly with Pepys's program. At the moment Pepys writes, Monck and his army are "in Scotland" no longer. The general has chosen New Year's Day to begin his march across the Tweed back into England, making of the river a cusp whose significance in political space matches that of the day in calendrical time, implying by such alignment a Providential sponsorship for his enterprise ("It was the Lorde's Day too, and it was his doing," declared Monck's chaplain, John Price), and accomplishing in public action that mesh of date and innovation that Pepys achieves as narrative in his newly opened private chronicle.[57]

After a second political paragraph setting forth what "is at present the desires and the hopes and the expectation of all," in the page's final passage Pepys shifts focus back to his own present predicament.

> My own private condition very handsome; and esteemed rich, but endeed very poor, besides my goods of my house and my office, which at present is somewhat uncertain. Mr Downing master of my office.

Here, present uncertainty is not merely asserted (as in the political passage) but performed. Pepys opens with a clear pronouncement, then dismantles it by a series of subversions. First, he shifts to the passive locution by which he has already several times signaled general public perceptions. As "my Lord Lambert is not . . . expected" to come into the Parliament, so Pepys is "esteemed rich" by unnamed observers. In turning the public perspective on his "own private condition," Pepys achieves a Heisenbergian result. The condition itself changes abruptly under observation, and "very handsome" becomes "endeed very poor." Or does it? The next phrase revises the self-assessment upward by listing, with pointedly repeated possessive pronouns, the author's most reliable assets—"my goods of my house and my office [i.e., my job]"—before yielding to the sentence's final self-subversion: "which at present is somewhat uncertain." Pepys extricates himself from this oscillatory field by a final phrase of fact—"Mr Downing master of my office"—but the move only adds to the data of instability. Downing, a temperamental employer who does not much care for Pepys, is the reason for the precariousness of Pepys's post.

On this first page, as in the bellman episode, Pepys creates an *inclusio* that figures the text as personal property: the page begins and ends with passages about the diarist himself, which thus enclose the other matter that transpires between them.[58] He constructs the symmetry, though, from matched indeterminacies, themselves similarly structured. In both the first and last pronouncements on himself, Pepys starts from a seemingly stable assessment ("without *any* sense of my old pain" / "my own private condition very handsome") which proves immediately subject to qualification ("*except* upon taking of cold" / ". . . but endeed very poor . . ."). The chief difference between these structures of uncertainty is that the second has also absorbed the slight indeterminacy of timeframe and tense that has marked the prose in the interim. Pepys writes up most of his "own private condition" in a neutral tense that floats free in time. Only in the last phrase does he commit himself to the present, naming and characterizing that frame of reference even as he deploys it: to live and to write "at present" is to dwell in the "uncertain," whose dominion extends so far as to include itself (just how certain, after all, is "somewhat uncertain"?). The action Pepys performs here, in the self-correcting report on himself, is among the diary's most characteristic and frequent moves. As this early instance makes clear, that action is the conceptual correlative of the diarist's decision to track and precisely manifest the sometimes urgent ignorance of the present moment, to write the moment as midst rather than as endpoint.

With the first page full and shaped, Pepys crosses to the second and enters the diary's fundamental time-form, the dated entry. In the first clause under the date, Pepys demonstrates another of his most characteristic devices for constructing the moment as a middle term:

> This morning (we lying lately in the garret) I rose, put on my suit with great skirts, having not lately worn any other clothes but them. (1.3)

"This morning I rose": the short clause defines a distinct beginning, but halfway through Pepys inserts a parenthetical phrase. Its syntax, wherein the present participle takes its own agent ("we lying"), is omnipresent in the diary because of its usefulness for a certain kind of timing and telling. Called the nominative absolute, it couples explanation with a kind of temporal inversion. It appears amid the narration of a more particular action (here "rising") only to include that action within its own larger compass. Pepys repeats the gesture, by means of a simple participial phrase ("having not lately worn"), before the sentence ends: his garment, like his rising, is contextualized within a larger span that is itself reckoned as local and evanescent (in the coming months Pepys will move out of the garret and change his suit). The nominative absolute and other participial phrases are a chief means for performing that temporal action in which the diary deals most often: embedding moments in the middle of a temporal continuum that extends indefinitely in either direction.

When, three lines later, Pepys miswrites the text of Gunning's sermon, he is making a temporal move of essentially the same kind, though not by the same syntax: he is shifting a narrated moment from the position of an endpoint ("when the fullness of the time was come") into the chronistic midst ("in the fulness of time"). And because the Biblical text concerns childbirth (the moment of the Messiah's arrival), much that has already appeared in the diary becomes significant here: the doubled New Year's Days; the distresses of the body that both Pepyses have endured contiguous with those days (Elizabeth's "terms" the day before one New Year's, Samuel's lithotomy the day after the other); the uncertainty of the present. Moments not embedded in continuum have produced disappointment: "the end of last year" brought with it an end to Pepys's current hopes for progeny, and Pepys may surmise what may have been medically true: that his lithotomy had caused his sterility. Pepys rewrites Galatians from the vantage of his own predicament, from with*in* a time whose "fullness" he wants to conceive of as in process. In the construction of new middleness lies his only hope for progeny.

In such construction, too, the context makes clear, Pepys finds an important means of securing time as property. His diary presents itself on its first page as a project for making permanent in text the present, uncertain time of a writer who has just discovered that he may not achieve that alternate durability proffered by a line of descendants. By the diary's second page, the process whereby this textual permanence is also to be construed as private property has already made itself manifest in several small strategies that will replicate throughout the text. They all derive from the same general principle: Pepys devises markers of enclosure—"wife and maid a-washing," "up . . . and to bed," calendrical dates—and then encloses *them* by various strategies—participial phrasing, adjacent entries, slippage or elision of verb tense—within a system that extends outward to that final textual enclosure specified in the bellman episode, the "writing of" orthographically occluded lines in a sequestered book.

•

In Pepys's diary, the dated entry is the fundamental unit of enclosure; the calendrical contiguity of the entries encloses each and enacts that calibrated continuity, that doubly constructed fullness, of textualized time that distinguishes Pepys from his predecessors and contemporaries. The diaristic item-izer John Evelyn at one point shuddered at the thought, in connection with his own traveling and travel writing, of moving, thinking, and writing "like a goose swimms down the river"; for him, such flow, such continuity, is inimical to judicious selectivity.[59] For Pepys, by contrast, continuity *conceals* selectivity. Selection must still take place if the day's representation is to fit onto the page, but the devices of enclosure and the strategies of middleness allow him to foster the illusion of writing the days, months, and years continuous and whole.

For time told intermittently, whether as occasion or as measure, the most familiar horological medium was the tower bell, still powerful in the culture. For time told *continuously* Huygens had just provided a new instrument, the pendulum clock with its minute hand and markings. For time told this way in *private* (the way Pepys tells it in his diary), the equivalent would be the pocket minute watch. In the 1660s this is not yet technologically feasible (Huygens and Robert Hooke are separately at work on the possibility). But Pepys gets hold early of an "advance simulacrum" of the technology and makes telling use and sense of it.

Time now to read Pepys reading his watch.

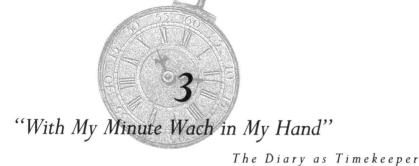

"With My Minute Wach in My Hand"

The Diary as Timekeeper

*P*epys first becomes fascinated with watches five years after starting his diary. In this chapter I shall show that he constructs time on the watch as he has constructed it for half a decade in his journal; he derives from it the same uses, pleasures, and privileges as a medium of precision, continuity, property, and self-possession. Pepys is especially responsive to Huygensian temporality in its early stages, because his particular place in the culture—his rank and aspirations, his professional involvements, his milieu and coterie—enable and even impel him early on to merge his diaristic reckonings of time, his shaping of narrative, and his apprehension of self and property, under the auspices of a new temporality; to experience, construct, and report a new structure of feeling about time that will matter increasingly, and publicly, over the decades to come.

WATCHES

When in the course of the diary Pepys first gets hold of a watch, his delight verges on embarrassment:

> To the Change after office, and received my Wach from the watch-maker; and a very fine [one] it is—given me by Briggs the Scrivener. Home to dinner; and then I abroad to the Atturny General. . . . So home, and late at my

office. But Lord, to see how much of my old folly and childishnesse hangs upon me still, that I cannot forbear carrying my watch in my hand in the coach all this afternoon, and seeing what a-clock it is 100 times. And am apt to think with myself: how could I be so long without one. (5.13.65; 6.101)

Enthusiasm here occludes specificity. Pepys does not say exactly what kind of timepiece he has received as gift from the scrivener; the description "very fine" leaves unclear whether the watch bears one hand or two, whether it marks the hours only or the minutes as well. What the entry does make clear is that he treats his watch on the Huygensian model that larger English clocks had made conspicuous for about eight years, consulting it as though at every glance it will tell anew "what a-clock it is," as though to look at the watch "100 times" will be to see a hundred "times" defined. The exclamation "But Lord, to see," one of the diary's most frequent phrases, enacts astonishment by syntactic incompleteness: it points out the marvelous phenomenon (the thing "to see") and implies, by the absence of full predication, that the marvel resists full analysis and explanation.

Still, the very diction of enthusiasm bears sufficient traces of specific causes and effects. For one thing, the watch's persistent chronometric report on the present ("what time it *is*") appears to exert a temporal pull on the prose. After Pepys has recounted the activities of afternoon and evening, the watch re-enters the narrative as an object of wonder, and the tense shifts from Pepys's customary combination of the verbless neutral ("To the Change after office") and simple past ("and received") into a rarer sustained present which subsumes both the past time of riding ("in the coach all this afternoon") and the present time of writing. For a short, unusual stretch, Pepys tells time on the watch's terms. His phrasing collates this brief insistence on telling time in the present with other pleasures that are apparently intensified by combination: in the comprehensiveness of the watch's temporal coverage ("*all* this afternoon"), in its portability "in the coach" as co-occupant of an enclosure moving through urban space, and in its status as emphatically personal property conferring special privileges ("my watch in my hand"). The diarist expresses in this first narrated encounter with the novelties of watch time, an almost violent affinity, a pleasure so intense as to incur a wary self-derision. Pepys mocks his reaction as "folly and childishnesse"— before narrating it (and, in the present tense, re-indulging it) in detail.

Four months later Pepys finds a way to sustain the pleasure less abashedly, by compounding it with use.

Up, and walked to Greenwich, taking pleasure to walk with my minute wach in my hand, by which I am now come to see the distances of my way from Woolwich to Greenwich. And do find myself to come within two minutes constantly to the same place at the end of each quarter of an hour. (9.13.65; 6.221–22)

Evidently the experiment, though completed on this particular day, has actually occupied several. Pepys has walked the route repeatedly with minute watch in hand, and has found his pace so regular as to match distance to duration with rough predictability: the first quarter-hour's walking delivers him "within two minutes constantly to the same place" every day, the second with equal consistency to a point farther along, and so forth for the whole route. This time, Pepys specifies the kind of watch he is using, because in the specifics inhere the whole possibility and point of his modest investigation. On the "way from Woolwich to Greenwich" minutes matter, and the watch, promising temporal precision commodified as portable property, provides not simply a cue for pleasure, but also an instrument for self-reckoning, for a quantitative study of the self's motions through space and time. The elements of watch time that entranced Pepys in the coach remain in play, but now they produce data. From this new reckoning of time and motion, shame is notably absent.

The experiment fulfills, among several subtler functions, a simple one. It offers diversion during what is for Pepys a new and long commute. He carries his watch in part to beguile as well as measure the time he is unaccustomed to spend in walking to work. For the past five years he has both lived and labored in the same building complex, the Navy Office near the City of London's center (hence his phrase in the earlier passage, "so home, and late at my office"). The plague, now at its height in the city, has prompted Pepys to move with his wife to Woolwich, and the Navy Office to relocate, at Pepys's suggestion, to a town a little farther upriver. "I think it will be necessary," Pepys had written to his superiors a month earlier, "that we remove to some place . . . such as Greenwich or the like." [1]

In that offhand phrase, Pepys establishes for the first time ever a link between the Navy and the town, a connection now so familiar as to seem virtually synaptic. It plays intriguing havoc with the hermeneutics of the present entry. Greenwich has become over the past three centuries a byword for the systematization of everything that engages Pepys on his riverside walk: for the reciprocal calibration and coordination of time, space, and motions, and for the advancement of minutely exact chronometry. In 1675, with Wren's construction of the Royal Observatory on Greenwich Hill, Greenwich became the site for the first methodical assault on the problem of the longitude, in the eighteenth century the center for its solution, in the nineteenth and twentieth (with the gradual dissemination of Greenwich Mean Time) the citadel for precision timekeeping. It has achieved, in reckonings of both space and time, a centrality amounting to hegemony, figuring as degree zero in cartographic space, and as global reference point for clock time.

The diarist knows nothing of this. When he writes "Greenwich" into his entry, the word possesses no chronometric associations, and even Pepys's own linkage of town and navy appears in retrospect a false start (Wren will build the Observatory there because the Hill affords a propitious situation, not because the navy has set up shop there once before). For Pepys Greenwich operates as an incidental destination in space. For the reader of Pepys, it can serve as a point of orientation in cultural and horological history—as guide and as corrective. In a way, Pepys's ignorance is the crucial datum. At Greenwich, Huygensian temporality will achieve hegemony, but not yet and not inevitably. The diary offers information valuable by virtue of its limitation: it records and (so I shall argue) embodies in its narrative what the watch means to the walker when Greenwich, in effect, means nothing. For Pepys the watch first means pleasure, founded in novelty and rather intricately compounded of precision, portability, and knowledge. By attending to the constituents of that pleasure, to their histories and their convergences in both the watch and the walker, we may catch the lineaments of an important temporality at the moment of its emergence.

In 1665, a minute watch was rare, expensive, and horologically hubristic.[2] With its separate minute hand and closely calibrated dial, it purported to emulate the precision of the new pendulum clocks without the least capability of matching their performance. Huygens's invention had instituted accuracy but precluded portability. The pendulum requires an absolutely stable and relatively spacious installation in order to work at all, and cannot function in so small and frequently agitated an area as a person's pocket. So watches could not yet partake of the innovation; they continued, as they had for the century or so of their existence, merely to miniaturize the old technology, which of course operated all the less reliably for the diminution. Well after larger clocks began regularly to display their new efficiency by the addition of a minute hand, the vast majority of watches still confessed their lingering limitations by a solitary indicator of the hour. Pepys, reading his instrument as though its differentiations of "two minutes" are reliable, in effect commits the same anachronism that Aubrey performs on Allen's watch, only from the opposite, proleptic vantage: he ascribes to the thing an accuracy it does not *yet* possess. The timepiece in which he takes pleasure looks in retrospect positively quixotic, its extra hand a tremulous lance tilted in vain against the creaking windmill of the old machinery within.

But like the lance, the minute hand indexes an aspiration, one which Huygens himself ardently entertained at this time: that the new precision of the pendulum clock might somehow be made portable after all. Huygens had for years pursued this possibility by experiment, and Pepys himself had recently participated in his quest. Both the inventor and the naval administrator stood to benefit enormously from the creation of a timepiece accurate to the minute and sufficiently self-contained to stay steady on board a ship. Such an instrument would solve at last that most costly navigational conundrum, the question of the longitude. Mariners had hitherto lacked a reliable means of reckoning the location of their vessels along the global axes running east and west, and so of determining exactly where they stood on the surface of the water and the world. (The north-south index, the latitude, they had long been able to find by gauging the angle to the ship of fixed marks like the North Star.)

For over a century sailors had suspected that they might more usefully construe the problem in terms of time rather than of space. Navigators, one speculator suggested in 1530, might be able to calculate the longitude by comparing the data from two unimpeachable timepieces.[3] One of these nature had already provided: the sun, coursing from east to west, appears to move steadily around the earth, traversing fifteen degrees of latitude (out of the globe's 360) every hour. The other timepiece humans would have to invent: a portable clock so reliable that, once synchronized with the time at the place of departure, it would continue to tell that time throughout the voyage, despite vicissitudes of waves, wind, and weather. A ship's navigator, traveling southwest from England, might examine this hypothetical chronometer and find that the time now in London was three o'clock; if the sun overhead (as read by a sophisticated kind of nautical sundial) declared shipboard time to be one o'clock, then the vessel must be on a longitude thirty degrees west of London. By coordinating this information with the readily determined latitude, the mariner could chart the vessel's exact position and distance from its point of origin, of destination, and from any known local dangers. Time would translate easily and usefully back into space.

The pendulum clock brought the prospect of such a solution tantalizingly close. It appeared to possess the accuracy necessary for the task, and Huygens set about redesigning it to achieve the portability as well. In 1663, with the help of Alexander Bruce, a founding Fellow of the Royal Society, he arranged to have two pendulum clocks, still very large but carefully modified for travel, carried and tested on expeditions to Portugal and to Guinea, under Major Robert Holmes. Holmes's glowing report appeared in the very first issue of the Society's durable *Philosophical Transactions* in March 1665.[4] These new clocks, he claimed, had surpassed in accuracy the earlier, unsatisfactory techniques by which the captains of his expedition's other ships had, like generations before them, gauged their positions. Huygens, wanting both to be "more particularly informed about the pendulum watches committed to Major HOLMES" and to have their merits officially ratified, had already entered into almost weekly correspondence with the Society. But at the meeting on 1 March "[o]ccasion was taken . . . by some of the members, to doubt the exactness of the motion of these watches at sea."[5] In order to learn more details about the expeditions from those who had actually sailed in them, they deputized a newly elected Fellow who, by virtue of his position as Clerk of the Acts for the Navy Board and his experience as an attendant at the Society's meetings since before its chartered inception, could be presumed conversant in matters nautical and scientific: "Mr. PEPYS was desired to visit the Major, and to inquire farther" concerning the voyage's elusive particulars, "for the satisfaction of the Society" (2.21) At the meeting a week later Pepys, conscientiously fulfilling this first assignment as a Fellow exactly a month after his election, reported that the results of the experiment, when more closely investigated, had indeed proven less encouraging:

> Mr. PEPYS gave an account of what information he had received from the master of the Jersey ship, who had been in company of Major HOLMES in the Guinea voyage, concerning the pendulum watches, viz. that the said master affirmed, that the vulgar reckoning [i.e., the older methods of charting] proved as near as that of the watches, which, added he, had varied from one another unequally, sometimes backward, sometimes forward, to 4, 6, 7, 3, 5 minutes. . . . (2.23)

A week later the Society, still desirous of details, closed its meeting by asking Pepys "to procure the journals of those masters of ships, who had been with

Major HOLMES in Guinea, and differed from him in the relation concerning the pendulum watches" (2.26).

Pepys's initial report would prove prophetic. The problem of the longitude had to wait almost another century for its solution, which took the form of a timepiece much more intricate, accurate, diminutive, and insulated than any pendulum clock: John Harrison's spring-regulated marine timekeeper. But Huygens's experiment appears to have prompted from Pepys a kind of recapitulation. Six months after he presents his first report to the Society, he records his watch-timed walk to Greenwich, a private experiment in the longitude of the self, his traveling vessel not a fleet but his own person, his instrument not a cumbersome clock made even heavier for transport but a watch small enough for holding in hand or pocket, its venue of report not a spoken address at a Society meeting nor a scientific periodical but some shorthand sentences in a secret book. Pepys shrinks the experiment from global to local space, and transposes it from a public to a private sphere, but every feature of his little project suggests that he conceives and conducts it along the same lines as Huygens's experiment.

The combination of Royal Society influence and private initiative accords a novel status to the minute watch, shaping the ways it operates as personal property and the extent to which it makes time property too. Watches, expensive and distinctive from the time of their first manufacture, had figured primarily as a sign of prosperity, and only secondarily (if at all) as a means of timekeeping. When Briggs the scrivener conveys one to Pepys as a kind of bribe, he is working within a durable tradition of the watch as prize. And working successfully: Pepys, initially troubled at the form of the gift,[6] is soon pleased at its worth ("a good and brave piece it is . . . worth 14*l*—which is a greater present then I valued it" [5.12.65; 6.100]). On the riverside walk, as earlier in the coach, emphatic possessives ("my . . . wach in my hand") manifest proprietary pride. Though the pride has ample precedent, the proprietorship takes on new forms and new meaning.

The earliest watches, first appearing more than a century before Pepys's, functioned more as ornament than as instrument. They were costly objects designed to declare their cost to public view. Small drum-shaped table clocks designed for traveling, or elaborately wrought ovals worn on a chain around the neck, they made available to the passing observer as well as to the owner an index not so much of the time as (more reliably) of the wearer's wealth. Since "for the first three-quarters of the seventeenth century there was no significant technical advance in watchmaking, . . . [i]nterest was . . . concentrated upon decoration, and it is during this period that the greatest variety of high-quality decoration is found, both in the cases of watches, and in the movements." The decoration took many forms: elaborate engraving on the metal without and within; scenes depicted by painting or by colored materials laid into the tortoise shell casing; emulation by the entire body of the watch "of irrelevant shapes such as those of books, skulls, dogs, birds, crosses, flower-buds. . . . Particularly popular were forms in the *memento mori* class, such as the skull and the cross."[7] Such watches mingled, in various proportions, a proclamation of piety with one of prosperity.

By their design and, in the early seventeenth century, their placement on the breast (often with the dial visible), watches committed themselves to public display, not private information. That the watch was never "mere" jewelry is suggested by its increasing marketability. Buyers were plainly willing to pay more for the combination of machinery *and* ornament than for a comparable adornment, such as an engraved and jeweled brooch. Clearly part of the watch's appeal resided in its claim to chronometry, in its capacity to suggest that the owner somehow possessed time as well as timekeeper, and this was doubtless true: the more expensive the watch, the wealthier the owner, and the more discretionary his or her time. But the elaboration of ornament, the open display, and the utter lack of technical advance in the interior suggest that the privilege of timekeeping was construed as secondary to the pleasure of display. By numerous decorative contrivances clockmakers contrived to beguile the observing eye, and (at the same time) to keep it distracted from the moving hand, to take the mind off the patently erratic motions; even the interior movements were often elaborately engraved and bejeweled, meant to be seen. They looked better than they worked.[8] The watch did not so much claim to render time as private property as to announce itself as private property, openly on show.

Before mid-century, this arrangement changed for men. About 1625, pockets appeared on clothing,[9] and men's watches disappeared into pockets. Women's watches remained more open ornaments a good while longer. The gendered distinction suggests a developing construction of chronometry as a figure for power rather than for mere wealth. An early exception may illustrate the rule: Elizabeth I possessed "a watch so small it fit into a ring; its tiny alarm announced the hours by scratching her finger."[10] In this instance private chronometry indexes monarchic privilege and the conventional emphasis on ornament over function gets redistributed. The watch-ring displays itself as ornament to all in sight, but reserves the privilege of its timekeeping to its owner alone, who receives private information without exerting visible (or indeed actual) effort; the time comes to her by a route accessible to no one else.

For most of the subsequent century Elizabeth's privilege—the semi-invisible timekeeper—was reserved largely for men, and was configured somewhat differently. With the pocket watch, visible effort was now part of the point. Pocket watches retained their tendency towards elaborate ornament, but the new choreography of consultation established a more even balance between show and use. A man withdrawing his watch from his pocket in order to tell the time might do so in the surreptitious hope that onlookers would admire its appearance, but what he enacted was privileged access to a private source of chronometric information. Display of the object—constant when the watch was worn upon the breast—became subsumed in a performance of which the object was a prop. With every withdrawal and return, the privilege of discretionary access would be reemphasized. Now that watches were private as well as portable, their function as timekeepers came farther to the fore (even though in fact they worked no better). The display of the watch was now (at least ostensibly) a correlative of its function: it appeared in order to tell time. The watch no longer represented (in the manner of jewelry) ownership *per se*; it manifested (as in Elizabeth's case) a particular chronometric privilege, privately possessed.

The privacy of that privilege became, in England as nowhere else, a selling point emphasized in the watches' design. At about the same time that watches began disappearing into pockets, English artisans took the structure of their casing to a complex and gratuitous extreme. They devised the "pair case," which encompassed the original watch—the lid (now sometimes made of crystal), dial, movement, and metal backplate—in a second hinged enclosure; sometimes the case-maker would add a third. Such a watch, purporting to confer a chronometric autonomy upon the owner, modeled self-containment by design. Ostensibly, the outer integument of the pair case protected the decorative details upon the inner one from the friction of the pocket. But since ornateness inevitably transferred to the outermost case, where it stood available for display (while the inner cases became simpler), these compound enclosures really served no practical purpose; indeed they made the watch thicker and harder to wind, and no other nation adopted them.[11] What they sacrificed in utility they made up for by a complexity that the English buyer evidently found compelling; the fashion for them lasted the rest of the century. On the one hand, the pair case appeared to surrender some of the watch's potential for secrecy; its design often left the dial open to view under a single lid of crystal. But what the case left visible, the owner's pocket would always obscure until the chosen moment of display. The pair case made of the pocket watch a sequence of layered secrets that began with the pocket itself. Withdrawing the watch, the owner could, at need or pleasure, lay some of its secrets bare, and find a different source of satisfaction in each subsequent revelation, passing from the adornments of the outer case to the simple sheen of the inner, and from there, by opening yet another hinged compartment, to the imposing intricacies, the partly visible wheels, shafts, and springs, of the movement itself. Owner and onlooker might take pleasure in still further revelations, as Pepys makes clear in an entry dated three months after his Greenwich experiment with pace and timepiece. He has called on "my Lord Brouncker," horological expert and president of the Royal Society, "and there spent the evening, by my desire, in seeing his Lordship open to pieces and make up again his Wach, thereby being taught what I never knew before; and it is a thing very well worth my having seen, and am mightily pleased and satisfied with it" (12.22.65; 6.337). On the walk to Greenwich, Pepys takes pleasure in what the watch reveals to him about the secret rhythms of his motion, here in what it discloses concerning the secret mechanism of its own. Here as often in the diary the discovery of secrets ("what I never knew before") propels Pepys into a language erotically tinged: the watch's compound enclosures invite serial disclosures; Pepys begins in "desire" and ends "mightily pleased and satisfied." The pair case figures the English watch as the site of secrets; the pleasure this time round consists partly in taking possession of them. Brouncker possesses them as commodity (it is "his Wach"); Pepys acquires them as knowledge ("what I never knew before").

Beyond such satisfaction, other desires persist. Brouncker and Pepys both understand, in December of 1665, that in watches the relation between commodity and knowledge remains uneasy. This year, Huygens's carefully wrought maritime pendulums have fallen short of desire, despite the satisfaction implied in Holmes's initial report. Any lesser timepiece must sustain much greater suspicion. Brouncker's watch (like any other in 1665) will readily enough yield up its secrets as an impressive mechanical artifact worth owning and understanding, but it does not yet offer accurately enough the very knowledge it purports to trade in: the metric grasp of passing time. It functions impressively as curiosity, inadequately as instrument.

For Brouncker, Pepys, and others in the Royal Society, the watch's inadequacy would likely have deepened its aura of the clandestine, its significance as private property. Huygens's quest after a portable, longitudinal timekeeper had given rise to secrets on every side. As Joella Yoder remarks, "the public record of [Holmes's] sea trial," in the first *Philosophical Transactions*, "leaves an impression of unqualified success"; only the attendees at Society meetings would become aware of unpublicized complications, of the gap between report and reality.[12] That breach had proven irresistible to Robert Hooke, who at the meeting on 15 March argued (as he had before) the impracticality of Huygens's design and hinted, grandly and darkly, at his own solution: "Mr. HOOKE declared, that he intended to put his secret concerning the longitude into the hands of the president [Brouncker], to be disposed of as his lordship should think fit" (Birch 2.24). Pepys, at the earlier meeting during which he had been elected to membership, had taken note of an intrinsic structure of secrecy in Hooke, whereby his odd appearance and behavior continually concealed real merit. In his entry for the day he wrote "Above all, Mr. [Robert] Boyle today was at the meeting, and above him Mr. Hooke, who is the most, and promises the least, of any man in the world that I ever saw" (2.15.65; 6.36–37). For Huygens, Hooke, Brouncker, Bruce, and other principal players, and for Pepys observing, the whole project of portable timekeeping—with its problems and its possibilities—unfolds within a constricted circle, in secret schemes and private hands.

PLEASURE

The emphatic privacy of English watches, as figured by the pair case, preceded the advent of pendulum-governed accuracy in clocks by several decades, and of a commensurate reliability in watches by half a century: pair cases appeared around 1625, pendulums in 1656, the balance-spring watch in 1675. I suggest, though, that the two developments—of privacy in the watch's form and accuracy in its function—though historically independent of each other, converge: that Huygensian precision, when it arrives, compounds the watch's significance and heightens its charge as private property. The proposition is obvious in two material ways. First, minute hands, and the machinery behind them, cost extra money; the more commonplace one-hand watches came cheaper. Whether the minute watch merely promised precision (1665) or actually delivered it (1675), it pointed to the prosperity of its owner. Second, the capacity to track minutes, first on clocks and eventually on watches, enhanced chronometric autonomy many times over. The owner of a patently imprecise watch would have to check it frequently against the "higher authority" of a sundial or (especially after 1660) of a standing clock.

There is a third sense, more elusive because less concrete, in which Huygensian precision conduces to privacy. It has to do with the status in the late seventeenth century of the minute as a unit of measurement, and with its consequent eligibility as a means of self-definition, a tool for self-tracking. The full meaning of the pleasure Pepys finds *en route* to Greenwich resides exactly here, in a convergence of precision (however illusory) with privacy that produces new data: "what I never knew before," this time not about the watch as mechanism (as at Brouncker's house), nor even about "what time it is" (as in the coach), but about the idiosyncratic motion of the solitary self through space and time.

The minute is the measure that makes such knowledge possible, that facilitates both the gathering and the possessing. If the pair case and the pocket privatized the chronometric instrument by sequestering it from public space, Pepys's minute watch privatizes the chronometric operation by distinguishing it from the familiar indices of public time. The watch's extraordinary extra hand purports to grant its owner private access to a temporal unit exotically small and still unusual even on public clocks. Most watches told time in the broad terms by which Londoners, tutored by steeple bells and house clocks, had long learned to regulate themselves: the hour, the half, the quarter. Well into the era of the pendulum, the quarter-hour retained its hold on the public mind as the smallest convenient unit for conceiving of and structuring social time; some of the earliest English pendulum clocks assign to it a remarkable pride of place on the dial. The minute, by contrast, often served to draw the fine, specialized distinctions required by the new science. William Harvey (so Aubrey reports) possessed "a minute watch with which he made his experiments" (*Brief Lives* 1.303). As Pepys demonstrates in his report to the Royal Society on his findings concerning Huygens's clocks, the disparity he describes between the two shipborne pendulum clocks, of "4, 6, 7, 3, 5 minutes," will eventually prove sufficient to mark the experiment a failure. Gerhard Dohrn–van Rossum has pointed out that "only since the so-called 'Scientific Revolution' in the middle of the seventeenth century can one speak of experimentally quantifying scientific procedures and of conceptions of time as a scaled continuum of discrete moments" (287). Minutes become tools, markers of phenomena, and thus a means of knowledge.

Appropriating Huygens's experiment, Pepys alters it two ways: he inverts the hierarchy of its categories, and shifts the meaning of its signifier. The measured minute still matters, but with a different application. In the search for the longitude, time serves space; Holmes tracks time in hopes of working out exactly where he is, and the Society, in order to verify Holmes's enthusiastic reports on the clocks' performance, had requested the "masters' journals" partly because a lingering disagreement over exactly where the ships had landed at one point on the expedition raised questions about the efficacy of the Major's vaunted instruments and calculations (Birch 2.21). In Pepys's short record of his experiment, details of space become secondary to those of time. Pepys names only his points of departure and of destination (and those confusedly: still unaccustomed to moving in these precincts, he begins his entry in the manuscript, "Up, and walked to Woolwich," before crossing out the final word and replacing it with "Greenwich"). Despite his opening announcement that "I am now come to see the distances of my way," Pepys delineates no "distances" reckoned as numbers of miles or as the names of fixed points along the route. Instead, he tells time. What interests him both in the walking and the writing is the relation of his movement to that of the watch, which he gazes at continually as its hands advance steadily through large spans and small. Even for these durations he offers no absolute numbers, nor does he say how long the journey takes him; he reckons them only relative to each other and to his progress, and gleans from them a layered self-knowledge: of the fundamental regularity of his pace (and, by reciprocal inference, of the watch's), of the inevitable and idiosyncratic variations of tempo within that steady structure, and even of the exact range of those variations ("within two minutes"). By writing up "the distances of my way" in minutes rather than in miles, Pepys manages both to make good on the odd plural in that phrase, and to give singular force to the possessive. The space he traverses along this public road belongs to all, but the timing of his trek belongs to him alone. "My" way consists of multiple temporal "distances" that vary from each other from day to day and from span to span: some occupy thirteen minutes, some seventeen, and some durations in between.

Announcing a pleasure, the passage limns the temporal aesthetic that underwrites it. The oddly fused wording in which Pepys reports his findings verges on paradox: "to come within two minutes constantly to the same place" is to come (by general reckoning) "constantly" and (by the specialized criteria of the minute watch) *not* constantly at the same time. The

pleasure that the watch makes possible consists in playing temporal uniformity against temporal inconsistency, the presumed steadiness of the watch's
Tick, Tick, Tick against the presumed flux of the walker's pace. Pepys has
given voice to a similar aesthetic a few months earlier in his account of a
"very strange" argument about rhythmic form in music: "[Captain Taylor]
sa[id] that the law of a dancing Corant is to have every barr to end in a
pricked Crochet and quaver [i.e., a dotted quarter and eighth note]—which
I did deny. . . . It proceeded till I vexed him; but all parted friends, for
Creed and I to laugh at when he was gone" (4.23.65; 6.88). In a dancing
courante the meter in every bar will be the same but, Pepys argues to the
point of vexation and laughter, the rhythm need not be—indeed (so the
laughter implies) it ought not to be identical, if monotony is to be avoided
and pleasure sustained. On the Greenwich walk, stability and variety derive
from slightly different sources, the one from a uniform duration (the quarter
hour), the other from a changing one (the time required "to come . . . to
the same place"). With erratic bodily motion to provide the desired irregu-
larity, measure itself becomes a source of pleasure.

The pleasure is, of course, contrived and constructed. In order to sustain
the satisfaction that arises from his measurings, Pepys manages to forget the
facts that complicate them. Though his watch does enable him to know better than before the regularity of his habitual pace, he also knows—who
better, in the wake of the Royal Society inquiry?—the likely unreliability of
the device he carries. Imprecise instrument, variable pace: nothing along the
road to Greenwich goes "constantly," even in relation to itself. Watch and
owner actually participate in a private relativity. The experimental procedure, though, pretends otherwise, by confining to one component an indefinition that is actually diffused throughout the system. It ascribes temporal
fixity to the watch, elasticity to the walker. Pepys construes "the distances
of my way" as variabilities of time over stability in space, as a mode of
temporal self-location. In his formulation, variance abets definition, definition possession, possession pleasure.

That abstract possession "my way" originates in property more palpable.
Earlier, in recounting the coach ride, Pepys wrote of "carrying my wach in
my hand," but there his eager proprietorship was offset by anxiety: he im-
puted "folly and childishnesse" to himself and so cast the watch as—what
watches had been for most possessors in their first century—a toy, its ostensible use (the tracking of time) reduced to visual display and idle activity
("seeing what a-clock it is 100 times"). In the walk to Greenwich "with my

minute wach in my hand" the phrase expands by a single word, but the word makes all the difference. Pepys figures the minute watch not as toy but as instrument, a possession of a very different order. In Pepys's experiment, the watch amounts to a kind of capital, whose yield is increased possession of time and self through an enhanced knowledge of the way the self operates over time. In the write-up, Pepys follows the triple possessives "my . . . wach," "my hand," and "my way" with a culminating reflexive: "And do find myself. . . ." The pronoun functions not as the direct object that closes the clause (as it does in the twentieth-century vocabulary of introspection), but as the subject of its own infinitive verb phrase: "And do find myself to come within two minutes constantly to the same place. . . ." The phrasing construes "myself" not as an abstract, conceptual being, but as an entity defined and determined by the particulars of its motion through time. It is by a similar construction, grounded in closely measured time, that Huygens's horological and Holmes's navigational successors, with watches in hands, would try—with eventual success—to find themselves on waters newly measured out in minutes. And it is by a comparable reckoning, of uniform durations played off against elastic motions, that Pepys makes of his diary a running exercise in temporal self-reckoning and self-location.

DIARY AND WATCH

For each of the three chief features Pepys values in the timepiece—its precise calibration, its privacy, and its consequent capacity to produce new data of the self—he has already incorporated a textual analog in his journal. First, the minute watch takes its name from its novel calibration, which divides time into small, uniform spans numbered and defined in continual succession, so that time is subject to comparatively rapid, systematic redefinition. Pepys's diary is comparably calibrated, by a different temporal unit but by a similarly comprehensive system. Pepys inscribes in the page's margin each date in succession, omitting none, and in the page's middle he produces a new narrative specification for each consecutive date. Second, the watch figures definition as complicatedly private, supplied by a device that (like larger clocks) delivers its data to the eye but (unlike them) reserves it to its owner by compound sequestrations. Pepys's diary engages in a secrecy comparably complex. He writes it in a shorthand that is not quite a secret cipher. Finally, in Pepys's particular use of the watch, the calibration and sense of privacy converge, so that the minute hand gauges both its owner's comportment with a common measure of time (the quarter hour) and the range of his idiosyncratic deviation from that conventional span. In the diary, similarly, the date identifies the measure common to all who operate under England's Old Style calendar; the narrative data, the particulars of movement through the day, belong to Pepys alone.

The pendulum clock tells out each minute in succession, Pepys's diary each day. On most of the new clocks, the minute markings were not interpolated between the hour markings (as on many twentieth-century timepieces). They appeared instead within a narrow ring of their own, the outermost on the dial. Within the much wider inner band appeared the twelve large roman numerals long familiar as indices of the hours. Around the slender outer circle the minute markings were numbered by smaller Arabic numerals (see Fig. 3). The arrangement, with two quantitatively and ortho-

Figure 3. One of the earliest pendulum clocks (1657), by Huygens's collaborator Salomon Coster (for interior view, see p. xvi). The dial consecutively numbers the minutes as well as the hours. Soon a less crowded format for the outer ring became fairly standard on both clocks and watches, with every minute marked by the type of small calibration here used for the quarter-hours on the inner ring, and with an Arabic numeral placed above the marking for every fifth minute (5, 10, 15 . . . 60). Photograph courtesy of the Time Museum, Rockford, Illinois.

graphically distinct series, for hour and for minute, arrayed along each of the twelve radii, was intended to facilitate the counting of minutes in a culture that had not yet mastered that collation (still difficult for children newly trying to read analog clocks) whereby the number 4, for example, represents both the fourth hour after noon or midnight, and the twentieth minute within any hour.

In Pepys's text, too, the markers of time occupy their own outer bands. The names of the months run across the tops of the pages, while days of the week and numbers of the dates run down the left-hand margin, opposite the units of prose that occupy most of the paper's space. The minute on the clock and the day in the diary function as the smallest integers of definition within their respective systems, from which larger spans will be composed: the clock tracks hours as well as minutes; Pepys tracks months and years as well as days. His diary tends towards calibration in narrative as well as number. Like many diarists he will often mark the ends of months and years by special narrative activities (for example, tallying up fiscal accounts and reckoning less quantifiable gains and losses). Unlike most he will mark the beginnings and endings of each day with like punctilio. On the clock, the completion of one integral span and the commencement of the next are signaled by the minute hand's arrival at the next calibration. Pepys's text proclaims the corresponding moment triply, by the new date, and by the formulas of closure and commencement that precede and follow it.

The new clocks changed not only the unit but also, in effect, the mode by which time was defined, and this too bears on the role of the day in Pepysian narrative as well as in the daily forms that followed. The minute markings map out in detail the hitherto untracked middles of the hours that were previously defined only by their beginnings, endings, and (sometimes) subdivisions. As Dohrn–van Rossum points out, the advent of the minute radically changed the construct of the hour. From the twelfth through the sixteenth centuries, "the clock-hour was the twenty-fourth part of the full day. . . . In everyday life this hour was divided into halves, thirds, quarters, sometimes into twelve parts, but it was not divided by sixty or understood as the period of sixty minutes" (282). Before minute markings, that is, the hour was (from the point of view of mechanical timekeeping) a monolith—the sole unit and term by which the time of day was reckoned. After Huygens it was a finite set, its elements articulated and itemized. The seventeenth minute after three o'clock could now be defined as precisely as three o'clock itself. The new clocks proposed a temporality in which "middle moments," identifiable by number but asymmetrical within the larger scheme, merited, and repaid, close attention.

Pepys writes middleness assiduously. This is partly a condition of his genre (the diarist neither knows in advance, nor can narrate in retrospect, the day of death), and it is partly a concomitant of the narrative's rigorous diurnality: most of the autobiographical story lines that Pepys tracks (his jealousy of his wife's dancing master, for example, or his conduct of a clandestine administrative scheme) take many days to resolve themselves, and may indeed begin and end almost imperceptibly. When Pepys writes up an entry at the end of a given day, or even after a cluster of days, he often knows only the story's middle, and not its conclusion. Three days before the Greenwich walk, for example, Pepys records "the most happy news" of his cousin and patron Lord Sandwich's naval success against a Dutch fleet, "his taking two of their East India ships and six or seven others, and very good prize. . . . [T]his news doth so overjoy me, that I know not what to say enough to express it . . ." (9.10.65; 6.219). The day's "most happy news" will beget years of trouble, here unforeseen. Sandwich's legally dubious seizure and distribution of the Dutch ships' prize goods caused a national scandal that threatened many careers, Pepys's included (6.231, n. 2). The diarist, though, records the day's data from the day's vantage.

Pepys's ignorance in the entry may seem simply unavoidable in a diurnal narrative. But his method of diary-keeping construes calibrated, numerated middleness also as a positive value, and not just a byproduct, of diurnal self-recording. The extant manuscript bears evidence that it is the product of multiple revisions, and in many cases (most notably that of the Great Fire) Pepys composed the final version of a given entry days, weeks, or even months after the date it records. Often, then, he possesses retrospective knowledge, but almost without exception he refrains from reporting or acknowledging it within the entry (though it may, of course, shape in ways often unguessable just how the entry is written). So the diary's middleness, ineluctable with respect to the narrative's place within the diarist's indeterminable lifespan, is also, in its local manifestations from entry to entry, partly a fiction, a contrivance, a deliberately chosen discipline of narrative time. The narrative in any given instance confines itself (regardless of the author's information) to the timeframe specified by the dated calibration at the page's edge; illumination as to the direction any given narrative is taking arrives in stroboscopic increments at intervals of a day.

The minute watch figures privacy as well as precision. Pepys's diary does this too. It secures its own operations from casual observation by com-pounded enclosures: a leather-bound volume (itself usually concealed within a desk drawer) containing the self-sequestering orthography of shorthand. Thomas Shelton, who devised and published the stenographic system that Pepys uses, reckoned secrecy as the first virtue of his method: "Sometimes a man may have occasion to write that which he would not have every one acquainted with, which being set downe in these Characters, he may have them for his owne private use onely. . . ." [13] In practice, though, the privacy of Pepys's timekeepers, chronometric and textual, is comparably ambiva-lent. The pocket watch could serve as prop in a conspicuous performance, while the pair case, however layered and intricate, usually left the dial on display.

So it is with secrecy in the diary. Pepys simultaneously seeks it and sur-renders it. Shelton's *Tachygraphy* ("rapid writing") was among the most popular forms of shorthand in its day (iv). It would have sufficed to keep the diary's contents secret from Pepys's wife, though not necessarily from his colleagues in the Navy Office (where he sometimes stored the journal). Many of them would have learned stenography, either (like Pepys) as an accomplishment popular among university men and *virtuosi* or as a useful tool in their clerical and administrative crafts (ii). When Pepys most desired secrecy, as in the accounts of his marital infidelities of thought and deed, he compounded the text's obscurity by setting in shorthand a *lingua franca* of his own devising, composed from a "basically Spanish" word stock into which he mixed English, French, and (in lesser proportions) Dutch, Italian, Latin, and Greek; to confute legibility further, he occasionally "insert[ed] between syllables the shorthand symbols for *l, r, m* or *n*" so that the diction would be at times not only polyglot and ungrammatical but also technically nonsense. But though he contrived at times to deepen the shorthand in this way, he also saw fit, at points on virtually every page, to shed orthographic concealment altogether. "The diary," its editors state, "employs a great deal of longhand, mostly for personal names, place names, names of ships, days, months and festivals, and titles of rank. Titles of plays, songs and books" also appear in plain script, as do words "apparently so written for the sake of emphasis." [14] As a result, the text reads tantalizingly (to the tachygraphically uninitiated), with persons, places, times, and enthusiasms clearly legible, but with their predication (their convergence in narrated action) obscured. Occasionally, the longhand runs counter to Pepys's ostensibly secretive pur-pose, blazoning some particulars of his errant sexual activities (the name of a mistress, the title of an erotic book) while obscuring others under the triple cover of the orthographically garbled code.[15] The complex secrecy of the diary's orthography, like that of the watch in some of its applications, operates for its proprietor as both a prize and a hurdle, to be both courted and counteracted.

The mixed secrecy of Pepys's orthography mirrors and facilitates that of his entire narrative endeavor. His simultaneous disclosure and sequestration of acts and thoughts too risky for more public revelation is to a great extent a correlative of his chosen temporality, of the way he constructs both fullness and middleness in the narrative. The intent to record—or to seem to re-cord—the whole of his conscious day necessarily entails inscribing or even highlighting those tracts of time that, if unwritten here, would be known to no one save the occasional co-conspirator—sexual partner or administra-tive crony. And the diary's secrets cluster thickest around issues that the rule of narrative middleness leaves necessarily suspended at day's and entry's end: for example, around the diarist's fears that he won't be able to pay a loan, to complete a scheme or a seduction, or to keep hidden a fact or act he needs concealed. Again, Pepys is true to these agitations even when writing or rewriting the entry after they have passed. The temporality in which Pepys writes thus produces a running, inexorable equation between self and se-crecy: the public Pepys appears in virtually every entry, speaking words and doing deeds that others witness, but he appears only intermittently; the tem-poral *continuum* of the day belongs to, and is inseparable from, the private Pepys. The diary figures the public self as intermittent and occasional, the private self as abiding and continuous: it is the secret self alone who fills the frame of the daily entry.[16]

On the Greenwich walk, I argued above, the watch's precision intensified the privacy of its data. To Pepys, the minute markings appear to facilitate the accurate measure of idiosyncratic motion. In the diary, the shorthand itself provides a medium in which secrecy and precision combine to produce knowledge as a form of tangible, permanent property. Shelton hints at this dynamic while crying up the "divers wayes" in which his technique can benefit his pupils. After secrecy, he enumerates several more advantages:

2. For brevity, it is of no small use: for by this Art, as much may be written in one page, as can be written in six, in another ordinary hand. 3. For the celerity of it, the rules being learned perfectly; one may write as fast as any man ordinarily speaketh. . . . 4. Many things of good use are, and have been

by this Art preserved, which otherwise had beene lost, as may appeare by the workes of divers worthy men by this Art taken, and published, which else had perished with the breath that uttered them. (A3r–v)

The benefits that Shelton represents as working in "divers wayes" operate, in Pepys's practice, combinatorially; they all come into play in the diarist's approach to textualizing time. Any kind of script, shorthand or long, can of course claim (as Shelton does here) the capacity to preserve "things of good use." The special boast implicit in Shelton's third and fourth points is that tachygraphy alone, by virtue of its "celerity," can make impalpable human speech permanent by preserving the evanescent products of "breath" in verbatim transcript. Shorthand came closer than any other technique in the culture to what we now call "real time recording"—the preservation (rather than the *précis*) of an action in its full temporal dimension. Of course, the technique operated within limits. The only action it could claim to represent so fully was speech, which it recorded by a process simultaneous and coextensive with the utterance ("What! Write as fast as speak?" begins a prefatory poem in another of Shelton's textbooks). Pepys used the method in this way to set down, for example, his manuscript "Account of His Majesty's Escape from Worcester, Dictated to Mr. Pepys by the King himselfe."[17] True, Shelton's method, working at about a hundred words a minute, probably could not quite make good his promise that the user might "write as fast as any man ordinarily speaketh" (*Tutor* 2). In the midseventeenth century shorthand could not actually keep pace with the speed of speech, as the minute watch could not match time *per se*. Pepys, though, deploys both instruments as if they could, ascribing to each a combination of privacy and precision that facilitates the tracking of human actions—motion, speech—over real time.

In Pepys's diary, shorthand bears as complex a relation to real time as it does to secrecy. Shelton's second boast, that shorthand takes up less space (one page in place of six) holds true for time as well. Tachygraphy need not always match real time, as when it transcribes dictation; it can, for other purposes of writing, compress time as well. Pepys, writing out his entries primarily in shorthand, performs in effect a double compression of time. The narrative, regardless of the shorthand, performs formidable compressions of its own. By the criterion of word count alone—a convenient common denominator between lived time and textual time—a Pepysian entry presents far fewer words than were spoken (let alone thought) over the course of the day it represents; it also consumes less than a day in the writing (here the tachygraphy's speed does matter) and demands less in the reading.

The term current in the seventeenth century for such textual compression, particularly in the clerical professions wherein Pepys was so well versed, is still in use: "minutes." The means by which Pepys tracks time in his diary bear the same name as the units by which he tracks his motion on the walk. But the written "minute" initially plays the figuration of time in the opposite direction, away from the fixities of chronometry towards the elasticities of narrative. Scribal minutes generally condense: they reduce longer utterances and larger actions to fewer words and smaller space.

At the same time, the practice of "minute-making" often evinces a propensity towards expansion, towards constitution (or reconstitution) into wholeness. A "minute" taken from a speech might (unlike Pepys's shorthand reproduction of Charles's "Account") aspire to preserve only the chief points; but "minutes of a speech" might also describe a set of notes made in advance by the speaker, "to be further elaborated" (*OED*) either by written revision or at the moment of oration. One who records the minutes of a meeting, like the stenographer who takes dictation, works in a process temporally coextensive with the session, noting (or recalling) actions and utterances as they arise in sequence over time. The very doubleness of the term, the fact that it can name both a process of compression and an irreducible measure of real time, fosters a sense of the possibilities for expansion, as though the written minutes of the record can adequately represent the lived minutes of the meeting. The relation between the two types of minutes is intrinsically synechdocal, but the scribe works as though the part will suffice for the whole. Still, textual minutes differ from chronometric as narrative time differs from measured: one is a phenomenon of nearly infinite (and ineluctable) elasticity (both elongations and compressions); the other is comprised of fixed durations.

This difference between minutes extends to the way the passage of time is represented, on the watch and in the diary, by visible arrangements in space. The minute markings on the edge of the dial, the dates on the edge of the page, define each duration by the number assigned to it in an established system of time measurement, calendrical or horological; the actual duration appears, in both timepiece and text, as a space between two indices. On the watch that space is blank. In the diary it is occupied by the text of the entry, the minutes of the day. Pepys defines duration doubly, by public integer and private account. On the watch the integers number time; in the diary, the numbers of time index narrative.

Yet this fundamental distinction between the minutes of watch and diary ends up, in Pepys's handling of both instruments, extending analogy. I argued above that Pepys's pleasure on the Greenwich walk derives from the play of temporal fixities against variabilities. His watch provides the fixity, his walking the variability, and his pleasure consists in working out the relation between the two. In the process the measured minute plays a double role. It offers a new fixity, a newly particularized duration made visible as marking and motion around the dial, but it enables Pepys (or so he supposes) to track exactly the range of his variances from a common measure (the quarter hour). In the diary too the numbers of time—the dates listed in unbroken series along the page's edge—identify the fixed duration and the common measure; here it is the narrative minutes that embody elasticity, index idiosyncrasy, and track variability from span to span. They do so in the plainest way (apparent even to the eye that cannot penetrate their shorthand) merely by their uneven distribution of the days over the page's space. In the diary the spaces between the integers vary (as they do not on the watch), as Pepys chooses to narrate each day at greater or lesser length. His diary's rules of engagement with real time stipulate that the durations represented be serial and calendrically isochronic, but not that the representation be (as on the watch) isotopic. The forms by which the diary pages translate time into space make clear the fundamentally chronometric grounding of the discipline. Every date without exception introduces a blank space that Pepys must fill with prose. But the arrangement also figures a corresponding freedom: Pepys fills the blank by forms and criteria of his own devising, even to the extent of determining its dimensions as a correlative of the day's abundance and significance, privately reckoned. The rigor of the temporal grid, the steadiness of the formal *Tick, Tick, Tick*, underwrite and highlight a certain suppleness in the narrative, whereby in the ten-year diary, as on the Greenwich walk, Pepys takes the divisions of time and construes them as his own.

PLACING PEPYS

Of all the many scholars who have cited Pepys on many topics, only one has invoked him on the texture of lived time. In his study *The Metronomic Society*, the sociologist Michael Young laments the current tyranny implied in his title, whereby clocks and watches, accurate, synchronized, and omnipresent, dominate the lives of the people who wear them. In a footnote to his per-oration, he invokes Pepys as a paragon of a near-pastoral indifference to clock time which, by Young's account, preceded the Industrial Revolution. Suggesting that "the happy mean seems to be to remain aware of the passage of time but to behave tranquilly as though one is not aware of it and has, at least on some occasions, all the time in the world," Young appends the following note: "A reminder is in Samuel Pepys' seventeenth century diary. His account is so engaging because he brought so much gusto to each new moment—every pretty woman seen through the window of his coach; each new dish of beef or even pease porridge; each song he sang, from a new composition of Purcell senior to a tavern ballad; and always the fact that every moment was different. . . . The diary is remarkable for what he had, and for what he did not have. He and his fellows did not have clocks as their constant companions." [18] Here again is the familiar "gusto" along with the customary inattentiveness to the forms by which it manifests itself in Pepys's book of time. Contrary to Young's assumption, the diarist behaves within his text as though he were inescapably aware of time; he accords to its steady measure a power of arbitration over his narrative structure that is un-matched in any predecessor. Similarly, he treats his clocks, if not as constant companions, at least as profoundly compelling ones. Young undervalues the diary's fundamental engagement with the measured passage of time.

In his discussion, Young sentimentalizes developments in "metronomic" cultural time that E. P. Thompson and Michel Foucault have analyzed more rigorously. The ways in which Pepys engages with time, in both his watch and his diary, help fill in the larger accounts of "time-discipline" that Thompson and Foucault establish. The two historians' commitment to un-derstanding late-eighteenth- and early-nineteenth-century developments in chronometry as a means of exploitation (Thompson) and subjugation (Fou-cault) focuses their attention on modalities and *milieux* rather different and distant from Pepys's. Thompson's article divides its history of clock-time consciousness into two basic phases. The first is between 1300 and 1650, when mechanical timekeeping lent "a new immediacy and insistence" to the sense of mortality, and hence to the figure of "time as a devourer" (352–54). The second phase covers a period when chronometric work-discipline was well under way: "We are entering . . . , already in 1700, the familiar landscape of disciplined industrial capitalism, with the time sheet, the time-keeper . . ." (385). Thompson's scheme, detailed and nuanced with respect to laborers' time, leaves little room for attention to other orders of society and orderings of time. The essay casts sidelong glances at prosperous people who value their clocks and watches as ornate objects (363, 366) but does not deal with more socially equivocal figures like Pepys, the son of a tailor who takes perpetual pleasure in conceiving himself (and hearing himself described) as "a very rising man" (8.20.62;3.172), and who learns from a coterie of aristocrats and inquirers (Boyle, Brouncker, Huygens, Hooke) to recognize in the minute hand a very new tool for new science, and so to discern in the close calibrations of his exotic watch not a means to manage others but an opportunity to amuse, to instruct—to acquire knowledge about—himself. Pepys, his diary, and his watch occupy a position and period that Thompson hurries past.

In Foucault's schema, Pepys's "very rising" career traces a trajectory more central, and more fully explained. Pepys's watch, remember, comes to him as a bribe, a measure of the distance he has traversed over the preceding five years from powerlessness (as Clerk of the Exchequer, with "Mr Downing master of my office") towards power; he will over the next decades travel farther still. It is the phenomenon of the diary itself that remains a little elusive in Foucault's explanatory paradigm. In *Discipline and Punish*, Foucault builds his account of subjectivity and subjection not from private writings but from public documents: the measures decreed by a seventeenth-century town council to contain the threat of plague by virtually incarcerating the citizens; military training manuals, school timetables, and other such testimony to "those minor processes" that, according to Foucault, "overlap, repeat, . . . converge and gradually produce the blueprint of a general [disciplinary] method." Foucault finds that culminating blueprint in Bentham's Panopticon, which subsumes the ever-increasing intricacy of regulation within an elegant economy of enforcement. "He who is subjected to a field of visibility, and who knows it, assumes responsibility for the constraints of power," writes Foucault. "He makes [those constraints] play spontaneously upon himself . . . he becomes the principle of his own subjection" and in this self-subjection, Foucault asserts, lies the central mechanism of a new, culturally pervasive technology of discipline (202−3).[19] Pepys's diary, an equivocally secret book that takes the self as subject, and his career as both accomplished public administrator and energetic self-chronicler, would seem to provide an instance for testing this claim derived from documents more public. During the 1660s (the decade from which Foucault begins his investigation of changes in the disciplinary pattern) Pepys produces a journal governed by the unusually systematic disciplines of time already discussed. In the seventies and eighties he rises to the top administrative position in the Navy, and from that place of power restructures the entire institution along new lines of highly articulated regulation, which he propounds by dispatching thousands of written directives in the very genre that *Discipline and Punish* most attentively investigates.

The sequence of Pepys's career figures the Foucauldian paradigm in reverse—solitary self-scrutiny first, massive regulatory apparatus second—and so opens a question of continuity: do the modes of discipline that operate in the diary bear a demonstrable affinity to those by which the diarist will later remake the Navy? The journal and the life, abundant though they are in Foucauldian cues, supply a fairly intricate answer, confirming Foucault's account in some ways, complicating it in others. For Pepys's public life, the Panopticon affords an instructive paradigm, but in the pages of his private narrative Pepys constructs autonomy in ways that the scheme can't fully compass.

Foucault's "minor processes" cluster particularly thick on the walk to Greenwich: the minute calibration of time and motion, convergent technologies of self and machine, observation, and documentation all come into play. Even the destination is suggestive: in a private recapitulation of Huygens's and Holmes's globe-compassing experiment, Pepys bears his minute watch towards the site of its Foucauldian apotheosis, the center point of the "Panchronicon" from which (in Young's "metronomic society") the world will eventually synchronize its clocks and actions. But the questions of surveillance and discipline arise most pointedly out of those junctures where the experiments with the timekeepers enter the record of timed documents.

The Royal Society's request that Pepys "procure the journals of those masters of ships, who had been with Major HOLMES" may have supplied the first impetus for a lifelong preoccupation. Over the ensuing decades, Pepys amassed a large personal collection of sea journals (eventually including Holmes's own account of this voyage), as a resource for the study of navigation and for a projected history of the Navy.[20] The collection bespeaks the sensibility that was to make Pepys so effectual, and so Foucauldian, an administrator. In 1665, Pepys mistrusted Major Robert Holmes on several grounds, both personal (he suspected that Holmes was trying to seduce his wife) and professional (he thought Holmes was cheating the Navy Office). To procure the masters' journals of the voyage was to retain over Holmes a power of surveillance, and potentially of discipline. Such documentary panopticism came early to the navy, whose administration depended on the control of activities over huge expanses of space by means of logbooks recorded in minute increments of time. As Secretary of the Navy, Pepys proved both ardent in his pursuit and expert in the deployment of such records. He dispatched many letters inquiring as to the exact hour of a ship's departure or arrival at a remote port or soliciting the ship's journal to corroborate, for example, a captain's suspect claim that, contrary to the testimony of observers, he "got timelily from shore." To counter slackness thus detected, Pepys drew up detailed schemes of discipline. "Pepys's whole plan" of naval reform, writes one of his biographers, "was to make a rule for all things, great or small." "Into the slipshod and rather chaotic organization of the Navy," writes another, "[Pepys] introduced a high degree of system and method, and so vastly increased efficiency in every direction." [21] "A rule for all things, great or small," a discipline that extended "in every direction"—the locutions, though casual, savor of the panoptic, and Pepys's acquisition of other men's logbooks confirms the impression. The collection of sea journals that Pepys bequeathed at his death to the library of his alma mater, like the experiment recorded in those he procured for the Royal Society, do point, as Foucault might suggest, towards a procedure whereby sharp definition and clear order radiate invisibly from a compact center— the clocks at Greenwich, Pepys's desk at the Naval Office—outward towards a control and efficacy "in all directions"—a system in which knowledge accumulates into power.

But alongside Holmes's and the other journals, Pepys bequeathed to Magdalene College his own diary, the one he'd kept during the decade in which he began his rise through navy ranks; the juxtaposition of manuscripts poses the question of their relation. The journal Pepys writes differs from the journals he collects in the same way that the private experiment he undertakes differs from the scientific project it mimics—by its elasticity, by the running interplay between numbered fixities in the time form and verbal variation in the narrative. The experiment of Huygens, launched in pursuit of new precision, and the journals of the ship's masters, composed in expectation of inspection and surveillance, all move conformably along the trajectory of discipline that Foucault maps across the subsequent century. But the more private enterprises—the riverside walk and its diaristic record—do not. Pepys's experiment partakes with Huygens's of the same materials and modes—watch, motion, time, and space—but with a different purport. For Huygens, as Pepys's investigation determines, a difference of "4, 6, 7,

3, 5 minutes" means failure: clocks so variable cannot fulfill their designated purpose. The precision Huygens seeks will, when found in the next century, abet the minutely articulated time-discipline that Foucault finds exemplified in the schedule at an eighteenth-century French school: "8.52 the monitor's summons, 8.56 entrance of the children and prayer, 9.00 the children go to their benches. . . ." The idea Pepys implements on his riverside walk, of measuring the body's motion in minutes, may promise, in Foucault's scheme, a future strategy of regulating that motion by even smaller intervals. But Pepys is bent on other business: he seeks to know his body's motion but not to regulate it. Any data will do: the variable of "two minutes" every quarter of an hour, fatal to Huygens, proves merely intriguing to Pepys. He neither announces nor will implement a program of perambulatory reform. The knowledge gained in the experiment conduces not to power but (in Pepys's word) to "pleasure."

That pleasure derives in part from the way the watch-timed walk conflates the component most central to the diary's structure—calibrated time—with the sensory capacity most productive of its substance—steadily exercised sight (both elements, of course, figure prominently in the operation of the Panopticon). The very word "watch," quickly followed as it is by the infinitive "to see," registers the fusion, and so the walk, by its preoccupations, recapitulates in miniature the workings of the private chronicle in which the diarist writes it down. In both the walk and the book, Pepys's pleasure does depend on the achievement of a new precision—on mechanical and private technologies for tracking the minutes and the days in close succession—but this is a precision complicatedly construed. What was perhaps most remarkable about the Huygensian clocks for their first enthusiasts was their *decentralization* of the temporal, their apparent disconnection from recognizable modes of discipline: the church tower and the *campanile* had for centuries monopolized chronometry, and had propounded a time that was measured and told in the service of explicit interests (dictating the times of prayer or the hours of labor). Earlier clocks and watches had followed suit, offering not accurate timekeeping but explicit visual representations of a heaven-directed temporality: sun, moon, stars, a case embossed with a crucifix or shaped like a death's head. The new clocks and watches often dispensed with such designations, supplanting them with plain black marks, regularly spaced and numbered. In the diary (a corresponding shift) the blank page declines the confident astrological and religious prolepses characteristic of the earlier almanac. The blankness and the unit (the minute, the day), or rather the blankness *of* the unit, appear to Pepys to offer both a space and an instrument for individual, idiosyncratic habitation and inscription along a continuum whereby he can appropriate public time for private use. The date at the beginning of every entry names a duration the diarist has occupied in common with everyone else in England. But no one else, the diary implies by its very existence, has lived these precise experiences or recorded them in exactly this way. The diarist both assumes and enacts an irreducible individuality and a variable (ultimately incalculable) freedom: the tools—date and language, paper and pen—are public artifacts of the culture, but their deployment within the diary is idiosyncratic to the extent measured by the difference (and the sameness) among actual diaries, a difference the diarists themselves perform and believe in without being able to gauge. By virtue of this practice, which is grounded in a temporality more rationalized but less centralized than that of preceding generations, Pepys can pursue a discipline of time without necessarily succumbing to one of actions, can observe and record himself in a time-ordered way without, in Foucault's words, becoming "the principle of his own subjection," and can even recognize within the discipline a means of liberation and autonomy.

Within the diary, the language of sight colludes with the structures of time to forestall a totalizing discipline. In an early entry Pepys describes himself as always "with child to see any strange thing" (5.14.60; 1.138), and the exclamation "Lord, to see [this or that]" reappears every few pages throughout the decade to record some new occasion of astonishment. Most often, Pepys applies the phrase to what he observes in the behavior of others, as during the Great Fire: "Lord, to see how the streets and the highways are crowded with people, running and riding and getting of carts at any rate to fetch away things" (9.3.66; 7.272). Sometimes he turns the locution on himself, as when living under threat of plague: "Lord, to see how I did endeavour all I could to talk with as few [people] as I could" (9.14.65; 6.224). In both cases the exclamation, by its grammatical incompleteness, its absence of predication, offers a syntactic analogue for the watch-measured walk to Greenwich: both experiment and exclamation register the data but relinquish a measure of control. The impulse is energetically panoptic— Pepys would like to "see any strange thing" he can—but its objective is not disciplinary. Pepys, observing, will accord the "thing" the full measure of strangeness, of deviance from the norm, that makes it valuable. In his diary, "to see" is not to regulate.

But in the pages of Pepys's diary, to see is to appropriate. By the very ink-act of exclamation, Pepys ushers the observed phenomenon into the closed domain of his secret book and its shorthand code. The diary manifests its preoccupation with the visible in two ways: by the way it privileges sight in its report, and by the way it resists it in its method. Pepys's procedure for recording his own time is almost explicitly antipanoptic: though his inscription of his experience and behavior will technically be visible to anyone who opens the book (as, in Bentham's design, the prisoners' cells can be plainly seen by anyone watching from the central tower), the code assures that to virtually everyone the record will be unreadable (as the prisoners' behavior will not, having been rendered "transparent" by Bentham's strategies for lighting the cells). Pepys's code achieves an opacity, an obscuring of private time and thought from more central instruments and systems; working within it, Pepys (again to borrow Foucault's terminology) knows himself *not* to be "subjected to a field of visibility other than his own."

That knowledge sustains the diary, as the document itself attests on its final page. In 1669 Pepys brings his diary to an end because his failing sight has rendered the shorthand code both difficult and dangerous to write. His last sentences reenact, by their ambivalence and ambiguity, the whole book's intricate commerce between the visual public world and the invisible occluded secret record. Pepys proposes to himself a plan "from this time forth to have [the diary] kept by my people in longhand, and [I] must therefore be contented to set down no more then is fit for them and all the world to know" (5.31.69; 9.504). Here at the diary's end, the notion that the document will continue in some form sustains that construction of middleness that has been so important to its operations from its inception. But Pepys will not pursue the plan, because it is inconceivable that he could be contented with the logistics he describes: to subject his secret narrative to fields of visibility other than his own—the eyes, ears, and minds of the amanuenses, and the legibility of the longhand—runs so contrary to the contours of his enterprise as to end it altogether. The next and final sentence counts the cost: "And so I betake myself to that course which [is] almost as much as to see myself go into my grave" (9.565). Pepys does not make clear whether he here refers to the loss of his sight or to the end of his narrative, so inextricably are vision and diary intertwined. And though the comparison declares the end of temporality and the advent of darkness, the diction retains the privileges that the sentence ostensibly abjures: Pepys conceives even death as a "course," a mode of motion over time, and in casting the image of "myself go[ing] into my grave" he retains his prerogative, pervasive through the diary and crucial in its making, "to see." The sentence, in its insistences and its resistances, makes a fit conclusion for a work that deals in pleasured sight but not a reformative surveillance, in measured time but not a relentlessly articulated self-discipline.[22]

•

The diarist's encounter with his watch, then, adumbrates a structure of feeling about time that emphasizes autonomy rather than subjection, property rather than discipline. Chronometry is now a private capacity; it can produce time, by various means of enclosure, as a private property: to read time as property on a watch, and to write it as property in a diary, is to attain knowledge (and hence possession) of the self in time, and this possession entails pleasure. In the timeframe of the 1660s Pepys's ability to inhabit this structure is privileged; it arises from his multiple positions in convergent hierarchies and from the techniques and perceptions attendant upon them: the clerk's bookkeeping, the student's and secretary's shorthand, the "rising man's" (and virtuoso's) passion for acquisition, the Navy administrator's venue of operation, and the Royal Society initiate's curiosity. In 1665 few could have construed watch time as he does; no one wrote diary time as he does. It is partly for these reasons that Pepys takes his feeling about time (as Williams's model predicts) "to be private, idiosyncratic, and even isolating"; indeed, Pepys compounds Williams's model in that for him these are not merely attributes of the *feeling* (as would be the case with a "private, idiosyncratic" feeling about a patently public phenomenon like the theater) but also components of the structuring instruments. Chronometry, on the watch and in the diary, is for Pepys intrinsically the tool of privatization: by indexing idiosyncrasy it also enacts a form of isolation—or at least, of differentiation—from contemporaries who share the span. As a way of identifying Pepys's temporal practices, Williams's alternate name for his model, "structures of *experience*" (italics his), works even better. For Pepys the measures of time, by structuring experience in narrative, thereby make it private. Williams rejects experience as rubric because "one of its senses has that past tense which is the most important obstacle to the recognition" of the novelty of the structures Williams is describing (132). With Pepys's present-focused diary that obstacle does not obtain: in Huygens's and in Pepys's hands, the structure of feeling about time is emphatically new.

In Pepys's case, a lifetime was long enough to see the structure move out of the realm of the "isolating" at least part way towards that of the "social." Just after his death, his nephew and heir John Jackson attached this memorandum to the autopsy report: "*May the 26th*, 1703. *Memorandum:* That the exact time of my Unkle Pepys's departure was 47 minutes past 3 in the morning, by his gold watch. J. J."[23] "We may be sure," notes Pepys's biographer Richard Ollard, that Jackson was acting at his uncle's instruction.[24] We may be sure also that the watch's data are more precise than any gathered on the walks to Greenwich. In 1675 Huygens had put the balance spring into place; it offered within the watch's small confines something like the isochronicity that the pendulum had made possible in larger clocks (the notion that a spring-governed watch might surpass the pendulum's precision awaited realization in the next century, with the renewed search for the longitude). Jackson evidently regards the watch as elegant enough for special remark; it is gold, and manufactured by Thomas Tompion, the most accomplished clockmaker alive. But the minute watch is no longer an oddity. Many watches in circulation now look and work this way, and the datum of "47 minutes past 3" is part of an increasingly familiar time form.

A year before Pepys's death, diurnal narrative had gone public too.

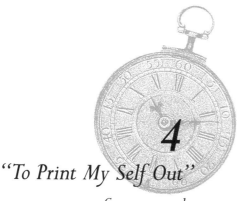

4

"To Print My Self Out"

Correspondence and Containment in the Spectator and Its Predecessors

*T*he *Daily Courant*, England's first daily newspaper, made its debut on 11 March 1702, from the press of Samuel Buckley. No other news-sheet rivaled it for timing until the *Daily Post* appeared in 1719.[1] The *Courant*'s first diurnal successor was neither a newspaper nor, strictly speaking, a rival. It was Addison and Steele's *Spectator*, first produced on 1 March 1711 by the same printer and booksellers and with a similar boast, "To be Continued every Day."[2] That phrase lingered in the mind of John Gay when he reported the new paper's success two months later, in a published "Letter to a Friend in the Country" about the tastes of periodical readers in the city. "[W]e were Surpriz'd all at once by a Paper called The SPECTATOR, which was promised to be continued every day. . . . We had at first indeed no manner of Notion, how a Diurnal Paper could be continu'd in the Spirit and Stile of our present SPECTATORS; but to our no small Surprize, we find them still rising upon us, and can only wonder from whence so Prodigious a Run of Wit and Learning can proceed. . . ."[3] What struck readers most, Gay makes clear, was not simply the paper's "Spirit and Stile." Those had in one form become familiar through the thrice-weekly *Tatler*, which had abruptly ceased publication at the beginning of this year and whose authors (Gay rightly guesses) had gone on to this new enterprise. The consensus Gay

reports centers on "our no small Surprize" at the paper's "Prodigious" timing. Gay describes a "we" that is unified in three ways: by its activity (reading periodicals), by its response (surprise), and by its occupation of a temporal continuum created by the paper and marked by its own reappearance
at regular intervals unprecedentedly small and steady for a work of "Wit
and Learning": the papers "still ris[e] upon us" like the daily sun, at a "Run"
which recalls the root meaning of that only other daily, the *Courant*.

By 1711, the "we" whom Gay describes as reading and responding were
coordinated in time by their scrutiny of another instrument as well, one of
metal rather than print. Pope, in a couplet published two weeks after Gay's
"Letter," found the two procedures close enough for simile.

> 'Tis with our *Judgments* as our *Watches*, none
> Go just *alike*, yet each believes his own.[4]

Pope here echoes a comparison used by Suckling in the epilogue to his play
Aglaura (1638):

> But as when an authentique Watch is showne,
> Each man windes up, and rectifies his owne,
> So in our verie Judgements.[5]

The differences in Pope's version measure considerable cultural change,
touching timepieces and opinions, over the intervening decades. In Suckling's milieu, as David Landes points out, "no one trust(s) his own watch"
to work; each owner willingly submits to a higher authority.[6] Pope's readers
manifest by contrast a confidence more like that which Pepys placed in his
minute watch on the walk to Greenwich, but it is now a confidence better
warranted, more generally distributed, and communalized. Other testimony confirms the impression. In 1698 the French traveler Henri Misson
depicted London as a place where timekeeping had become extraordinarily
privatized: "There are not a great many large [i.e., tower] clocks in *London*,
so that you have little Advantage by them in your Houses; but the Art [of
clockmaking] is so common here, and so much in Vogue, that almost every
Body has a Watch, and but few private Families are without a Pendulum."[7]
Like Misson's observation and John Jackson's memorandum, Pope's figure
makes clear that the minute watch, which was rare forty years before, is
now a familiar commodity widely possessed, at least within that circle to
whom Pope addresses his poem.[8] Pope further takes for granted that these

watches work well enough to approximate each other but not well enough to "go *just* alike," and that the small discrepancies have themselves become a familiar datum to his readers, who have had the experience of checking their watches against each other. The couplet conjures up a milieu in which watches shuttle easily between secret and social spaces, ticking in many pockets, emerging often for consultation and comparison—a milieu in which time, measured in minutes on private timepieces, is subject to both a general consensus (detectably inexact, but more closely and widely coordinated than fifty years ago) and a residual, insistent idiosyncrasy—a proprietary pride (*my* watch tells *the* time).

Further signs of change inhere in the way Pope redistributes Suckling's pronouns. In Suckling the watches are individualized ("his") and the judgments communalized ("our"). Pope distributes things more evenly: both watches and judgments are at once "our" property and "each his own." Yet Pope's structure finally plumps for community, not simply because of the doubled *our* but because of the figure it serves. The very act of making the metaphor increases the number of things that hold together over those that pull apart: our telling of time does "go just *alike*" our forming of judgments, even though the times and judgments are not identical. We are very like ourselves (so the involuted simile seems to say). The *Essay*'s opening gambit is to provoke consensus on the subject of divergence—to dissolve by one degree the solipsism it describes by enabling each reader to recognize (and possibly to laugh at) the solipsism itself as common ground, and to see the place of the "each" within the "our."[9]

What Pope performs as simile, historians of his period have reconstituted as argument. By his remaking of Suckling, Pope confirms Jürgen Habermas's account of the development of the public sphere, away from a realm defined by display (where monolithic authority "is shown" and duly acknowledged) and toward that conversational region where private property holders gather in order to compare their judgments, seek consensus, and sustain a sense of both their individual autonomy and their collective authority. In this world neither watches nor judgments submit to authority; collectively they constitute authority, though a vexed and complex kind. In this newer order the time of the minute watch, in both its consistency and its variance, is familiar and pervasive enough to serve as emblem for the ongoing activity of the owners: the forming of opinion.

Pope's couplet not only maps a process, it points to origins as well. In early eighteenth-century England new conceptions of community took shape at a nexus of print and place: in the periodical papers on coffee house tables. The two strongest analyses of how this happened emphasize the very activities that Pope yokes in simile: the telling of time and the forming of judgments. Benedict Anderson shows how the newspaper synchronized the community in time, while Jürgen Habermas demonstrates how the periodical essay, which was "an immediate part of coffee-house discussions and considered [itself a] literary piece," focused its readers' attention and judgment on themselves as a newly defined entity.[10] Both scholars make important and persuasive arguments; each (as is the wont in such mighty overviews) gets wrong a small but significant point. For Habermas "the moral weeklies were a key phenomenon" in the formation of the public sphere—but "weeklies" is a misnomer for papers that appeared three or six days a week (42). Habermas argues that these papers mapped a new social configuration by taking their readership as their topic: "In the *Tatler*, the *Spectator*, and the *Guardian*, the public held up a mirror to itself; it [came] to a self-understanding through entering itself into 'literature' as an object" (43). One of the key components of this mirroring involved sound as well as sight—a print simulation of speech. By various strategies the periodicals "attested to their proximity to the spoken word." The papers "were not only made the object of discussion by the public of the coffee houses but were viewed as integral parts of this discussion. . . . One and the same discussion transposed into a different medium was continued in order to reenter, via reading, the original conversational medium" (42).

For Anderson, on the other hand, the newspaper helps form the imagined community far less through its content than by its timing. "The date at the top of the newspaper" is "the single most important emblem on it," Anderson argues, because it "provides the essential connection—the steady onward clocking of homogeneous, empty time" (33). It works, that is, like the watch in Pope, but at the level of the calendar, by coordinating a daily "mass ceremony" whose "significance . . . is paradoxical. It is performed in silent privacy, in the lair of the skull. Yet each communicant is well aware that the ceremony he performs is being replicated simultaneously by thousands (or millions) of others of whose existence he is confident, yet of whose identity he has not the slightest notion. Furthermore, this ceremony is incessantly repeated at daily . . . intervals throughout the calendar. What more vivid figure for the secular, historically clocked, imagined community can be envisioned?" (35). Anderson here does justice to the timing but underestimates the complexity of the newspaper's initial context.[11] Doubtless the papers—news and essays—were often read in "silent privacy," but the evidence confirms Habermas in suggesting that their venues of absorption were not only the "lair of the skull" but also the noise, community, and conversation of coffee houses and tea tables, whose habitués read them aloud and talked them over. Anderson and Habermas agree that the papers did much to foster in their readers a sense that they were part of a community by virtue of their engagement with the printed sheet, both as its readers (according to Anderson) and as its topic (according to Habermas). The two accounts, though, evince complementary blind spots: each is most revealing where the other is least exact. Habermas ignores the true timing of the papers he discusses, while Anderson overlooks the complex traffic that they facilitated among silence, print, and speech.

By innovations on precisely those two points, the *Spectator* effected a unique intervention in the process that interests both Anderson and Habermas: the construction of identity among its readers. As Habermas suggests, the *Spectator* does mirror and define its readership by making them a constant presence in the paper, as subjects of stories, as objects of judgment, and as writers of letters that Mr. Spectator prints and answers. But in the *Spectator* the metaphor of the mirror works perhaps more literally than Habermas specifies; like actual mirrors, the paper enacts a reversal of the image it presents to those who stand before it. Mr. Spectator imagines his readers as talkative and intensely sociable. Isaac Bickerstaff, the supposed author of the *Tatler*, had done so too. As his paper's title suggests, he mirrors his readership not only by his subject matter but also by his persona; he is gregarious like them, cast in their image. Mr. Spectator, by contrast, depicts himself, in the first number and in the 554 to follow, as different from his audience in one central respect. He is preternaturally private, a "Silent Man" who has never "spoken above three sentences" in his whole life, and who has chosen now to write instead.[12] The paper's first readers understood themselves (within the fiction) to be receiving through print a daily, current report from an intensely private consciousness. The rhetorical strategy produces in effect a new hybrid of genres. The *Spectator* read like an essay, came out like a daily newspaper, and looked like one too in its typeface and general design.[13] From the vantage, though, of its first readers and of its putative author, its most surprising innovations—its timing and persona— gave it the salient features of a diary, but of a diary turned inside out: the work not of a public or social figure composing a more secret version of the self in a single, sequestered manuscript, but of a wholly secretive sensibility imparting itself in print, to be read by a wide and varied public in the diurnal rhythm, and at the running moment, of its making.

Nothing like this had been attempted before and nothing before had succeeded like this. The evidence suggests that the *Spectator* matched or outdid all contemporary papers, news or literary, in sheer number of copies sold.[14] The importance of the paper's timing to its initial success is difficult to recover, in part because the *Spectator*'s very popularity put it through quick and abiding transformations. Before the end of its two-year run its publishers began reissuing the papers in indexed volumes, and the consequent emphasis on topicality over temporality has affected the reading of them ever since. Two years after the paper's final number, the merchant Joseph Collet could suggest that his daughter read the essays as a combination of wisdom and conduct literature by selecting those on the right subjects: "I enjoyn you to study the Spectators, especially those which relate to Religion and Domestick Life. Next to the Bible you cannot read any writings so much to your purpose. . . ."[15] Twentieth-century readings tend to follow Collet's counsel in form if not in spirit. The *Spectator* is most often read and taught, whether in anthologies or in the definitive edition, by topical clusters—on wit, Milton, social mores, Sir Roger, imagination. The paper's timing, which most "Surpriz'd" its first readers, is the feature least conspicuous to later ones. Yet Addison and Steele were doing something emphatically new with diurnal publication. Mr. Spectator is the first figure, real or feigned, to appear in print day by day, and is also the first print *eidolon* to define his whole character in terms of an obsessively cultivated privacy about his own experience.

What follows is an inquiry into the force of this fiction: how this figure, produced with this timing, achieved this preeminence. The oddity of Mr. Spectator's self-containment was of course a joke, but it was a joke that lasted and thrived over the longest series of papers that any non-news periodical had yet produced. Plainly, in yoking a practice of daily writing with the embodiment of a profoundly secretive self, and in making these the constant components of the paper (whatever topic it happened to be taking up on any particular day), Addison and Steele had hit upon a combination and configuration that many readers wished to buy into. I argue that the combination made possible a transaction between paper and audience which incorporated both the Habermasian imaging and the Andersonian "clocking" of the readership, but with unprecedented rhetorical intricacy and appeal. The paper cultivated a new correspondence with its readers, as both a communication (corresponding *with* them) and a mirroring (corresponding *to* them).

The *Spectator* mapped the grounds of this correspondence differently from any predecessor. It offers to mirror its readers not in their social mode, as they move through that "Talking World" where, Bickerstaff once estimated, they spend "one third Part of the Day" (*S* 264, 3.337), but in their private mode, at the level of consciousness that continues through each waking day whether they are engaged in talk or not. Mr. Spectator posits his self-containment as a heightened reflection of a universal condition—a condition founded in the way the mind functions over time. His paper enacts both continuity and containment by its own exacting calendar: it too operates every day, as no "reflective" paper had before, and (again like no predecessor) presents itself from the start more as monad than miscellany.

By its fusion of silence with diurnal form, the *Spectator* fosters a fiction of reciprocity between itself and its readers, in which each party not only mirrors the other but appears to occupy the other's place in space and over time. Readers occupy Mr. Spectator both as objects of his attention and as presences in his paper. He occupies them—or rather "informs" them—as the figure of that silent part of themselves which they, as gregarious social beings, least recognize. In a reckoning to which the paper repeatedly returns, he fills their space, time, and mind at every stratum from the secret to the social (he fills the "lairs of their skulls," the talk in their gathering places, the succession of their days) and they fill his (his essays, his thoughts, his days). The daily paper becomes not merely the medium for this reciprocal filling, but also a running argument in favor of a diurnal paradigm for achieving, recognizing, and inhabiting the fullness of time.

Since self-containment is an intrinsic condition of the mind in time, time becomes the means of management. By precept and example, the *Spectator* advocates a reckoning by days. The calibrations of the calendar are both narrow and contiguous enough to constitute ready-made containers, easily filled; the paper argues that to fill them in succession, from the resources of a contained and continuous consciousness, is to possess a life in full. By its fiction of reciprocity, the paper undertakes to induct its readers in this process. To read Mr. Spectator's daily self-rendering will be in some sense to compose it, to inhabit it, and even to recognize and accept his public prose as a comprehensive account of oneself; Mr. Spectator's public journal becomes a version of, or surrogate for, the reader's private diary. Absorbing the journal and absorbed in it, readers become diurnalists too.

The *Spectator*, then, bears the same relationship to the minute watch in its culture that Pepys's diary bears to the much rarer private timepieces in his.

In a world where minute watches are rarities, Pepys performs in secret manuscript a newly serial, precise, and private rendition of the self in time. In a culture where the possession of a private timepiece has become an increasingly widespread social practice, particularly among the *Spectator*'s literate and prosperous audience, the paper performs in print a subjectivity that is recognizably akin to Pepys's in its secrecy and its sense of time. With the *Spectator*'s success, the discourses of time and self that Pepys reads on new clocks and writes in his private book go influentially, abidingly public.

PREDECESSORS

The *Spectator* pursues unity with its reader by means of an unprecedented cluster of unities in its design: one voice delivering one discourse, usually on one topic, on one folio half-sheet appearing once each day (Sundays excepted). In the *Spectator*'s tenth number Addison surveys the first successes of this scheme, and touches for the first time on an argument to which he will often return. "I shall not be so vain as to think, that where the Spectator appears, the other publick Prints will vanish; but shall leave it to my Readers Consideration, whether, Is it not much better to be let into the Knowledge of ones-self, than to hear what passes in *Muscovy* or *Poland . . .*?" (*S* 10; 1.45). Here is Habermas's periodical mirror privatized, a promised image not only of the outward community ("my Readers") but of the inner psyche of each member. "Publick Prints" deal in events remote, dispersed, and various; they are plural in number and nature. The singular *Spectator* works on a matter more unified, and so close at hand as to be contained within: self-knowledge, to be effected by a one to one correspondence (figured as both exchange and match) between Mr. Spectator and "ones-self." The oddity and impact of the new paper may perhaps best be understood in the ways that it set itself up against and within the periodical traditions of the public prints that had preceded it. By the time the *Spectator* appeared, almost a century of news-books and newspapers, news letters and literary periodicals, had produced various formats for representing heterogeneous material within the unity of the printed product, and for constructing correspondences with both its contributors and its readers. In the makeup of the *Spectator*, a much more recent tradition proved equally important: Steele and Addison's *Tatler* had gradually developed away from heterogeneity towards the figures of unity and containment that the *Spectator* would in turn intensify.

The date on the top of the newspaper, which is for Anderson an emblem of the nation, was at its first appearance in the early seventeenth century a signifier of something else: the new prevalence of measure over occasion as a paradigm for the production and distribution of news. Occasional news texts—broadsides and pamphlets prompted by specific events—had existed long before and would persist for another century and more. On 23 May 1622 there appeared a quarto pamphlet displaying signs of a new scheme on its title page. It was called *The Weekly Newes* and the specific month and date of issue appeared below the name. The promise of periodicity had come to English print. In the months that followed, the promise was equivocally fulfilled, with the pamphlets published irregularly, usually twice a week. In mid-October, though, the news-books began to be numbered consecutively and to be issued at approximately weekly intervals.[16] The *Newes*'s identity resided almost exclusively in the regular sequence of its dates and serial numbers, rather than in its title, which its publishers chose to alter often as a sales strategy. Apart from their numbering, these news-books were designed and sold as ordinary books, and in the paradigm of that practice new titles sold faster than old.

Among the favorite alternative rubrics in this early period were "coranto" (i.e., a "running" account) and "The Continuation of our weekly Newes." The wording makes clear that the new periodicity developed out of a desire, on the part of both makers and readers, for a sense of narrative continuity. Still, the continuity (such as it was) came in clumps. *A Perfect Diurnall of the Passages in Parliament* (1643–9) was the first of many mid-century papers to feature "Diurnall" in its title, but it appeared, like most of its contemporaries, at intervals of a week.[17] It narrated parliamentary proceedings day by dated day, but its readers took in that information at a rate seven times slower than that at which it had been gathered. The *Diurnall*, like most news-books, bore *two* dates in its heading, to denote the time span covered: "From the 16. of Ianuary to the 23. of Ianuary."

With an increase in the number of news-books, the pace of reader intake quickened. The Civil Wars gave rise to so many new weeklies that in 1644 it was briefly possible for an avid (and nonpartisan) London news reader to simulate "diurnality" by reading a different paper (or even several) every day of the week save Sunday.[18] During the Commonwealth, Protectorate, and Restoration, government suppression drastically reduced the number of licensed print venues until, beginning in 1665, there was only one, with a new format and frequency. *The London Gazette* was, as Sutherland remarks, "a complete innovation" (11). Unlike the earlier periodicals it was a folio half-sheet rather than a book, and it appeared twice a week (on Mondays and Thursdays). In 1679 the lapse of the licensing act coupled with the news cornucopia in the wake of the Popish Plot supplied the *Gazette* with sudden and plentiful competition, but for the rest of the century all newspapers imitated the *Gazette*'s format and most copied its timing, until in 1695 three new papers increased their output to three sheets a week (Tuesdays, Thursdays, Saturdays). When in 1702 Buckley achieved real diurnality with *The Daily Courant*, he duplicated the *Gazette*'s format even more closely than most, with one pointed substitution. The *Gazette*'s design was calculated to display the crucial words "Published by Authority" as prominently as possible in every number. The phrase appeared in authoritative black-letter font just below the title, framed above and below by emphatic horizontal lines; beneath this the paper's span dates ("From Monday February 22. to Thursday February 25.") appeared in smaller typeface. In the line-framed space that the *Gazette* gave over to "Authority," Buckley simply placed his *Daily*'s single date, as if to say that that alone was authority enough—an impression that the paper's serial numbers, situated (like the *Gazette*'s) in the upper right-hand corner but ascending day by day at twice the speed of any rival news-sheet, might be expected to confirm.

In Buckley's paper, the temporal unity represented by the date at the top presided over considerable geographic heterogeneity, with many short reports datelined to many points in Europe and beyond. Like the corantos of a century before, the *Courant* depended heavily on published news shipped from the continent; unlike any journalist before him, Buckley acknowledged his indebtedness by heading each cluster of reports with the name of the European paper from which he had translated it. The visual effect was to bring together a multitude of authorial sources under the *Courant*'s single rubric. Throughout the seventeenth century, the proportions of foreign and domestic intelligence in newsbooks and papers had varied wildly, but by Buckley's time the sequence of such reports had been widely established. Foreign news came first, domestic news second (usually on the verso of the news-sheet and often in the last column). The arrangement was expedient for the compositor, who could not conveniently insert late-received news anywhere but at the paper's end. Since the freshest news was likely to be local, it made sense for the compositor to save the London news for last, where accumulation would not disrupt coherence. To read from start to finish a paper so laid out was to begin with events comparatively long ago and far away (at Paris or Prague, or in countries even more remote) and to approach ever closer to one's own situation in time and space. The date at the top of the morning's paper, then as now, acted as asymptote, approached but rarely broached by the events reported; the imprint at the bottom of the verso offered a corresponding anchor in space: the bookseller's address would be, for many (perhaps most) of the paper's readers, very familiar and very near. This spatialized self-definition had, for English readers, a temporal correlative that the *Courant* frequently signaled. Since all its continental source papers were datelined in the New Style calendar, eleven days later than in England's Old Style, many of the dates that headed reports from Europe were subsequent to that on the top of the paper. With every such discrepancy the English reader would be reminded (however subliminally) of the nation's calendrical insularity and idiosyncrasy. Addison and Steele, in *Tatlers* and *Spectators* that resembled Buckley's paper and proceeded from the same press, would make much of both this spatialized focus and this perceived insularity.

From the beginning, the ways that journalism moved through space and time, and the ways it represented them, were deeply influenced by the kinds of delivery services, incoming and outgoing, available to the paper's makers. In the early coranto and many of its successors, the shipping news was not only a staple source of copy but also a brief genealogy: the boats whose arrival the paper announced to its mercantile readers had also supplied the information, by way of foreign prints and sailors' talk, that brought this number into being (Sutherland 123–31). Within England, postal arrangements did much to structure the timing involved with both getting news and spreading it. Until 1680, London had no internal system of delivery other than the "occasional": porters for hire carried what needed carrying. The sudden advent of the penny post, a system of hourly delivery, greatly increased the speed and efficiency with which the papers could gather news, while the countrywide postal schedule determined the rate at which they could put it out.

The appearance in 1695 of three papers with the same new word in their title—*The Post-Boy, The Flying Post,* and *The Post Man*—established a new kind of synchrony between print and delivery, and with it a new frequency of output. The papers "were published on Tuesday, Thursday and Saturday, the three days on which the mails left London in the late evening for all parts of the country" (Sutherland 26). The thrice-weekly pattern remained in

place for most newspapers for over twenty-five years. Competition produced two other *Posts*—the *London* and the *English*—with the same frequency on the alternate timetable: Mondays, Wednesdays, and Fridays. Perhaps because they appeared on the three non-post days of the week (their
imitative names were misnomers), they did not do as well or last as long.
But they did make it possible, for the first time since mid-century, to read a
different newspaper every day. When the *Courant* appeared during their run,
its novelty and its greater success consisted in its unification of disparate time
and print elements already in play. Readers could now take in the same paper
every day.

The post assured the papers a means of delivery, the papers guaranteed
the post a steady source of income (then as now there were special newspaper rates), and the symbiosis between the two affected not only the papers'
timing but also their form and meaning. A widespread perception developed, which Steele and Addison would soon exploit in new ways, of the
periodical as a site for correspondence between writers and readers—for an
exchange more fluid and reciprocal than that figured by the "letters" department in modern magazines. The phenomenon began in necessity. The
early domestic papers (those that promised "News both from City and
Country") depended in part on their readers to supply the news and rewarded them with free copies of the paper. For London news the correspondence might be conversational, and the item prefaced "We hear . . ."; country news came in by post, and might be datelined thus: "Essex, By Letters
from a place called Much Waltham in this County, we have this strange but
true Relation . . ." (Sutherland, 102–3). Non-news periodicals made letters from readers an even more conspicuous component of their form.
The Royal Society's monthly *Philosophical Transactions* gave over considerable
space to direct transcriptions of their correspondence, and Dunton's *Athenian
Mercury*, like its modern descendants the advice and information columns
(e.g., Ann Landers or "The Straight Dope"), treated questions sent in by its
readers as its necessary point of departure, its *raison d'être*. These might be
brief queries, but as the paper prospered they sometimes ran longer, into a
kind of casuistry: substantial autobiographies leading up to a moral quandary.
The format made Habermasian mirroring particularly explicit. The paper's
readers saw themselves made over as potential writers, and saw the "Athe-
nians" (the putative committee of teachers and counselors who answered
the queries) refigured as attentive and responsive (though still authoritative)
readers.[19]

In the newspapers, the phenomenon of mixed authorship became manifest in a visual correlative: by the time the papers arrived in the hands of their intended readers, they often bore a combination of print and script. The practice began as an attempt to make the news as current as possible. "The term 'Postscript,'" writes Morison, "dates from the later seventeenth century. . . . [It] was applied to written additions of late news inserted in the margins of printed papers by the clerks of the booksellers through whom the subscribers received their copies" (63). Some papers left space blank in anticipation of this later filling. Even after the "Postscript" became formalized as a printed addendum on a separate sheet (sold either separately or enfolded in the parent paper), the blank space remained in place. It had turned out to be a strong selling point. Londoners could buy and read the paper, fill the blank space with news (personal or otherwise) that they wished to convey, and dispatch it to friends in the country at the newspaper rate, which was cheaper than the regular post. The recipient took in a paper in which the offices of writer and of reader visibly converged.

For many, the presence of script on the printed news-sheet must have seemed the residuum of an older, still flourishing news medium created exclusively by scribal hands and pens. The news letter was produced in scriptoria that might contain as many as fifty clerks writing out copies simultaneously. It looked like a letter and moved like one. It arrived by post, handwritten and headed with a date and a formal, elaborately calligraphic greeting "Sir," "Madam," "My Lord." Its readers thus saw themselves made present in the letter from its outset. They paid well for this privilege, and for the larger one that manuscript made possible: letters could legally convey information that the government did not allow to appear in print. Newsletters had existed in England since the 1630s (Sutherland 6), but perhaps the output of the formidable journalist Henry Muddiman best exemplifies their place and process. In late 1659 Muddiman was designated by General George Monck as a kind of press agent for the incipient Restoration. He was soon made assistant to the new secretary of state Sir Edward Nicholas, and given control of all news media, both print and script.

The former office sustained the latter. In the Secretary's service, Muddiman had access to all domestic correspondence and much foreign information supplied by the Secretary's vast intelligence network; he also received "free postage not only for his own letters and news-letters, but for those letters . . . addressed to him." From the information he gathered by these means, he printed two weekly news-books (one on Mondays, one on

Thursdays) of government-sanctioned reports, as well as a newsletter (once, twice, or thrice weekly, depending on the subscriber) that revealed much more about parliamentary proceedings and other matters to a wide variety of subscribers paying £5 apiece: "peers and members of parliament, post-masters and country booksellers, clergymen and doctors, army officers, merchants, innkeepers and others" (Sutherland 7). With some of them, the correspondence was genuinely reciprocal: Muddiman asked for news and subscribers supplied it. The peculiar appeal of the newsletter, and the appe-tite for the kind of news that only it could supply, buttressed it for several decades against increasing competition from print. Although some newslet-ters succumbed to the pressure, many continued to thrive into the second decade of the eighteenth century, well past the introduction of the thrice-weekly papers and the *Daily Courant*.[20] The newsletters by now ordered their topics as did the newspapers: foreign news first, London last—with late-breaking stories often inscribed vertically down the margins. Impossible in print, this epistolary effect, like the vocative address and the idiosyncratic handwriting, confirmed in the reader a sense of receiving privileged infor-mation privately dispatched—of participating in a personal conversation on matters of moment.

That more people wanted this experience than could afford it is indicated by the long-running success of a paper that contrived to fulfill the desire by simulacrum. *Dawks's News-Letter* (1695–1716) was an extraordinary hy-brid of many of the elements that the century's journalism had put into play: novel timing and salable spacing; print and script; privacy and publication. The first evening newspaper, it looked like an elegantly handwritten letter but was made entirely by the press. Ichabod Dawks had devised a typeface that mimicked manuscript.[21] As a piece of print, his paper could not deal in forbidden news, but it offered (with the reader's mild connivance) most of the newsletter's other gratifications. *Dawks's* prefatory "Sir," printed in cal-ligraphy as elaborate as that in the newsletters, was now impressed by type-block and addressed to no one in particular, but any male who bought the paper might choose to recognize himself in the vocative. He might also, in keeping with the year-old practice of the written postscript, extend the *News-Letter* by one link into a chain letter of his own: "This letter will be done upon good writing paper," Dawks promised in an early number, "and blank space left that any gentleman may write his own private business."[22]

The paper's innovative timing abetted this purpose. It appeared between four and five on Tuesdays, Thursdays, and Saturdays, and in its ample blank

space London buyers could inscribe their very latest "private business" before dispatching the paper to the country by the post that night; sometimes
too booksellers would add written postscripts of their own. The recipient
would hold a paper that displayed two manuscript styles, one of machine-
made uniformity, with "a very settled appearance, as settled and as formal
as an Indenture"; the other more erratic and (in most cases) personally familiar. Dawks, though, infused familiarity into his copy, as did the newsletters he imitated. His odd enterprise thrived, Morison argues, because Dawks
understood what some of his competitors in both manuscript and print did
not: "that in this time of transition there was not one public but two publics,
corresponding to two habits of reading. The cheapness and dispatch of the
printer had brought into existence a fresh market for news, but there remained numbers of older readers who were used to the more personal tone
of the written newsletters and they preferred them if they could get them at
the cost and with the speed of the newspapers. Thus with these two traditions, there were two styles of news-writing."[23] Dawks wrote the old style
in a newly invented typeface that simulated old script, and by that stratagem
appealed to several audiences: London as well as country, street buyers as
well as subscribers, young as well as old.

The paper ran twenty years, long enough to be laughed at in mid-career
by Richard Steele in a still newer kind of paper, the *Tatler*. Isaac Bickerstaff
reports on a day spent in the coffeehouse among news readers. He mocks
the inaccuracy of *Dawks's* foreign news; in this regard it resembles all the
other papers. In other ways it differs: "But Mr. *Dawks* concluded his Paper
with a courteous Sentence, which was very well taken and applauded by the
whole Company. *We wish*, says he, *all our Customers a merry* Whitsuntide, *and
many of them*. Honest *Icabod* is as extraordinary a Man as any of our Fraternity
[i.e., newsmongers], and as particular. His Style is a Dialect between the
Familiarity of Talking and Writing, and his Letter such as you cannot distinguish whether Print or Manuscript, which gives us a Refreshment of the Idea
from what has been told us from the Press by others. This wishing a good
Tide had its Effect upon us, and he was commended for his Salutation, as
showing as well the Capacity of a Bell-man as an Historian."[24] Steele's last
comparison may possess a particular resonance. In the years since the bellman passed Pepys's window only to be apprehended in secret script, the
profession had added to its tasks of night-watching, well-wishing, time-
telling, and information-giving a new enterprise: letter-gathering. From the
beginning of the seventeenth century, the bell's sound makes its way from

the street into letters as it did into Pepys's diary, but now as an enforcer of conclusion, rather than a figure of middleness. "The bell rings for my letter," writes Mary Coke to her husband Thomas in 1701, "and makes me lose the happiness of fancying I am talking with my dear," because she must now hurry to get the missive into the hands of the passing bellman, who will bear it either to a nearby receiving house or directly to the recipient.[25] "The post-bell rings," wrote Mary Wortley Montagu in 1712, bringing her letter to a sudden close, "my next shall be longer. . . ."[26] At the time of *Tatler* 178, the bellman's activities as postman had just changed from ad hoc arrangement to an elaborately articulated new institution, Charles Povey's half-penny post. Steele compares Dawks to a bellman at just the moment when the bellman had become an instrument—and hence a figure—of that epistolary community of correspondents into which *Dawks's News-Letter* has for ten years made a curious intervention.

Perhaps it is because he fosters community that Dawks here subtly alters Steele's tone. Bickerstaff has mocked pretty severely the contentiousness and gullibility of the coffeehouse news readers. Here, though, a tincture of kinship tempers the amusement. "This wishing . . . had its Effect upon *us*," he writes; the pronoun joins Bickerstaff with the objects of his recent derision, as "*our* Fraternity" joins him with "Honest *Icabod*" in the brotherhood of newsbearers. One hundred seventy-eight numbers in, the *Tatler* has made the grounds of such a kinship fairly clear. Bickerstaff too has pursued some of the same ends that he attributes to Ichabod here: the fostering of "Familiarity" in print, a sense of "Talking and Writing" mixed (or, as Mary Coke puts it, a "fancy" that writing *is* "talking"), a community fused by correspondence. Like *Dawks*, the *Tatler* makes ingenious use and combination of the expectations and desires its readers bring to reading. But Steele and Addison have devised means more intricate, in their rhetoric and print format, than script-like font and hearty tone.

When Steele started the *Tatler*, on 12 March 1709, he had been editing the *London Gazette* for two years, and would continue to do so for most of the new paper's run. The *Tatler* fell heir to two concurrent periodical traditions that were sometimes intertwined: that of the printed news-sheet, of which the *Gazette* was the oldest and in many ways the stodgiest surviving specimen, and that of the periodical literary miscellany, of which the *Tatler* immediately established itself as the most successful enterprise yet launched.[27] Both traditions supplied the *Tatler* with strategies of containment and correspondence: ways of arranging mixed materials on the page and construing them as a unity; ways of simultaneously addressing and mirroring the readership. The *Tatler* slightly altered every familiar strategy it took up. The early numbers make clear how carefully (and accurately) Steele had worked out a set of variants on tradition that would heighten the paper's appeal by sharpening its definitions of itself, its apparent author, and its audience. Yet these definitions changed substantially during the paper's twenty-two-month run, especially as Addison began to participate actively in the paper's making. He and Steele now took the paper's own initial tradition and developed it in directions that would ultimately make their shift from the *Tatler* to the *Spectator* less a contradiction than a continuation. The *Tatler*, that is, gradually initiates constructions that the *Spectator* would take up—constructions of time and audience, talk and print, silence and self-possession.

The vast majority of readers who picked up the *Tatler's* free first number would not have known that its maker was also the Gazetteer. Nonetheless, they might have detected at a glance the free sheet's print genealogy, its formal kinship with newspapers and literary periodicals. Like the *Gazette*, the *Courant*, and the thrice-weekly *Posts*, the *Tatler* divided its copy into sections, with headings that specified the place and date of the report (the first dateline, for example, read "*White's Chocolate-house, April 7*"). In the paper's preamble, Bickerstaff laid out the *Tatler's* particular geography, its spatial scheme for putting the world into print. Before "I had resolv'd upon" this work, Bickerstaff writes,

> *I had settled a Correspondence in all Parts of the Known and Knowing World. . . .*
> [I] *shall divide* [my] *Relations of the Passages which occur in Action or Discourse throughout this Town, as well as elsewhere, under such Dates of Places as may prepare you for the Matter you are to expect, in the following Manner.*
>
> *All Accounts of* Gallantry, Pleasure, *and* Entertainment, *shall be under the Article of* White's Chocolate-house; Poetry, *under that of* Will's Coffee-house; Learning, *under the Title of* Graecian; Foreign and Domestick News, *you will have from* St. James's Coffee-house; *and what else I have to offer on any other Subject, shall be dated from my own* Apartment. (*T* 1; 1.16)

Miscellanies like the *Gentleman's Journal* had dealt in "Matter" just as variegated, though more diffusely. Comic periodicals like the *English Lucian* (1698) had mildly mocked the newspapers by dating preposterous reports from familiar local neighborhoods rather than exotic distant cities; others, like Ned Ward's *Weekly Comedy* (1699) and *Humours of a Coffee-House* (1707) had made a fictional coffeehouse the setting for extravagant serial narratives. What is new with Steele is his specificity, and the uses to which he puts it. By datelining from actual coffeehouses long associated with particular activities, Steele manages not only to categorize and hence contain his subjects more precisely than had the earlier miscellanies, but also to set up his paper from the start as a particularly polished, comprehensive, and multifaceted social mirror. He claims, that is, that the categories of person and experience in which he will deal originate not with him but with his readers, who already occupy them as actual, physical spaces—local habitations with well-known names. The mirroring, he implies here, is about to become animated into a more kinetic two-way traffic. About four-fifths of every *Tatler* will originate at the very coffeehouse tables where the paper will be read a day or two later.

Such reciprocity refigures too the city in which the coffeehouses are located. As government Gazetteer Steele dealt almost exclusively in foreign rather than domestic news. The *Tatler*'s datelines, so like the newspaper's in form and so different in content, enable him to present London—and by extension, Britain—as a world unto itself, "Known and Knowing," a container in which a continuous exchange of "Action" and "Discourse" is about to commence. Even the news of the larger world becomes a particular London property. "You will have" news, Bickerstaff promises, not from foreign ports (as in the *Gazette* or *Courant*) but from St. James's, the Whig coffeehouse near Whitehall and Parliament, where the business of knowing the world, transacted through reading and conversation, shapes what is known about it. From the construction of London as a sealed container, two corollaries develop, one of time and one of space. First, the paper's datelines will deal exclusively in the local time of the world it addresses. Even in the reports of foreign news, narratives of New Style events on the continent will appear under Old Style headings, whose dates (unlike those in the *Courant*) will always make sense within the calendrical timing that Britain now uniquely inhabits. These are the dates of this place alone. Second, Bickerstaff lays out a sequence of datelines that recapitulates the ordinary newspaper's familiar motion even as it miniaturizes its scope: the *Tatler* will enact over the course of its columns a sequential closing in from the larger world to the local—from the continent to London in the newspapers, from the sociability of the coffeehouses to the privacy of "My Own Apartment."

Isaac Bickerstaff, who occupies the apartment and authors the paper, had in fact made his name as a figure for self-containment of another order. Swift had invented him a year earlier in order to mock the pretense of the astrological almanacs in general, and of the popular astrologer John Partridge in particular, to push past the ordinary limits of human time and write the future. "Isaac Bickerstaff, Esq." had first appeared as a rival astrologer who, in an almanac-pamphlet of his own, foretold the death of Partridge on 29 March 1708, and who in subsequent publications affirmed repeatedly and hilariously, over the vociferous objections of the real Partridge, that his prediction had come exactly true. He had, in effect, put Partridge in his proper temporal place, insisting on time limits where Partridge acknowledged none. In the *Tatler* Bickerstaff refers occasionally to his astrological prowess, but rarely exercises it. Mostly, he reaffirms the death of Partridge (as at the end of *Tatler* 1, in the first dispatch from his apartment). His method has become local and empirical rather than prophetic. As Swift's anti-astrologer, he has found more suitable employment outside the world of the annual almanac in the rhythm of a periodical that deals exclusively with the present and is timed to travel with the post.

Steele marked the change from Swift's initial conception another way as well.[28] Bickerstaff's new title, *The Tatler*, appeared above his name on the masthead, and from the first Steele used it to signal a new mode of correspondence with his readers, a way of making them present in the paper. Earlier personal titles (the tradition was a long one) denoted solo acts that the papers performed for their readers: the *Spy* spied, Mr. *Review* reviewed. "Tattling," by contrast, necessitates community; it requires both listeners and speakers, often in alternating roles. Steele's title implies that the paper's "Action and Discourse" will be addressed *to* its readers, and more important, undertaken *with* them. As Bickerstaff claims in the preamble, the title is also calculated to widen the circle of participants until it encompasses "all Persons, without Distinction"—particularly of gender. "I resolve also to have something which may be of Entertainment to the Fair Sex, in Honour of whom I have invented the Title of this Paper" (*T* 1; 1.15). This is the first of many moves that the *Tatler* and the *Spectator* will make to invite women readers to see themselves mirrored in the paper's masthead, substance, and method. The strategies are complicated (and, from a present viewpoint, compromised); but they hinge on a suggestion of androgyny in the authorial *eidolon*, here represented by the conjunction at the top of the paper of Bickerstaff's masculine name and feminized title.[29] He does not merely write a *Tatler*, he *is* one—loquacious, gregarious, "the greatest wit in his club"—

as readers soon recognized and long remembered: Bickerstaff "understood himself very well," wrote one reader to Steele five years later, "when he called himself *Tatler*." [30] The paper's success (and the correspondent's nostalgia) suggests that Bickerstaff understood his audience as well. By many strategies in the early *Tatlers* Steele establishes a passion for talk as the common ground on which his audience, male and female, can unite: here the distinctions between the gendered modes of talk (feminized "tattle" and masculinized "wit") dissolve sufficiently so that a self-proclaimed *Tatler* will be applauded (as Gay and countless others applauded Bickerstaff) for a wit. In its initial conception and opening numbers, the *Tatler* takes farther than any predecessor the strategy of "attest[ing its] proximity to the spoken word," which Habermas calls crucial in the formation of the public sphere (Habermas 42). By its title and its coffeehouse dateline, it constructs a correspondence between author and readers based on talk: talk transpiring in houses, public and domestic, on the street, and in corresponding spaces on the page; talk contained but unconstrained.

With Addison's increasing collaboration, Steele began to experiment with the paper's prose containers, to re-evaluate the sources by which they were to be filled, and to alter the model of correspondence that the paper set forth. The first changes involved the relations between Bickerstaff's most remote news, channeled through "St. James's," and its most local, "From my own Apartment." When Steele started the *Tatler*, he had plainly counted on occupying many inches of its columns with foreign intelligence gathered from his sources at the *Gazette*.[31] Addison, though, in his debut as Isaac Bickerstaff in *Tatler* 18, abjured this dependency on distant events. The news writers, Bickerstaff notes, are frantic at the prospect of a peace with France; with no more wars to misrepresent they will lose their livelihood. At paper's end, he excepts himself: "I cannot be thought to speak this out of an Eye to any private Interest; for, as my chief Scenes of Action are Coffee-houses, Play-houses, and my own Apartment, I am in no Need of Camps, Fortifications, and Fields of Battle, to support me. . . . I shall still be safe as long as there are Men or Women, or Politicians, or Lovers, or Poets, or Nymphs, or Swains, or Cits, or Courtiers, in Being" (*T* 18; 1.151). The passage restates the contract of correspondence laid out in the first number, whereby Bickerstaff will draw his matter from places and persons close by (and redistribute it accordingly), but it also reaffirms a desire Steele had expressed three weeks earlier for an even greater self-sufficiency. "[W]hen we have nothing to say to you from Courts and Camps," Bickerstaff had written in

number 11, "we hope still to give you somewhat new and curious from our
selves" (*T* 1.102). Because the "we" here is clearly editorial, the phrase
"from our selves" points to a source more solitary than "Lovers," "Poets,"
or "Cits." It echoes the dateline Bickerstaff originally listed last—"From
my own Apartment"—at a point when he has started to give that heading
new priority. In the *Tatler* just preceding (no. 10), this dateline had appeared
at the start of the paper for the first time, as it would often in the months to
follow, sometimes extending its dominion to include topics that Steele had
originally assigned to other departments. In *Tatler* 64 (5 September) Steele
datelined one of the year's biggest stories, Marlborough's victory at Mal-
plaquet, from Bickerstaff's residence. On this occasion even news "from
Courts and Camps" reaches the *Tatler*'s reader directly "from our selves,"
not from St. James's.[32]

When Addison returned from Ireland (whence, as secretary of state, he
had sent in his first contributions to the *Tatler*), he and Steele developed
Bickerstaff's journalistic self-sufficiency further through a shift in form. Their
first collaborative *Tatler*, no. 75, set a precedent that most subsequent
numbers would follow: the coffeehouse datelines disappeared, and the dispatch from Bickerstaff's apartment occupied the entire paper. The *Tatler*,
within six months of its debut, had changed its structure. In its early numbers, it had taken as its motto a line from Juvenal, *"Quicquid agunt Homines
nostri Farrago Libelli"* [Whate'er men do, or say, or think, or dream, / Our
motley paper seizes for its theme].[33] Steele had at first planned to embody
the farrago of topics by a multiplicity of venues and headings. Such subdivisions now gave way to a unity differently shaped: the paper presented, more
often than not, a single essay on a single topic. The new form refigured the
correspondence between the paper and its readers. *Homines*—"Lovers,"
"Poets," "Cits"—would still read representations of their doings in the
Tatler's pages, but all shunted through a single switching house: Bickerstaff's
"Apartment," which is to say his experience, his judgment, his mind. Addison and Steele had in effect exchanged their motto from Juvenal for its
ancestor in Terence: "Nothing human is alien to *me*." In *Tatler* 1, for example, readers had received an account of a theatrical benefit for Thomas
Betterton under the literary dateline of Will's coffeehouse. A year later they
could read of Betterton's death and funeral in a dispatch Bickerstaff wrote
from his own apartment, a narrative whose form insisted on the priority of
the perceiver as determinant of the thing perceived. Bickerstaff reported not
so much the public mourning as the private thoughts and memories of the

actor that preoccupied him on his walk to the burial in Westminster (*T* 167; 2.422 – 26). Addison in his first contribution had listed "the Coffee-Houses, Play-houses, and my own Apartment" as the *Tatler's* three chief "Scenes of Action." Now he and Steele had subsumed the first two under the third, where one mode of "Action" performed by one actor mediated all others: "The Lucubrations of Isaac Bickerstaff."

That phrase soon became an alternate title for the *Tatler*, whose new structure and terminology highlighted, in contrast with the original format, the solitude of the *eidolon* rather than his gregariousness. The now-dominant dateline places him "Apart" from the world he writes about; "Lucubration" (which Samuel Johnson would later define as "anything composed by candle-light") encloses him even more tightly, in the illuminated circle in which he works. This is a space not for talk, but for inscription. By displacing the coffeehouse datelines, the *Tatler* now represented its correspondence with its readers less as conversation than as written exchange. The timing of the writing had shifted contours, too. Where the multiple datelines bore mul-tiple dates, the unified essays bear only one, and often offer an extended, diary-like account of what Bickerstaff calls (in the first *Tatler* headed wholly from his apartment) "the History of the Day."

The *Tatler* had now introduced a discernible dissonance between its title and its form, between idle and variegated chat and unified essay, but this seems to have played as yet another of those doublings that had been selling points from the start. If Bickerstaff could "correspond to" women as well as men, could parade as both wit and tattler, then his mock-solemn night-written lucubrations might, in their affability, be taken as just one step re-moved from talk. Addison and Steele had mastered a dialect more subtle than Dawks's (and this is part of Steele's condescension to his periodical sibling), able to move more smoothly along the spectrum "between the Familiarity of Speech and Writing," and the paper's popularity, which was immense from the start, continued to increase. Steele's motives in ending the *Tatler* rather abruptly on 2 January 1711, after a twenty-month run, seem to have had little to do with commerce, and much more to do with politics. The election of October 1710 had put the Whigs out of power. Steele had given up control of the *Gazette* to the Tories, and may have agreed to end the *Tatler* too (which had satirized Harley over the summer) in ex-change for retaining his office as commissioner of stamps. He and Addison may also have already conceived the new undertaking of the *Spectator*.

That possibility gets support from what appears to be the *Tatler's* implicit dramatization, in its closing numbers, of its reasons for coming to an end. Steele stages, in Bickerstaff's voice, a critique of talk in the culture which leads up to an abandonment, in his own voice in the final number, of Bickerstaffian talk altogether. Political overtones are audible: a certain kind of satiric tattling had gotten Steele into trouble and now he terminates its medium. He develops the motifs of talk versus silence, copious chat versus self-containment, in ways that suggest that political pressures may have converged with a self-reckoning on the part of the authors. First, he and Addison may have become dissatisfied with "tattling" as a model for the form of correspondence and communion between author and reader that they had developed, and second, they may have had the silent Mr. Spectator and his daily schedule already in view. Bickerstaff undertakes to cure his readers of loquacity. He deems it a problem in terms that call his whole successful project into question. He prescribes for the loquacious a method of self-containment that relies on a form of time-reckoning that has not mattered much in the *Tatler* but that the *Spectator* will make central to its composition: small steady measures, closely and continually tracked.

In *Tatler* no. 264, which appeared two and a half weeks before the series' end and bore the motto *Favete Linguis* [Be silent] (Horace, *Odes* 3.1.2), Bickerstaff analyzes loquacity as a form of robbery: "A Man that talks for a Quarter of an Hour together in Company, if I meet him frequently, takes up a great Part of my Span. A Quarter of an Hour may be reckoned the Eight and fortieth Part of a Day, a Day the Three hundred and sixtieth Part of a Year, and a Year the Threescore and tenth Part of Life. By this moral Arithmetick, supposing a Man to be in the Talking World one third Part of the Day, whoever gives another a Quarter of an Hour's hearing, makes him a Sacrifice of more than the Four hundred thousandth Part of his Conversable Life" (*T* 3.337). By Bickerstaff's own calculations, the charge falls fairly close to home. The *Tatler* required about "a Quarter of an Hour's hearing" three times a week[34]—though Bickerstaff may feel that he has already exonerated himself by pointing out that "An Author [as opposed to a talker] may be . . . thrown aside when he grows dull" (*T* 3.335−36). As punishment for talkers, Bickerstaff has devised an instrument of close temporal confinement:

For the utter Extirpation of these Orators and Story-Tellers, which I look upon as very great Pests of Society, I have invented a Watch, which divides the Minute into Twelve Parts, after the same Manner that the ordinary

Watches are divided into Hours; and will endeavour to get a Patent, which shall oblige every Club or Company to provide themselves with one of these Watches (that shall lie upon the Table as an Hour-Glass is often placed near the Pulpit) to measure out the Length of a Discourse.

I shall be willing to allow a Man one Round of my Watch, that is, a whole Minute to speak in. . . . (*T* 3.337)

Old tradition, new technology: what is striking is the shift in scale. Bickerstaff's invention abbreviates sixtyfold the duration measured out by sermon-glass and ordinary watches alike, but it is not really an invention at all: the seconds hand, which is in Steele's world what the minute hand was in Pepys's, tracks time just this way. Bickerstaff conjures up, for comic purposes, a culture-wide application (in "every Club and Company") of the latest chronometry for a time-discipline articulated, in Foucauldian fashion, literally down to the minute. "*Methusalem* might be half an Hour in telling what a Clock it was," Bickerstaff has just remarked, "but as for us Post-diluvians, we ought to do every Thing in Hast" (*T* 3.337). Within this history, Bickerstaff figures his watch as the defining instrument of the new epoch, arbitrating containment and continuity in the age of haste, and performing Anderson's "clocking of homogeneous, empty time" at a lively clip: one talker one minute, another the next.

Within the essay, Steele keeps the alignments among the watch, the paper, and the author pointedly uncertain. On the one hand, the paper has long done for Bickerstaff what he now wants his watch to do for others: it has "measured out," more palpably than an actual watch could do, "the Length of [his] Discourse": two columns on two pages, one prose unit (essay) on one half-sheet. Towards the end of the essay, Bickerstaff pushes the comparison: "I shall only add, That this Watch, with a Paper of Directions how to use it, is sold at *Charles Lillie's.*" The watch does not exist, but the "Paper of Directions" does. Readers now hold it in their hands, where it embodies the self-contained discourse it advocates, and directs them, as would the timepiece for which it serves as surrogate, to mimic its own measured utterance. Having brought the analogy so far, though, Steele all but undoes it in the following sentence. Having exhorted others, Bickerstaff registers discomfort at the unavoidable equivocation with which his paper's title, and his own identity, infuse his present counsel: "I am afraid, a *Tatler* will be thought a very improper Paper to censure this Humour of being Talkative; but I would have my Readers know, that there is a great Difference between Tattle and Loquacity, as I shall show at large in a following Lucubration, it being my Design to throw away a Candle upon that Subject, in order to explain the whole Art of Tatling in all its Branches and Subdivisions." By its shape and length the sentence sustains the very sense of unease, voiced at its outset, which it endeavors to offset.

In the remaining *Tatlers* the unease never lifts; instead it closes in, and down. The promised paper fails to deliver the promised distinction. Bickerstaff again censures the loquacious, this time as murderers rather than thieves (he ends by quoting Horace's first *Satire*, in which the poet, trapped by a talker, fears that "he shall die by an eternal Tongue"). But Bickerstaff does not demonstrate the "great Difference between Tattle and Loquacity." Instead, a week later, he himself falls silent. The last *Tatler* displays none of the familiar certifications of his authority: no masthead, no motto, no "Apartment," only the serial number and, heading the prose, the date of issue. In the paper's first sentences Steele explains these absences. "I . . . have nothing further to say to the World under the Character of *Isaac Bickerstaff*" (*T* 271; 3.362). His diction, substituting "say" for "write," is commonplace enough, but may work particularly here. Steele sustains to the end the equivocation between "the Familiarity of Talking and Writing" which the paper capitalized on at the start, and now lets go the *eidolon* who made that confusion rhetorically rich and financially lucrative. This last paper, dated "today" and bearing Steele's own signature, is more explicitly a letter than anything the *Tatler* had previously produced—and in that way too it brings the *Tatler*'s mode of correspondence to an end. In two months, Steele and Addison will launch a new *eidolon* who only writes, rarely talks.

A year and a half later, Nahum Tate looked back to this time of transition in a celebratory poem published in *Spectator* 488:

> WHEN *first the* Tatler *to a Mute was turn'd,*
> Great Britain *for her Censor's Silence mourn'd.*
> Robb'd of his sprightly Beams she wept the Night,
> Till the Spectator *rose, and blaz'd as bright.*
> So the first Man the Sun's first setting view'd,
> And sigh'd, till circling Day his Joys renew'd . . .
>
> (4.233)

The metaphors are rather a mess, but a significant one. They render accurately the key transformations in *eidolon*, in timing, and in the mode of correspondence between paper and reader. Tate's first line pinpoints a moment—when Steele had "nothing further to say"—but it elides a process. The *Tatler* had been "turning mute" by stages almost throughout its run, from the varied venues and their chatty paradigms in the early numbers, to the solitary "Lucubrations" of the later, and finally to the critique of talk at the close. If Tate's line, poised at the transitional cusp, slightly misrepresents the past, it compactly adumbrates the future: when next the *Tatler* "to a Mute was turn'd," it was by means of a definitive mutation: gregarious Isaac Bickerstaff became silent Mr. Spectator.[35] The mutation entailed a change of timing, too, enacted here in the shift from imagery of silence to that of sun. Mr. Spectator reappears every day. With the shift in *eidolon* and schedule, the audience alters too. Tate figures the readership of the *Tatler* as a collective ("Great Britain"), as had the paper itself, especially in its early days, but he figures the admirers of the *Spectator* as individuals ("The *First Man*"), thus registering some of the novelties in the later paper's mode of address. Yet the sun metaphor accords the *Spectator* enormous power over the collective as a decisive agent in the Andersonian imagination of community; Gay had used it too, in describing the daily papers "rising upon us," and uniting "us" in admiration as they rise. The *Spectator*, these figures argue, now defines its readers' days, and may even make them too (no sun, no day).

In a short preamble, Addison praises Tate's epigram as "ingenious"; the fact that he publishes it suggests that he deems it accurate too. In devising and disseminating the *Spectator* eighteen months earlier, he and Steele had mirrored to some extent the predicament shared by themselves and many in their audience: as Whigs, they were suddenly outsiders, politically muted by a shift in power. Making muteness the occasion for mutation, they now set about discovering what power could be attained, what transactions with the polity could be achieved, by a figure of silence played out over continuous, calendrically calibrated time.

"TO PRINT MY SELF OUT"

The *Spectator* establishes from its outset, and as the absolute condition of its existence, that self-containment towards which the *Tatler* had been tending late in its run. The motto atop the new paper's first number casts the undertaking as a kind of metamorphosis:

> *Non fumum ex fulgore, sed ex fumo dare lucem*
> *Cogitat, ut speciosa dehinc miracula promat.*

[Not smoke after flame does he plan to give, but after smoke the light, that he may set forth striking and wondrous tales.]

(Horace, *Ars Poetica,* 1.143 − 44)[36]

Horace here writes about beginnings but casts them metaphorically as moments of transmutation—from fire to smoke (in the case of bad beginnings) or from smoke to firelight (in the case of good ones). He has just condemned, in language appropriate to Addison and Steele's new tight-lipped persona, the empty boasting, the pointless "opening of the mouth" on the part of the poet who begins his epic with a promise to narrate the entire Trojan War. He here praises the comparatively restrained narrative contract Homer subscribes to in the opening lines of the *Odyssey* (from their modest smoke he will produce a lasting light); a few lines further on, Horace will make that praise proverbial by commending Homer's way of plunging the reader *in medias res.*

The whole passage, Addison apparently realized, bears directly on his new enterprise (he would often use it as epigraph later in the paper's run), and particularly on the curious combination of fictional autobiography and manifesto which the first *Spectator* sets forth. There Addison depicts his emergent *eidolon* in the midst of a metamorphosis of his own, brought about by the converging pressures of past and future upon the present. Mr. Spectator, recollecting his "very first Appearance in the World" and anticipating his eventual disappearance from it, determines upon a course wholly new to him, one which his first essay both announces and initiates. In the very act of writing this, his "very first Appearance in the World" of print, he shifts from near-perfect silence into a highly idiosyncratic kind of utterance, from a mode of existence elusive and evanescent, like that of smoke, to one potentially more abiding and effectual, like that of fire and light, or print on paper.

The *Spectator's* silence begins as jest, then shifts to something more substantial. Mr. Spectator relates "that when my Mother was gone with Child of me about three Months, she dreamt that she was brought to Bed of a Judge," and that he himself, once born, "seemed to favour my Mother's Dream" by such "Gravity of . . . Behavior" as "[throwing] away my Rattle before I was two Months old," and refusing to use "my Coral 'till they had taken away the Bells from it." Towards the essay's end, though, mortality shades the joke. In Mr. Spectator's initial outing, thoughts of birth and death not only pervade the prose, but appear to account for it—to have prompted its sudden inception.

When I consider how much I have seen, read and heard, I begin to blame my own Taciturnity; and since I have neither Time nor Inclination to communicate the Fulness of my Heart in Speech, I am resolved to do it in Writing; and to Print my self out, if possible, before I Die. I have been often told by my Friends, that it is Pity so many useful Discoveries which I have made, should be in the Possession of a Silent Man. For this Reason therefore, I shall publish a Sheet-full of Thoughts every Morning, for the Benefit of my Contemporaries. . . . (*S* 1.5)

From its inception in lifelong silence to its prospective prolificity in print, Mr. Spectator conceives this whole project in terms of "Fulness," the optimal reciprocal relation between a container and the thing contained. He proposes to "communicate the Fulness of my Heart," not in the unregulated flow of speech but in a well-defined "Sheet-full of Thoughts every Morning." As silence has bounded the life, paper will portion out its revelation. Like Samuel Pepys, Mr. Spectator chooses a single, short, precisely dated unit, defined by the shape and size of a piece of paper, as the ideal vessel for the self; and in the daily repetition of that unit he hopes to fashion an instrument of the self's continuance and, ultimately, its completeness.

Mr. Spectator, of course, writes from a different vantage in time than Pepys. For Pepys, even at his diary's inception, each day provides its own narrative; its amplitude fills the entry. The fullness Mr. Spectator intends to communicate, on the other hand, is cumulative. It has gathered over a lifetime of days, and what he promises now are "Thoughts," not linear narrative. It is instead the paper's readers who will experience these disclosures in diurnal sequence. The passage (and the paper) figure them as Mr. Spectator's "Contemporaries" not so much in that they have occupied the same span of life (as beneficiaries and legatees ordinarily do not; Mr. Spectator will often make clear that he is addressing an audience younger than himself) as in that they occupy with him the exact time of its revelation; they will receive his "Discoveries" "every Morning," in the same putative rhythm in which they are written.

What that rhythm is supposed to render, Mr. Spectator touches upon in the passage's most striking clause. "I am resolved . . . ," he writes, "to Print my self out, if possible, before I Die." The word "out" does double duty. It traces the self-reversal Mr. Spectator now proposes, whereby he will turn himself inside-out and lay open his private consciousness to public scrutiny. But it also suggests completion, even exhaustion (as in to "wear out"), and so writes into the undertaking the same strict equation between person and page that operates in Pepys's diary. By its logic, each successive daily entry constitutes a piece of the self, and the aggregate contains the whole. In both Pepys's formulation and Addison's, the equation proves reversible. Diarists stop writing only when they die, and to cease before that is in effect to die betimes. Pepys in his final sentence betook himself "to that course which [is] almost as much as to see myself go into my grave." [37] Mr. Spectator anticipates a slightly different order of events, hoping to "Print my self out . . . *before* I Die." His words, though, portend not sequence but synchronicity. In them, Addison provides the earliest of countless signals throughout the paper's run concerning this creature's peculiar propensity for evanescence. A real-life diarist may survive his final page by many decades, but Mr. Spectator can exist for only as many days as he writes. On this day, prose and the press have brought him into being; on the date he last prints himself out he will die like a diarist, leaving only his book of days behind him.

At the same time, the conditional interjection "if possible" insists on Mr. Spectator's "actual" existence by raising a question of timing that could only apply, albeit comically, to a living person. With so much accumulated "self" to "Print out," at the rate of a "Sheet-full . . . every Morning," Mr. Spectator wonders whether his life-span will allow him enough days to complete the task. His speculation lends urgency to the enterprise, and offers a tacit explanation, founded in the character's predicament, for the novelty of daily publication.

The urgency of the new project (the question of whether it will be possible to complete it in time) accounts, within the fiction, for the *eidolon's* choice of the medium as well as the timing by which he now undertakes to correspond with his readers. Mr. Spectator initiates his printed journal as the ideal middle way between "Taciturnity," which he here abjures, and "Speech," for which he has "neither Time nor Inclination": it will allow him to deal in words without agitating his vocal cords. Part of this reasoning is absurd. Composition generally consumes more time than talk (and Mr. Spectator will often, as in *Spectator* 24, draw attention to the time his papers cost him). The real logic lies in the passage's quick sequence of displacements—"Speech," "Writing," "Print"—in which one mode of correspondence gives way to another more rapid and more public. Speech and writing reach only those who can hear the words or read the page the pen has crossed; but through print Mr. Spectator can address multitudes while keeping technically silent. The distribution of his "Possession[s]" will thus match the mode of their accumulation. Indeed, this paradoxical process has already begun. Somehow, Mr. Spectator's friends have become aware of his "Discoveries" despite the fact that, as he avers, "[I] do not remember that I ever spoke three Sentences together in my whole Life" (S 1.2). The contradiction hints at a possible parallel in the author's transactions with his audience, whereby the paper will conduct not so much a linear discourse in which Mr. Spectator "speaks" and readers attend as an osmotic transfer of material from his mind to that of his reader, a correspondence enacted in an instant (like the reflection in a mirror) rather than one transacted over time (like that of speech or writing). By this reckoning the odd phrase "to Print my self out" becomes more literal still, and the sheet that readers purchase contains not a transcription of thought but a direct impression of it, struck off in a moment. Print can, after all, make possible such contractions of time. Writing demands duration, but whole pages of prose can be pressed onto paper in an instant, and a reader can absorb words faster than a speaker can say them.

In *Spectator* 4, the first essay of the series' first full week, Steele develops the hint at length in Mr. Spectator's first detailed narrative of an encounter between himself and a fellow mortal: a curious "Conversation" he engaged in with Will Honeycomb, the now-elderly Restoration rake, "the other Night at a Play" (S 1.20). Steele traces with comic precision the gradients by which Mr. Spectator's capacity to receive impressions in silence readily converts into an ability to convey them without speech, and even to inculcate them in whatever companion comes under his power.

Steele encapsulates this involuted process in the double-jointed sentence of transition with which he begins the scene. Mr. Spectator has just finished explaining that as a "dumb Man," he can with "more than ordinary Penetration" and "without being admitted to their Conversation" perceive "the inmost Thoughts and Reflections of all whom I behold." At the start of the new paragraph he makes clear that such acuity is not only a privilege he exercises, but also one he can confer on others who behold him: "Those who converse with the Dumb, know from the Turn of their Eyes and the Changes of their Countenance their Sentiments of the Objects before them" (S 1.20). The process is the same, the practitioners reversed. The "dumb Man" now allows himself to be understood by the same mute signs he reads in others. But in this case the person reading and the person read collaborate in an exchange (rather than a mere "Penetration") of "Thoughts and Reflections" in which Mr. Spectator attains a peculiar ascendancy he has barely hinted at before. "I have indulged my Silence to such an Extravagance, that the few who are intimate with me, answer my Smiles with concurrent Sentences, and argue to the very Point I shak'd my Head at without my speaking." "Extravagance": the sentence duly plays out the motion mapped by the word's Latin roots. So forceful has Mr. Spectator made his "Silence" that it can push past its own confines and "wander outward" into the speech of another, who thus answers wordless "Smiles" with "concurrent Sentences." Eighteenth-century typography, with its capitalized nouns, emphasizes the alliterative *s*'s by which Steele points up the sequence of translation: from silence through sight to sound in speech.

When Will Honeycomb first speaks, he bears out what Mr. Spectator has just made clear: that this odd kind of exchange entails dialogue and even disagreement, so that Mr. Spectator's points, when rendered audible in the answers of his interlocutor, are subsumed in sentences that take issue with them. "Upon my looking with great Approbation at a blooming Beauty in a Box before us, [Will] said, 'I am quite of another Opinion: She has, I will allow, a very pleasing Aspect, but methinks that Simplicity in her Countenance is rather childish than innocent.'" The utterance includes six words "attributable" to Mr. Spectator ("She has a very pleasing Aspect") to twenty-one of Will's. The pattern of objection and subsumption continues as the two men "discuss" the woman further, but as they turn their attention to another, the conversation changes shape altogether. "When I threw my Eye towards the next Woman to her, Will. spoke what I looked . . . in the following Manner: 'Behold, you who dare, that charming Virgin. . . .'" Dialogue and disagreement give way to a concord between the wordless observer and the companion who puts his observations into words. Mr. Spectator practices a kind of animate ventriloquy. The "dumb Man" speaks his thoughts through another man's mouth.

In a last touch, Steele makes those voiced thoughts themselves the final piece in a pattern involving silence, spectatorship, and speech. Speaking what Mr. Spectator "looks," Will can hardly be expected to recognize that he is summing up the curious dynamic that has driven the whole exchange: ". . . How is the whole Woman expressed in her Appearance! Her Air has the Beauty of Motion, and her Look the Force of Language" (*S* 1.21). In short, the woman exerts the same powers of silent self-expression over Mr. Spectator that he exerts over Will. Within the sequence, he acts as versatile, indispensable middleman. First, he interprets the woman's "Look" and then, by a look of his own, he transmits his interpretation to Will, who then fulfills the potential "Force of Language" in both looks by putting them into actual, audible words. For the first time, though, Mr. Spectator demonstrates in action that odd evanescence that he has hitherto only hinted at in his self-descriptions. Though he alone has exercised the full range of spectatorial powers (reading the thoughts of another and broadcasting thoughts of his own), he manages in the end almost to disappear from the sequence in which he has seemed an essential term. Will, in speaking the "Sentiments" that Mr. Spectator has formed about the "Object" before him, in effect, makes them his own. Steele clinches the point by posting a kind of eavesdropper at the outset of the scene. "WILL. HONEYCOMB was very entertaining the other Night at a Play to a Gentleman who sat on his right Hand, while I was at his Left. The Gentleman believed WILL. was talking to himself . . ." (*S* 1.20). Will's early, disputative utterances ("I am quite of another Opinion . . .") might well entertain the gentleman as the monologue of a man apparently at odds with himself. But the speech Will delivers in concert with Mr. Spectator's final look makes considerably more sense; by its opening imperative ("Behold, you who dare . . ."), it might even be construed as an invitation to the gentleman and anyone else within hearing to partake of the challenges and pleasures of acute observation. For by now Will has absorbed and appropriated the spectatorial powers of two formidable practitioners— the "Woman" who can give "her Look the Force of Language," and his companion who can both read and speak the language of sight with unmatched ability. So, for the moment, can Will, who in accurately interpreting his friend, finds himself decoding the woman more deftly too: Steele implies that the old rake has in his previous utterances, and throughout his life, been judging women peremptorily rather than reading them attentively.

In this tacit critique, and in the transactions of silence, sight, and speech that give rise to it, Mr. Spectator hints for the first time at the complexity of his own stance towards women, and of his strategies for addressing what would soon become a large audience of female readers. On the one hand, the "charming Virgin," though celebrated for possessing a "Force of Language," is not permitted to speak for herself; she remains the object of a collective male gaze. On the other, her powers surpass those of all the men involved except Mr. Spectator, with whom she is in some respects equated. By identifying himself with her and construing their shared silence and seeming passivity as sources and proofs of acuity and linguistic force, Mr. Spectator might well appear to invite his women readers into a particular and potentially appealing mode of correspondence: relegated like him to seem-

ingly marginal roles in the bustling public sphere, they share with him powers that the common run of men like Will have yet to attain. In the opening
paragraph of his earlier periodical, Steele had teased women as "Tatlers" (he
named the paper, he says, in their honor); here, though, he identifies them
as potential fellow spectators.[38]

The construction of such a fellowship, among both women and men, is
the chief purpose of the scene at the playhouse. There Steele dramatizes a
mode of interaction in which anyone who picks up the paper will participate.
Like Will at the theater, readers of the *Spectator* engage in intimate discourse
with a "dumb Man," and receive his revelations by an unaccustomed exer-
tion of their own faculties. Like Will, they use their eyes as instruments
more of listening than of seeing—as the means to take in words that, since
Mr. Spectator does not speak, the ears alone would be helpless to hear.
Steele develops the analogy between Will and reader further by the essay's
end. Mr. Spectator voices the hope that his attentive readers, like his clubfellow, will not only register his thoughts but speak his words: ". . . I shall
take it for the greatest Glory of my Work, if among reasonable Women this
Paper may furnish *Tea-Table Talk.*" (*S* 1.21). As the authors will make clear
again and again, that talk is furnished in two ways. First, like other papers,
the *Spectator* was often read aloud, the words entering the eye and leaving
the mouth of a single reader, to enter at the ears of several hearers; like no
other paper, it managed to image, in the person of its sharp-eared, silent,
and visually expressive *eidolon*, a synthesis of sight and sound like the one
that made possible its rapid dissemination among a large audience. In these
circumstances, as in Honeycomb's final speech, the "*Talk*" is direct translation: like Will the reader speaks, and like the Gentleman the listeners hear
precisely what Mr. Spectator "looks"—what he sees, thinks, and makes
visible in print. But of course the *Spectator* may prompt a second kind of talk,
in which readers and listeners, like Will in his earlier remarks, contribute
more material of their own: they may discuss what the paper says. In both
cases Mr. Spectator exerts his powers of ventriloquy over a numerous audience far more significant and substantial than his silly clubfellow. The "Silent
Man" produces speech without moving his mouth: his readers, whether they
speak "from" him (in reading his works aloud) or "give Answer to" him,
will inevitably speak *for* him, and make his thinking heard.

When Mr. Spectator observes, at the end of the scene in the playhouse,
that "the working of my own Mind, is the general Entertainment of my
Life," he has already complicated the sentence's implicit solipsism by a signal

act of inclusion. In context, the formulation proposes a reflexive relation not within one mind but between two. For Mr. Spectator, mental activity serves as mirror: he finds his greatest pleasure in the scrutiny of his own thought's "working." The reader who has found entertainment from the same source in effect stands before the same mirror, with eyes fixed (at this stage of the encounter) not upon his or her own image, but upon this curious new figure who has just emerged into view. Already, though, Mr. Spectator has imparted to his performances a second thrust as well. In delineating the peculiar powers that derive from his silent self-containment, he implicitly presents himself not merely as an object of entertainment, as a provider of particular delights, but as a paradigm for the proper use of private thought. By attentively observing him, his readers might conceivably take their mirroring one step further, might learn to appropriate his self-sufficiency and find in the "working" of their own minds the chief entertainment of their lives, and so reduplicate his pleasurable reflexivity by a matching self-awareness of their own.

Such a possibility gives point to the requirements for readership at which Steele has hinted in this essay's opening sentences. Though Mr. Spectator welcomes among his readers both the "Blanks" of society, those clones of Will Honeycomb and models of receptivity who "when they first come abroad in the Morning" are "utterly . . . at a Stand till they are set going by some Paragraph in a News-Paper," he aspires also to a more able audience whom he describes indirectly in terms of the unworthy readers who are their opposites: "These are Mortals who have a certain Curiosity without Power of Reflection, and perused my Papers like Spectators rather than Readers" (*S* 1.18).

Here, for perhaps the only time in the whole series, the paper's title is used pejoratively, to suggest emptiness rather than fullness. But Steele invokes this connotation in order expressly to abjure it. The purpose of the sentence, of the essay, and indeed of the whole enterprise is to remake the meaning of the paper's title so that it conjures up not a purely passive onlooker, but the active practitioner of a demanding craft; as Steele insists at this essay's conclusion, "the World . . . shall not find me an idle but a very busy Spectator" (*S* 1.22). In the essay itself, the author has warranted the worth of his spectatorship by establishing himself first as an acute reader of silent signs, then as a being endowed with extraordinarily kinetic powers of reflection: he finds pleasure in his own mind, he discerns his own image everywhere in the external world, and he prompts from his companions an audible echo of his silent musings. He now seeks readers similarly empowered, who will peruse his papers as "Spectators" in the new, richer sense he has imparted to the term.

If he cannot find them, he has already, in effect, undertaken to create them. He will remake in his own image the mind of anyone who reads him; indeed, he has already begun that transformation. By the peculiarities of his own presence in print, he has enforced upon his audience a profound attentiveness analogous to his own: they hearken to the inflections of his rarefied whisper, the sound not (as with Pepys) of subdued speech but of articulate silence—of a voice so private that it can be heard only upon the page. In doing so, they become privy to the working of his mind not merely as consumers of its product (that is, as receivers of his published thoughts), nor even as informed observers of its process, but as almost involuntary fellow practitioners, whose own perceptions have become attuned to the nuanced modulations among silence, sight, thought, and talk which form not only fit matter for the mind's working, but also an apt model of its operations, and a limitless resource for its entertainment. Taking in the *Spectator* through their eyes and ears, allowing its words to echo in their mouths and minds, they provide living testimony to its author's powers of ventriloquy and reflection: they become the real-life avatars of a wholly fictional creation.

"TO FIND THEIR ACCOUNT":
THE DAY AS PROPERTY, THE *SPECTATOR* AS DIARY

By such strategies of reflection and ventriloquy, the *Spectator* transmutes self-containment into a mode of correspondence. By its diurnal schedule, it models calibrated continuity as a paradigm for possessing time as property, and for managing it well. In *Spectator* 10, the most famous of the paper's pronouncements on itself, Addison touches in the first sentence on the rhetorical significance of the *Spectator*'s diurnal timing. "It is with much Satisfaction that I hear this great City inquiring Day by Day after these my papers. . . ." The words "Day" and "daily" pervade the essay, appearing some fifteen times, closely followed by smaller subdivisions, "Morning" and "Hour." In his first number, Addison had argued the urgency of the paper's daily publication from the vantage of its putative author; now he argues from the need of its readers: "To the End that their Virtue and Discretion may not be short transient intermitting Starts of Thought, I have resolved to refresh their Memories from Day to Day, till I have recovered them out of that desperate State of Vice and Folly into which the Age is fallen. The Mind that lies fallow but a single Day, sprouts up in Follies that are only to be killed by a constant and assiduous Culture" (1.44). The mind, always active, must always be watched. Mr. Spectator's "constant and assiduous" attention to his readers' minds will provide not only a means of correction but also a pattern of proper behavior, the very opposite of the "short transient intermitting Starts of Thought" that may be the best that they can manage now.

The paper's motto, from Virgil's *Georgics*, presents in simile this argument for unremitting endeavor, an unbroken series of repeated efforts:

> *Non aliter quam qui adverso vix flumine lembum*
> *Remigiis subigit: si brachia forte remisit,*
> *Atque illum in præceps prono rapit alveus amni.*

> [As if one, whose oars can scarce force his skiff against the stream,
> should by chance slacken his arms, and lo!
> headlong down the current the channel sweeps it away.]
> (*Georgics* 1.201–3)[39]

The intermittent oar strokes of a paper like the *Tatler* or the *Post-Man* will not suffice for the sustained project of psychological and social transformation which Addison here proposes. Part of the ingenuity of *Spectator* 10 lies in the way it grounds its argument for a genuine daily paper, a "journal" true to the etymology of the name, not (as Buckley did) in the urge to keep up with fast unfolding external events, but in the need to enact over time an ongoing narrative of internal reform.[40] "Knowledge of ones-self," which Addison deems more important than information about *"Muscovy* or *Poland,"* requires even steadier study.

But Addison supplants Virgil's simile of the stream with his own metaphor of the field ("The Mind that lies fallow but a single Day . . ."), and the shift is significant. Neither oar strokes nor daily newspapers are, after all, truly "constant." They both simulate continuity by regular repetition, but they always entail a vacant interval between one oar stroke and the next, the appearance of this morning's paper and tomorrow's. The agricultural figure forestalls the danger of such a gap. Seeds once set in earth grow continually, and the ones Mr. Spectator speaks of seem designed to expand not in size but in duration, to fill the hours that follow their planting. This figure of temporal insemination, in which small things grow to great, sets a pattern Addison repeats throughout the paper: he guarantees explicitly to the "Blanks," and implicitly to "Families," "the female World," and all his fellows in "the Fraternity of Spectators," that by spending "a Quarter of an Hour in a Day on this Paper," they will receive "a good Effect on their Conversation for the ensuing twelve Hours" of their waking lives (*S* 1.44–47).

Here, however, the rustic metaphor begins to fall apart. Mr. Spectator outstrips the ambition of ordinary farmers; he plans to reseed the same furrows every day. He thereby posits a kind of double almanac: the daily planting of a diurnal crop ("twelve Hours'" worth of good conversation), synchronous with a longer-term project designed to yield a larger harvest in the season when he will have once and for all recovered his readers "out of that desperate State of Vice and Folly into which the Age is Fallen" (45). *Spectator* 10 is usually read as boasting of its ubiquity in space ("in *London* and *Westminster*," "at Tea-Tables, and in Coffee-Houses") but it makes much more of its ubiquity in time. Mr. Spectator undertakes to accompany his readers not only wherever they wander, but also whenever they are conscious. And so he acquires the lineaments of consciousness itself, quiescent by night, renewed each morning, and operant all day.

Accompaniment, after all, is not exactly what he is up to. Mr. Spectator insists that he aspires not to mere proximity with his readers, nor even to ordinary intimacy, but to a kind of self-infusion. He plants his ideas in their minds; they "imbibe" his "Notions" and he "instil[s]" into them his "sound and wholesome Sentiments" (46); indeed, he will later boast that like a "Chymical" doctor he condenses "the Virtue of a full Draught" of moral medicine into the "few Drops" of his "little Diurnal Essays," and so works all the more effectively "to diffuse good Sense through the Bulk of [the] People" (*S* 124; 1.506–7). (Hence, perhaps, his remarkably recurrent interest in tea, coffee, and tobacco: his readers take them into their systems, as he wishes them to absorb his papers, regularly and with relish.) The more frequent the infusions, the more potent and sustained their effects. Will Honeycomb at the playhouse enjoyed only a "short transient intermitting Start" at becoming like Mr. Spectator through exposure to him. But readers who take in the *Spectator* every day will prosper from a far more abiding transformation: they will be subdued to what they read. In the end, the arguments in favor of diurnal publication from the author's vantage (in *Spectator* 1) and from the reader's (in *Spectator* 10) converge. The daily paper will allow Mr. Spectator to "Print my self out" in the sense both of representing himself completely and of impressing his own identity and way of thinking upon his readers, as though they were soft metal fit for coining, or sheets of paper, *tabulae rasae*, awaiting the imprint of a particularly valuable text.

Time, profit, and property dominate the figure of speech by which Addison first describes the service he aspires to perform for his readers. Just before Mr. Spectator turns to the metaphor of the mind as field, he expresses the hope that his readers may "find their Account in the Speculation of the Day" (*S* 10; 1.44). The idiom means merely "to get one's money's worth," or, sometimes, "to collect a profit"; so Addison is simply promising that his paper will amply repay the penny's cost and the "Quarter of an Hour's" time that it asks of its readers. But the term "Account" also names the fiscal document, often diurnal in its rhythm, by which merchants and clerks calculate the prosperity and prospects of their enterprises. Readers of the *Spectator*, so the locution implies, can find a collateral moral reckoning in its serial pages, can set the credits of their "Virtue and Discretion" against the debits of their "Vice and Folly." What's more, the frequency of calculation will tend to better assure a net profit in conduct as in commerce.[41]

The phrase implies more still. Pepys, working first from his fiscal tabulations, produced an account of another kind, a running narrative in daily installments that summed up experience less systematically but more abundantly than ledgers alone could do. Addison's phrase makes a parallel promise: that in the *Spectator* readers will find their own narrative, written and issued every day by a tantalizingly elusive narrator, but somehow inscribed by themselves, reflecting and recording their actions, their thinking, their secrets. Like all puns, "Account" here suggests at least the possibility of coherence among its several significations. Mr. Spectator, like Pepys before him, undertakes to negotiate anew the intricate relationships among property, private experience, and serial, secret prose. But what Pepys discovered by way of solitary practice, Addison and Steele render as a public performance—almost, indeed, as a public service in which the audience participates perforce. In Mr. Spectator's diurnal writings, readers will discover not only his diary, but their own.

Between Pepys and Addison, Locke effected a significant intervention. Walking with his minute watch, writing in his diary, Pepys discovered to his pleasure that time could be constructed as a kind of private property. In the *Essay Concerning Human Understanding*, Locke rewrites that volitional pleasure into a potential doom. He insists that time can only be private property; whatever clocks or watches may declare, the mind can only reckon time with reference to the rhythmic succession of its own ideas.[42] By Locke's logic, what Mr. Spectator calls "the working of my own Mind" becomes not only "the general Entertainment of my Life" but also its chief time-keeper. Addison declares his allegiance to Locke's notions in *Spectators* 93 and 94, discussing how his readers may "travel through Time" most pro-ductively, and fill up the "Spaces of Life" that they now leave idly empty (*S* 93; 1.395): "Mr. *Lock* observes, 'That we get the Idea of Time, or Du-ration, by reflecting on that Train of Ideas which succeed one another in our Minds. . . .' To which the Author adds; '. . . [W]e see, that one who fixes his Thoughts very intently on one thing, so as to take but little Notice of the Succession of *Ideas* that pass in his Mind whilst he is taken up with that earnest Contemplation, lets slip out of his Account a good Part of that Duration, and thinks that Time shorter than it is'" (*S* 94; 1.399).[43] Addison proposes to "carry this Thought further" by developing from Locke's reasoning "a Method of lengthening our Lives, and at the same Time of turning all the Parts of them to our Advantage," by "employing [our] Thoughts on many Subjects, or by entertaining a quick and constant Succession of Ideas" (398–9). Ad-dison's words aptly describe his own enterprise. The *Spectator*, now nearing its hundredth number, has already proven the worth of such a method by putting it into practice. "A quick and constant Succession" of single sheets, dealing in "Ideas" and "Thoughts on many Subjects," the series has im-parted its own variety to its readers, and thereby, in Addison's present ar-gument, made their lives seem longer and more plentiful, while its punctual reappearances every morning have rendered the regular, real pulse against which the relative, subjective time of mind and memory unfolds. Those who read the *Spectator* regularly will have already found their own minds drawn into that most pleasurable and profitable way of working in time which Ad-dison here propounds in his optimistic extrapolation from Locke.[44]

In the peroration of this essay, Addison fuses the images of time as pecu-niary property and of the mind as a field to be attended "with a constant and assiduous Culture": "How different is the View of past Life, in the Man who is grown old in Knowledge and Wisdom, from that of him who is grown old in Ignorance and Folly? The latter is like the Owner of a barren Country, that fills his Eye with the Prospect of naked Hills and Plains which produce nothing either profitable or ornamental; the other beholds a beautiful and spacious Landskip divided into delightful Gardens, green Meadows, fruitful Fields, and can scarce cast his Eye on a single Spot of his Possessions, that is not covered with some beautiful Plant or Flower" (1.401–2). Like Locke's argument, Addison's final simile overlays the operations of time and mind in such a way that the two become virtually indistinguishable. Time has metamorphosed from money into something less liquid but more valuable: real estate. Like the mind in the earlier figure, time is here a tract of arable land idiosyncratically farmed by every owner—the inviolable but also ineluctable property of fool and sage alike, who hold it under lifelong lease and cannot wish it away even should they want to. But the mind too has remained, as before, the site of cultivation—and has become the creator and surveyor of its own landscape as well. Only the mind's fecundity can transmute time into a cluster of "Possessions" worth possessing.

If, conversely, the mind should fail its mission and let itself and its span of life lie fallow, then time will turn on its possessor to become a prison. So asserts one of Mr. Spectator's fictitious correspondents, Samuel Slack, at the outset of a letter in which he will argue from his own case the desperate and widespread need for an instructive *Spectator* paper on the "general Distemper" and "universal" affliction of "Idleness": "The regaining of my Liberty from a long State of Indolence and Inactivity, and the Desire of resisting the farther Encroachments of Idleness, make me apply to you; and the Uneasiness with which I recollect the past Years, and the Apprehensions with which I expect the Future, soon determin'd me to it" (*S* 316; 3.148). Locke has here become, in effect, the keeper of a lockup, a kind of temporal gaoler. He has decreed, after all, that the mind, even when it does not occupy time with ideas, must nevertheless inhabit it. Samuel Slack has evidently found such habitation a state of bondage, and though he claims to have recently regained his "Liberty," he finds in "Idleness" a source of prospective as well as recollected horror. His claim to "Liberty," in fact, is mildly equivocal in its wording; the opening phrase might plausibly be read to mean that "*the hope* of regaining my Liberty" has prompted the letter. And indeed the letter itself constitutes the only warrant of the claim. The writing of it is an undeniable action; it separates past years and future dangers. At the moment of writing Slack stands imperiled in the middle of a desert of wasted time, past and future. This preamble initiates an exchange whose format is unusual for the *Spectator*: without directly acknowledging Slack's letter, Addison will reply to it in the next number. Letter and reply enact a collaboration between the fictional reader Slack and the fictional author Mr. Spectator. For his optimistic reading of Locke in the earlier paired essays, *Spectator*s 93 and 94, Addison resorted to lectureship and direct didacticism. But here, confronting the anguish that is the underside of Locke's argument, he resorts to something more subtle: an exchange between fictional author and fictional reader in which daily writing itself, in public *Spectators* and in private diaries, becomes the means of escape from the wasteland of lost time.

The exchange turns upon a distinction between the life experiences of author and reader: by virtue of his containment and acuity, Mr. Spectator has dealt all his days in "Fulness," in the "secret Satisfaction" of a lifetime well spent (*S* 1; 1.5); Slack, by his own account, has known only emptiness. Now he surpasses Mr. Spectator in his capacity to tally up the cost of time misspent. In the last paragraph of *Spectator* 94 Addison conjured up the oppressive uniformity of a wasted "past Life" in his image of a "barren Country, that fills [the Eye] with the Prospect of naked Hills and Plains." Slack describes a vista even less differentiated and more primal.

> The Occasion of this [Slack's condition] seems to be the Want of some necessary Employment, to put the Spirits in Motion, and awaken them out of their Lethargy. If I had less Leisure, I should have more; for I shou'd then find my Time distinguish'd into Portions, some for Business, and others for the indulging of Pleasures: But now one Face of Indolence over-spreads the whole, and I have no Land-mark to direct my self by. Were one's Time a little straitned by Business, like Water inclos'd in its Banks, it would have some determin'd Course; but unless it be put into some Channel it has no Current, but becomes a Deluge without Use or Motion. (*S* 316; 3.148–49)

The language here passes seamlessly from that of business to that of Genesis, and so posits a cosmological correlative for the writer's private but universal problem. Slack, echoing the Authorized Version with remarkable consistency, in effect rewrites the biblical narrative in reverse, and as autobiography: he presently finds himself beneath a "Deluge" and in need of a new Creation. "One's Time," copious and inchoate, has itself become the form-destroying flood. By way of recovery, Slack must reshape himself as his maker first shaped the world. As "the spirit of God moved upon the face of the waters" in the opening sentences of Genesis, so Slack seeks a means to put his own "Spirits in Motion" over the "Face of Indolence" in order, like God, to effect useful and redemptive divisions, to "distinguish" "my Time" "into Portions" (as the Lord distinguished the waters by establishing dry land). The Noachian phrasing that ends the paragraph carries with it the suggestion of a punishment in which Slack operates as both avenging justice and suffering culprit. The Deluge, after all, dissolved a world already created, which would have abided indefinitely had mortals inhabited it aright, but which God reduces instead to its original condition—"without form, and void" (in the Bible's wording), "without Use or Motion" (in Samuel Slack's). Time and mind, according to Slack's implicit allegory, constitute a kind of private cosmos ripe for shaping. They provide humanity (as Locke has argued and Addison has affirmed) with a medium and a tool sufficient to produce fruitful distinctions and so to make of life a pleasing form, a satisfying fullness. Slack by his idleness has worked his own unmaking.

For this apocalyptic affliction, he seeks a homely but a potent remedy: to distinguish his time into those natural "Portions"—days, seasons, years— whose definition and distinction constituted the very first business of Creation, and, by attending consciously to these segments of time, to make each productive in its turn. The idea of apportioning leads Slack to both of the *Spectator*'s familiar tropes for time as property: land and money.

> The Time we live ought not to be computed by the Number of Years, but by the Use has been made of it; thus 'tis not the Extent of Ground, but the yearly Rent which gives the Value to the Estate.
> . . .
> Wretched and thoughtless Creatures, in the only Place where Covetousness were a Virtue we turn Prodigals! Nothing lies upon our Hands with such Uneasiness [as does Time], nor has there been so many Devices for any one thing, as to make it slide away imperceptibly and to no Purpose. A Shilling shall be hoarded up with Care, whilst that which is above the Price of an Estate, is flung away with Disregard and Contempt. (3.150)

By the end of the essay, though, the discussion of time's proper use modulates (as often happens in the *Spectator*) away from the analogy with land and money, and towards the redemptive efficacy of daily reading and writing: the day itself supplants the shilling and the acre as the unit of property. Slack, intent upon goading himself into reformation, cites the examples of those ancient paragons who pursued the "Improvement of every Part of Time" by means of thought and language, ink and paper: "*Seneca* in his Letters to *Lucelius* assures him, there was not a Day in which he did not either write something, or read and epitomize some good Author; and I remember *Pliny* in one of his Letters, where he gives an Account of the various Methods he used to fill up every Vacancy of Time, after several Imployments, which he enumerates; Sometimes, says he, I hunt; but even then I carry with me a Pocket-Book, that whilst my Servants are busied in disposing of the Nets and other Matters, I may be employed in something that may be useful to me in my Studies; and that if I miss of my Game, I may at least bring home some of my own Thoughts with me, and not have the Mortification of having caught nothing all Day" (3.150–51). These ancients have achieved that steady, diurnal rhythm of endeavor with which Addison has proposed to enrich his readers' lives. Like Seneca the paper's audience can assert that "there [is] not a Day in which" they do not "read and epitomize" at least one "good Author."

Hence the peculiar force of the request with which Slack begins to bring his letter to a close: "Thus, Sir, you see how many Examples I recall to Mind, and what Arguments I use with my self to regain my Liberty: But as I am afraid 'tis no ordinary Perswasion that will be of Service, I shall expect your Thoughts on this Subject with the greatest Impatience, especially since the Good will not be confined to me alone, but will be of universal Use" (3.151). Ancient examples will not suffice for his dire need, Slack suggests; he seeks instead a present encounter. As arbiter of temporal wisdom Mr. Spectator outqualifies Seneca and Pliny. In their letters, they merely report their strategies for the "sollicitous Improvement of every Part of Time"; in his papers, Mr. Spectator has given proof of his in a public performance every day for the past year. In requesting Mr. Spectator's "Thoughts on the Subject" of idleness, Slack is seeking not so much an acquaintance with particular precepts as an induction into Mr. Spectator's method of moving through the days and making them productive. Oppressed all his life by a time "without Use," Slack now wishes to inhabit the opposite kind of time, the kind he sees incarnate in Addison and Steele's diurnal paper: a time so richly varied and sharply differentiated as to be of "universal Use." He wishes, in effect, to be like Mr. Spectator.

It is the prevailing irony of this number that Slack partly achieves his wish simply by expressing it. Goaded by his distress, he raises himself momentarily, in this single outpouring of his pen, to the ranks of those paragons of "Labour and Assiduity" whom he invokes as models. Like his heroes Seneca and Pliny he has written a letter, and in writing has found a sure protection against the danger of this day's futility. But he surpasses even them to stand with their superior in these matters—Mr. Spectator—and has even, for an interval, supplanted him. Slack has, after all, authored the *Spectator* for the day. He has written the "Speculation" against idleness that he so ardently desires to read and now, with its publication, he has seen it pass into "universal Use" in coffeehouses and at tea tables.

By tacitly answering Slack's appeal simply by publishing it, the *Spectator* implies two arguments about its own enterprise. First, the paper's method of distinguishing time into "Portions" and ordering them in writing affords a ready refuge for readers who find such discipline difficult to attain. Second, so honed is Mr. Spectator's alertness to the needs of his audience, so supple is his reflexivity, and so capacious are his pages, that his readers can in effect practice his kind of ventriloquy in reverse. They can "Print *their* selves out" in his paper, can trace "the Workings of *their* own Minds" for their "Entertainment" and enlightenment, and can observe and address their own shortcomings from his vantage and his lectern. They can furnish—and become—their own *Spectators*.

In this reciprocal ventriloquy, reader's voice and author's inevitably mingle, sometimes indistinguishably: a correspondent will appear to speak for Mr. Spectator, Mr. Spectator for his readers. This continuity of identity and voice takes an unusual form in the next paper: Addison continues Slack's topic without acknowledging his letter, as though the train of thought had passed unmediated from reader to author. By the essay's end, Mr. Spectator makes explicit the remedy for empty time that he has hinted at from its outset: "I would . . . recommend to every one of my Readers, the keeping a Journal of their Lives for one Week, and setting down punctually their whole Series of Employments during that Space of Time" (*S* 317; 3.156). Recount every day, for one complete cycle of days; even after so short a "Space of Time," "the keeping a Journal" will banish idleness. The *Spectator*, having drawn from the diary paradigm some of its own most distinctive elements (its containment, its continuity), now advocates the practice *per se*.

It does so by means of a monitory fictional simulacrum. Addison has given over most of *Spectator* 317 to the transcription of one week's entries from the journal of "a sober Citizen, who died a few Days since," and who, "being of greater Consequence in his own Thoughts, than in the Eye of the World, had for some Years past kept a Journal of his Life." As the scholar of diary fiction Lorna Martens has pointed out, this journal marks a signal moment in the mixing of narrative modes: this is "the first day-to-day fictive diary that appeared in print."[45] The fiction here operates as negative exemplum: this journal has failed to bring about in its idle author the reformation that Addison will shortly promise to all his readers who keep a similar chronicle.

MONDAY . . .

One a Clock in the Afternoon. Chid *Ralph* for mislaying my Tobacco-Box.
Two a Clock. Sat down to Dinner. *Mem.* Too many Plumbs, and no Sewet.
From Three to Four. Took my Afternoon's Nap. (*S* 317; 3.153)

Addison accounts for this sterility in the tiny biography with which he prefaces the extract: ". . . the Deceased Person had in his Youth been bred to Trade, but finding himself not so well turned for Business, he had for several Years last past lived altogether upon a moderate Annuity." The supposed diarist, then, incarnates Samuel Slack's nightmare of an entire life lived in undifferentiated time, without distinctions between business and pleasure, and therefore ultimately without distinction of any kind. The journal maps out the "barren Hill and Plains" that Addison described, in *Spectator* 94, as the arid desert of a fool's "past Life."

In a strategy of self-advertisement, Addison attributes the vacuity of this diarist's time partly to contamination by text. The Citizen reads, and discusses with his friend Nisby, the news of the world. "*Hours Ten, Eleven and Twelve.* Smoaked three Pipes of *Virginia.* Read the *Supplement* and *Daily Courant.* Things go ill in the North. Mr. *Nisby's* Opinion thereupon." That short reading list, of course, discloses a significant omission. The Citizen studies the daily newspaper and also (in his insatiability) the thrice-weekly *Supplement*—but he does not read the *Spectator.* Rather than pursue the "Knowledge of ones self" that Addison has advertised as his paper's chief commodity a year earlier, the Citizen invests in stories heard from afar.

> TUESDAY . . . *From Four to Six.* Coffee-house. Read the News. . . . Grand Vizier strangled. . . .
> *Ten.* Dream of the Grand Vizier. Broken Sleep.
>
> WEDNESDAY . . . Mr. *Nisby* of Opinion, that the Grand Vizier was not strangled the Sixth Instant.
>
> FRIDAY . . . *Twelve a Clock.* Went to Bed, dreamt that I drank Small-beer with the Grand Vizier. (3.154–55)

The rumors of Mehemet Bashaw's death, on which the *Courant* and other papers had been running frequent and contradictory reports in recent months (3.154, n. 2), posit a question closer to home. Of the sober Citizen as well as of the Grand Vizier it may be asked, is the man alive or dead? The last lines of the diary extract supply both answers:

> SATURDAY . . . *Six.* Went to the Club. Like to have faln into a Gutter. Grand Vizier certainly Dead.
> &c.

So, of course, is the sober Citizen—figuratively dead at the time he writes, and literally dead on the day Addison's audience reads. Addison suggests by the final "&c." that the journal will continue, but he makes clear by his timing that it will not do so for long. On the day this *Spectator* came out, rumors of the Vizier's death were only three months old; in view of this *terminus post quem*, the late Citizen must here be recording, all unwittingly, the idle expenditure of his own near-final days. His certainty about the Vizier's death in the last line of the diary extract effects an interesting inversion. Readers of this day's *Spectator* did not yet know for sure that the Vizier had died (confirmation would come a full month later), but they could see that the Citizen had died. He has mused on the wrong mortality—another's, not his own—and so missed the urgent point that Slack and the *Spectator* have been expounding on this and the previous day: that a life misspent in inattention to the proper disposition of private time amounts to a kind of living death, an uncreating like the Flood, which reduces the self to a primal chaos, or to a state near non-existence, "as tho' [it] had never been."

At the essay's end, Addison shifts focus to the reflexive realm of the private self. He argues that in mocking the idle Citizen he is advocating not the pursuit of social "Consequence" but the cultivation of inner worth. "I do not suppose that a Man loses his Time, who is not engaged in Publick Affairs, or in an Illustrious Course of Action. On the contrary, I believe our Hours may very often be more profitably laid out in such Transactions as make no figure in the World, than in such as are apt to draw upon them the Attention of Mankind. One may become wiser and better by several Methods of Employing ones self in Secrecy and Silence, and do what is laudable without Noise or Ostentation" (3.156). Two familiar modes of discourse reemerge here, restoring Addison's prose to that accustomed fullness it has conspicuously lacked during the fragmentary interlude of the mock journal: the notions of time as capital (whereby "Hours may . . . be . . . profitably laid out in . . . Transactions"), and of secrecy and silence as the seat and source of personal power. Addison here reminds his readers of their autonomous capabilities as investors of their own time and spectators of their own selves. Having done so he delivers, in his essay's last lines, his culminating counsel: "I would, however, recommend to every one of my Readers, the keeping a Journal of their Lives for one Week, and setting down punctually their whole Series of Employments during that Space of Time. This kind of Self-Examination would give them a true State of themselves, and incline them to consider seriously what they are about. One Day would rectifie the Omissions of another, and make a Man weigh all those indifferent Actions, which, though they are easily forgotten, must certainly be accounted for." Here Mr. Spectator echoes John Beadle urging his Puritan reader to keep a continuous record of the self founded on the model of the account book. In life as in commerce, the *Spectator* argues, it is not sufficient merely to conduct prudent "Transactions"; one must also record them in order to attain that honed consciousness of purpose and productivity on which every enterprise depends for its success. The setting down of "indifferent Actions" commonly performed unconsciously salvages them from oblivion, making them permanent and hence available for scrutiny. It allows the journalist to "weigh" activities that in their ordinary evanescence acquire no mass, and makes possible a reckoning of the density of endeavors in proportion to the volume of hours, the "Space of Time" they occupy. On this temporal scale, for example, the Citizen's two hours spent "read[ing] the News" and drinking "a Dish of Twist" register a contemptibly inconsiderable density. Keeping a journal will help the diarist spend "Hours" profitably as mere good intentions (and even good actions) may not, and will bring within reach the goal Slack yearns towards, the "sollicitous Improvement of every Part of Time."

Mr. Spectator argues by implication that any "one of *my* readers" will make better use of a journal than did the Citizen in the sample. He buttresses this claim exactly a week later by publishing a five-days' diary he has received in a letter from a young woman named Clarinda, who remarks that she has "perform'd . . . according to [his] Orders," by composing "the following Journal, which I began to write upon the very Day after your *Spectator* upon that Subject" (*S* 323; 3.181–82). As Mr. Spectator notes in his preamble, Clarinda's journal too chronicles a life of idleness (e.g., "*From Eight to Nine.* Shifte a patch for half an Hour before I could determine it. Fixed it above my Left Eyebrow" [184]). The difference this time lies in the new awareness of the self in time that the journal produces in its author. "Upon looking back into this my Journal," Clarinda concludes, "I find that I am at a loss to know whether I pass my Time well or ill; and indeed never thought of Considering how I did it, before I perused your Speculation upon that Subject. I scarce find a single Action in these Five Days, that I can thoroughly approve of. . . . I will not let my Life run away in a Dream" (184–85). To encourage this correspondent "in her good Inclinations," Mr. Spectator ventures a further recommendation: "I would have her consider what a pretty Figure she would make among Posterity, were the History of her whole Life published like these Five Days of it"—that is, as a diary put into print. The suggestion enacts yet another fusion between *eidolon* and reader, by inviting Clarinda to project herself imaginatively into the scheme Mr. Spectator undertook for himself at his paper's inception: "to Print my self out," in daily installments, "before I die." When introducing Clarinda's letter, he refers to his own publishing project as "my Journal" (181).[46] The wording clinches the connection between the public and private genres: author and reader are diurnalizing in tandem. The periodical essay engages with the diary form, and the *Spectator* corresponds with its audience, at precisely that point where the Habermasian and Andersonian elements of the project mesh, in an operation where the text functions as mirror, and the acts of written reflection take place at intervals evenly measured and continuously tracked.

•

When, after twenty-two months of daily papers, the *Spectator*'s creators decided to bring the series to a close, Addison devised an indirect way of conveying their intention. In *Spectator* 550, Mr. Spectator announces that he will soon start to speak. "I think I have so well preserved my Taciturnity, that I do not remember to have violated it with three Sentences in the space of almost two Years. . . . Now in order to diversify my Character, and to shew the World how well I can talk if I have a Mind, I have thoughts of being very loquacious . . . (4.470–71). Isaac Bickerstaff had ended by abjuring loquacity; Mr. Spectator will end by aspiring to it. Though he promises to publish a "very useful Paper" when "*the* SPECTATOR*'s Mouth is to be opened*" for the first time, his readers, alert all along to the symbiosis between silence and spectatorship, immediately understood that the paper would not outlast its putative author's first attempt at speech; his amusing plan was nothing to their purpose. Three days later, Addison gave voice to their disappointment by printing a valedictory letter of affection and regret from a group of Mr. Spectator's admirers. Dated from Oxford and addressed to Mr. Spectator, the letter insists that

> IN spight of your Invincible Silence you have found out a Method of being the most agreeable Companion in the World. . . .
>
> It was . . . a matter of great Grief to us, to think that we were in danger of losing so Elegant and Valuable an Entertainment. And we could not, without Sorrow, reflect that we were likely to have nothing to interrupt our Sips in a Morning, and to suspend our Coffee in mid-air, between our Lips and right Ear. . . . (*S* 553; 4.485–86)

That last phrase touches precisely upon the method by which Mr. Spectator has endeavored—not "in spight" of but because of his "Invincible Silence"—to become "the most agreeable Companion in the World." He has pitched his ventriloquial voice at that exact locus where the coffee cup now hovers in this elegiac image: "mid-air, between our Lips and right Ear," so that, like Will Honeycomb at the playhouse, his readers may lose track of the distinction between hearing Mr. Spectator's thoughts (through their eyes as well as their ears) and speaking them for themselves; if his "Chymical Method" works, his readers will absorb his speculations imperceptibly, as if they were the fruits of their own acuity. From this delicate suspension the *Spectator* derives its remarkable rhetoric of transparency, which conveys the impression that the paper's readers are seeing through Mr. Spectator in two senses—by means of his acuity, but also by means of their own, as if he were merely a window (and not a lens that artificially enhances sight), and the power of perception were theirs alone.

For Mr. Spectator, then, "to print my self out" is a program not merely of self-presentation but of self-transfusion; his readers and not only his page will serve as receptacles for the print, and hence for the self it encodes. Such a method readily opens questions of volition and subjection, and Scott Paul Gordon has written well about the Foucauldian, disciplinary dimension of the *Spectator*'s program.[47] "Mr. Spectator," he begins, "seems to anticipate precisely the 'Eye of Power,' the voyeuristic gaze which disciplines subjects by observing them" (3). Gordon goes on to argue that Mr. Spectator deploys this power more aggressively than critics have recognized heretofore, displaying it as "a capacity *unique*" to himself, unattainable by his readers (20; Gordon's emphasis). Gordon is right, I think, about the aggression, but wrong about the "uniqueness." The formulation overlooks the intricate combination of invitation and argument proffered in the paper's figuration of the ways in which it will "correspond" with its readers. The *Spectator*'s aggression, which Gordon rightly pinpoints, addresses the reader by a running subtext to the effect that "You *must* become like me": Mr. Spectator's prose does undertake to fill "Blank" minds as though they were blank paper; and to "improve" also the full minds that encounter it. The paper's promise, though, consists in the invitation "You *can* become like me" and its argument develops the claim that "You are *already* like me": my silence figures the continual, ineluctably secret state of your own consciousness; "the working of my own Mind" is my chief entertainment, the working of yours may become yours. The success of Addison and Steele's spectatorial program

depends not on the uniqueness of powers in the author but on their repro-
ducibility, first in print and then in the reader.

The disciplinary program that Foucault outlines depends on reproduc-
ibility too. The denizen of the Panopticon takes on the observer's task to
become "the principle of his own subjection" (*Discipline* 203). Gordon argues that the *Spectator's* aggressive program failed. He cites a contemporary
attack on the new paper, *The Spy upon the Spectator*, as evidence for what he
deems the readership's chosen opacity, their refusal to lay themselves open
to the gaze. "This Spy," he writes, "must stand in for the many readers who
resisted [what the *Spy* called] Mr. Spectator's 'Tyranny'" (20). There is evidence to suggest, though, that if the *Spectator's* aggression sometimes failed,
its promise often allured and its argument swayed its audience. As Gordon
notes, the *Spy* itself, a projected series, failed after the first number, while
the *Spectator* went on selling at a spectacular rate. And it is not altogether
necessary to let the anonymous assault "stand in" for real readers. The reaction of one at least is elaborately documented—though he is admittedly
an extreme case. When Boswell came to London in 1762, he arrived eager
to emulate Addison, Steele, and their *eidolon*. In the *London Journal* his many
assertions to that effect, and enactments to that end, make clear that he
conceives of himself not as buying into subjection, but as acquiring power
and self-possession: "I think myself like [Mr. Spectator]," he writes, "and
am serenely happy. . . ."[48] Boswell ardently pursues that correspondence
between real reader and putative author which Addison and Steele had constructed as strategy, medium, and object of aspiration fifty years before.

One point of resemblance could not have escaped Boswell's notice. He
too was now producing, in his newly launched journal, a substantial tract of
self-recording prose under each successive date.

But the model on which he did so was a hybrid, compounded of the
Spectator and of other precedents. Boswell posted his daily narrative to a
friend in his native Scotland. By the 1760s, this diurnal tempo of address no
longer belonged solely to the periodical press; it was also much in use among
travelers writing home.

5

Travel Writing and the Dialectic of Diurnal Form

*I*n his preface to the final volume of his last long work, *A Tour Thro' the Whole Island of Great Britain*, Daniel Defoe tells this anecdote about time, text, and form in travel writing:

> I knew two Gentlemen who travelled over the greatest Part of *England* in several Journies together; the Result of their Observations were very different indeed; one of them took some Minutes of Things for his own Satisfaction, but not much; but the other, as he said, took an exact Journal; the Case was thus:
>
> He that took Minutes only, those Minutes were very critical, and upon some very significant Things; but for the rest his Memory was so good, and he took so good Notice of every thing worth observing, that he wrote a very good and useful Account of his whole Journey after his Return . . .
>
> The other Gentleman's Papers, which I called an exact Journal, contained the following very significant Heads:
>
> I. The Day of the Month when he set out.
>
> II. The Names of the Towns where they din'd every Day, and where they lodg'd at Night.
>
> III. The Signs of the Inns where they din'd and lodg'd, with the Memorandums of which had good Claret, which not.
>
> IV. The Day of the Month when he return'd.[1]

Defoe takes sides. He admires only the account by the first, "critical" traveler, and has even consulted it in order to "correct and enlarge" his own
book, which he trusts "shall not be a Journal of Trifles" like that of the
second traveler.

At the same time, Defoe acknowledges that his preference is not univer-
sally shared. "The Moral of this brief Story, which I insist that I know to be
true, is very much to my Purpose. The Difference between these two Gentlemen in their travelling, and in their Remarks upon their Journey, is a good
Emblem of the differing Genius in Readers, as well as Authors, and may be
a Guide to both . . ." (4). By Defoe's reckoning, the difference between the
two modes of writing pervades the literary culture. I shall argue in this
chapter that the preferences Defoe polarizes in his anecdote converged more
complicatedly in actuality. The two travelers embody a dilemma deeply important in eighteenth century writing but underattended to in recent scholarship: a conflict between the attractions of the "exact Journal" as a tool
for representation and those of earlier "critical" modes that established the
"significance" of "Things" (to borrow Defoe's key criterion) by structures
other than a steady succession of days and dates. As Defoe's small anecdote
suggests, the dilemma often operates as a dialectic, in that "Authors and
Readers" (whatever their "Genius") find it difficult to conjure up—even to
advocate—one of the two terms, without thinking of and contending with
the other.

On the one hand, the very phrase that Defoe applies with opprobrium to
the prose of the second traveler also functioned throughout the century as a
term of advocacy. "Keep an exact Journal," John Ryther advised in *A Plat
for Mariners* (1672), echoing the precept of countless other Puritan conduct
books.[2] Ninety-nine years later Samuel Johnson supplied the same counsel
as his friend Joseph Baretti set off for Italy: "I hope you take care to keep an
exact journal, and to register all occurrences and observations."[3] On the
other hand there persisted the conviction, to which Defoe gave voice, that
an "exact Journal" must become "a Journal of Trifles"—that a registry of
"*all* occurrences" will inevitably record many too many. The conflict between these positions sometimes transpired (as in Defoe's schema) between
opposed factions made up of "Authors and Readers" whose "differing Genius" manifested itself as differing taste in the textualization of time and
experience. More often, though, the dialectic makes itself apparent as an
ambivalence within individual writers and readers, and as a principle of

structure within particular texts whose writers strive to synthesize the antithetical extremes. The evidence suggests that many "Authors and Readers" sought to combine the mind-sets of Defoe's two travelers in the texts they wrote and read, while remaining aware that such a combination was no simple thing. Johnson himself (as I shall show in the next chapter) registered the attractions and liabilities of diurnal form in ways that operated powerfully in both his life and his work.

By drawing a general distinction, Defoe was also bucking a particular trend. After daily periodicals like the *Courant* and the *Spectator*, the travel book was the first print genre to accommodate diurnal form, and the first to elevate the successive "Day[s] of the Month" to the status of "very significant Heads" (in Defoe's sarcastic phrasing), as chief arbiters of structure in the traveler's narrative of his or her experience. The strategy proved popular. In increasing numbers throughout the century, English presses produced volumes whose titles announced their contents as a *Voyage* (or *Journey*, or *Tour*) and their format as a *Journal*. Such journals constituted a thriving, steadily expanding subgenre within the burgeoning phenomenon of travel literature in general, a category that by mid-century bestrode the book market like a colossus.[4] Within that category, the travel journal appeared alongside alternate structures for representing remote spaces, such as the one Defoe had devised in the *Tour* as a kind of countermove: a series of long, markedly non-epistolary "Letters," bearing only consecutive Roman numerals for their headings (no "Day of the Month"), and dealing so extensively in description and so minimally in narrative that even Defoe's biographers are hard-pressed to pinpoint the dates of their composition.

Within another category, the published travel journal exercised a near monopoly. For most of the eighteenth century it was virtually the only kind of journal to find its way from manuscript to print; the diaries of stay-at-homes remained unpublished until the end of the century. As a popular mode of travel literature, and as almost the sole representative of journal literature, the travel journal focused the wider debate about the viability of diurnal form for representing phenomena in space and experience over time. It offered both an object of dispute and a site for its working out.

The travel journal, then, represents an important stage in the emergence of diurnal form as a familiar practice, a next step after the *Spectator*, and one that spans the century. I want to look in this chapter at two adjacent facets of the phenomenon—the textual telling of new time and the debate it instigated—before turning in the next to two texts that, in the century's final quarter, enact that debate with unprecedented complexity, clarity, and consequence: Johnson's *Journey to the Western Islands of Scotland* and Boswell's *Journal of a Tour to the Hebrides*.

First, the travel journal furthers a process that I have tracked from Aubrey's onomatopoeia and Pepys's diary: the textualization of a new horology. The travel journal coincides with and enacts as form eighteenth-century England's central innovation in the technology of timekeeping. The project for calculating the longitude by chronometry, which Huygens (helped by Holmes, Hooke, Pepys, and others) had pursued unsuccessfully in the mid-seventeenth century, became over the course of the eighteenth first a national mania and then (with its completion) a national triumph, eventually establishing Greenwich, Pepys's chance-chosen destination, as the center for world time. The travel journal, whose popularity increases along with this preoccupation, enacts the project's premise as textual form: it too plots motion through remote space by a structure of incremental time.

The parallel is of course imperfect. As with Pepys's diary, the language and structure of narrative involve complexities that the numbers of time do not, and those complexities form the second object of this chapter's inquiry. Here the focus widens to encompass several modes of writing, including manuscript as well as print, because (as Defoe suggests) the traveler's journal forms part of a larger opposition within the literary culture. The debate among "Authors and Readers" as to the usefulness of the "exact Journal" extended to other incarnations of diurnal form: the daily newspaper, the private diary, the journal letter. I propose to offer (in Defoe's phrase) a "Guide to both" positions in the debate, and more importantly to their several syntheses. The travel journal, as the preeminent print journal, customarily sought to mediate the debate, paying at least lip service to both sides in its preface, and seeking by various strategies to mingle the sense of dates, sequence, continuity, exactitude, and comprehensiveness associated with the exact journal with that of critical selectivity. The published travel journal holds these concerns in common with its manuscript counterpart the journal letter, a daily narrative dispatched to a distant friend (usually in batches determined by the schedule of the post); this was perhaps the most pervasive, and socially sanctioned, mode of diurnal writing throughout the eighteenth century. A two-way traffic linked it with the published travel journal, whose writers usually insist at the outset that their text originated as a series of journal letters never intended for print; these "reluctant" publications in turn influenced the private practice from whence they claimed to come. The published travel journal and the private journal letter, then, mirrored each other in a way comparable to what the *Spectator* envisioned when it advised readers to keep diaries of their own: "Authors and Readers" of *similar* "Genius" tracking time by the same template. The travel journal becomes the print paradigm for a whole set of practices, and as such the object of both suspicion and celebration.

LONGITUDE: PLOTTING SPACE BY TIME

During the final years of Queen Anne's reign the problem of the longitude returned to the center of scientific and national attention, where it would remain until its solution half a century later.[5] The experienced diurnalist Joseph Addison made himself instrumental in putting it there. On 22 October 1707, a cluster of navigational mistakes made by a crew under the command of Admiral Sir Clowdisley Shovel caused the loss of four ships and nearly two thousand lives (including the commander's). The incident brought pressure on the government to do something new and conspicuous about navigation. As years passed and pressure mounted (due in part to further accidents at sea), Addison made public the first conspicuous new scheme for a solution. In the *Guardian* of 14 July 1713, he introduced with solemn praise a letter "on no less a Subject, than that of discovering the *Longitude*," written by William Whiston, former Lucasian Professor of Mathematics at Cambridge, and Humphrey Ditton, Mathematical Master at Christ's Hospital. The letter began by reviewing the problem and ended by announcing, without describing, a solution: "We are ready to disclose it to the World, if we may be assured that no other Persons shall be allowed to deprive us of those Rewards which the Publick shall think fit to bestow for such a Discovery; but do not desire actually to receive any benefit of that Nature till Sir *Isaac Newton* himself, with such other proper Persons as shall be chosen to assist him, have given their Opinion in favour of this Discovery."[6] After Whiston was dismissed from his post for doctrinal eccentricities, Addison and Steele helped arrange for him a series of lectures on astronomy at Button's coffeehouse, the social center of their Whig world. Their endorsement in the *Guardian* served their own ends. At this point both editors were planning to run (successfully, as it turned out) in the August elections for the House of Commons. The question of the longitude made a useful, if minor, opposition issue; the Tories had not yet done anything distinctive to address it.

Whiston and Ditton's solution, published in 1714, involved the mooring of small vessels in charted positions at close intervals along trade routes all over the globe: each was to fire a rocket 6,440 feet into the air every night at midnight, so that it could be seen by passing ships that would take their bearings from it. In April the two mathematicians applied to Parliament for "those Rewards" that (as they had intimated in the *Guardian*) they felt were coming to them. Their petition coincided with another, urgently worded, from a group of merchants and seamen, beseeching the government to supply "due Encouragement" for a true solution. In response, the House created a committee of scientists including Sir Isaac Newton, whose report on 11 June prompted its hearers to produce *A Bill for Providing a Publick Reward for such Person or persons as shall Discover the Longitude at Sea*. It offered £20,000 to the "First Author or Authors" of any method capable of determining longitude to within thirty geographical miles (about thirty-five statute miles), with smaller rewards (£15,000 and £10,000) for techniques with larger margins of error. Addison was one of the Members assigned to write the bill. The Whiston-Ditton scheme that he had sponsored the year before had not after all concluded the quest for the longitude (as its projectors had plainly hoped) but had initiated it anew, with unprecedented fervor and encouragement.

The competition for prize money that ensued over the next fifty years struck many as a mania. The Scriblerians, now firmly entrenched against Addison's circle, found Whiston and Ditton's proposal hilarious, not so much the butt of satire as a real-life rival to it.[7] "Whiston has at last published his project on the longitude," Dr. John Arbuthnot wrote to Jonathan Swift, "He has spoiled one of my papers of Scriblerus', which was a proposal for the longitude not very unlike his . . . that all the Princes of Europe should joyn & build two prodigious poles upon high mountains with a vast Light house to serve for a pole Star."[8] Nevertheless, satire persisted. Arbuthnot used some of his material after all, Hogarth derided the project in the final print of *A Rake's Progress*, Prior parodied it in *Alma*, and much later Pope and Swift published (in the *Miscellany* for 1735) a scatological verse, probably by Thomas Parnell, which had diverted the group in 1715 by repeatedly rhyming the designers' names with "bepi-t on" and "besh-t on."[9] Swift, to whom several longitude projectors applied for help, considered the enterprise "as improbable as the Philosopher's Stone, or perpetual Motion" and knew its cost first-hand. His friend Joseph Beaumont had become immersed in the problem and (as a result, Swift thought) gone mad.

The competition provided the British press with an inexhaustible source of copy, and followers of the long-running story found much to warrant suspicions of lunacy. The *Gentleman's Magazine*, for example, published numerous proposals, but announced in August of 1752 that it would henceforth limit itself only to those most "worthy," having been prompted to that decision by a spate of submissions that included "some in Hebrew and other mysterious characters . . . some under the form of an algebraic equation, in which neither the name nor value of any one of its terms is expressed; some for effecting utter impossibilities, as finding the sun's true place . . . by observation at midnight." [10] The more plausible proposals tended to fall within one of three categories: those based on measurements of time, those based on measurements of space, and those based on measurements of force. The time-centered solutions conformed to Huygens's original conception of a clock reliable enough to track the time at a prime meridian; clockmakers energetically set about devising one in pursuit of the new rewards. The space-centered solutions depended in some cases on cumbersome terrestrial and aquatic arrangements (like Whiston's rocket launchers), in others on more sophisticated readings of celestial positions: the apparent angles of the stars, and the moon's motion relative to them (it was in pursuit of this method of "Lunar Distances" that Charles II had founded Greenwich Observatory in 1675, and this line of inquiry produced enormous advances in astronomy and navigation). The solutions based on force theorized that variations in magnetism, if measured correctly, might supply an accurate reading of the longitude; Whiston and Ditton's comeback proposal, on the use of the "dipping needle" (a magnetic pointer that moved up and down with changes in the force field), was of this kind.

Despite the variety of schemes, though, the nature of the problem focused attention from the start on timekeeping. Newton had pointed out, in his seminal report to the House in 1714, that of the four kinds of solutions then under consideration, three required the use of at least one accurate watch, and even Whiston's scheme (of the fourth kind) decreed that rockets rise all over the globe when it was midnight at the Peak of Teneriffe (his candidate for the prime meridian). It was clear to some involved in the quest that the solution to the longitude, if ever achieved, would amount to the apotheosis of clockwork as arbiter of global space and time.

The Yorkshire clockmaker John Harrison brought this about, working much of the century (from 1730 to 1772) to produce a timekeeper reliable enough to meet the Board's requirements. In 1749 Harrison received the Copley Award, the Royal Society's highest prize, for having developed three instruments (H1, H2, and H3), each more exact than any predecessor; he had not yet qualified for the larger rewards promised by the Longitude Act. In 1755 he began work on H4, the watch that would (after four years' further effort) solve the navigational problem and (after another fourteen years' petitioning) secure for its maker most of the long-sought prize. In the quest for the longitude, mechanical chronometry had prevailed; nothing had proven necessary beyond Huygens's original conception, made actual by the gradual refinement and elaboration of his now-primitive technology. Huygens's cumbersome shipboard clocks had deviated by several minutes during Holmes's year-long voyage to Guinea (1664); an exact copy of H4—compact enough to rest across an open palm (though not in a normal pocket)—varied by no more than eight seconds in its decisive trial during the three years of James Cook's second voyage (1772–75), which compassed both the Antarctic and the tropics.[11]

Harrison's sustained, well-publicized endeavors brought the portable time-keeper to the center of public consciousness as an instrument that could now pinpoint the present moment, and track the succession of such moments, more precisely than ever before.[12] It also made each tracked moment more momentous: the central point of reference within the nexus of science, trade, navigation, and conquest in which Britain was increasingly construct-ing its identity. Benedict Anderson suggests that Harrison's chronometers, by carrying Greenwich time to remote reaches of the globe, brought to a "zenith" the "accumulation of technological innovations in . . . navigation, horology and cartography, mediated through print-capitalism," which made possible the "synchronic novelty" whereby "substantial groups of people were in a position to think of themselves as living lives *parallel* to those of substantial other groups of people" (*Imagined Communities* 188). From Brit-ain's point of view parallelism was perhaps the least of it; the quest for the longitude encoded hierarchy as well. First, it appeared to clinch the nation's stronghold on the technology of timekeeping; the concurrent French con-test for the longitude appeared markedly less successful.[13] Second, it traced larger possibilities of dominion on the world's maps by establishing Green-wich as degree zero, the prime meridian from which the remainder of the numbers of space (and, eventually, of time) were to be reckoned around the globe.[14] In her book *Imperial Eyes*, Mary Louise Pratt argues that a "Euro-centered form of . . . 'planetary' consciousness" developed during the sec-ond half of the eighteenth century, in which the local particulars of remote spaces were abstracted and "rewoven into European-based patterns of global unity and order."[15] The meridian at Greenwich enacts such a pattern as pure, all-encompassing numeration, nationalized as specifically British rather than "European."[16] The quest for the longitude established the British watch as the necessary referent for time, a British town as the necessary referent for space. In tandem the two now functioned as the indispensable tools of navigation, preserving lives and safeguarding wealth, abetting empire as both practice and schematic construct.

In many respects, as Pratt points out, the way for this "planetary consciousness" had been prepared by text. Anderson's argument that print capitalism mediated the new simultaneity centers on the novel and the newspaper, but another print mode bears an even closer relation to the constructs of time and space that emerged from the quest for the longitude: the sea journal, a date-structured narrative of navigation or (most popularly) circumnavigation. Apart from the excerpts from religious diaries incorporated into spiritual autobiographies, these texts were the first sustained journal narratives of any kind to find popularity in print (they figure as forebears of the non-nautical travel diaries that became popular in mid-century). They form a kind of conduit whereby the book of continuous days (what I have cast as the Pepysian paradigm) emerged into public consciousness. The form first appears sporadically in the late seventeenth century (at a time when Pepys is assiduously collecting sea journals in manuscript); it achieves secure (and abiding) popularity in around 1709–12, at a time when newspapers and *Spectators* are accustoming their readership to absorbing narratives and self-representations in daily installments.

Over the course of this early phase, the form accords the journalistic succession of dates an increasing prominence and structural power. Unlike the manuscripts in Pepys's collection, the bulk of the early published sea journals are clearly the products of retrospect. Though they draw heavily on logbooks written day by day (and hour by hour) over the course of the voyage, and retain from these texts a plethora of dates and details, they conspicuously recast them from what Lorna Martens calls "an armchair perspective," omitting some dates, running others together within a paragraph, and leaping ahead from the inception of a "story-line" on a particular date to narrate its completion months later. In 1712 (concurrently with the *Spectator*), published sea journals begin to adhere more closely to the Pepysian rule of writing to the ignorance of the moment, within the limitations of the knowledge available on the date that heads the entry.[17]

Increasingly, then, as the form develops, the numbers of time structure the narrative of motion through space. In his *Cruising Voyage Round the World* (1712) Woodes Rogers writes,

> Dec. 20 [1708]. This day, according to what our Committee agreed at *Grande*, we exchang'd Mr. *Vanbrugh* for Mr. *Bath* Agent of the *Dutchess* [the companion ship]. Easy Gales of Wind, but very veerable . . .

> Dec. 21. Easy Gales of Wind, but very veerable. We have seen a deal of Rock-Weed for some days past, of a great length and generally found in large Branches. Lat. 48.50.S.

> Dec. 22 Fair Weather with Rain, Wind very veerable. The Water is generally discolour'd. We had a good Observ. Lat. 49.32.S.[18]

The navigator-narrators of these texts generally justify their choice of diurnal form as a doubly efficient mode of representation. It re-enacts the "real," originary documentation of the ship's log, and it allows for the greatest comprehensiveness of coverage; it can contain and place data of all kinds. William Dampier explains in the opening paragraph of his circumnavigation narrative that his book "is composed of a mixt Relation of Places, and Actions, in the same order of time in which they occurred: for which end I kept a journal of every days Observations."[19] The wordy title page of Edward Cooke's *Voyage to the South Sea* (1712) suggests that the journal form encompasses not merely a "mixt Relation" but a heterogeneity of genres. After first specifying the book's central referent, "A VOYAGE to the South Sea, and Round the World," the title goes on to itemize the various genres and techniques by which the representation is to be accomplished: "Containing A JOURNAL of all memorable Transactions during the said VOYAGE . . . A DESCRIPTION of the *American* Coasts . . . an ACCOUNT . . . of Mr. *Alexander Selkirk* . . . Illustrated with CUTS and MAPS."[20] The small caps unite these six elements while distinguishing them from the rest of the page's copious verbiage. That the journal comes first among the representational modes suggests both its priority and its comprehensiveness: the description and the account, the cuts and maps will all appear in their appropriate places within the succession of dates that structures the whole. The calendar here serves as chief arbiter of the order of things; it holds in place all the elements of the narrative's "mixt Relation," and so facilitates that prehensile textuality whereby, in Pratt's argument, voyages performed and written conferred "planetary consciousness" and world possession on both the navigator and the reader (29–30).

The calendar's primacy as axis appears even more conspicuously in a familiar component of the published sea journal, a chart that William Dampier calls "a particular Table of every days run": the leftmost column lists successive dates, the remainder of each row enumerates the course, distance, latitude, and winds that obtained on the day specified. Dampier, like many other authors of sea journals, includes his Table partly "for the satisfaction of those who may think it serviceable to the fixing the Longitudes of these Parts"; he offers the chart, that is, as a help in constructing the one category of information most conspicuously missing from it (1.284).

If sea journals were published in part to assist in the solution of the longitude, they also inculcated that solution's *modus operandi* as a familiar strategy of narrative. By virtue of their structure, they constantly collate the data of exotic space with that of familiar time—with dates that their first readers had simultaneously occupied at home, and could recall. Anderson's terms apply here: the sea journals mediate a growing sense of "simultaneity" between the sedentary reader and the outwandering narrative. In the published sea journals, the dates of the calendar function as will the minute and second hands on shipboard watches later in the century. In the maritime journal as on the marine chronometer, time organizes the perception and the charting of motion, and situates the British subject near the center of the reading. In the *Compleat English Gentleman* Defoe makes that centrality explicit: "[The English Gentleman may] make the tour of the world in books, he may make himself master of the geography of the Universe in the maps, attlasses and measurements of our mathematicians. . . . He may go round the globe with Dampier and Rogers. . . . He may make all distant places near to him in his reviewing the voiages of those that saw them . . . with this difference, too, in his knowlege, and infinitely to his advantage, viz. that those travellers, voiagers, surveyors . . . etc., kno' but every man his share . . . But he recievs the idea of the whole at one view." [21] Defoe's examples are not random: Dampier's was one of the earliest published sea journals, and one of the most popular; Rogers's one of the most innovative in its commitment to diurnality (and also tremendously successful); both impart "master[y]" of the "globe" by a diurnally structured narrative. The privileged English centrality that Defoe here posits as a function of text, Harrison will eventually actualize as a consequence of technology: the whole of the world on one time grid (the writer publishes this passage in 1730, the year the clockmaker begins his attempt). Invoking Dampier's and Rogers's narratives of global navigation, Defoe here gainsays his remarks about the "two Gentlemen" a few years earlier, and so manifests his own ambivalence as to the viability of diurnal form. This time round, he construes the "exact Journal" as an attractive instrument and index of national power.

THE TRAVEL JOURNAL: PLOTTING PRINT BY TIME

During the same decades in which the watch began to image dominance abroad, it was acquiring hegemony at home. In 1726, nearly half a century before John Harrison put the marine chronometer on the map (or rather, enabled it to generate and articulate the map), Jonathan Swift noted that many people already accorded their watches an extraordinary authority—if not in discovering their place at sea, at least in ordering their lives on land. In *Gulliver's Travels* Lemuel Gulliver, global navigator and no stranger to shipwrecks, demonstrates his timepiece to the Lilliputians, who write up their impressions in an inventory of his effects: "He put this Engine to our Ears, which made an incessant Noise like that of a Water-Mill. And we conjecture it is either some unknown Animal, or the God that he worships: But we are more inclined to the latter Opinion, because he assured us (if we understood him right, for he expressed himself very imperfectly) that he seldom did any Thing without consulting it. He called it his Oracle, and said it pointed out the Time for every Action of his Life."[22] Swift's satire here suggests the third stage in Raymond Williams's paradigm for emergent structures of feeling. The watch, which Pepys construed as private and Pope as social, is here described in terms that make it explicitly dominant. No longer, as in Pope's simile, do "our Watches" appear as a (plural) figure for social exchange, their differing data as a metaphor for our differing "Judgments." Here the singular watch functions in the capacity that Pope himself aspires to in the *Essay*: as an "Oracle," sole and infallible dispenser of truth. Gulliver and his kind allow it to dictate "the Time for" their "every Action," with respect both to themselves and to each other. The watch no longer images the social; it organizes it.

The Lilliputians' write-up offers a small datum about the large process that E. P. Thompson has tagged as both crucial and elusive in eighteenth-century England: the transformations by which "the inward notation of time" became entrained with, and even subordinated to, the outward movements of the watch. Commonplace outward notations of time supply further evidence. In the first decades of the eighteenth century, almanacs, long the repository of such notations, began to change their format. The astrological "Prognostications" that Swift had mocked astringently in the guise of Bickerstaff fell sharply out of favor. Some very successful almanacs now helped their readers tell a different kind of time:

1	a	New-Years-Day: or the Circumcision of Jesus Ch
2	b	*Good Watches should be* **9** *minutes too fast for the Sun.*
3	c	Sun rises at 8, sets at 4. [Days 8 h. lo Night 16 h. lo.]
4	d	Watches and Clocks 10 minutes faster than the Sun.
5	e	Days increased half and [*sic*] hour in length.
6	f	Epiphany: or, Twelfth Day.
7	g	*Watches* 11 *minutes too fast.*[23]

Couched among Messianic calendar markings, the table intersperses instructions whereby the reader may effectually divorce sublunary timekeepers from the movements of celestial bodies. Solar time had always varied (on a predictable curve that was repeated annually) from the machine-told time of fixed durations. Here, though, the machine begins to take precedence. (By century's end British law would underwrite the precedence, establishing "mean time"—in effect, clock time—rather than solar time as the legal standard.) Where the older almanac purported to help its buyers foresee the future with the aid of astral signs, the newer kind helped them construct the present moment by means of a machine. The future ebbed from the text in other ways as well. Successful innovators renounced prediction altogether, and gave the space over to history, fiction, recipes, and verse "enigmas" to which readers would send in solutions in the hopes of winning a cash prize and seeing themselves in print. The present continuum of an ongoing correspondence between the almanac and its readers supplanted the future tense of prognostication.[24]

By mid-century the almanac encountered serious competition from another kind of publication that was even more open to the immediate needs and impulses of its readers. Robert Dodsley's *Memorandum-Book* first appeared in 1748 and remained a tremendously profitable and popular publishing phenomenon for the rest of the century. Forebear of the Filofax, the book afforded for each date a space available for inscriptions that, whether anticipatory (such as for an appointment) or retrospective, generally arose from the moment and kept account of it. Using this book in conjunction with the watch (usually located in a nearby pocket), readers could, and did, project and record their movements with new abundance and precision.[25]

They thus participated in the trend that J. Paul Hunter traces in texts over the course of the preceding decades. According to Hunter, "detailed circumstantiality was triumphing in the culture," and he ascribes this triumph to a growing appetite for "contemporaneity," "a large cultural embracing of the present moment" with (again to recall Johnson's phrase) "all the occurrences and observations" that attend upon it (*Before Novels* 168, 167−93, and passim). Just after mid-century Harrison's chronometer materialized this "embrace" as new technology, by pinpointing the moment more precisely and positing a "contemporaneity" operant around the globe (this may also explain the hold it took on the public imagination). Memorandum books inscribed the watch's oracular status more locally. In them, the new particularity took a simple form: more people writing more moments into more blank page space.

The memorandum book functioned as a social tool, but not as a social text; its notations of time remained in the pocket, inscribed and consulted solely by its owner. The triumph of circumstantiality occurred in texts whose authors intended them to be read by other eyes, and it took place (as Hunter shows in detail) against energetic opposition. Parties to the dispute recognized at least two components to the question: the new *mode* of time ("contemporaneity") that the literary culture craved, and the *forms* of time (often diurnal) by which the makers of texts sought both to satisfy and to sustain that craving. Hunter concentrates productively on the dispute about mode; I want here to focus on the disagreement about form. Opponents of "circumstantiality" (notably the Ancients engaged in battle with the Moderns) often cast diurnal narrative as a chief culprit. Yet as I've suggested, the dialectic took place within individual writers as well as between parties. Opponents of diurnal form acknowledged and even succumbed to its attractions, while champions confessed its liabilities. I want here to trace the dispute as it touched on three new modes of diurnal narrative that emerged in the first half of the century: the daily newspaper, the journal letter, and the published travel journal.

The charges against diurnal narrative stuck earliest and hardest to the daily newspaper, where the critique often took the form of a trope so commonplace that it was sometimes invoked by the journalists themselves. "We

News-Writers," wrote one of the fraternity in the *Daily Post* (the *Courant's* first diurnal competitor), "like Stage-Coaches, must go our Stages, even tho' we have no Passengers; but with this Disadvantage on our Side, that they may go empty, we not." [26] Since the daily sheets cannot travel "empty," particulars must be produced; under the pressure of time, they make their way into print. What the *Daily Post* voices as excuse, critics of the diurnal press commuted into satire. In *Spectator* 452 Pope joins Addison in an all-out assault on "our Modern News-mongers." "I have Thoughts," Pope writes, "of Publishing a daily Paper, which shall comprehend in it all the most remarkable Occurrences in every little Town, Village and Hamlet, that lie within ten Miles of *London*, or in other Words, within the verge of the Penny-Post. I have pitched upon this Scene of Intelligence for two Reasons; first, because the Carriage of Letters will be very cheap; and secondly, because I may receive them every Day. By this means my Readers will have their News fresh and fresh . . ." (4.92). Describing his mock project, Pope makes clear that the pointless comprehensiveness of the information ("all the . . . Occurrences" in "every little Town") will follow as a direct result from the compulsion to gather and distribute it every day. The daily paper virtually demands this descent into triviality because there is not worthwhile matter sufficient to meet so insistent a schedule of publication.[27] The imperative of the time form has now trumped the question of what might be fit (or in Defoe's term, "useful") to print. "Fresh and fresh," an expression widely current, captures by its form the appetite for news delivered rapidly, serially, and paratactically, regardless how "remarkable" the "Occurrences" really are.

It is this rhythm for gathering particulars that Addison mocks in his preamble to Pope's letter. Readers of "History, Travels, and other Writings of the same kind," he argues, will "meet with much more pleasure and improvement, than in these Papers of the Week." History writing compacts, selects, and connects; the reader may take in "the News of a whole Campain, in less time than he now bestows upon the Products of any single Post . . . [His] Curiosity is raised and satisfied every Moment . . . without being detained in a State of Uncertainty from Day to Day. . . . [T]he Mind is not here kept in a perpetual Gape after Knowledge, nor punished with that Eternal Thirst, which is the Portion of all our Modern News-mongers and Coffee-house Politicians" (4.91). Addison here anticipates Defoe's distinction between the maker of the "critical Minute" and the keeper of an "exact Journal." That his critique appears within the medium of a daily

Spectator, with visual and commercial links to the *Daily Courant*, accords with the paper's—and the Augustans'—long-standing strategy with respect to "News-mongers": adopt the format to subvert the substance and deride the practice. At the same time, the kinship of venue gives vent to possible ambivalence: Addison and Pope are participating in the diurnal rhythm whose narrative consequences they energetically mock.

Pope's satire, though, registers the power of the phenomenon it opposes. In manuscript as well as print, the culture's participation in diurnal texts was becoming so wholehearted, varied, and widespread as both to motivate the mockery and call its efficacy into question. The daily paper Pope derides had firmly demonstrated both the possibility and the commercial appeal of continuous narrative unfolding over successive days. In the course of the century, readers and writers manifested their pleasure in the paradigm several ways. First, they supplied an expanding market for the diurnal paper itself: in 1703 London had one daily paper, in 1741 six, and in 1792 there were twelve (some of which now appeared on Sundays as well).[28] Second, in increasing numbers, writers narrated their own lives day by day in manuscript journals, recounting all days (and in some cases "all" of each day) for the full duration of the manuscript; the present-focused particularity in which Pepys had dealt with unprecedented abundance a century before was now a fairly familiar practice.[29] Third, and perhaps most significant, the keepers of manuscript journals now often wrote not merely to record a diurnally structured narrative but also to impart it, in the hybrid form colloquially called a journal letter. When Pope keys his mock newspaper to the operations of the "Penny-Post" and the inexpensive daily "Carriage of Letters," he is touching upon one of the main prompters for the presence of detailed circumstantiality and diurnal form in manuscript narrative. The post office functions as middle term in Pope's derisive précis of the new dispensation whereby ephemera achieve unwarranted permanence. As mere gossip, "the most remarkable Occurrences in every little Town, Village and Hamlet" would be trivial but evanescent. As "Letters" they become lasting; as print they are laughable.

By Swift's reckoning, on the other hand, the distinction in modes made a genuine difference: a manuscript letter might justify detailed diurnality in ways that print could not. In print, for example, Swift uses the journal form satirically (as did Addison in the journal of the "sober Citizen") as a means of mocking the culture's predisposition to the inconsequential. In his verse "Journal of a Modern Lady" (1729) Swift deploys the journal's characteristic attention to the temporal and the particular to itemize the ways in which the lady and her companions contrive to misspend their time ("how should I, alas! relate, / The Sum of all their senseless Prate" [140−41]).[30] Even the title links diurnal structure with the "Modern" mode. In his manuscript journal letters to Esther Johnson, though, Swift produces a copious, even compulsive, day by day account of his own doings. Two stretches of such text survive, both published posthumously: the two-year tract (probably incomplete) now called the *Journal to Stella* (composed 1710−13) and the much shorter "Holyhead Journal" (1727). Hunter remarks that Swift's ambivalence about "modernist values" surpasses Pope's in two ways: he is "more divided temperamentally," experiencing a stronger attraction to them, but (perhaps for that reason) "even more ruthless" in his denunciations (163). Swift's two surviving clusters of journal letters both show him to be deeply engaged in the modern practice of daily particularizing, but each cluster enacts one side of his ambivalence: in the earlier text he delights in the practice; in the later text he reviles it. The different circumstances that produce these opposed responses, and the language that enacts them, suggest how strongly the journal form has become identified for Swift as exclusively a medium of the social, as distinguished from the solitary (e.g., Pepys's diary) or the public (Pope's imaginary gossip paper). Only as a means of intimacy, couched in a manuscript dispatched by its author to a cherished recipient, can a minutely detailed daily narrative purge the taint of modernity to fulfill a viable function. Swift's conduct of his journal letters, inflected by his ambivalence as an Ancient, enacts responses to diurnal form that would become more widespread later in the century, bringing pleasure and misgiving to the increasing numbers who produced journal letters in both manuscript and print.

The *Journal to Stella* unfolds in the years when the *Courant*, the *Tatler*, and the *Spectator* had brought both the narrative of news and the discourse of the self up to diurnal speed. The *Journal* is mindful of its print counterparts (Swift, involved with Addison and Steele as friend and occasional contributor, mentions the essay papers often) and it strives to outdo them in frequency and continuity: "I always begin my last [i.e., my next letter] the same day I ended my former," Swift writes, so that "I shall always be in conversation with MD, and MD with Presto."[31] Swift comes close to Pepys in some of the rules governing paper space and time. He often writes both evening and morning, mails each sheet as it is filled, and narrates each succeeding day for more than two years (until an attack of shingles forces him onto a slightly more sporadic schedule). Early letters express misgivings about the way the timing of the text dictates its length. At one point Swift asks, "Tell me, do you like this journal way of writing? Is it not tedious and dull?" (20). And later he comments, "I can't tell whether you like these journal letters: I believe they would be dull to me to read them over; but, perhaps, little MD is pleased to know how Presto passes his time in her absence" (35). Even before receiving what was doubtless a reassuring response, Swift goes on to experiment with ways in which the temporality of the new form might abet the intimacy of the correspondents. Like Harrison later in the century, he seeks to parlay a steady continuity into a space-subsuming contemporaneity by constructing textual moments that he in London can occupy in tandem with Rebecca Dingley and Esther Johnson in Dublin. He contrives, for example, to simulate second sight and inform the women of what they are doing at the exact instant of his writing, and later gloats at having done so: "Did you smoak [guess] in my last how I told you the very day and the place you were playing at ombre? But I interlined and altered a little, after I had received a letter from Mr. Manley, that said you were at it in his house, while he was writing to me; but without his help I guess'd within one day" (51). By the same token, he often narrates the moment of writing with as much immediacy and particularity as he can muster. He begins an entry "Is that tobacco at the top of the paper, or what? I don't remember I slobbered" (56), and goes on to report the opening of a letter from Johnson and Dingley: "Oh, I won't open it yet! yes I will! no I won't; I am going; I can't stay till I turn over [i.e., to the next page]. What shall I do? My fingers itch; and I now have it in my left hand; and now I'll open it this very moment.—I have just got it, and am cracking the seal, and can't imagine what's in it . . ." (57). The narrative tempo (Genette's term for the proportion of word count to duration narrated), along with the implicit physical awkwardness attendant on writing while doing something else at the same time, anticipate by nearly half a century not only Samuel Richardson's policy of writing "to the moment" but the comic excesses of slow motion present-tense reportage by which Fielding (in *Shamela*) and Sterne parodied this new textual timing. In the other historical direction, Swift replicates the premise that underlies Pepys's uncharacteristic account of the passing bellman (i.e., "this is going on while I write")—but with significant variation. Pepys writes to enclose the moment, Swift to transmit it. Pursuing those ends, Pepys writes in the past tense, Swift in the present, which allows no distance between the doing and the writing, the writing and the reading. By textual tricks of contemporaneity, Swift enacts intimacy.[32]

Swift's only other surviving diurnal dispatches, published posthumously as the "Holyhead Journal," mark the collapse of this construct. Rushing from London to Dublin in September 1727 in hope and fear at the news of his beloved Stella's mortal illness, Swift found himself stranded by bad weather at Holyhead for six days, each of which he accounts for in prose inscribed on some loose leaves of paper and addressed to Stella, who he greatly fears will not live to see the narrative or its author: the question of contemporaneity is now wide open, and fraught with pain. As in his earlier journal from London, Swift deals abundantly in particulars, but this time he repeatedly recoils from them, and apologizes for them.

> Tuesd. 26th. I am forced to wear a shirt 3 days; for fear of being lowsy. I was sparing of them all the way. It was a mercy there were 6 clean when I left London . . . I got anoth^r Loyn of mutton, but so tough I could not chew it, and drank my 2d pint of wine. . . . It raind all night, and hath rained since dinner. But now the sun shines, and I will take my afternoons walk. It was fairer and milder weather than yesterday, yet the Captain never dreams of Sailing. To say the truth Michaelmas is the worst season in the year. Is this strange stuff? Why, what would you have me do. I have writt verses, and put down hints till I am weary. I see no creature, I cannot read by candle-light. Sleeping will make me sick. . . .
>
> The Days are short, and I have five hours at night to spend by my self before I go to bed. I should be glad to converse with Farmers or shopkeepers, but none of them speak English. A Dog is better company than the Vicar, for I rememb^r him of old. What can I do but write every thing that comes into my head. . . .
>
> [M]y hat is worn to pieces by answering the civilityes of the poor inhabitants as they pass by. The women might be safe enough, who all wear hats yet never pull them off, if the dirty streets did not foul their petticoats by courtisying so low. Look you; be not impatient, for I onely wait till my watch marks 10, and then I will give you ease, and my self sleep, if I can.[33]

The question "do you like this journal way of writing?" so early and easily laid to rest in the *Journal to Stella*, reappears here as a source of constant vexation, to be answered only in the negative. Michael Rosenblum has argued well that the crises of narrative self-doubt in the "Holyhead Journal" reflect larger, pressing cultural uncertainties about the emergent role of detailed circumstantiality in storytelling.[34] Swift, he suggests, here "writes against his own intuition about what is worth remarking upon," and is "uneasy that his performance has fallen below the threshold" that divides those matters that merit narration from those that do not. I think that the precedent of the *Journal to Stella* complicates this claim, because there Swift deals at the same level of personal detail, but with a very different affect. It is true (as Rosenblum suggests) that the exciting years in London supplied narrative matter far more appealing to Swift than anything he can find during the dismal week at Holyhead. Still, Rosenblum's threshold of significance does not appear to account for the difference between the tobacco and slobber that Swift is pleased to note at London, and the sweaty shirt he apologizes for mentioning in Wales. The distinction between the journals seems to have less to do with the question of the "tellable" and more to do with the circumstances of the "telling-to"—the question of whether the text will find its audience. Swift is fairly sure that the page mentioning (and marked by) tobacco will reach Stella (only the inefficacy of the post could interfere). He knows, though, that the sheet mentioning the shirt may not, and that even if Stella still lives, she will not receive these pages until he delivers them himself (they cannot stand in for him).

In the "Holyhead Journal," the ebbing of the journal letter's social function recasts its temporal form as an embarrassment and a catastrophe. In the *Journal to Stella*, the writing up of each day fills time three ways, first as duration, then as representation, then as transmission. The act of writing takes time, which Swift often delights to detail in slow motion, as in his description of opening the letters; it represents time, as prose fills the page in sections headed by successive dates; and the page once filled transmits Swift's time to Esther Johnson in the running simulation of simultaneity he contrives. Now that the prospect of transmission stands under the local curtailment of the weather and the larger threat of death, all that is left of the earlier journal letter's process is duration and representation; deprived of its third support, the structure topples. Scribbling "till my watch marks 10," Swift makes clear that he writes not because the day demands prose representation, but because it allows no other activity but such representation: "What can I do but write every thing that comes into my head." It is the solitude of the production, and not the "untellability" of the particulars, that pulls the text below Rosenblum's threshold of acceptable endeavor. Swift's recurrent self-reproach implicitly rejects the narrative contract that produces a diary like Pepys's, which abstracts the continuous temporal from the social, which must record the day simply because it is a day, and which must be inscribed in the invisibility of code so that it can be written down fully (Swift's little language, by contrast, is a means of textual intimacy among several psyches—"PMD"—rather than secrecy within one). In the "Holyhead Journal," the dilemma of diurnal form, shorn of its sole solution in the social, intensifies into nightmare. Writing up the days and scorning himself for doing so, Swift produces an essay in—and explicitly about—the futility of recording diurnal details without the clear prospect of imparting them. The solitary setting down of small things in daily measures, which pleased Pepys (an early Modern), torments Swift (a central Augustan).

If Swift's journal letters reject the model of the private diary, they resist also the opposite extreme: the possibility of publication. At one point in the "Holyhead Journal," Swift remarks sarcastically that he "will have [the journal] printed to satisfy the Kingdom" (205). The joke smacks of overcompensation, substituting a mass audience for the one reader whose imminent disappearance he dreads. In practical reality, of course, Swift envisioned no such destiny for any of his journal letters. His biographer Irvin Ehrenpreis surmises that Swift held onto the *Journal to Stella* (while destroying the rest of his correspondence with her) because he "planned to use these letters as sources" for a projected history or memoir (lightly marked excisions in the manuscript suggest that Swift may have begun to winnow away the intimacies that would be irrelevant in such a book).[35] Such culling of personal manuscripts had long formed part of history writing (Pepys had projected a similar process), and accorded well with the widespread conviction, voiced by Addison and implied by Pope in the *Spectator* quoted earlier, that almost any selective narrative ("History, Travel, and other Writings") was to be preferred over indiscriminate "Day to Day" installments delivered by the "Post." By such a reckoning, journal letters ran much the same risk as newspapers and newsletters: of a detailed circumstantiality that rendered them unfit for print.

That Swift concurred in this view is suggested by evidence both within his journal manuscripts and beyond them. The "Holyhead Journal," with its passing joke about publication, begins with a paragraph whose historical relation to the rest of the text is uncertain, but whose thematic connection is strong. In it, Swift decries Pope, Gay, and others for naming in print too many hack writers, and thereby according them undeserved access to the attention of posterity.[36] As in the journal that follows, Swift argues here that some things ought perhaps to go unwritten, and certainly unpublished. In print, Swift like Pope pits "detailed circumstantiality" against itself, deploying it not only as an all-purpose satiric tool for itemizing sundry follies and indulgences, but also (and often in the same breath) as a means for mocking his culture's growing appetite for published minutiae.[37] The wholesale purveyance of particulars by the press is a "Modern" madness. In a world so perversely inundated with unsorted minutiae, the published journal letter (quite apart from any question of unwanted self-revelation) can find no honorable place.[38]

It does, though, find a comfortable commercial niche. By mid-century the published collection of a traveler's journal letters had supplanted the navigation-centered sea journal as the most popular diurnal mode in travel writing. In their highly conventionalized prefatory remarks, the writers in this new mode tell roughly the same story, epitomized here by one of the most successful of them, Patrick Brydone: "The Author wrote [these journal letters] for the amusement of his friends, and as an assistance to his memory . . . he can with truth declare that they never were intended for publication."[39] The text "never should have seen the light" but for the insistence of its initial readers; deferring to their wishes, the author now presents his letters "to the Public with the greatest diffidence" (A3r, A4r). This rationale sustains some differentiation between the categories of social manuscript and public print, but with a view towards their continuity rather than their containment. Jonas Hanway, for example, first addresses his journal letters to individual friends, then has them privately printed for distribution as gifts, and only then ushers them into the bookseller's hands as A Journal of Eight Days Journey. This sequence articulates with unusual clarity the thinking common to most of the preambles, in which the journal lettrist depicts the original recipient (or circle of recipients) as a kind of market test group, a miniature public whose enthusiastic response has warranted (or even demanded) a wider publication.

Nonetheless, as the Swiftian distinction between the social and the public began to dissolve, Popean misgivings about the consequences persisted. The journal lettrists readily reiterated the sea navigators' rationale that diurnal writing offered them the most commodious structure available. Copiousness and variety were their selling points too, and the succession of dated days offered the most convenient kind of packaging. Still, the liabilities of such abundance were recognized by those who chose to publish in the form as well as by those (like Swift and Pope) who ridiculed such publication: a structure capable of accommodating "*all* occurrences and observation" stipulates no theoretical limit as to what the day's text can contain, how long it should run, or at what narrative tempo. In a literary culture where much in the way of detail was desired, and where diurnal form seemed peculiarly able to deliver it, how much was too much? No journal lettrist published without parading his or her alertness to this problem of plenitude as a kind of credential, a reason to read further.

One line of argument held that the hybrid genre itself imposed redemptive constraints. Hanway makes this case in his opening letter:

> I was in a mood to scribble; and I had a further reason for writing, and that
> not the worst: *I had something to say.*
>
> But, Madam, a mere journal, without any striking occurrence, could
> have given me as little pleasure in writing, as you in reading. I therefore
> threw this in the form of *letters*; if there is any spirit in them, it is derived
> entirely from the persons to whom they are addressed.[40]

The letter's concern for the attention span, interests, and "spirit" of its reader will offset the "mere journal's" potential for quotidian prolixity.[41] Even the term "journal" as then understood could accommodate a measure of retroactive self-restraint. In Johnson's *Dictionary* definition—"an account of daily transactions"—the placement of the adjective leaves open the length of time between the event and the record (the account itself need not be written daily) and the unspecified interval might allow for retrospective mediation between the infinite particularity of the original transaction and the judiciously culled (though still date structured) narrative.

When ushering their manuscripts into print, most journal lettrists felt compelled to promise their readers such mediation in some form. The conventional topos of modesty (e.g., Brydone's insistence on his "diffidence") customarily came packaged with what might be called a redaction trope: the author's assertion that the original letters had been remade on their way to publication. This practice, too, had clear precedent in the sea journals, whose captain-composers presented themselves as mediating between the forms of text produced by seamen aboard ship and those savored by readers on land. Dampier explains that "I have frequently . . . divested my self of Sea Phrases, to gratify the Land Reader" (A3v). Cooke assures his reader first that "the Journal it self . . . was exactly kep't all the Time we were Aboard," and then that he has substantially remade the text out of fear that "a continu'd Account of Winds, Latitudes, Longitudes, and such other Maritime Particulars . . . might prove heavy and tiresome" to most who bought the book (1.B3v). The idea that continuity combined with particularity might produce weariness passed readily into the prefatory rhetoric of the later land-based travel journal. In his non-epistolary *Journal of a Voyage to Lisbon* (1755), Henry Fielding presents as his first qualification a propensity to leave things out:

> To make a traveller an agreeable companion to a man of sense, it is neces-
> sary, not only that he should have seen much, but that he should have over-
> looked much of what he hath seen. . . .
>   [Many travel writers] waste their time and paper with recording things
> and facts of so common a kind, that they challenge no other right of being
> remembered than as they had the honour of having happened to the author,
> to whom nothing seems trivial that in any manner happens to himself. Of
> such consequence do his own actions appear to one of this kind, that he
> would probably think himself guilty of infidelity should he omit the minut-
> est thing in the detail of his journal. That the fact is true is sufficient to give
> it a place there, without any consideration whether it is capable of pleasing
> or surprising, of diverting or informing, the reader.[42]

Here (as in similar remarks in *Tom Jones*) Fielding treats "overlooking" as a talent that should precede composition, so that no "merely common inci-
dent" will find its way onto the page in the first place (188).[43] In the absence of that gift, the journal writer's personal particulars threaten to become not merely tedious but opaque: they preclude the reader's view of the country traversed or of the culture encountered. This was Defoe's point too in mocking the "exact Journalist" who names his dates, inn, and wine, but nothing beyond them.

Fielding's denunciation found many echoes. The charge of an occlusive egotism dogs travel journals and journal letters to the end of the century. " 'I said, and I did, and I went' " exclaims the fictitious, Shandean sojourner in Samuel Paterson's parody of travel books, *Another Traveller!* "—[H]ow shall I get rid of it?—for the soul of me I can't tell!"[44] To echo the phrase Johnson used in advising his friend Baretti, a structure of time that is open to "all occurrences and observations" within the writer's experience is in danger of textualizing far too many, and of burying the way things *are* (in that country now) under a heap of details about the way things *were* (on the particular cluster of days the writer traveled there). Journal lettrists, though, were in a position to promise a kind of double winnowing: first at the moment of composition, next at that of revision. Many aver, with

Samuel Sharp, that their manuscript letters have been "altered and curtailed" for the reader's sake; they assume that such trimming is a requisite component of the transition to print.[45]

Curtailment, though, is not the only mode of redaction; often the original text undergoes expansion. Cooke, for example, inserts long chapters of "Description" derived from other authorities in order (he says in his preface) to break the monotony of "continu'd . . . Maritime particulars" that were intrinsic to the sea journal; Brydone notes that "in transcribing [his journal letters] for the press, he found it necessary both to retrench and amplify" so that "some of the letters have been extended much beyond their original length" (vi); Samuel Sharp insists that "had I foreseen . . . Publication [which, like so many journal lettrists, he did not], I might . . . have been circumstantial in many Particulars where I am now superficial" (A2r). Whatever the promised mode of redaction—abridgment, enlargement, or some combination—the recurrence of the topos underscores the widespread assumption that a manuscript narrative structured by days and dates should not pass into print without careful mediation. Even here, though, the dilemma of diurnal form registers strongly, for the journal lettrists often work to dissolve the impression of redaction. A few lines after Brydone declares that he has "found it necessary to retrench and to amplify," he contrives to limit the effect of the admission: "But he would not venture to new-model [the letters]; apprehending, that what they might gain in form and expression, they would probably lose in ease and simplicity; and well knowing that the original impressions are better described at the moment they are felt, than from the most exact recollection" (vii). Brydone here fosters the impression that he has left his original descriptions largely intact. The move exploits the doubleness intrinsic to the eighteenth-century conception of a journal as the product either of immediacy (an account written daily) or of retrospective reconsideration ("an account of daily transactions" produced at a remove). The journal lettrists want it both ways. Most often, they cultivate the sense that the text they offer both is and is not "the Journal it self" (in Cooke's half-promissory phrase). In the redaction topos journal lettrists found a way out of the dilemma without really resolving it. They just passed it on to their readers, who were left to surmise at every passage as to what may have been "altered," "curtailed," enlarged, or cut.

In the rare instances where the redaction topos was not invoked, the author was left to work out the dilemma another way. Giuseppe Baretti, for example, took Johnson's advice, kept "an exact journal," and produced the "book of travels" his friend had foreseen: *A Journey from London to Genoa, through England, Portugal, Spain and France* (1770). The text takes the form of copious daily letters addressed to the Italian friends who await Baretti at the end of his journey. He says nothing about the amount or kind of redaction that has preceded publication. He justifies his choice of form another way—by the dignity of the Johnsonian imprimatur: "It was he [Johnson] that exhorted me to write daily, and with all possible minuteness. . . . To his injunctions I have kept as close as I was able. . . ." Immediately, though, Baretti begins to reckon up the possible costs of this obeisance: "[M]y only fear upon this occasion, is, that some want of dexterity in the management of my narratives may justly have subjected me to the charge of egotism, as I am convinced that I have passed too frequently from my subject to myself, and made myself as much too often the hero of my own story. Yet this fear is not so predominant, as to exclude the hope that such an impropriety will be overlooked if I have but succeeded in the main point, and effectually assisted the imagination of my reader to form an idea tolerably just of Spain. . . ."[46] Baretti expresses the now familiar fear associated with diurnal travel writing: that the exact journal (as Defoe and Fielding foretold) attracts particulars concerning "myself" over those concerning "my subject," and so its "narratives" (the odd plural is significant) need careful "management" if they are not to occlude the unified "idea" of the place that is the professed goal of the prose. Yet as Baretti observes, the fear does not predominate. It is mitigated by the hope that the method of "writ[ing] daily, and with all possible minuteness" provides a matchless means of "assist[ing] the imagination," and it is overruled by the hint that the potential "impropriety" of the process is actually a key element in its efficacy. Baretti speaks (to reverse Defoe's phrasing) for a now expanding group of "Authors and Readers" of *kindred* "Genius." Decades after the deaths of Defoe, Swift, Pope, and Fielding, their darkest forebodings were confirmed by the writers and readers of travel journals, who purported to find in the detailed circumstantiality of the daily account a source of both entertainment and instruction. As Charles Batten observes, Sterne's *Sentimental Journey* had extravagantly upped the ante on autobiographical particulars in books of travel; and in the 1770s many authors followed suit in journal form.[47]

When, in the middle of that decade, Samuel Johnson undertook to write his only book of travels, both his method and his structure differed drastically from those he had recommended to his friend a few years before.

Diurnal Dialectic in the Western Islands

Johnson and Boswell traveled together through Scotland in the fall of 1773, both of them writing all the while. In a letter to Hester Thrale written about halfway through the journey, Johnson notes, "I keep a book of remarks, and Boswel writes a regular journal of our travels. . . ."[1] In Johnson's phrasing, he and Boswell become Defoe's "two Gentlemen" incarnate, the one critical and selective, the other copious and exact. In the century's final quarter they play out with unprecedented intricacy the tensions of time and form that Defoe had laid out in its first.

Each writer went on to produce a print account of the trip grounded in the mode of his own manuscript, and each had read a version of the other's account before revising and publishing his own. The intricate, intertwined production of the two texts culminates and transmutes the century's debate about the diurnal. In their collaborative process of writing, rethinking, and revising the accounts, both Johnson and Boswell are clearly drawn towards the other's mode of recording, and so they manifest the ambivalence that marks so much of the debate about diurnal form. Their finished texts, though, pull pointedly in opposite directions, Johnson's towards the critical, Boswell towards the diaristic. As the contemporary response to the books makes clear, their dialogue did not resolve the debate, but it enlarged the field of possibility. Boswell's *Journal* and the *Life of Johnson* (for which the

Journal is a calculated test of both narrative and commercial possibilities)
extended the culture's apprehensions (both its understanding and its alarm)
as to what diurnal form could do in print.

"THE NEGATIVE CATALOGUE":
JOHNSON'S *JOURNEY* AND THE CHOICE OF FORM

In *A Journey to the Western Islands of Scotland* (1775) Johnson suppresses the
indices of time and favors those of space. He heads each section of his account with the name of the town or island visited; he deals so scantily in
dates and durations that it becomes much easier for the reader to gauge
where the travelers went than when they were there. Johnson's headings
aspire to show the reader Scotland itself rather than the recent trip through
it—to emphasize what is there now rather than what (briefly) happened
there then. Johnson's choice of form seems unremarkable; it simply accords
with Defoe's prescription in the *Tour* half a century earlier. The *Journey* tacitly takes its place within the long-running tradition of critical travel writing
that now opposed the more recent journalistic tradition by emphasizing the
transparency of description, analysis, and discourse over the opacity of particularized narrative.

Johnson's choice is worth investigating, however. Not only does it stand
in opposition to the advice he often gave to others—advice that in Baretti's
case had recently produced a travel book in the newer, journal letter mode;
it also sorts oddly with a discovery of form that Johnson made during the
trip itself. When informing Thrale about his "book of remarks" and Boswell's "regular journal," he does not mention the most unusual of the journey's documents—the one he is writing at that moment. The sentence appears in one of the continuous, copious journal letters that Johnson wrote
and dispatched to Thrale throughout the Hebridean tour—the only sustained diurnal narrative of the self that he would ever produce. Johnson,
that is, had produced a travel text in the newer mode—a mode also radically new for him—before publishing one, only a year later, in the older. At
one point, he probably envisioned a continuity between the texts: he asked
Thrale pointedly to keep his journal letters, apparently expecting to draw
on them for the published *Journey*. Yet the book differs so drastically from
the letters that scholars dispute the degree to which Johnson used the manuscripts, or even whether he used them at all.[2]

Johnson presents perhaps the most fully documented instance in the eighteenth century of the dilemma of diurnal form as it operated within a single

reader and writer. In his journal letters to Thrale he resolves the dilemma one way; in the published account another. I want to argue that the life-long dilemma that precedes the book and the choice of form within the book shape the *Journey* in ways hitherto unexamined. They inform Johnson's presentation of himself and of Scotland, and they constitute one of the most important, and hidden, links between the two. For Johnson, questions that had long been active and agitating in connection with writing about himself carry over into his writing about Scotland, both during the process that produces the *Journey* and in the published text. Over the decades that preceded the *Journey,* such questions often presented themselves as an ambivalence about the value and viability of diurnal form.

Traces of the dilemma appear early in Johnson's career. In a 1743 letter to Edward Cave, editor of the *Gentleman's Magazine*, Johnson contemplates his projected history of the British Parliament (never completed) and puzzles over the question of structure, page arrangement, and dates: "I think the insertion of the exact dates of the most important events in the margin or of so many events as may enable the reader to regulate the order of facts with sufficient exactness the proper medium between a Journal which has regard only to time, and a history which ranges facts according to their dependence on each other, and postpones or anticipates according to the convenience of narration. I think our work ought to partake of the spirit of History which is contrary to minute exactness, and of the regularity of a Journal which is inconsistent with Spirit. For this Reason I neither admit numbers or dates nor reject them" (*Letters* 1.34). The passage outlines advantages and liabilities for both methods, but its structure provides clues as to which will dominate. In the first sentence, Johnson limns the conditions governing "history" at more than twice the length he devotes to the "Journal," and the proportion accords with his claims for the greater intricacy and authorial freedom of the former (his thinking here echoes Addison's three decades earlier, in the *Spectator*'s mockery of the daily newspaper). The journal, which "has regard only to time," deals in "regularity" and "minute exactness" at the expense of elasticity and "Spirit" (expressively capitalized). The first sentence's tentative findings in favor of history, though, fade in the careful balance of the second sentence, and the deliberate irresolution of the third. Having explored the puzzle, Johnson expressly leaves it unsolved; he even implicitly retracts at the end of the paragraph the solution (dates in the margin) he proposed at the start.

In connection with published narratives, the dilemma is familiar enough.

For Johnson, though, it extended into the sphere of private, manuscript self-recording. "He told me," Boswell reports in the *Life*, "that he had twelve or fourteen times attempted to keep a journal of his life, but never could persevere." [3] The attempts date back at least to 1729 (his twenty-first year) and persist until his death in 1784. Johnson's explanation for the pattern—his failure to "persevere"—is at once authentic and insufficient. As both a mode and a sign of self-discipline, the idea of a regular journal exerted genuine appeal. Sloth per se would not likely have been the sole preventative. Johnson often saw and depicted himself as an idler, even in connection with authorial work that had made his perseverance legendary (the *Dictionary*, for example). Johnson's resistance to "the regularity of a Journal," a practice "which has regard only to time," derives at least in part from conflicts about the proper use and inscription of time itself, conflicts then at large in the culture between the new fascination with the present moment and long-standing religious traditions that stipulated a focus on futurity and eternity. Johnson's highly charged and abundantly documented engagements with both temporalities make his particular approach to the diurnal dilemma an interesting index—partly typical, partly idiosyncratic—of the shifts in time consciousness that were taking place around him.

A few passages from his surviving diaries will suggest both the persistence of Johnson's attempts to keep a regular journal and the characteristic temporal gestures that undo them.

> Jan. 1, 1753, N.S. . . . I hope from this day to keep the resolutions made at my Wife's death
>> To rise early
>> To lose no time
>> To keep a Journal.

> Sept. 18. 1760 . . .
>> To keep Journal.
>> To oppose laziness, by doing what is to be done.

> January 2. [1781] I rose according to my resolution, and am now to begin another year. I hope with amendment of life.—I will not despair. Help me, help me, O my God. My hope is
> . . .
>> 3 To keep a Journal.
>> 4 To study Religion
>> 5 To avoid Idleness

[next entry in MS:] APR. 13 GOOD FRIDAY 1781. I forgot my Prayer and
resolutions till two days ago I found this paper.[4]

At these moments and at many others like them, the diaries serve as a repository of resolutions, which is to say that they pointedly select as their
topics those activities and routines that are not yet in place, which do not
obtain in the present. Pitching the temporal focus forward, the resolutions
leave the present unaccounted for, except (by implication) as a site of emptiness, failure, and intent. When Johnson opts instead to write the present
rather than the future, he often inscribes emptiness by a different strategy—
that of omission. On his birthday in 1780, for example, he laments that "I
have not at all studied; nor written diligently. I have [the lives of] Swift and
Pope yet to write . . ." (1.301). As his editors point out, Johnson here
neglects to mention that these two are the only *Lives* left to write in the
series of fifty-two, and that (his exaggerated self-reproach to the contrary
notwithstanding) he has already been working on them for some time
(1.302). Whether by the tacit elimination of accomplishments, or the express enumeration of resolutions, Johnson's entries write the present as
empty, and only the future as (potentially) full. But his diaries most often
index emptiness by mere absence, by establishing a plan in which every day
is to be registered as text, and then for most days supplying no text at all.

    As the 1781 entry makes clear, the desire to "keep a Journal" always
forms part of the larger resolve "to study Religion" (in the sense of pursuing
it by all means available). For Johnson the imperative to keep a diary is
roughly the same as that enunciated by John Fuller more than a century
before: "Thy Audit will be strict, so should thy accounts be." This formulation pitches the entire diaristic endeavor towards the future, infusing piety
with panic at the audit yet to come, and produces in Johnson some of the
same effects I traced earlier in connection with the Puritan diarists. The
writer's aspiration towards comprehensiveness in the record ("*all* God's gracious dealings," writes Beadle to his followers; "*all* occurrences and observations," writes Johnson to Baretti), coupled with a discouraging experience of the task's impossibility, produces in practice an occasionality often
laced with self-reproach. Johnson's attempts at self-recording cluster thickest
around certain signal dates—New Year's, Easter, the anniversaries of his
wife's death and of his own birth—all the while declaring his resolve to
escape from occasion into continuity. The pressure of futurity, invoked to
ensure piety, renders the present-centered diary problematic.

In Johnson's world, the ideas of futurity and continuity occupy a far more cluttered landscape of textual forms and time forms than they had a century before; within this new configuration Johnson's temporal dilemmas appear distinctive and in some respects retrograde. J. G. A. Pocock has argued at length that in the early eighteenth century, the new commerce of speculation produced "something society had never possessed before, the image of a secular and historical future" that posed a danger by its attractiveness: "Government stock is a promise to repay at a future date; from the inception and development of the National Debt, it is known that this date will in reality never be reached, but the tokens of repayment are exchangeable at a market price in the present. . . . Property . . . has ceased to be real and has become not merely mobile but imaginary. Specialized, acquisitive and post-civic man has ceased to be virtuous, not only in the formal sense that he has become the creature of his own hopes and fears; he does not even live in the present, except as constituted by his fantasies concerning a future."[5] The dissolution of classical civic virtue in the sea of speculation, Pocock argues, necessitated a countermove aimed at "the stabilisation of this pathological condition": a new construction of virtue that focused attention away from the future and towards the present moment (113). If "the secular future was open and indefinite," the model for moving towards and through it might be found in "the frugal merchant . . . whose willingness to invest in the future was the product of his confidence in the present" (100). In another work, Pocock points out that "the Augustan journalists and critics were the first intellectuals on record to express an entirely secular awareness of social and economic changes going on in their society"; he repeatedly shows Addison and Defoe diagnosing the "pathological condition" of rampant futurity and prescribing the remedy of a prudent focus on the present.[6] Though Pocock doesn't say so, the time form of Augustan journalism did much to abet these economic ministrations. The close succession of dates at the top of the thrice-weekly *Review* and the daily *Spectator* consistently grounded their "Speculations" (in Addison's frequent term) about trade (and everything else) within the local limits of the present.

By contrast, when Johnson takes up the periodical essay (on the same thrice-weekly schedule as Defoe), he turns it to a different temporal purpose. Early on in *Rambler* 5 he diagnoses roughly the same "pathology"—a nearly irresistible attraction to the promises held out by an imaginary future—but he construes it less as a function of the local economy than as a universal condition of the psyche.

Every man is sufficiently discontented with some circumstances of his present state, to suffer his imagination to range more or less in quest of future happiness, and to fix upon some point of time, in which, by the removal of the inconvenience which now perplexes him, or acquisition of the advantage which he at present wants, he shall find the condition of his life very much improved.

   When this time . . . at last arrives, it generally comes without the blessing for which it was desired.[7]

In the passage from the *Rambler*, as in Johnson's diaries, the designated "point in time" is the least stable and substantial element in the scheme. It figures first as the object of anticipatory illusion (thereby emptying the actual present of all activity but the future preoccupation); when it arrives, it figures only as the site of lack, the place from which to register the absence of the "blessing." As remedy, Johnson prescribes not a renewed attention to the present (as do Pocock's Augustans), but an alternate, radically religious preoccupation with the future. Two *Ramblers* later he sets down a proposition he will frequently repeat, within the paper and beyond: "The great task of him, who conducts his life by the precepts of religion, is to make the future predominate over the present . . ." to the extent that "temporal hope or fear" will hold no sway over the mind (3.37–38). Where Addison and Defoe seek to stabilize the "pathological condition" of their culture's obsession with the future by cultivating a fruitful tension with the present, Johnson sees the solution in a contest between two futures: the fallible prospects conjured up by human imagination and the sturdy course constructed by the Christian God. The distinction between the sobriety and weight of the *Rambler* and the comparative lightness of its pre-eminent predecessor the *Spectator* became a commonplace among readers in the eighteenth century and after; it derives as much from a fundamental difference of temporality as of prose style.[8] Johnson imports a seventeenth-century sense of time, steeped in the tradition of *memento mori*, into an eighteenth-century periodical medium.

   The same mixed temporality that shaped Johnson's practice in periodical texts informed his encounters with chronometric tools. At age fifty-nine he bought his first watch, an expensive and efficient instrument adorned in such a way as to provide both a modern tracking of time and a pre-modern vision of temporality. It bore, Boswell reports, "a short Greek inscription, taken from the New Testament, Νυξ γαρ ερχεται, being the first words of our

SAVIOUR's solemn admonition to the improvement of that time which is allowed us to prepare for eternity: 'the night cometh, when no man can work'" (*Life* 2.57). The three Greek words, encircled by the dial's twelve numbers and traversed by the mechanism's two hands, enforce as visible sign an admonition that Johnson cites repeatedly in his periodical prose;[9] they insist that the data of the minute hand be construed *sub specie aeternitatis*. The dial plate prompts the mind to a series of actions, demanding first that it reinterpret the precisely marked present point of time as part of an inexorable movement, by which multiple nights and manifold endings—of a day, of a life, of all sublunary time—are always approaching; next, that it conjure up yet another, collateral ending—the uninscribed second clause of Christ's sentence—and so experience, through an instantaneous act of verbal memory, the incipience of all closures, syntactic and apocalyptic; and finally, that it bring this fresh apprehension to bear upon the present reckoning so that the telling of time may conduce to the fullness of time, by prompting the watch's wearer to "prepare for eternity." About three years later Johnson chose to "la[y] aside this dial-plate," reasoning (as he explained to Boswell) that the inscription "might do very well upon a clock which a man keeps in his closet; but to have it upon his watch which he carries about with him, and which is often looked at by others, might be censured as ostentatious" (2.57). Johnson's misgiving arises in effect from an odd anachronism in his timepiece. Before the pendulum and the balance spring, when watches were even more often "looked at by others," the ornamentation of the instrument as a *memento mori* was commonplace. In an early seventeenth-century context, Johnson's inscription would not be ostentatious at all; only the inner machinery, steadily ticking, would astonish. Where for Pepys the minute hand was the hypnotic innovation, by Johnson's time the mechanism and its accompanying markings were altogether familiar; the Greek inscription was the novelty, and so would naturally compel the most attention (thus once again according the future priority over the present). Johnson's encounter with the dial plate—its costly acquisition and its deliberate laying aside—indicates both his attraction to the modes of modern chronometry and his alienation from them.

That alienation comes through even more explicitly in Johnson's one intervention into the protracted quest for the longitude. In 1755, he published a pamphlet entitled *An Account of an Attempt to Ascertain the Longitude at Sea, by an Exact Theory of the Variation of the Magnetical Needle*. He signed it not with his own name but with that of his housekeeper's father, Zachariah Williams, who had worked on a magnetic theory for nearly half of his eighty-odd years and for whom Johnson now sought to secure some recognition and reward. Johnson begins the pamphlet by writing off the two alternative categories of solution to the scientific problem. The approach through measurements of space, by readings of the sky, is "utterly impracticable to the Sailor, tost upon the Water, ill provided with Instruments, and not very skilful in their Application." In Harrison's approach through measurements of time, it is the instruments themselves that are at risk: "The Hope of an accurate Clock or Time-keeper is more specious. But when I [i.e., Williams] begun these Studies, no Movements had yet been made that were not evidently unaccurate and uncertain: And even of the mechanical Labours which I now hear so loudly celebrated, when I consider the Obstruction of Movements by Friction, the Waste of their Parts by Attrition, the various Pressure of the Atmosphere, the Effects of different Effluvia upon Metals, the Power of Heat and Cold upon all Matter, the Changes of Gravitation and the Hazard of Concussion, I cannot but fear that they will supply the World with another Instance of fruitless Ingenuity, though I hope they will not leave upon this Country the Reproach of unrewarded Diligence." [10] In the fantasy Johnson here sets forth, new instruments matchless for their capacity to track the present are utterly annihilated by the "Obstruction," "Waste," "Pressure," and "Hazard" of a projected future. Time and circumstance destroy the timekeeper. Johnson casts Williams's "autobiography" in the same temporal mold. Having begun the project fifty years ago, imbued with "incessant Diligence" and "the Zeal of Enquiry," Williams now writes in despair of present recognition, to inform fickle "Posterity . . . that Mankind had once within their Reach an easy Method of discovering the Longitude" (14, 16). By pamphlet's end, he has run the course that Johnson forecasts from the beginning for Harrison and his watches: from a state of "specious Hope" to one of "fruitless Ingenuity." Johnson's ways of constructing in text the time of Harrison's watches and of Williams's "autobiography" contrast sharply with the newer temporality, centered on the present, that the longitude problem was pushing towards the center of public attention. The clockmaker's "mechanical Labours" are in Johnson's words "*now* loudly celebrated" precisely because they may produce a newly reliable definition of the *now*. Contemplating this present-centered project, Johnson writes only an imaginary future, generated by oscillations between "hope" and "fear." For many of Johnson's potential readers, the long-running competition and the newly precise chronometry that came out of it had helped to cultivate a conception of time different from that set forth in Johnson's *Account*: as a medium of tangible precisions and uses, not large cruelties and betrayals. Where the culture increasingly construes time as sheer *chronos*, newly powerful and enabling, Johnson insistently reinstates the long-standing (classical, medieval, and Renaissance) paradigm of *tempus edax*, debilitating and destructive. Johnson pitches his *Account* against the chronometer in more ways than one—not only against its prospects as a solution to the longitude, but against the kind of time it was widely understood to tell, the model of time, *now*-centered, that it was helping to propound.

As we have seen, that model of time was evident everywhere in texts. In the *Account*, Johnson objects to Harrison's timekeepers on the same general principle by which he resists the structure of the "regular Journal" in his letter to Cave: both methods, "having regard only to Time," accord time too much power. In his published writings, as on his pocket watch, Johnson tempers eighteenth-century constructions of a secular temporality (imaged in the watch's now commonplace *Tick, Tick, Tick*) with seventeenth-century visions of eternity (when "the night cometh"). He contrives by text "to make the future predominate over the present," and this temporal predilection, I have suggested, undoes his diary-keeping despite (even during) his repeated attempts. But Johnson's resistance to diurnal form—even in the teeth of his own desire to write it—is rooted not only in his religion but in his literary and social convictions as well. As he suggests to Cave, a form that regards only time precludes that subtler selectivity "which ranges facts according to their dependence on each other." Yet when Johnson recommends journal-keeping to others (as he often does), he advocates no such selectivity. Instead, he figures the form as a repository of indiscriminate plenitude: "you should write down every thing that you remember, for you cannot judge at first what is good or bad" (*Life* 2.217); "keep a journal fully and minutely" (2.385); "do not remit the practice of writing down occurrences as they arise, and be very punctual in annexing the dates" (*Letters* 3.69). The enthusiasm here runs counter to other convictions Johnson voiced as to how writing should work. Like Pope in his mockery of the daily press, Johnson perceives that a prose form produced daily positively invites an indiscriminate choice of subjects that can easily become ridiculous, pointless, or even dangerous. In his *Rambler* essay on novels, for example, Johnson argues that "If the world be promiscuously described, I cannot see of what use it can be to read the account; or why it may not be as safe to turn the eye immediately upon mankind, as upon a mirror which shows all that presents itself without discrimination" (*R* 4; 3.22). That "promiscuous description" that Johnson here abjures for other written accounts of reality forms the chief feature of diary-keeping as he envisions and recommends it.

What partly exempts the journal from this general censure is (once again) a question of futurity—in this case, of the text's envisioned destiny. In Johnson's usual reckoning, journals (unlike novels) were to be read by no eyes other than the author's own. As a means of keeping the practice private, Johnson repeatedly recommended that the manuscript be destroyed at the writer's death (advice he eventually followed, burning two volumes of autobiographical writings during his final illness). Once submitted to public scrutiny, the journal risks the charge of "promiscuous" description. "It is a very good custom to keep a journal for a man's own use," Johnson remarks, and cites a specific example: "There is nothing wonderful in the journal which we see Swift kept in London, for it contains slight topicks, and it might soon be written" (*Life* 4.177). The problem is not that he kept it but that we see it (it had first appeared in 1766), as Johnson explains while elaborating this dismissal in his "Life of Swift" (1781): "In the midst of his power and his politicks, he kept a journal . . . and transmitted it to Mrs. Johnson and Mrs. Dingley, to whom he knew that whatever befel him was interesting, and no accounts could be too minute. Whether these diurnal trifles were properly exposed to eyes which had never received any pleasure from the presence of the Dean, may be reasonably doubted. They have, however, some odd attraction . . ." (*Lives* 3.23). With that "however," the dilemma of the diurnal returns, and suggests an affinity between the authors which the posthumous publication of the *Journal to Stella* slightly obscures, but which the unseen "Holyhead Journal" helps to highlight. For Johnson as for Swift, the activity of keeping a diary is hedged about with problems of literary decorum—questions as to what all those "diurnal trifles" are for, and misgivings that they may be for naught.

The two writers construct diaristic decorum differently—for Johnson, the journal's proper venue is purely solitary, while for Swift it is purely social—but they concur in precluding publication. In the "Holyhead Journal" Swift speaks derisively of publication ("I will have it printed to satisfy the Kingdom"), as a way of dispelling the pressing question of decorum, of whether he should be writing the text at all ("What would you have me do[?]"). In Johnson's attempts at journal-keeping, I think the counter-mode of publication pressed more constantly. Johnson's own rules for diary-keeping ("write down everything") ran counter to those he had implemented in a long career as published author ("range facts according to their dependence on each other"); for him the decorum associated with print helped frustrate the aspiration towards diurnal manuscript. At the same time, by viewing the diary as purely private, Johnson effectively sealed the genre off from his steady attention and best endeavor; he writes a fuller, more fluent manuscript prose when he is addressing an audience, as in letters or on those religious occasions in his diary when he transmutes his entries into prayers, which are directed to God rather than himself. In Swift's short "Holyhead Journal" and in Johnson's lifelong diary attempts, we can see the dilemmas of diurnal form played out in two different directions, each unsatisfactory to the author. Bereft of an audience, Swift thinks he shouldn't write a journal, and compulsively does. Johnson thinks he should, and mostly doesn't.

The lives of the two writers each provided a single period of exemption from these concerns. Johnson's journal letters from the Hebrides to Hester Thrale are for him what the *Journal to Stella* was for Swift: a stretch of time and text in which journalizing became a matter of ease rather than anguish. In Johnson's case, this aberration arose from a combination of three factors having to do with his concept of the travel journal, his circumstances in the Hebrides, and his choice of correspondent. First, Johnson conceived the travel journal as the sole exception to his rule of diaristic secrecy, viewing it as a social rather than private text, written to be read, not concealed. To an old friend traveling the continent with his daughter Johnson writes: "Miss Nancy has doubtless kept a constant and copious journal. She must not expect to be welcome when she returns without a great mass of information. . . . If she has satisfied herself with hints, instead of full representations, let her supply the deficiencies now while her memory is yet fresh, and while her father's memory may help her" (*Letters* 3.107). As a repository of experience gathered abroad, potentially collaborative in itself, the "constant and copious journal" is to function as a means of social transmission, bearing information and securing welcome. In Johnson's constructions of the diary, distance makes a difference.

So, on the tour to Scotland, did the logistics of transmission. Upon arriving in the Hebrides, Johnson discovered that the post came "but once a week" (*Letters* 2.69). That tempo was too slow, and the distance from London too great, to allow for the rapid exchange of letters to which he and Thrale had become accustomed during the previous eight years of their friendship. Having been caught short in one letter, with little time to write and much to say before the weekly post departed, he resolved in the next to try a new rate of output. "I am so vexed at the necessity of sending yesterday so short a Letter, that I purpose to get a long letter beforehand by writing something every day, which I may the more easily do, as a cold makes me now too deaf to take the usual pleasure in conversation" (2.71). The plan to write something every day promptly materializes as a novel design for writing the day itself: the letter goes on to provide the longest, most detailed account of a single day (1 September 1773) to be found anywhere in Johnson's writings, and it initiates a series of letters that cover the remainder of the trip in a calendrically ordered sequence of dated entries—the closest thing to a "constant and copious journal" that Johnson was ever to produce.

The language in which Johnson stages this turning point helps reconcile the singular journal practice he here commences with his long-standing scruples about the form. He portrays himself as writing from a position of silence and solitude (he is "deaf" and bereft of "conversation"). By this reckoning the act of writing something every day will remain the sustained, solitary action that Johnson construes as necessary but burdensome in diary-keeping; this time, though, the endeavor will be punctuated, and the burden relieved, by the weekly postal action of dispatch and transmission. At the same time, by depicting himself as withdrawing from "conversation" into daily self-recording, Johnson can construe himself as solving another problem of long standing. Reckoned by a page count of published output, the previous eight years have been the least productive of his career. During that period (as Boswell amply documents), Johnson has emphatically given over his time to the "usual pleasure" of conversation rather than the pain of writing, troubled all the while by the conviction that when the day produces no text, it is doomed to evanescence. A large part of the diary's appeal for Johnson inheres in its potential to counter such oblivion. In his hands, though (as we have seen), the practice exacerbates the problem rather than solves it, both because he writes up particular days as empty (rich in resolutions for the future but devoid of present particulars) and because he leaves most days unwritten altogether. Now sequestered in a double silence, "deaf" and therefore dumb, withdrawn from the local conversation of his cohorts, and deprived even of his customary epistolary "conversation" with Thrale (enacted as the quick exchange of shorter letters), Johnson finds it necessary, possible, and pleasant to write his days as full.

The final decisive factor in the fullness of the journal letters is their recipient. Beginning long before the tour, as Bruce Redford shows, the act of
writing to Hester Thrale had elicited from Johnson a prose unmatched in all
his oeuvre for ease and transparency: particular, paratactic, and personal.[11]
In the letters from the Hebrides, the journal structure, the daily schedule,
and the week-long installments afforded this unique register of writing the
widest scope of operation it was ever to attain. Both travelers saw that something extraordinary was taking place in Johnson's new, abundant manuscript.
"Dr. Johnson wrote a long letter to Mrs. Thrale," Boswell remarks in his
journal. "I wondered to see him write so much so easily."[12] Writing to
Thrale's husband towards the end of the trip, Johnson expressed the hope
that "my mistress keeps all my very long letters, longer than I ever wrote
before" (2.100). What had made them so long (and prompted Johnson's
pleonastic modification here) was their hybrid status as both journal and
letter. In later years, when traveling with the Thrales to Wales and to Paris,
Johnson would produce a much scantier diary; his auditor accompanied him,
and conversation reasserted its ascendancy over self-recording in script.

In his travel letters to Thrale, Johnson rejoices at his new, prolific incur-
sion into diurnal form, but even here he keeps track of the dialectic. Early
in the trip he sets down a small, temporal self-deprecation. "We dined at
York, and went on to Northallerton, a place of which I know nothing but
that it afforded us a lodging on Monday night, and about two hundred and
seventy years ago, gave birth to Roger Ascham" (2.48). Johnson here casts
himself in the role that Defoe mocked in the person of the *Tour's* "exact"
journalist: the superficial traveler who notes everything about his own movements, and only the most obtrusive facts about the place he moves through.
Johnson too had made fun of this figure in periodical prose. In *Idler* 97 he
decried those travel writers who "crowd the world with their itineraries":
"Those who sit idle at home, and are curious to know what is done or
suffered in distant countries, may be informed by one of these wanderers,
that on a certain day he set out early with the caravan, and in the first hour's
march saw, towards the south, a hill covered with trees . . . that an hour
after he saw something to the right which looked at a distance like a castle
with towers. . . ."[13] The satire here works partly by syntax. The traveler
himself appears as the subject of every sentence ("he saw . . . an hour after he saw . . ."), while *what* he saw languishes in subordinate clauses. By
preoccupying himself too minutely with the temporal details of his particular sojourn, the traveler has rendered the significant life of the place

visited inaccessible to the reader. Johnson levels against all itinerists the same charges that were long lodged specifically against those who chose to publish their travel journals.

When reading particular travel journals, Johnson drew sharper discriminations. He despised, for example, Jonas Hanway's coy implementation of the "my-friends-forced-me-to-publish-this" convention.[14] He admired, though, the book of travel letters Brydone had produced by amplifying his manuscript representations of the terrain he traveled through, and thus enhancing the transparency of his text (*Life* 2.346). When he set about writing his own *Journey*, he extended the policy of amplification much farther, shedding the time structure of the journal letters in which he had first recounted his experience. His book's opening sentence propounds a tacit credo, a subliminal topos of redaction: "I had desired to visit the *Hebrides*, or Western Islands of Scotland, so long, that I scarcely remember how the wish was originally excited. . . ."[15] Johnson deals generously in geographical appositives (giving the reader both names for the Islands) but restrainedly in autobiography: what he "scarcely remembers" he will not trouble to reconstruct. This book, he implies, will narrate not the time of the writer, but the time of the place: it will be a *Journey*, not a journal. His ambivalence about diurnal form allows him to admire Brydone's travel diary (which had successfully countered the "egotistic" dangers of the diary form); but it precludes his publishing in such a form himself. Read alongside the journal letters to Thrale, the *Journey* seems to constantly strip away particulars: names, dates, and the details of dinners and conversations, which are abundant in the manuscript, disappear in the book in favor of sustained meditations (greatly expanded in comparison with the letters) on the history and culture of the people and the place.

Dropping the diurnal form almost altogether, Johnson pursues (more zealously than the itinerists he has mocked) the rewards of amplification by a strategy of omission. In the course of the *Journey*, though, something curious happens which became central to the controversy the book soon aroused among Scottish and English readers. As the book progresses, the Englishman's amplifications focus with increasing intensity on what he construes as Scottish omissions—on those things that in his opinion the people of the Highlands have failed to do: plant trees, open windows, write history. In one of the book's most persistent strains, Johnson meditates on Scotland as a place of lack. I want to consider here the ways in which the cultural omissions that Johnson perceives in Scotland align with the long history of textual omissions which has produced the present book: the diaries that construct emptiness either by writing away the present or by leaving it un-written altogether, the sudden, surprising abundance of the journal letters to Thrale, and the subsequent "emptying" of personal particulars that John-son deems necessary in the production of the present book. In the making of the *Journey*, Johnson's recent constructions of Scottish "vacuity" (a re-current term) converge with his lifelong agitations in the dialectic of diur-nal form.

In his *Journey* as in his journals, Johnson is preoccupied with two kinds of relations between writing and vacuity: with the noting of phenomena that are not (or not yet) present (as in the diaries' recurrent clusters of resolu-tions), and with the failure to write the present (as in his many unrecorded days) that results in its effectual annihilation. In the *Journey* as in the diaries, Johnson approves of the former mode and is alarmed at the latter. To reckon present lacunae may promote future fullness, but to leave the present un-tracked as text is to lose it altogether.

By Johnson's own criteria, noting absences forms part of the travel writ-er's project of transparency. He takes the absence of trees, for example, as a cue for an admonitory lesson in transcultural imagination. To the armchair "speculatists" who "hastily . . . censure that . . . laziness that has omitted for so long a time so easy an improvement" to the landscape as the planting of trees would provide, Johnson responds with a rhetoric meant in part to convey the particular time consciousness that poverty enforces in Scotland:

> [T]here is a frightful interval between the seed and timber. He that calcu-lates the growth of trees, has the unwelcome remembrance of the shortness of life driven hard upon him. . . .
>
> Plantation is naturally the employment of a mind unburdened with care, and vacant to futurity, saturated with present good, and at leisure to derive gratification from the prospect of posterity. He that pines with hunger, is in little care how others shall be fed. The poor man is seldom studious to make his grandson rich. (*Journey* 116)

Johnson aims here to reap the fruits of his own choice of form. He has resisted the preoccupation with the particulars of his own temporal experi-ence precisely in order to imagine—and to adjure readers to imagine—what it is like to inhabit a texture of time other than their own. Yet the passage ends up constructing a temporality closely in accord with Johnson's own. It contrasts two ways in which futurity impinges on the present, one beneficent ("the prospect of prosperity"), the other immobilizing ("the shortness of life"). Immobility prevails: the paragraph closes with the failure of permanence and a lack of legacy. In the sequence of the prose, alternate futures converge in present vacancy; just such a structure produces the emptying of the present in Johnson's attempts to keep a journal, to record himself.

Earlier, in discussing the "incommodiousness of the Scotch windows" (which he says are built in such a way as to make opening them both difficult and rare), Johnson makes explicit the link he sees between his practice of noting omissions and his desire for transparency in travel writing, in the name of an accurate anthropology:

> The necessity of ventilating human habitations has not yet been found by our northern neighbours; and even in houses well built and elegantly furnished, a stranger may be sometimes forgiven, if he allows himself to wish for fresher air.
>
> These diminutive observations [about the windows] seem to take away something from the dignity of writing, and therefore are never communicated but with hesitation, and a little fear of abasement and contempt. But it must be remembered, that life consists not of a series of illustrious actions, or elegant enjoyments; the greater part of our time passes in compliance with necessities, in the performance of daily duties, in the removal of small inconveniencies, in the procurement of petty pleasures; and we are well or ill at ease, as the main stream of life glides on smoothly, or is ruffled by small obstacles and frequent interruption. The true state of every nation is the state of common life. (*Journey* 16)

The argument here echoes closely that of *Rambler* 60 twenty years earlier, in which Johnson exalts as the most valuable elements of any biography the "domestick privacies" and "minute details of daily life" (3.321). In context, though, the passage in the *Journey* also inverts the *Rambler*'s argument in a way that accords with Johnson's long resistance to setting down the "minute details" of his own daily life. "These diminutive observations" deal (again) with what is not there: open windows, "fresher air." A little later in the *Journey*, when he and Boswell arrive "weary and peevish" at an inn, eagerly hoping for sustenance, Johnson sums up the innkeeper's response in the form of a small joke: "Of the provisions the negative catalogue was very copious" (38). The humor of the line arises first from the push of the modifiers, the surprise yoking of the idea of plenitude with that of absence. But the real curiosity inheres in the noun that comes between. Johnson conjures up a document devoted exclusively to enumerating not a collection of things that exist (which is what catalogues usually count), but an aggregate of things that do not. In the next sentence, Johnson provides a sample: "Here was no meat, no milk, no bread, no eggs, no wine." The joke on the innkeeper adumbrates a crucial component of Johnson's own method in the *Journey*. Where other travel writers catalogue the "minute details" of their private itineraries to the point of opacity, Johnson intermittently produces a "negative catalogue," "very copious" in "diminutive observations" aimed at delineating—but also, as in the joke, deploring—"the state of common life."

By the ornate phrasing of the joke, Johnson maintains his distance from both the innkeeper and his own predicament at the inn. When he shifts his attention to another kind of link between writing and negation, the difference between himself and the Scottish culture he observes narrows considerably. The *Journey* treats as a recurrent theme an argument that had inflected Johnson's many attempts to keep a journal, and that had also cropped up constantly in his advocacy of diary-keeping to others: that manuscript, and not memory or speech, offers the only safe repository for experience and knowledge; and hence that those "occurrences and observations" that pass into either silence or talk but not into text are as good as lost. Late in the *Journey*, recounting a day's sailing among several islands, Johnson advances this argument as a way of explaining the inaccuracy of most travel writing, and then implicates himself in the problem:

> An observer deeply impressed by any remarkable spectacle, does not suppose, that the traces will soon vanish from his mind, and having commonly no great convenience for writing, defers the description to a time of more leisure, and better accommodation.
>
> He who has not made the experiment, or who is not accustomed to require rigorous accuracy from himself, will scarcely believe how much a few hours take from certainty of knowledge, and distinctness of imagery; how the succession of objects will be broken, how separate parts will be confused, and how many particular features and discriminations will be compressed and conglobated into one gross and general idea.
>
> . . .

I committed the fault which I have just been censuring, in neglecting, as we passed, to note the series of [i.e., the names of the islands passed during] this placid navigation. (122–23)

Here near the end of the book, this mild but deep-rooted self-censure links Johnson not only with other travel writers, but also with the Highland culture he is writing about. For Johnson, one of the defining features of Scottish culture is its absence of written records and its consequent reliance on the unstable continuities of orality and memory. Johnson sounds the note early, lamenting the limitations of the first book about the Hebrides, Martin Martin's *Description of the Western Islands of Scotland* (1703), which, though written by "an inhabitant of *Sky*" who "lived in the last century when the chiefs of the clans had lost little of their original influence," fails to provide details about a clan culture that the Union and Culloden have now utterly transformed.

> [Martin] probably had not knowledge of the world sufficient to qualify him for judging what would deserve or gain the attention of mankind. The mode of life which was familiar to himself, he did not suppose unknown to others, nor imagined that he could give pleasure by telling that of which it was, in his little country, impossible to be ignorant.
>
> What he has neglected cannot now be performed. In nations, where there is hardly the use of letters, what is once out of sight is lost for ever.
>
> (*Journey* 52)

Here, as in the passage on the absent trees, Johnson essays an empathic psychology, reconstructing the motives that account for the gap. The passage on Johnson's own failure to note the details of his navigation turns empathy into identification: Johnson too commits the fault that he here regrets in Martin.

Between the two passages, though, the argument about the impermanence of the unwritten becomes the central instrument in the *Journey*'s central negation: Johnson denies, over the vociferous objections of his Scots hosts, the authenticity of the *Ancient Poetry* of Ossian, which James Macpherson had published (and in Johnson's opinion forged) to great acclaim during the previous decade.

> I suppose my opinion of the poems of Ossian is already discovered. I believe they never existed in any other form than that which we have seen. The editor, or author, never could shew the original; nor can it be shewn

by any other. . . . [The poems are] too long to be remembered, and the
language formerly had nothing written.
. . .

   The Scots have something to plead for their easy reception of an improbable fiction: they are seduced by their fondness for their supposed ances-
tors. A Scotchman must be a very sturdy moralist, who does not love *Scotland* better than truth. . . . To be ignorant is painful; but it is dangerous to
quiet our uneasiness by the delusive opiate of hasty persuasion.
   . . . If we know little of the ancient Highlanders, let us not fill the vacuity with *Ossian.* (98–99)

This time, the exculpatory psychologizing excuses the "easy reception" by a
combination of overt insult and sharp contrast: the sturdy *English* moralist
loves truth better than Scotland, and insists on the "vacuity" of Scottish
history.

For readers late in the eighteenth century and for critics late in the twentieth, the Ossian controversy operates as the test case through which to
assess the whole function of the *Journey*'s "negative catalogue." In recent
years Johnson's stance against Macpherson has attracted much astute political
and historical commentary. Kathryn Temple, for example, depicts his rejection of the Ossian poems and of the oral culture they purported to represent
as an attempt to impose, through English "cultural authority," a "construction of literary property" that emphatically valued writing over speech, an
attempt which Katie Trumpener sees as inadvertent proof "that it is possible
to observe with considerable precision the material conditions of a culture
without understanding the life, the dynamic or the possibilities of the culture
at all." [16] In order to situate Johnson's response to Ossian within the context
of the questions of writing and time that I have been exploring here, I would
like to make three observations. The first is that, as Trumpener suggests,
Johnson is correct on his own terms: James Macpherson drew on oral culture to create the poems, but he was also perpetrating a technical fraud, and
Johnson, by applying the deductive imagination to a question of time and
text, discovered more documentary "truth" than did Macpherson's adher-
ents. But the new scrutiny of the literary and national politics underlying
Johnson's rejection usefully points up the extent to which he is here diverg-
ing from his own precepts about travel, travel writing, and imagined time.
By constructing an opposition between a love of Scotland and a love of truth,
Johnson preempts the possibility of any sustained, sympathetic imagining of

the ways in which those who love Scotland imagine the Scots' past; the temporal transparency that Johnson advocates for the traveler in *Idler* 97 gives way to a kind of temporal opacity. Where the Scots, aided by Ossian, imagine past time as a plenum of talk and poems, Johnson insists, in the *Journey*'s last words on the subject, on a temporal "vacuity."

Second, the terms in which he dismisses Ossian align the gesture with a construction of time that operates (as I have tried to show) through much of the *Journey*, and through much of Johnson's other writing as well: the process whereby the imagination, operating upon time, discovers vacuity rather than fullness. As he examines local ruins and inquires into local self-deceptions, Johnson perceives again and again what he perceived also in Harrison's time-keepers twenty years before: instances of "fruitless Ingenuity" and of the inevitability of decay, surrounded and indeed produced by oscillations between hope and fear. In this way too the argument for temporal transparency in *Idler* 97 gives way to a practice more complex. Johnson reads into Scotland a particularly constructed tragedy of time that he has often read and written before.

Finally, I suggest that for Johnson, the question of the evanescence, permanence, or legitimacy of an oral culture is inextricable from issues of time and self-recording that have run through his own life, and that in a certain way culminate in Scotland. Johnson's diaries, I have shown, are haunted by the sense that not to write experience—to leave it oral, aural, and evanescent—is at the very least to register a vacuity in time, or worse to create one by textual silence. Like Swift, though, Johnson is also haunted by a set of literary values that regard "promiscuous" narrative with suspicion. In the later years of his career, Johnson has by his own severely critical analysis allowed his life of talk (long conversations late into the night) to preponderate over his life of writing. In Scotland, though, circumstance has presented Johnson with a solution to these quandaries unmatched in his experience before or after. Like Swift in the *Journal to Stella*, he is performing with ink and paper the particulars of his days for a distant, valued reader, and he is at the same time watching Boswell write his talk abundantly into text every evening. Through Boswell, Johnson's private oral culture that is for him a point of anxiety is being translated into a written system, day by day, in Scotland as never before. In rejecting the oral culture of the Highlands, he is consigning it to the doom he has himself momentarily escaped: the doom of the unwritten, of time left vacuous by the absence of text.

The questions of silence, speech, and writing, of negation and affirmation, converge again in a moment at the very end of the *Journey*. Johnson records his visit to Thomas Braidwood's Edinburgh school for the deaf, and narrates his encounter with a student there: "One of the young Ladies had her slate before her, on which I wrote a question consisting of three figures, to be multiplied by two figures. She looked upon it, and quivering her fingers in a manner which I thought very pretty, but of which I know not whether it was art or play, multiplied the sum regularly in two lines, observing the decimal place; but did not add the two lines together, probably disdaining so easy an operation. I pointed at the place where the sum total should stand, and she noted it with such expedition as seemed to shew that she had it only to write" (136). In the last moments of the book's last narrative, Johnson concentrates, as he did in the analysis of Ossian, on the transmutation of the unwritten into the written, on the way inscription fills vacuity. As with Ossian, Johnson assumes that only text can transform a void into a plenum: he points "to the place where the sum total should stand," desiring to see the blank space filled. He delineates a different mode of filling than the one that (as he sees it) produced Macpherson's poems. The Braidwood pupil writes not a historical fiction but a fresh reality: the "sum total" that solves the problem Johnson just set for her, a text whose truth is easily established within the terms of the system in which it appears. The mute pupil's final inscription fills an audible as well as a visible void. Like the *Spectator*'s prose, it articulates discoveries that must otherwise have remained sequestered; it reaches past speech (which Johnson distrusts as a venue of truth) into silence (where truths may repose uncorrupted, awaiting articulation). But what interests Johnson most about her writing is that it is so "easy an operation." At Johnson's request, she inscribes what is already present in her mind: "she had it only to write," and "with such expedition" as compels Johnson's sustained attention.

In the next, penultimate paragraph, the Braidwood pupil becomes an emblem for the potential of plenitude in a place beset by "vacuity": "after having seen the deaf taught arithmetick, who would be afraid to cultivate the *Hebrides*?" (137). For Johnson as writer, the Hebrides themselves have already become a site for accomplishments that the pupil reenacts in miniature: a site for writing a running account of present realities in his journal letters to Thrale, and thereby filling a textual void that he had felt all his adult life, the absence of a "constant and copious" record of the self. At the inception of the first journal letter, Johnson described himself as momentarily "deaf": foregoing conversation, he is working directly from silence into script (like the Braidwood arithmetician), and for once in his life he

does so with "expedition" (recording "so much so easily," as Boswell remarks). The history of the *Journey*'s making suggests that Johnson also projects onto the Braidwood pupil (and hence onto the Hebrides) an image of
himself as writer, struggling with the problem of self-inscription and (provisionally) solving it.

"THE OCCURRENCES OF EACH PARTICULAR DAY": BOSWELL'S JOURNALS AND THE DISCOVERY OF FORM

Gathering and writing the material for his *Journey*, Johnson effectively sorts
the dialectic of diurnal form into its opposing terms. He dispatches something like an exact journal to Thrale, and a book of critical observations and
analysis to the public. At the same time, in his journal letters, Johnson participates (with a pride and satisfaction that surprised him) in the century's
most familiar way of accommodating and reconciling the dialectic: the hy-
bridization made possible by those two mixed forms, the journal letter addressed to and sculpted for a particular recipient, and the published travel
journal or (more often) the travel journal letter, accompanied through the
press by a redaction topos calculated to indemnify it against charges of over-
particularity, opacity, and egotism.

Boswell's *Journal of a Tour to the Hebrides with Samuel Johnson, LL.D.* (1785)
appears to play out the dialectic in the direction opposite to that Johnson
takes in the *Journey*. Published ten years after Johnson's book (and a few
months after his death), the *Journal* performs the travelers' companionship
as contrast: where Johnson's headings replicate those of the map, Boswell's
reproduce those of the calendar. By its structure of long entries under successive dates, the *Journal* bespeaks a simple, uncompromising commitment
to a particularized diurnal form. In fact, though, Boswell arrived at his
choice for the *Journal*'s form after decades of assiduous experimentation, in
manuscript and print, with the narrative possibilities of diurnal structure.
He is perhaps the century's most prolific inventor of new journal hybrids,
adding at least four combinations of his own to the catalogue. With each
invention, and increasingly over the series, Boswell sought to accommodate
the dialectic while giving its diurnal component a wider scope and larger
authority, allowing it to encroach upon, even to colonize, territory and tasks
traditionally reserved to other genres. The *Life of Johnson* is the last term in
the series, but the *Journal of a Tour to the Hebrides* is, I think, the most critical,
for two reasons: it claims the fullest print authority for diurnal structure
(allowing it to govern virtually the entire book) and it develops over the

longest time out of the most complex circumstances. Boswell writes it both with and against Johnson, whose *Journey* opts and argues for the opposite temporality, and whose intense ambivalence about diurnal form made him the incarnation of the dialectic. I want in this section to trace the route by which Boswell arrived at the structure of the published *Journal,* and to look at what he did with it once he had devised it.

In an essay on diaries composed in 1783, Boswell declared his devotion to the form.

> It is a work of very great labour and difficulty to keep a journal of life, oc-
> cupied in various pursuits, mingled with concomitant speculations and re-
> flections, in so much, that I do not think it possible to do it unless one has a
> peculiar talent for abridging. I have tried it in that way, . . . and I have thought
> my notes like portable soup, of which a little bit by being dissolved in wa-
> ter will make a good large dish; for their substance by being expanded in
> words would fill a volume. Sometimes it has occurred to me that a man
> should not live more than he can record, as a farmer should not have a
> larger crop than he can gather in. And I have regretted that there is no
> invention for getting an immediate and exact transcript of the mind, like
> that instrument by which a copy of a letter is at once taken off.[17]

In some respects, Boswell's theory of the genre here comes closer than any other pronouncement to the temporal practice that Pepys had devised 123 years earlier. Boswell, too, prizes complete and continuous representation so highly that he comes up with three metaphors in one paragraph—soup, crop, and cerebral transcript—in his attempt to express how those goals should be attained by text (and to acknowledge, in a rueful undertow, that they really can't). Like Pepys he recognizes the necessity "for abridging" but pursues the fiction that the abridgment can be reconstituted into fullness. And like Pepys in his final entry, Boswell plays figuratively with a parallel between the limits of the diary and those of the life it records. But Boswell goes further. Pepys tentatively equated the diary's ending with his own ("that course which is almost as much as to see myself go into my grave"). Boswell imagines granting the diary continuous arbitration over how much life he can live on any given day ("not . . . more than he can record").

By the time Boswell wrote the passage, it probably possessed for him a tincture of nostalgia. He had most fully realized its precepts twenty years earlier, at the very start of his career as diarist. The *London Journal* (1762), Boswell's first experiment in continuous and complete self-textualization, might best be described as an anti-hybrid. The process of its production separated out the two textual elements that had become fused in the now familiar structure of the journal letter. Boswell devised instead the journal with cover letter. He wrote up his days in great detail (now at leisure in London, he often had little else to do) and mailed the document in weekly packets, each accompanied by a freestanding letter, to John Johnston, a close friend who had remained in Scotland. Part of the point was to reinstate the autonomy of the journal. In his letters, Boswell addressed Johnston warmly, but in the pages of his diary he purported to write for himself, as though conscious of no other audience or addressee, though it is often easy to detect the points where the prospect of Johnston's reading put pressure on the discourse.[18]

Leisure was not the only factor in the *London Journal*'s copiousness. The scheme of postal "publication" fostered it too. In the journals that Boswell later wrote for himself alone, he did not write so fully. It is partly as a performance for Johnston that Boswell begins to absorb other genres within the *Journal*, establishing hegemony by heterogeneity. His imitations of the *Spectator* derive directly from a wounding remark of Johnston's: "my friend Johnston told me one day after my [previous] return from London that I had turned out different from what he imagined, as he thought I would resemble Mr. Addison. I laughed and threw out some loud sally of humour, but the observation struck deep" (*London* 62). By way of rebuttal, Boswell contrives a pointedly precise mimicry. In *Spectator* 1 Addison remarks that "Sometimes I smoak a Pipe at *Child's* [coffeehouse]; and whilst I seem attentive to nothing but the *Post-Man*, over-hear the Conversation of every Table in the Room" (1.4). Boswell devises a matching ritual, going to Child's every Saturday, eavesdropping on a conversation, and transcribing it for Johnston's delectation. The *Journal* incorporates the periodical essay in other ways as well, often suspending narrative for a few paragraphs of reflective and speculative essay-writing for which Addison clearly serves as model. Other genres too make their way into the entries. Boswell writes up his conversations in the format used for dramatic dialogue in play texts, and in less visible but more pervasive ways, he constantly attempts to approximate the narrative conditions of the novel, trying to plot a grand conclusion for his life story from the limited vantage of its early middle.[19] At the same time he assiduously adheres to Pepys's policy of accurately representing the ignorance of the designated moment, even when writing it up in retrospect.[20] More than any diarist of the period, perhaps, Boswell melds the temporality of *Tick, Tick, Tick* with an overriding impulse towards the sense of an ending.

Taken together, Boswell's fervent theory and lavish practice bespeak a deep engagement with diurnal form. At one point or another he manifests all the misgivings associated with the redaction topos: he decides that he will no longer set down "mere common trifling occurrences," determines that proceeding "regularly through the day would be too formal for this my journal," and fears on the other hand that the dull days of his convalescence from gonorrhea will not furnish substance for the entries he writes (*London* 274, 183, 178). Invariably, though, the practice itself pulls him back to plenitude and particularity, and so he rejoices, near the end of his London year, to discover that Johnson (whom he has recently met) appears to endorse precisely the kind of text he is composing:

> I told him that I had [kept a journal] ever since I left Scotland. He said he was very happy that I pursued so good a plan. And now, O my journal! art thou not highly dignified? Shalt thou not flourish tenfold? No former solicitations or censures could tempt me to lay thee aside; and now is there any argument which can outweigh the sanction of Mr. Samuel Johnson? He said indeed that I should keep it private, and that I might surely have a friend who would burn it in case of my death. For my own part, I have at present such an affection for this my journal that it shocks me to think of burning it. I rather encourage the idea of having it carefully laid up among the archives of Auchinleck. . . . I told Mr. Johnson that I put down all sorts of little incidents in it. "Sir," said he, "there is nothing too little for so little a creature as man." (*London* 305)

The conversation displays all the earmarks of Johnson's customary advocacy: the journal should be private, particular, and destroyed at death. As the passage proceeds, Boswell finds himself both rejoicing in Johnson's counsel and resisting it. He tentatively violates Johnson's injunction of secrecy by imagining his journal "among the archives," and he also defies it in the act of writing. Johnston will read this entry within the week—although Boswell does not admit as much to his new mentor. Eager for Johnson's unqualified approval, Boswell keeps secret his journal's lack of secrecy. The diurnal dialectic here becomes an element in Boswell's incipient friendship with Johnson.

In his second journal hybrid, Boswell sought to discover what the form could accomplish in print. At the age of 29, four years before the tour to the Hebrides, Boswell achieved literary fame and a lasting epithet ("Corsica Boswell") by a book whose title promised three genres in one volume: *An Account of Corsica; The Journal of a Tour to that Island, and Memoirs of Pascal Paoli*, the country's liberator. In fact the book was split into two sections rather than three. Boswell's *Journal* of his trip encompasses and includes his *Memoirs* of the hero; for the first time in public, he extends the territory of journal form in the direction of biographical portraiture. At the same time, he pointedly circumscribes his claims for the diurnal. He offsets his journal of personal travels and encounters by his more comprehensive and objective *Account* of the island, with which the book begins. Boswell is the first travel writer to accommodate the diurnal dialectic by this half-and-half structure of sutured forms; the success of *Corsica* made the strategy popular.[21] The book's design assumes, with Johnson, that a travel diary in its original form will impart an inadequate representation of place—and (as Fielding forewarned) a possibly boring one as well. Introducing his *Journal*, Boswell presents a rather extreme version of the redaction topos: "In writing this Journal, I shall not tire my readers with relating the occurrences of each particular day. It will be much more agreeable to them to have a free and continued account of what I saw or heard most worthy of observation."[22] The passage appears to promise some of that authorial transparency that Johnson advocated in the *Idler* and would try to implement six years later in the *Journey*. Although Boswell was working from copious diaries (now lost), he drops dates from his published book more thoroughly than even Johnson will. But Boswell performs his redaction with a difference. His editor Frederick Pottle notes that by emptying his account of particular dates, Boswell managed not to subdue self-celebration but to enhance it, for "by this method Boswell is able to give readers the impression that he spent a long time with Paoli. Actually he spent only about a week with him" (*Grand Tour* 154, n. 2). By many phrases in the published *Journal*, Boswell contrives to make the days of his visit seem more numerous than seven: "[Paoli] often talked to me of marriage . . ." (170); "I so far presumed upon his goodness to me as to take the liberty of asking him a thousand questions with regard to the most minute and private circumstances of his life" (184); "I thought him more than usually great and amiable when I was upon the eve of parting with him" (189). By such iterative formulations, Boswell stakes the *Journal*'s claim to work as *Memoir* too—by seeming to compass more time, the text doubles its identity as genre. Far from reducing the importance of the journal function, Boswell's redaction topos actually aggrandizes it.

This time, too, Johnson's reactions to Boswell's journal work effectively reanimated the questions surrounding the diurnal dialectic. While on Corsica, Boswell sent Johnson a letter containing a précis of his travels, followed by a characteristically jaunty and anxious toss of the gauntlet: "I dare to call this a spirited tour. I dare to challenge your approbation" (*Life* 2.3). Johnson's reply rehearsed old ambivalences a new way: "When you return, you will return to an unaltered, and I hope unalterable, friend. All that you have to fear from me is the vexation of disappointing me. No man loves to frustrate expectations which have been formed in his favour; and the pleasure which I promise myself from your journals and remarks is so great that perhaps no degree of attention or discernment will be sufficient to afford it. Come home, however, and take your chance" (*Corsica* 194). Here are all the familiar elements: the distinction between journals and remarks; the imperative to write extensively; the threat of disappointment, long operative in his own attempts to keep a diary, here emphatically projected onto Boswell—a threat founded in the fear that "perhaps no degree of attention" can fulfill an expectation insatiably "great." When *Corsica* came out, Johnson's reaction was again mixed. "Your History [i.e., the *Account*] is like other histories but your journal is in a very high degree curious and deligh[t]ful. There is between the history and the journal that difference which there will always be found between notions borrowed from without, and notions generated within. Your history was copied from books. Your journal rose out of your own experience and observation. You express images which operated strongly upon yourself and you have impressed them with great force upon your readers. I know not whether I could name any narrative by which curiosity is better excited or better gratified" (*Letters* 1.329). Johnson here praises Boswell's published *Journal* as he earlier (in the *London Journal*) endorsed his private diary-keeping. In doing so, he momentarily resolves the ambivalence he expressed decades before in his letter to Cave, on the basis of new criteria. There, the journal structure, "which has regard only to Time," precluded that "Spirit" that "History" achieves by selection and arrangement. Here, it is the history that lacks spirit and the journal that possesses it, by virtue of the immediacy and force of its images. As we have seen, though, the *Journal* that Johnson read supported this apparent reversal by suppressing its "regard to Time," omitting and rearranging (in Boswell's words) "the occurrences of each particular day."[23]

   Suppressing dates and details, Boswell acquired Johnson's approval of a hybrid *Journal* that doubled as biographical *Memoir*. In Boswell's next book of travels, where Johnson himself serves as subject, the questions of form, strategy, and decorum become more complex. They eventually produce the new hybrid of the *Journal of a Tour to the Hebrides*, in which, by contrast to *Corsica*, a scrupulously dated narrative of "the occurrences of each particular day" constitutes the text's structure, credentials, and main selling point. Late in 1784, in the days immediately following Johnson's death, Boswell received letters from his publisher imploring that he "hasten" both to prepare a large volume of Johnson's conversations and to announce his intention of writing a full biography. He proposed in reply a more measured undertaking. He would publish an account of his tour with Johnson as "a good Prelude to my large Work his *Life*." [24]

The question of how to make the tour into a book had intermittently preoccupied Boswell for the previous ten years. It persists even onto the published *Journal*'s title page, where Boswell quotes a querying quatrain from Pope's *Essay on Man*:

> O! while along the stream of time, thy name
> Expanded flies, and gathers all its fame,
> Say, shall my little bark attendant sail,
> Pursue the triumph and partake the gale?
>
> (*Essay* 4.383−86)

Pope seems confident (as usual) that the addressee (Bolingbroke) will answer in the affirmative. Boswell has reason to ask the question more urgently. A decade earlier, Boswell had summoned the passage to mind in connection with the confused beginnings of his book's gestation. It now compasses and epitomizes the long series of consultations, rethinkings, and reversals that produced the innovative hybrid of the published *Journal*.

Early on, Boswell conceived of his book in terms not of an intricate hybrid but of a simple pairing: he wanted to publish a text that would be read alongside Johnson's *Journey*. From the day of that book's publication (18 January 1775) Boswell began struggling to find a form of writing by which he could forge an alliance between the recollections of his daily record and those contained in Johnson's account. Having organized the tour in the first place, he now wanted to participate in its public rendition. Immediately upon receiving the proofs of the *Journey*, Boswell set about compiling and dispatching to the author a list of "Errata and Observations" which devoted special attention to correcting Johnson's vagueness or mistakes in narrating the particulars of the trip's timing. Where Johnson mentions a moment "early in the afternoon," Boswell queries, "Do you call it the *afternoon* before dinner?"; where the printer mistranscribed some of the few dates in Johnson's account, Boswell rushes in to set them right.[25] His corrections generally suggest the "regular Journalist" polishing the temporal particulars in a book that has less regard to time than does his own manuscript. His final emendation, though, reverses the pattern. Where Johnson in the *Journey*'s last words remarks that he has "seen but little," Boswell demurs: "Is not your concluding paragraph rather too modest? . . . [I]t is wonderful to consider the number & variety of minute objects which you have exactly delineated. . . . I can hardly conceive how in so short a time you acquired the knowledge of so many particulars."[26] The gesture combines reciprocity with denial. Boswell counters Johnson's closing construction of "vacuity" by insistently projecting the textual plenitude that has always constituted the chief principle of his own writing. He praises Johnson's *Journey* in the same terms that Johnson has used to praise his journals.

The "Errata," a series of short items indexed by the page and line numbers of Johnson's book, hardly constitute a literary performance in their own right, and as Boswell suggests in several letters to friends, his ambition soon turned to something more substantial: a book of "Remarks" to be published as a "Supplement" to Johnson's narrative.[27] Johnson, though, intended no such companion for his *Journey*, as Boswell learned on his next visit to London, two months after the book's publication: "As Mr. Johnson and I came along in the hackney-coach, he advised me not to show my journal to anybody, but bid me draw out of it what I thought might be published, and he would look it over. This he did upon my telling him that I was asked to publish; but he did not seem desirous that my little bark should 'pursue the triumph and partake the gale.' "[28] Boswell receives a disappointing negative in answer to Pope's question, and even Johnson's tepid encouragement appears to assume that this new text, like the Corsican *Journal*, will require careful extraction (he "bid me draw out of it what . . . might be published"), to the detriment of the diurnal form that structured the original. Yet as the day's narrative reveals, Boswell defies Johnson's injunction "not to show my journal to anybody" just minutes after he hears it. The hackney-coach in which the two converse is carrying them to Joshua Reynolds's where, with Johnson out of earshot, Boswell seizes the opportunity to read to the painter "some passages of my journal on the tour with Mr. Johnson, and he said, 'It is more entertaining than his' " (101–2). Boswell discerns that his small craft of daily narrative surpasses, in at least one respect and in one man's judgment, the formidable vessel it proposes to accompany. When the epigraph from Pope appears ten years later in the published *Journal*, it sustains this tacit gesture of defiance: Boswell has chosen to launch the "little bark" that Johnson did not encourage.

Even so, Boswell's first notion of how best to win approbation for his book, whether from Johnson or the public, entailed following Johnson's advice and recasting his raw travel diary into a form that Johnson had endorsed by example. There are two surviving manuscript leaves of a draft that Boswell wrote, perhaps as part of his projected "Supplement" in the year after the tour, or perhaps ten years later, in the months after Johnson's death, as an initial attempt at the book he had promised his publisher.[29] In either case, the draft takes a form different from that of Boswell's eventual book, but identical to Johnson's. Boswell has dropped the dates from their privileged position at the head of his diary entries and supplanted them with Scottish place names, a move that almost automatically reshapes the narrative beneath by prompting Boswell, as Pottle observes, "to select and condense." The draft manuscript dispenses with whole pages of conversation that the original diary had recorded as taking place along the road between "St. Andrews," Boswell's (and Johnson's) first heading, and Laurencekirk, Boswell's second heading; topography takes precedence over talk. In this design, as in his book on Corsica, Boswell defers to that argument within the diurnal dialectic that Johnson, Fielding, Defoe, and many others had endorsed: good travel writers subordinate the temporal particulars of their own experience to the "full representation" of what they have seen and heard.

Nevertheless, Boswell begins to register intimations that another mode of narrative might work even better. As he renews his attention to his travel journal in the months after Johnson's death in December 1784, he finds Reynolds's enthusiasm for the book in its original, time-focused form echoed on many sides. Boswell's summary journal entry for this period records his willing embrace—indeed, his active courting—of the suggestion by friends that his raw diary might not need extensive restructuring after all: "During [January] and February (till the 23 of that month, on which I am now writing), I had upon the whole a pretty good life, though not quite as I could wish; for I could not apply to the writing out of my *Tour to the Hebrides in Company with Samuel Johnson, LL.D.*, as I hoped I might do. Fortunately for me, Mr. Baron Gordon and Dr. Blair, to the first of whom I read a good deal of my original MS in the forenoon of Monday the 21 and to the latter in the afternoon, confirmed me in thinking that it might be printed with little variation; so (writing 27 February) I resolved that I would set myself down quietly in London and get the work executed easily" (*Applause* 276–77). The un-Johnsonian punctilio with which Boswell notes precise details of time and date ("Forenoon," "afternoon," "21," "27") enacts within the confines of this entry the choice towards which Boswell is tending with respect to his book—that is, to publish it as a diary, a narrative governed by the sequence of dates and the shape of days. More than anything he has published hitherto, the new *Tour* is to resemble the manuscript record he has written for most of his life. Even the proposed title here suggests the change; what Boswell now calls a *Tour* he will shortly rename, by way of clinching his decision, *The Journal of a Tour.*

The new title encapsulates the literary and commercial strategies that underlie the new hybrid Boswell has produced. The title of the Corsican book separated out its formal constituents, hedging the journal form on either side with a genre meant to offset its liabilities. Here instead the *Journal* governs all. It controls the syntax of the title as it will the structure of the book. At the same time, Boswell enacts a formal modulation and appropriation—a smuggling operation across the borderlines of genre. The travel journal was by now among the most familiar kinds of publication, and that is the genre that the first phrases in Boswell's title appear to proffer. A travel journal that functioned as biography was at this point a thing unknown—and that is what the title's final phrase (*with Samuel Johnson, LL.D.*) effectually promised. Nine months after Johnson's death, his name in the title sold the book. As Boswell partly implies in his letter to his publisher, his *Tour* will make "a good Prelude to my large work his *Life*" because it appropriates a tremendously popular mode of writing and exploits it for a new purpose. It thereby tests the commercial waters for the bigger book that Boswell plans to construct from the several decades' worth of diurnal texts whose time form the published *Journal* replicates.

Within the *Tour*, Boswell inverts the conventions of the published travel journal in order to accommodate the shift in substance. He does something new and highly calculating with the redaction topos. Up until the last days before publication, Boswell thought fit to include within the book a short account of how it had evolved first away from, and then back to, its original diary form—the form in which, he reminds his reader at once, Johnson himself had read it while on tour. Though Boswell admits that, because he kept the journal "imperfectly" on the first days of the trip, he has now "filled up and corrected" from memory the early portion of the narrative, he points out that "it gradually grows more perfect, and by and by will be found to be verbatim as printed, with only small insertions of words and omissions of passages not fit for publication. I once thought of writing it anew, but Sir Joseph Banks, Sir Joshua Reynolds, and other friends thought it would be better to give the genuine transcript of what passed at the time and add notes to explain or enlarge. A great part of its value is its authenticity and its having passed the ordeal of Dr. Johnson himself." [30] By "the ordeal of Dr. Johnson" Boswell emphasizes the fact that Johnson read the journal as a manuscript in progress at several intervals during the actual tour. Boswell returns to this point repeatedly in the text of the published *Tour*. In doing so, he reinscribes a familiar travel journal imperative by a new means. The traditional redaction topos tries to warrant both the authenticity and the transparency of the narrative in complicated combination. The writer pares away gratuitous detail, and/or inserts necessary amplification, in order to provide a fuller, more attentive account of the place visited than what obtained in the manuscript. The peculiar circumstances and purpose of the Hebridean *Journal*, however, permit Boswell to shift the grounds of authenticity and transparency off of the writer and onto the subject of the biography. The book's professed purpose being to provide a full and "genuine" representation of Johnson himself (and the Hebrides only secondarily), it repeatedly submits the questions of authenticity and transparency to Johnson's enthusiastic arbitration. "Mr. Johnson said [this journal] was a very exact picture of his life," writes Boswell in the journal, in a sentence that Johnson will later read—and leave intact (*Hebrides* 245). In the published *Tour*, the Johnsonian imprimatur largely supplants the redaction topos.

As the example of Brydone suggests, the customary redaction topos produces a small paradox: the published journal text both is and is not the original. Boswell's new dispensation focuses on only one side of the paradox. The need to convince the reader that the text is a "genuine transcript" of the manuscript Johnson read becomes imperative. Shortly before publication, Boswell decided that the above account was not convincing enough and canceled the whole paragraph. By this sleight of hand, he strengthened the illusion of authenticity that the vanished passage had proclaimed. Lacking the benefit of this explanation, with its attendant admission of gaps early in the original account, the book's readers would naturally take even the lengthy, date-capped narratives of Johnson's first days in Edinburgh as authentic entries, inscribed at the time and not reconstructed later. Boswell eliminates the last traces of the redaction topos in order to produce its exact opposite. This is *"the very journal,"* Boswell deceptively asserts and italically emphasizes, *"which Dr. Johnson read"* (*Journal* 5.78, n. 5).

On one point, though, Johnson's approval of the journal was notably equivocal: "It might be printed," he remarks to Boswell during the journey, "were the subject fit for printing" (5.227). The subjunctive leaves him uncommitted (he has, after all, introduced the possibility before not quite retracting it). As first reader of Boswell's travel diary, Johnson provides what Boswell wants to construe as the text's decisive endorsement. As writer of his own *Journey,* though, he influences the *Journal* in more complex ways: the books stake out opposite positions in the dialectic of diurnal form. In accord with the tradition of critical travel writing, Johnson pursues a transparent representation of the Hebrides by omitting the dates and details of his own itinerary. Seeking to extend the tradition of the "exact Journal," Boswell pursues a transparent representation of Johnson by reinscribing those particulars at every turn. On the tour the two writers moved in tandem. In the *Journal,* Boswell represents them as conducting what amounts to a running argument. It begins in the book's first sentence: "Dr. Johnson has said in his 'Journey,' 'that he scarcely remembered how the wish to visit the Hebrides was excited;' but he told me, in summer, 1763, that his father put Martin's Account into his hands when he was very young, and that he was much pleased with it" (5.13). The sentence lays out a clear line of succession—Johnson received from his father one book on Scotland and wrote another, Boswell has read that and responded with a third. It also lays out a more complex line of authority. In the *Journey* Johnson frequently corrected Martin in matters of Scotland's history; Boswell here corrects Johnson on his own. The sentence economically establishes Boswell's mastery over both his time and Johnson's: he notes not only what Johnson said about this episode of his early youth, but when he said it—"in summer, 1763," the first season of their acquaintance, the point of origin for Boswell's present privileges as Johnson's biographer. In the process he calls into question the strict precision of the *Journey*'s opening utterance: did Johnson, writing, really not recollect the anecdote, or did he only refrain from reciting it? In any event, Boswell's memory, so the language quietly argues, will not only supplement Johnson's, it will supplant it. What Johnson "scarcely remembers" Boswell readily recalls. Where the older author elided autobiography, the younger biographer sets himself up as broker of particulars.

Boswell's opening gambit mounts a political argument as well. In the *Journey,* Johnson repeatedly decries Scotland's failure to write its own history, not only in the age of Ossian but within the present century, when Martin himself "neglected" to record the "customs" and "wild opinions" of a clan culture now vanished: "What he has neglected cannot now be performed. In nations, where there is hardly the use of letters, what is once out of sight is lost for ever" (52). Boswell was more privy than most to the ways in which these pronouncements resonated with Johnson's self-reproach at his failure to record his own life in diaristic detail. In response to this mix of political pronouncement and personal predicament, the *Journal* enacts another kind of hybrid. It crosses boundaries and reverses roles, confronting Johnson with a combination of political rebuttal and personal compensation. In contradiction to Johnson's claim, but as solace for his self-reproach, the Scot here "performs" those particulars that the Englishman has neglected to set down for himself.

Several times in the published *Journal*, Boswell suggests that Johnson's role in this transaction was not merely receptive but collusive. When Boswell ran short of paper, Johnson procured him a blank book in which to write. Later, reading what Boswell had "written in [the] small book with which he had supplied me, [he] was pleased, for he said, 'I wish thy books were twice as big.' He helped me to fill up the blanks which I had left in first writing it, when I was not quite sure of what he had said, and he corrected any mistakes that I had made" (5.307). The "constant and copious journal" that Johnson often recommended, and never wrote, he here enables, sustaining constancy by supplying paper, encouraging copiousness by wishing the book bigger and by filling up its blanks. At one point during their travels, Boswell remarks in his journal that "I looked on this tour to the Hebrides as a co-partnery between Mr. Johnson and me" (*Hebrides* 243). The wording applies equally to the trip and the text, in which, by the intricate workings of this Anglo-Scot alliance, Johnson sees himself written down with unprecedented particularity.

The response of Boswell's contemporaries to the published *Journal* suggests that the dialectic of diurnal form had found no synthesis. Readers divided over the book's time-driven structure and insistent copiousness. John Wolcot ("Peter Pindar"), among the most caustic of Boswell's detractors, mocked in heroic couplets what he saw as a preposterous opacity, an egregious failure of selection and arrangement:

> How are we all with rapture touch'd, to see
> Where, when, and at what hour, you swallow'd tea! [31]

In the face of such charges, the *Journal*'s advocates often constructed defenses couched in terms set by the text itself. "Dr. Johnson's opinion of the Journal was somewhat different" from that of Boswell's assailants, notes Walter James. "I cannot but subscribe to Dr. Johnson's opinion, 'that it might be printed'; and to Mr. Boswell's, that the subject was fit for printing." [32] James here warrants the *Journal*'s worth by trying to reconcile Johnson's and Boswell's fundamental disagreement as to the viability of diurnal form in print. In the same paragraph, though, James resuscitates ambivalence. He assumes that the chief merit of a journal will always inhere in copiousness and comprehensiveness, not craft: "Who . . . ever talked about the *style* of a JOURNAL? The nature of the work admits of no such thing as fine style. You might as well talk of the style of an *Index*." The analogy stipulates order without form: what the alphabet is to the index, the calendar is to the journal. Trying to free the *Journal* from inappropriate expectations, James plays into the argument of its detractors, and sustains the dialectic he is seeking to resolve.

In the middle of the Scotland journey, Johnson had voiced one "opinion of the Journal" that remained a secret from Boswell until after he published his own account twelve years later. In the passage from his journal letter with which this chapter begins, Johnson explained to Thrale the different methods by which he and his companion were recording their experiences, paying more protracted attention to Boswell's work than to his own: "I keep a book of remarks, and Boswel writes a regular journal of our travels, which, I think, contains as much of what I say and do, as of all other occurrences together" (2.95). On the trip, Johnson had come to see for the first time how extensively, through the medium of Boswell's aptitude for journal-keeping, his own words and actions had found their way into the diurnal form he himself had often assayed and never mastered. Taken in tandem with a remark Johnson has made just a paragraph earlier, this description of Boswell's diary amounts to a quiet, half-amused concession: of the two authors, one engaged in a book of "remarks" and one in a "regular journal," Boswell has chosen the worthier task. "You remember the Doge of Genoa who being asked what struck him most at the French Court, answered 'Myself.' I can not think many things here more likely to affect the fancy, than to see Johnson ending his Sixty fourth year in the wilderness of the Hebrides" (2.94). Johnson here defies his own critical dictum: this time, he admits, the traveler himself is more interesting than the scenes he views. Foreseeing Boswell's narrative, Johnson momentarily adopts both Boswell's technique (inserting the temporal particular of his own age, which he will omit from his book) and Boswell's stance: for an instant he is not "Myself" but "Johnson," observed and wondered at from without. That something more than mere playfulness is transpiring here Johnson signals by an oddly floating phrase appended to the end of the passage. Having noted that Boswell's book "contains as much of what I say and do, as of all other occurrences together," Johnson draws a dash and inscribes a quotation: "For such a faithful Chronicler as Griffith" (2.95). Here Johnson recalls, with significant inaccuracies, lines from Shakespeare's *Henry VIII*, addressed by Katherine to Griffith himself, who has just given her a moving account of the death of Wolsey:

> After my death I wish no other herald,
> No other speaker of my living actions
> To keep mine honour from corruption,
> But such an honest chronicler as Griffith.[33]

Johnson, misremembering the line as he applies its praise to Boswell, substitutes "faithful" for "honest," and so manages by his mistake to touch upon an essential element of Boswellian narrative—its temporality. A writer may achieve honesty in a moment, by writing even a single true sentence, but "faithfulness" involves process and demands diligence over time. Boswell's "regular journal" enacts such faithfulness as literary form.

In the event, Boswell fulfilled this passage's forecast before he read it. He published the *Journal* in 1785, shortly after Johnson's death; only in 1788, when Mrs. Piozzi published her collection of Johnson's letters, could he see this praise of his journal. He promptly made use of it in his next and final journal hybrid. Three years later, at the beginning of his *Life of Johnson*, just after the prefatory material and just before the first sentence of the biography proper, Boswell inserted the four lines from Shakespeare, while refraining (with uncharacteristic modesty) from noting the particular, personal praise that Johnson had made of them. The lines had come to embody for Boswell the ultimate imprimatur for his massive undertaking. Having conducted, in his *Journal of a Tour*, a dialogue of form and a textual partnership with Johnson's *Journey*, Boswell was now in a position to enact a short dialogue of epigraphs with his own previous book. On the title page of the *Tour* he had addressed to Johnson, using Pope's words, his own urgent, half-exasperated question:

> Say, shall my little bark attendant sail,
> Pursue the triumph and partake the gale?

Though Boswell didn't know it, Johnson had already, from the midst of his travels, answered in the affirmative, by way of the line from Shakespeare. Writing to Thrale, he had implied that the small craft of the diary might suffice to limn a life and to outlast it, sailing beyond death "along the stream of time." Exchanging Pope for Shakespeare, Boswell once more expands his claims as to what diurnal form can do. It has already served as structure for his *Journal of a Tour*; now it will furnish both substance and shape for his long-projected "larger *Life*."

Writing a century and a half earlier, John Evelyn had expressed his preference for itemization rather than continuity in his record of the self by invoking the figure of "a goose swim[ming] down the river": the image argues that continuity in narrative—among and within days—risks silliness through an absence of discrimination. Pepys by contrast pursued such continuity, closely calibrated in his diary and on his watch, as an instrument for the possession of time and self. Now, near the end of a century that has witnessed the commodification and widespread dispersal of both minute watches and daily prose, Boswell invokes both Griffith's chronography and Pope's "stream of time" as public credentials, as warrants for the worth and fullness of his diurnal form.

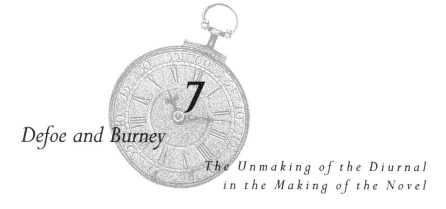

7

Defoe and Burney

The Unmaking of the Diurnal in the Making of the Novel

Novel time is different. In her essay on Addison, Virginia Woolf disputes Thomas Macaulay's claim that, had this prodigious diurnalist "written a novel on an extensive plan it would have been 'superior to any that we possess.'" The *Spectator*'s diurnal form, Woolf argues, prevents it from functioning as a proto-novel in any way. Each paper, she writes, "can be detached from the rest without damage to the design or harm to [it]self. In a novel, where each chapter gains from the one before it or adds to the one that follows it, such separations would be intolerable. The speed, the intricacy, the design, would be mutilated." [1] By this argument the intrinsic parataxis of diurnal form decisively differentiates it from the novel. The "merit" of Addison's papers "consists in the fact that they do not adumbrate, or initiate, or anticipate anything; they exist, perfect, complete, entire in themselves. . . . Each of these essays is very highly finished" (103). Though Woolf directs her argument solely to the *Spectator*, it comes close to encompassing other diurnal forms, narrative (like Pepys's) as well as discursive (like the *Spectator*'s). The individual entries of a diary may not be as "highly finished" as Addison's essays, nor as "entire in themselves"; they deal more markedly in "adumbrations" and "anticipations," incompletions and continuities. Still, the circumstances of their production in a textual system having regard (as Johnson noted) "only to time" appear to tell against "the speed, the intricacy," and above all "the design" that in Woolf's opinion the novel requires. Woolf's own career confirms the sense of generic disparity she sketches here. As a prolific diarist, literary journalist/essayist, and novelist, she not only wrote but read extensively in diurnal form (she is perhaps the only critic in the first half of this century to have produced essays on Pepys, Evelyn, Boswell, and Burney). As a maker of many fictions, though, she left one boundary of genre uncrossed: she never cast a novel in diary form.

As it happens, neither did the novelists of the eighteenth century. Only in the 1790s, after Boswell makes diurnal form viable for biography, do a few novelists begin to structure entire fictions in diary form in the way that Boswell built his Hebridean *Journal*. Nonetheless, the diurnal paradigm matters deeply in the novel from its inception, in ways that neither Macaulay's complacent fusion nor Woolf's deft sundering really get at. The real relations are intricate, charged, and consequential, and merit a book of their own. Before ending this one, I would like to sketch a few of them. This is my argument: that the dialectic of diurnal form—the opposition between copious continuity and critical selectivity—carried over into the novel early, and shaped it in important ways.

Working within the hundred years that had already produced the diary, the daily newspaper, the periodical essay, and the published travel journal, the first makers of novels were mindful of diurnal form as a limit case—the most commodious vehicle—for the kinds of copious and continuous narratives with which they too were working in new ways. The calendar's succession of dates supplied a plain grid that appeared capable of arranging, containing, and sustaining any kind of data, in any quantity and at any narrative tempo whatever. At times the novelists seek to approximate this limit case by incorporating diurnal structure in their texts. Crusoe keeps a journal, as do H. F. (in *A Journal of the Plague Year*), Pamela, and the eponymous narrator of Frances Sheridan's *Memoirs of Miss Sidney Bidulph*. In all these cases, though, diurnality dissolves in one way or another: Crusoe's and Pamela's journals end soon, H.F.'s shows signs of drastic redaction, and Bidulph's has clearly been excerpted (her text is marketed as *Memoirs . . . Extracted from Her Own Journal* rather than the journal itself). Other novelistic structures, too, suggest both a gravitation towards the diurnal form and a calculated resistance to it. In the epistolary novel, the letters allow for dates, continuity, and copiousness but also for selectivity (the journal letter itself, as we have seen, was often construed as a judicious compromise between a narrative of "all occurrences" and of those worth telling). In the titles of *Tom Jones*'s chapters and "Books," Fielding boasts of how assiduously he is tracking certain significant stretches of time, but also of how diligently he is discarding others that don't matter (no stagecoach driver he). Pope had predicted that any narrative committed to representing *"every* Day" must inevitably deal in details not worth reading, and the novelists devise strategies that take that danger into account. Their practice suggests that as a structure of time in text, they found the diaristic limit case both compelling and confining. Diurnal imperatives needed working with, but also working against.

It is this double operation of attraction and resistance that makes diurnal structure a crucial, insistent temporal language within the novel's heteroglossia of time. In "Discourse in the Novel," his seminal account of novelistic heteroglossia, Mikhail Bakhtin establishes that what he calls the "everyday genres" (*bytovoj vanr*)—"diaries, confessions, journalistic articles and so on"—"play an especially significant role" in the making of the novel, "bring[ing] into it their own languages."[2] He posits a modern chronotope (i.e., a time-space matrix) grounded in "everyday life" as a defining feature of the novel: in the novel, "such elements . . . as food, drink, the sexual act, death . . . enter *everyday life*, which is already in the process of being compartmentalized" (211; Bakhtin's italics). As a single word, the term "everyday" operates as a kind of mass noun and (if such a thing existed) mass adjective: it identifies phenomena—objects, habits, practices—which have become familiar by frequent use over extended time.[3] When "compartmentalized"—separated into "every day"—it points to something slightly different: the successive but separate units of time in which such familiarity develops. It is in this form that the term best incarnates the new compartmentalizations—in clocks, calendars, texts, and consciousness—that I've tried to trace throughout this book. I'd like now to track the traffic some early novels conduct between the term whole and the term sundered—to show how novelists produce the *everyday* by working with and against a form of narrative that operates and represents *every day*, how the absorption and the unmaking of diurnal structures come to constitute significant activities in the new genre.

I propose to do so by looking chiefly at the work of Daniel Defoe and Frances Burney, the two eighteenth-century novelists perhaps most engaged with calendrical, serial form even before they took up fiction—Defoe through his nine years' authorship of the thrice-weekly *Review*, Burney through the plentiful journals and journal letters that absorbed much of her writing attention throughout her career. Defoe is the first writer to incorporate a journal into fiction, and in *Robinson Crusoe* and *A Journal of the Plague Year* he sets up many of the patterns and problems by which the dialectic of diurnal form will help shape novels throughout the century. Burney takes up several of Defoe's precedents (and she caps her career in fiction by acknowledging the debt explicitly, in her last novel's last paragraph), but deploys them to new purpose. Her involvement with diurnal forms in both manuscript and print constitutes a critique of the ways in which the culture has gendered its constructions of time both within texts and beyond them.

DEFOE: "THE JOURNAL" AND THE "COPY"

Early in his account of his solitary island life, Robinson Crusoe boasts of the activity that his creator Defoe will later decry: the keeping of an "exact Journal." A few weeks after coming ashore, Crusoe explains, "I found Pen, Ink and Paper, and I husbanded them to the utmost, and I shall shew, that while my Ink lasted, I kept things very exact . . ." (48). A few pages later, Crusoe will show his exactitude by importing the text of his year-long island journal into his larger autobiography. "I shall here give you the Copy," he writes (52), and in doing so marks a first for fiction. At the date of *Crusoe's* publication, fictive journals had made only the slenderest incursions into print: *The Spectator's* "sober Citizen" was the first, to be followed by a few others, none longer than a pamphlet.[4] In *Crusoe*, by contrast, "The Journal" (so designated in a centered headline above the first entry) takes up about a ninth of the whole work; here for the first time, a faux diary forms part of a larger fiction. At the date of publication, then, Crusoe's "exact" journal was *sui generis*. Whatever Defoe may have later thought of such a writing mode as an adjunct to traveling, in his first long fiction he clearly expects it to do important narrative work.

Important, but circumscribed: one year into his journal-keeping, Crusoe runs out of ink, which "I could not make . . . by any Means that I could devise," despite his stunning efficacy in reproducing virtually all other components of domestic technology (48). Nor is this abrupt cessation the only evidence that the dialectic of diurnal form has carried over into fiction. The "Copy" Crusoe gives us reads like anything but a direct transcription of an original manuscript written day by day: it deals conspicuously in omissions and compressions, as well as in retrospective interpolations that give signs of having been composed years after the dates that head the entries. In the printed text, then, Defoe's making and unmaking of the journal transpire concurrently. Given the primacy of Crusoe's journal in the history of fiction, it is worth inquiring into the thinking that lies behind both of these entwined activities. Why does Crusoe keep a journal? Copy it in this form? Run out of ink? The answers illuminate the workings of narrative time not only in *Crusoe* but also in Defoe's subsequent novels, and in the novelistic traditions that followed them.

The presence of "The Journal" has long been attributed to *Crusoe*'s Puritan roots. It is "the Puritan tradition of diary-keeping," writes Paul Alkon, "that underlies Defoe's impulse to provide a journal."[5] In fact, Crusoe's journal differs significantly from this putative antecedent. In Puritan diaries, as Hunter points out, "conversion is almost always the central event," but it is also more than that: it is the recurrent, even pervasive, point of reference for the narrative. Generally, the diarist begins the diary as a consequence of conversion, and writes up subsequent actions and feelings in an urgent attempt to discern how strongly he or she has held to the condition of conversion, and how far fallen away from it.[6]

Crusoe's journal, by contrast, diverges from this pattern from its inception, and Defoe takes pains to point up the difference. Just before Crusoe begins to reproduce "The Journal," he conjures up an alternate version. He points out that he began to keep the diary several weeks after he arrived on the island, "for indeed at first I was in too much Hurry . . . and my Journal would ha' been full of many dull things: For Example, I must have said thus. *Sept.* the 30th. After I got to Shore and had escap'd drowning, instead of being thankful to God for my Deliverance, . . . I ran about the Shore, . . . exclaiming at my Misery . . ." (51). The passage has generated much comment about its inconsistencies with Crusoe's other accounts, earlier and later, of his first day,[7] but so far as I can determine, a more pressing (because more local) inconsistency has gone unnoticed. The phrase "instead of being thankful to God" is emphatically not what Crusoe would have written on his first day (or even in his first months), because it interpolates into the text a perspective he did not achieve until his fever-dream conversion exactly nine months later. When the "actual" entry appears three paragraphs later, it concerns itself exclusively with Crusoe's material predicament, and makes no mention of God or of thankfulness. Crusoe's *imaginary* first entry, then, corresponds with the Puritan precedent of the self-reproachful past-contrafactual ("what I didn't know or do or think or feel, though I could and should have"). His actual writing, though, breaks that precedent. If, as Hunter suggests, conversion is "central" to the Puritan diary, then, as Leopold Damrosch shrewdly observes, Crusoe produces a very different kind of text: "He keeps his diary *before* conversion. . . . At the very moment when the Puritan's continuous self-analysis begins, Crusoe's ends." [8] Damrosch exaggerates slightly: Crusoe narrates the crucial moment of conversion near the end of the journal, but still within its confines; the relation between the text and the event is one of overlap rather than separation. In Defoe's handling, the journal form and the conversion narrative will turn out to bear important relations to each other—just not the ones conventionalized in Puritan diaries and autobiographies.

The innovative representation of conversion is only one among many narrative problems to which Defoe and Crusoe address themselves in the making of "The Journal." When Crusoe first indicates his intention to reproduce his journal, he has in mind a narrative problem of an entirely different order: the near impossibility of telling his peculiar experience. "And now being to enter into a melancholy Relation of a Scene of silent Life, such perhaps as was never heard of in the World before, I shall take it from its Beginning, and continue it in its Order. It was, by my Account, the 30th of *Sept.* when, in the Manner as above said, I first set Foot upon this horrid Island . . ." (47). The passage hints at an elusive logic of representation. The faint tinge of the theatre ("a melancholy . . . Scene of silent Life") calls up the conundrum of a dumb show that must somehow be made audible if it is to become intelligible. By a confusion of representational modes, Crusoe seizes upon chronological sequence and continuity as the likeliest means to make his story "heard." "Order" will make for audibility.

This is neither Crusoe's first attempt at narrative ordering nor his last. At this point Crusoe has already been recounting the early weeks of his island life for several pages. Until now, both the substance and the form of his account have partaken of that mode of time and work that E. P. Thompson dubs "task-orientation," familiar in "peasant societies" and "important in village and domestic industries," in which "the day's tasks . . . seem to disclose themselves, by the logic of need, before the [laborer's] eyes." [9] Crusoe's activities on the first island days take the "logic of need" to an extreme that has achieved the status of myth; their sequence is dictated by necessity—by what he must do first, and what next, in order to survive. His narrative too moves by this logic, particularly at moments of transition:

"My next Care was for some Ammunition and Arms" (38); "My next Work was to view the Country, and seek a proper Place for my Habitation, and where to stow my Goods" (39). This "task-oriented" narrative allows the reader to determine the order of Crusoe's accomplishments—and to recognize its origins in practical necessity—but not to gauge the specific durations of each endeavor.

Gradually, though, the accumulation of *narrative* tasks produces its own discernible tangle: "Having now fix'd my Habitation, I found it absolutely necessary to provide a Place to make a Fire in, and Fewel to burn; and what I did for that, as also how I enlarg'd my Cave, and what Conveniences I made, I shall give a full Account of in its Place: But I must first give some little Account of my self, and of my Thoughts about Living, which it may well be suppos'd were not a few" (46). This encounter between the logic of practical need ("I found it absolutely necessary . . .") and the logic of narrative need ("I must first give some little Account . . .") prompts Crusoe both to backtrack (in order to retrieve his "Thoughts about Living") and to postpone (the task-narrative about "Fewel"). When, only a page later, he commits himself to a strictly chronological, date-structured account of his experience, "tak[ing] it from its Beginning and continu[ing] it in its Order," he is opting away from the task-oriented model that has posed his present narrative problems in favor of a time-governed form better suited to the representation of concurrent tasks and "Thoughts."

At the same time, through this shift in narrative mode, Defoe recapitulates an important economic development that is historically concurrent with Crusoe's exile. As Thompson points out, it was in the mid seventeenth century that prosperous farmers began the shift from task-oriented to time-measured reckonings of their employees' labor, from the "logic of need" to "dayworkes" or day labor (the agricultural manual Thompson cites as articulating the practice dates from 1660, the year after Crusoe lands).[10] Crusoe's decisions to keep and to present his journal reenact this shift as an experience first of writing, then of reading. Starting the island story again "from the Beginning," Crusoe's journal maps onto the calendrical time grid the tasks he has already narrated another way (Damrosch is at least partly right when he dubs the text a "time-and-motion study"). By first making, and then transcribing, the pages he calls his "Journal of Every Days Employment," Crusoe refigures task time as tasks timed.

By Crusoe's own account, the making of the journal serves more intricate purposes as well. It is a singular feature of Crusoe's island life (before Friday's arrival) that he operates as both sole laborer and sole freeholder; his journal's implications as a narrative figure of economy double correspondingly. Michel de Certeau, interested in those implications, jumps the gun a bit when he argues that "in Defoe's work, the awakening of Robinson Crusoe to the capitalist and conquering task of writing his island is inaugurated by the decision to write his diary, to give himself in that way a space in which he can master time and things, and to thus constitute for himself, along with the blank page, an initial island in which he can produce what he wants." [11] Crusoe's "awakening," "conquering," and even "writing" (in de Certeau's figurative application) have in fact begun some time before he starts his journal, in the tasks by which he appropriates the resources of the island for his survival, and marks its space with his habitation. Still, de Certeau identifies accurately those elements that make the function of the journal continuous with that of the tasks that precede it. As he crosses from task time to journal narrative, Crusoe writes in such a way as to make this connection explicit and concrete. His announcement of a new narrative scheme that is committed to chronology as its source of order precedes the "Copy" of his journal by several pages. In the interim he engages in rapid succession with a number of different methods of order, temporal (for the first time he specifies the date and season of arrival, and details his construction of a calendar), spatial (he supplies the island's longitude), and topical (he writes up his situational balance sheet, cited earlier [p. 62], sorting out his experience under the headings "Good" and "Evil"). Unlike the earlier account of tasks, these paragraphs aim at situating the self rather than narrating its activities. Crusoe locates himself on many of the grids that according to Foucault were combining to produce a new order of things, and that according to de Certeau were facilitating the "scriptural economy," under whose auspices the writing class was able to commute the blank page into a tool of cultural control.

Like task-time narrative, though, self-location proves problematic. Having placed himself on all those abstract grids, Crusoe becomes preoccupied with the difficulty of locating himself in his actual, physical home, amid the many objects he has salvaged from the wrecked ship. "At first," he writes, "this was a confus'd Heap of Goods, which as they lay in no Order, so they took up all my Place, I had no room to turn my self . . ." (50). The language momentarily inverts de Certeau's account of Crusoe's "conquering" agenda. At this point, Crusoe's "things" have "mastered" him, by denying him any empty space in which "to turn my self." Crusoe reclaims his "Place" by means of order.

> But when I had wrought out some Boards, as above, I made large Shelves of the Breadth of a Foot and a Half one over another, all along one Side of my Cave, to lay all my Tools, Nails, and Iron-work, and in a Word, to separate every thing at large in their Places, that I must come easily at them; I knock'd Pieces into the Wall of the Rock to hang my Guns and all things that would hang up.
>
> So that had my Cave been to be seen, it look'd like a general Magazine of all Necessary things, and I had every thing so ready at my Hand, that it was a great Pleasure to me to see all my Goods in such Order, and especially to find my Stock of all Necessaries so great.
>
> And now it was when I began to keep a Journal . . . for indeed at first I was in too much Hurry, and . . . too much Discomposure of Mind. (51)

The shift of topic in the last sentence enacts a logic of association. De Certeau explains how the journal enables Crusoe "to master time and things," but Crusoe here articulates a fuller relation between two technologies. The journal masters time as the shelving masters things: by compartmentalization, by "separat[ing] every thing at large in their Places." Both the diction and the sequence construe journal-keeping as the *next* task dictated by the logic of need, the temporal correlative of the spatial order Crusoe has just established.[12]

Crusoe's wording and logic also resonate with the work of a real-life diarist: Pepys. Crusoe's new orderliness allows him to speak of "great Pleasure" for the first time since the shipwreck; Pepys uses the phrase with astonishing frequency to express (as Crusoe does here) his satisfaction at the ways in which order—of private space and private time—enables him to enjoy both space and time as venues visibly filled with property. For that reason he, too, rejoices whenever he installs new shelving, and his enthusiasm for orderly storage, recurring in the diary at markedly regular intervals, suggests that it functions for him in ways analogous with diurnal form. Crusoe voices a perception common to both: "to see all my Goods in such Order" is thereby "to find my Stock of all necessaries so great"; subdivisions of space on the shelves and time in the journal promote the perception of fullness. For Pepys as for Crusoe, spatial and temporal order is an instrument of ownership. Crusoe and Pepys are near contemporaries, not only by their birthdates (both are born in Old Style 1632) but also in their texts. Crusoe's journal, begun late in 1659, predates Pepys's by only a few weeks. The two diarists participate in the same new phase of the "scriptural economy"; both perform, in Damrosch's phrase, a "time-and-motion study" designed in part to track productivity and possession. The making of their journals facilitates a mastery of time by means of orderly appropriation. Their "blank pages," once filled with prose under the signs of successive dates, define their "time" as the shelving clears their "Place." For most entries in Crusoe's "Journal of Every Day's Employment," the more useful explanatory paradigm is not Puritanism but Pepys.

Yet this fit too is far from perfect. Though comparable in intent and originary impulse, the textual timing in Crusoe's journal differs markedly from that of Pepys's diary. What I have called the unmaking of Crusoe's journal begins early, and works several ways. The text sometimes conflates several days in a single summary: "The 7th, 8th, 9th, 10th, and Part of the 12th. [of November] (for the 11th. was Sunday) I took wholly up to make me a Chair . . ." (54). Sometimes it interpolates retrospective observations, as in the continuation of the above entry: ". . . and with much ado brought it [the chair] to tolerable Shape, but *never* to please me . . . I *soon* neglected my keeping Sundays, for omitting my Mark for them on my Post, I forgot which was which" (emphases added). Often, Crusoe announces excisions from the original manuscript in order to avoid repeating details he has already provided in the narrative that preceded his presentation of his journal: "*Jan. 3.* I began my Fence or Wall . . . *N.B.* This Wall being describ'd before, I purposely omit what was said in the Journal . . ." (56). The further we read, the clearer it becomes that this copy differs significantly from the original manuscript, which Crusoe has now revised many decades after its composition.[13] For readers familiar with the sea journals of Dampier, Cooke, and Rogers, such redaction would not be surprising in itself, but Defoe's text generates surprise by other means. On the verge of presenting his "Copy," Crusoe explains that "in it will be told all these Particulars [i.e., the details of his early months] over again" (52). He forecasts, that is, a more complete transcription—and a fuller account of his time—than he actually provides. Crusoe's journal thus confounds expectations three ways: in its time structure it deviates not only from the Puritan diary and (less markedly) from the secular time record, but also from the promised structure by which its author ushers it in. Defoe constructs a text shaped (and misshaped) by its engagement with (and hence its difference from) each of the three paradigms, a heteroglossia of temporal templates unprecedented in print or manuscript. Defoe exploits the convergence to make points about the possibilities and problems of representation in the new textual time forms now emergent in the culture. I want to look briefly at two particularly productive dialogues of temporality: one between the secular setup of Crusoe's journal and the Puritan conversion narrative it comes to encompass; the other between Crusoe's unseen manuscript and the journal he remakes and unmakes for purposes of print narrative.

In most Puritan diaries, the conversion experience organizes the text and is present everywhere within it, both as a reiterated narrative and as a pervasive point of view: like Crusoe in his hypothetical first-day entry, the Puritan diarist writes up even pre-conversion events from a post-conversion point of view (Hunter calls this the "before and after" effect). Defoe, by contrast, arranges Crusoe's journal so that conversion will occur as a disruption: the entries for the dates of Crusoe's religious revelation (27 and 28 June) read like nothing that has gone before. The difference consists partly in the sheer quantity of words: these are by far the longest entries in the journal, and Defoe heightens the contrast by preceding them with some of the shortest:

June 23. Very bad again, cold shivering, and then a violent Head-ach.
June 24. Much better. (64)

The abrupt shift in tempo correlates with a modulation in textual authenticity. These tiny entries seem the most plausible direct "Copy" in the whole text; they appear to reproduce a manuscript composed by someone who is eager to track the course of his illness but who lacks the energy to do so in detail.[14] The conversion entries, by contrast, contain the most drastic, extensive, and sharply marked *post facto* interpolations of all. This shift away from momentary scribal realism corresponds with a change in narrative venue. All previous entries have concerned themselves with the "Day's Employment"; the first conversion entry tells instead the "terrible Dream" that comes to Crusoe "far in the Night," adjuring repentance (64). The sudden advent of the supernatural prompts Crusoe to a new and problem-ridden mode of interpolation as he labors both to represent and to interpret his experience in retrospect. "No one, that shall ever read this Account, will expect that I should be able to describe the Horrors of my Soul at this terrible Vision . . . nor is it any more possible to describe the Impression that remain'd upon my Mind when I awak'd . . ." (65). Here the journal's familiar mode of simple editorial intervention ("I shall omit them here") gives way to a topos of narrative futility: no redaction, Crusoe avers, will achieve the desired effect, or accomplish the sought-for transmission. Earlier, Crusoe lit upon his journal as the likeliest solution to the problem of the untellability of his "silent Life"; with the advent of his conversion, the journal itself confronts the problem and (Crusoe here suggests) cannot solve it.

Crusoe's reader does not arrive at the conversion entries wholly unprepared: Defoe adumbrates their substance in two earlier entries (themselves the journal's longest at their respective points). In one, the unexpected sprouting of some grain strikes Crusoe as providential (57–59), in the other a terrifying earthquake prompts him to thoughts of repentance. In all three cases—corn, earthquake, conversion dream—the providential signifiers operate as sudden eruptions that provoke first surprise, then meditation. The corn, "shooting out of the Ground," produces in Crusoe "Astonishment and Confusion" (58); the earthquake, shaking the ground, renders him "stupify'd" (59); the dream, in which "I thought the Earth trembl'd," awakes "the Horrors of my Soul" (64, 65). In all three figures, the seemingly stable "Ground," literal or (in the third case) psychological, bursts open to produce astonishment, and Hunter has shown how deeply this imagery is steeped in the Puritan emblem tradition.[15] In the time structure of the journal itself, Defoe produces a fourth figure of eruption, one that encompasses the other three and communicates the idea not by the data of narrative but as an experience of form. The secular *Tick, Tick, Tick* of days and labors successively numbered and succinctly narrated gives way to a providential temporality that brooks no resistance. A last touch at the end of the conversion entries confirms the pattern by a further dismantling. Crusoe confesses that amid his fever and his dreams, he may have lost track of calendar time altogether: "nay, to this Hour, I'm partly of the Opinion, that I slept all the next Day and Night . . . for otherwise I knew not how I should lose a Day out of my Reckoning in the Days of the Week, as it appear'd some Years after I had done" (70). Henceforth, then, even the dates on the journal entries will be unreliable. There are in any event few to come: starting here, Crusoe leaves many dates unnumbered and unnarrated; three months and seven pages later, he is almost out of ink, and the journal ends. In direct opposition to the Puritan tradition, Crusoe's journal provides the time form that conversion tears apart.

Religion is not the only mode of its unmaking. As I have already suggested, Defoe keeps the reader mindful almost from the start that "The

Journal" both revises and occludes the original of which it purports to be a copy. This second dialogic encounter, between the seen and unseen texts, operates even more directly on the reader's experience than does the first (between Puritan and secular modes). First, it produces a running index of narrative labor. With every explicit omission and conspicuous interpolation, the reader becomes increasingly aware of the strenuousness of Crusoe's mediation, of the effort he puts into imagining what the reader wants, doesn't want, and needs to know. The mere fact of the unseen manuscript, and the visible strategies of its revision, concretize and allegorize a problem that besets Crusoe as it does all of Defoe's subsequent narrators: the immense difficulties involved in simply telling their stories, transmitting evanescent experience in palpable, permanent text. Crusoe at first introduces his diary as an escape from such difficulties. It ought to make narration simpler by providing a surrogate for the initial, exclusive island experience. It has already abducted his abstract (and "silent") experience into text in a way that Crusoe warrants as "exact," whole, and orderly. Yet it too turns out to require laborious mediation, tinged by intimations of futility. In this sense too "The Journal" figures as one of a large number of tasks—narrative and otherwise—that Crusoe must undertake in his big book of work.

Crusoe's redactions in the journal make work for the reader too. Crusoe doesn't always signal his interventions by a note or an *N.B.*; it is often difficult to determine just where plausible copy from the original journal gives way to interpolation; even Crusoe's formula for concluding his "asides" ("But to return to my Journal") can occasionally come as a surprise when the aside itself is not conspicuous. Here too "The Journal" embodies a larger problematic in Defoe's fiction: the recurrent question of whether the reader is meant to accept the text as true history (figured by Crusoe's original journal) or palpable fiction (embodied by the obviously remade journal). Defoe's commercial and artistic intentions in this regard have been the subject of long debate.[16] "The Journal" seems to me to suggest, early in the career, that what Defoe actually purveys (very successfully in *Crusoe*'s case) is puzzlement: an ongoing uncertainty as to the authenticity of the particulars (here the exactness of the copy), which ends by producing a heightened awareness of the degree to which mere textualization is a form of fiction, and all narrative making demands remaking. The reader of Crusoe's journal, uncertain perhaps as to whether it is history or fiction, can nonetheless conclude that it is opaque: parts of the "silent Life" that the journal was to relate remain silent, occluded by a redaction that is itself at times uncertain in its procedures. Crusoe's original journal remains as elusive as the experience it once transmuted into text.

When Crusoe runs out of ink, diurnal form gives way to other time structures. Crusoe narrates the long remainder of the book in a mode somewhere between the "task-orientation" of his early island narrative and the continuous chronology of his journal. While on the island, he devises new patterns of time dictated by various "logics of need." He works out an alternate calendar in which alterations of climate take precedence over the months:

Half   *February* ⎫
        March   ⎬ Rainy, the *Sun* being then on, or near, the *Equinox*
Half   *April*   ⎭

(78)

On the other hand, he names his sole companion by the European designation for their day of meeting (a name and time scheme that Friday at first knows nothing of). And he recognizes a Providential pattern of time in a nexus of anniversaries that links up his birth-date, his island arrival and departure, and other turning points in his life. In these ways, the calendar persists as an important presence in the novel, serving both practical and narrative purposes: as a tool for cultivation (in seasonal reckoning), for asserting political power (over Friday), and for recognizing divine Providence. But it no longer structures narrative as in the continuous, dated entries of the journal.

Critics have sometimes seen Crusoe's journal as a failed improvisation, a strategy that Defoe expected to work a certain way and discarded when it didn't.[17] They do not take account of the work that it accomplishes precisely by virtue of its agitations and inconsistencies, its mixed allegiances to several paradigms: it dramatizes by eruption the pivotal conversion narrative; and concretizes by occlusion problems of telling and reading that will remain central to all the novels that follow. These critics also overlook a more fundamental affinity between the emerging paradigm of diurnal form and the construction of *Crusoe*'s fiction. Like the *Spectator*, *Crusoe* recombines in its central premise components that had earlier converged in the texts of manuscript diaries: constructs of solitude, of "silent Life," and of slow time minutely tracked. The oft-remarked mythic quality of Defoe's first novel derives in large measure from the way it forces the reader to re-imagine as solitary and slow processes and products long familiar through commodification and acculturation: to re-imagine what it is to make a chair, a table, a shelf, a house, a boat; to find redemption, acquire a servant, teach a language, save a soul, construct an army, create (and replicate) a culture.

Crusoe's island labor produces objects and power. His textual labor results in a kind of temporal microscopy, a deep, repetitious attention to these objects and the processes of their creation (often recounted not once but twice or three times) that makes the small large and the familiar strange. It is in this sense that Crusoe becomes a true contemporary—a co-constructor of time as well as a cohabitant of the calendar—with Pepys's diary, Hooke's *Micrographia*, Huygens's minute hand, and the Royal Society's minutiae, with all those minutely attentive subdivisions and enlargements, both temporal and spatial, that abetted empiricism en route to empire. In the end, the temporal idea of diurnal form, the exact tracking of the day's endeavors and results, proves as compelling as the money Crusoe apostrophizes aboard the wrecked ship: "O Drug! said I aloud, what art thou good for? Thou art not worth to me, no not the taking off of the Ground . . . I have no Manner of use for thee, e'en remain where thou art. . . . However, upon Second Thoughts, I took it away . . ." (43). Crusoe reasons himself into leaving the money alone, then takes it anyway; it remains with him throughout the island years and accompanies him back to Europe (where it increases). In a world where time was becoming money, Defoe's ambivalence about textual temporality plays out a little differently than Crusoe's ambivalence about coins, but has similar results. The book takes up the journal, sets it aside, but then keeps it too. When Crusoe moves into other narrative rhythms and tempos, summarizing whole years in sentences, then slowing conspicuously for detailed recountings of signal moments (like his first sighting of an alien footprint), these modulations enter inexorably into a dialogue with the time form by which he first contrived to order, and first attempted to communicate, the puzzle of his unprecedented "silent Life." The template, once introduced, cannot altogether disappear: Crusoe's reckoning of the island year as a cluster of numbered repetitious days bringing small increments of progress becomes part of the reader's equipment for imagining the more swiftly recounted later years. His actual "Journal of every Day's Employment," out of reach behind his redaction of the "Copy," remains all the more compelling as paradigm, as narrative possibility, and as index of slow time. Diurnal form is first reworked and then discarded, but its dialectic persists.

The dialectic operates still more insistently and pervasively in *A Journal of the Plague Year* (1722). Critics have often remarked how the chronological confusion of H. F.'s narrative—the mass of anecdotes undated, interrupted, repeated, and postponed—builds into readers' experience a temporal cor-relative for the bewilderment of Londoners in the plague of 1665.[18] No one has noted, though, how thoroughly Defoe structures this experience as a dialogue, or (more accurately) as a constant, highly charged struggle be-tween modes of narrative committed to different figurations of time. The strategy begins on the title page: *A Journal of the Plague Year: being Observations or Memorials, Of the most Remarkable Occurrences, as well Publick as Private, which happened in London During the last Great Visitation in 1665.* The title promises chronology and continuity (*A Journal*), while the subtitle promises selectivity (not "all occurrences and observations," as per Johnson to Baretti, only the "most Remarkable"). Five years later, in the anecdote of the two travelers, Defoe presents himself as keenly sensitive to the difference between modes, and opts for the more "critical." Here by contrast he proffers both, and assigns priority to the more continuous. The title limns the dialectic without resolving it.

So does the text. From beginning to end, it repeatedly reawakens the expectation and desire for chronology implicit in the title's first term, with-out ever precisely fulfilling it. The first such stimulus appears in the first sentence: "It was about the Beginning of *September* 1664, that I, among the Rest of my Neighbours, heard in ordinary Discourse, that the Plague was return'd again in *Holland*. . . ."[19] The engagement with the calendar evinced in the opening clause persists for several pages, becoming even more sys-tematic and particular in the process. As his first strategy for representing the plague's progress, H. F. transcribes data from the weekly bills of mor-tality, which in fact constituted the first print periodical to track a "story" (albeit couched in number rather than narrative) continuously across the calendar:

From *Dec.* 27 to *Jan.* 3	St. *Giles's* [parish] ... 16
	St. *Andrew's* 17
Jan. 3 to — 10.	St. *Giles's* 12
	St. *Andrew's* 25
	(3)

For a little while, dates dominate H. F.'s prose as well ("It was very strange to observe that in this particular Week, from the 4th to the 11th of *July* . . ." [14]), but as he modulates from statistics into anecdote, the calendar recedes and a new, less lucid mode of narrative time takes over, teeming with half-completed gestures of forecast and retrospection, postponements, asides, and backtrackings:

> But we perceiv'd the Infection kept chiefly in the out-Parishes, which being very populous, and fuller also of Poor, the Distemper found more to prey upon than in the City, as I shall observe afterward; we perceiv'd I say, the Distemper to draw our Way. (14)

> But I must go back to the Beginning of this Surprizing Time. . . . (19)

So numerous are the chronological dislocations that the phrase "I say" becomes a kind of watchword, repeatedly invoked (as in the first of the passages above) to reseal the rifts produced by H. F.'s self-interruptions, his quick leaps back and forth across the timescape of his tale. These rapid reversals produce two types of disorientation: it becomes difficult both to locate events on the grid of the calendar and to predict their narrative advent in the confused sequence of the text. In the most extended instance, H. F. first promises a narrative:

> I have by me a Story of two Brothers and their Kinsman . . .
> The Story of those three Men . . . I shall give as distinctly as I can, believing the History will be a very good Pattern for any poor Man to follow. . . . (57–58)

He promptly postpones it:

> I say all this previous to the History, having yet, for the present, much more to say [i.e., on the subject of my own activities] before I quit my own Part. (57–58)

Then he abruptly takes it up again many pages later: "I come back to my three Men . . ." (122). The distance between preamble and narrative covers about a fifth of the entire text. By such strategies, Defoe enacts the temporality he describes: the reader, too, dwells in "Surprizing Time."

At irregular intervals throughout the *Journal,* the calendar briefly reasserts its primacy. H. F. dates an action or transcribes more data from the mortality bills in such a way as to track the plague's chronological progress ("It was about the 10th of *September,* that my Curiosity led . . . me to go and see this Pit again . . ." [60]). By returning to the calendrical paradigm while at the same time keeping it at bay, Defoe develops a temporal analogue for the spatial questions that most preoccupy H. F. throughout his account: whether London's policy of shutting families into houses to prevent the spread of plague was practicable (it required watchmen everywhere), and whether in the end it succeeded in containing the contagion. H. F. returns to these questions repeatedly without ever definitively answering them. The efforts at containment were enormous, their success equivocal; they were no match for the human resistances and restlessness they sought to curb. A related restlessness infuses H. F.'s transactions in narrative time. Both the plague policy and the calendar present a paradigm for control, a "dream of discipline" (in Foucault's words) that falls quite short of fulfillment. The calendrical grid establishes a presence in the *Journal* sufficient to act as counterpoint to the diffuse and erratic narratives that H. F. weaves around and through it, but insufficient to contain them, to lock them into place. By the logic of the text, no straightforward *Journal of the Plague Year* could tell the time of that year truly. The failure of the title's promise becomes the title's point.

Defoe takes pains to establish a local logic, a plausible fiction as to how H. F.'s journal acquired its present form. Where Crusoe explains in detail the origins of his journal before he presents his copy, H. F. sketches them more casually and incidentally, in the midst of his account: "Such intervals as I had, I employed in reading Books, and in writing down my Memorandums of what occurred to me every Day, and out of which, afterwards, I [took] most of this Work as it relates to my Observations without Doors: What I wrote of my private Meditations I reserve for private Use, and desire it may not be made publick on any Account whatever" (76–77). The passage suggests a drama of redaction and excision, in which H. F. later reworks the sequential, continuous "Memorandums of what occurred to me every Day" into the expressive temporal disorder of the present narrative; by every "I say," he testifies to the struggle with which troubled memory relives and redistributes the materials of the first manuscript.[20] As in *Crusoe* we read only a much-altered copy of the journal; the original account, though promised in the title, remains insistently out of reach. This time, though, the distance and the difference between the two are much greater, and more pervasive. In *Crusoe*, the dissonance and the dialectic between the "exact Journal" and its "critical" reworking dominated only a portion of the novel. Here it occupies the whole, and defines it too.

By simultaneously presenting and occluding his narrators' journals, Defoe produces two effects that I have not yet discussed, and that I think hold useful implications for an understanding of temporality both in his other fiction and in the novels which came after his over the course of the century. The first is an effect of isolation—an experience of reciprocal, unbridgeable separation in calendrical time in which he involves both his narrator and his reader. The second I'll call the temporal reality effect (adapting Barthes), a textual representation of time specifically keyed to the way temporality was "really" conceived, written, and practiced in the culture.

Defoe himself presented a remarkably extensive commentary on the effect of isolation in the third and last of his *Crusoe* books, *Serious Reflections During the Life and Surprising Adventures of Robinson Crusoe*, in which Crusoe presents (as the title suggests) not a further narrative but a series of essays reflecting upon his past experience. In his opening essay, "Of Solitude," Crusoe interprets his "long tedious life of Solitude . . . the Life of a Man in an Island" as emblematic of a condition common to all: "Sometimes I have as much wonder'd why it [i.e., my island life] should be [i.e., should have been] any Grievance or Affliction; seeing upon the whole View of the Stage of Life which we act upon in this World, it seems to me, that Life in general is, or ought to be, but one universal Act of Solitude. . . ."[21] The voice is the voice of Crusoe, but the argument is that of the *Spectator* (while producing the *Review*, Defoe had read that preeminent rival attentively and commented on it often). As Crusoe's essay proceeds the echoes get stronger: "What, then, is the Silence of Life?" Crusoe asks, implying, like Mr. Spectator, that his own long silence simply reflects his reader's ongoing predicament. Finally, like Addison and Steele, he suggests that this inherent sequestration may be made useful: "A Man under a Vow of perpetual Silence, if but rigorously observed, would be, even on the Exchange of *London*, as perfectly retired from the World, as a Hermit in his Cell . . . and if he is able to observe it rigorously, may reap all the Advantages of those Solitudes" (3). The wording closely recapitulates one of Mr. Spectator's most frequently cited celebrations of his peculiar state: "There is no Place in the Town," Addison wrote in No. 69, "which I so much love to frequent as the *Royal-Exchange*," where "I am known to no Body."[22] Pat Rogers has made the general observation that "in some ways . . . the contemporary writer closest to Defoe is Joseph Addison."[23] Their deep engagement with questions of solitude and silence constitutes one of the largest tracts of common ground.

They develop the ground differently. In "Of Solitude" Crusoe argues with some ambivalence (witness the tangled syntax and oscillating convictions of the "Act of Solitude" passage) that isolation produces some "Advantages" (notably an opportunity for "the Contemplation of sublime Things"). The *Spectator* argued more forthrightly and systematically that human solitude can serve as a means of achieving order, pleasure, and power. In Defoe's fictions, though, it is far more often a source of pain and bafflement. An incident from *The Journal of the Plague Year* provides a compact instance of a kind of sundering that operates everywhere in Defoe's novels. H. F. encounters a waterman who supplies his plague-stricken wife and children with money and food he earns by delivering supplies to boats anchored in the river; the ubiquitous fear of infection forces him to interpose some space between himself and both the vessels he supplies and the family he sustains. "I fell into some Talk, at a Distance, with this poor Man . . . *Why, says he, that's my House*, pointing to a very little low boarded House, *and there my poor Wife and two Children live*, said he, *if they may be said to live; for my Wife and one of the Children are visited, but I do not come at them.* And with that Word I saw the Tears run very plentifully down his Face; and so they did down mine too, I assure you" (106). The plague in the *Journal*, like the ocean in *Crusoe* (and like other formidable factors in Defoe's other novels), acts as an arbiter of isolation. It imposes barriers and frustrates empathy. "This poor Man" (who by trade specializes in fluidity, mobility, and access) fears contact with his family, as H. F. does with the man. Talking and shedding tears, the two men's faces mirror each other, but "at a Distance."

In the last clause H. F. explicitly, if casually, draws the reader ("you") into this troubled system of relations. The reader, though, occupies it differently. The distance that divides H. F., the waterman, and his family is spatial. That which separates the reader is fundamentally temporal, and it is in that respect that this moment serves as emblem for a larger time effect of isolation that governs much of Defoe's fiction.

A Journal of the Plague Year is an intensely occasional work. It appeared in 1722, at a moment when signs of the plague's return were compelling much attention. The text's title and timing proffer a clearly defined temporal divide (fifty-seven years, spanning two calendrical centuries) that is offset by a kinship of situation. The book's initial readers might expect to find in H. F.'s account a mirror of their own potential predicament as (on a smaller scale) the waterman witnesses in his face a reflection of his own grief. Very late in the book, though, Defoe abruptly introduces a small complication into this imaginary communion. When H. F. mentions a burial ground at Moorfield's, his text gives way to the sole editorial intrusion in the book: "*N.B.* The Author of this Journal, lyes buried in that very Ground, being at his own Desire, his Sister having been buried there a few Years before" (233). Up to this point it has been possible to imagine a contemporaneity between the narrator and his audience. What Genette calls the "narrating instance"—in this case the moment at which H. F. has remade his "Memorandums" into the present text—remains unspecified. If (as the details of the narrative suggest) H. F. is roughly Crusoe's contemporary (born *ca.* 1632), then the *Journal's* first readers would have reckoned with the possibility that what they hold is a recent redaction of an older manuscript by a still living (but aged) man. Defoe's abrupt cancellation of that possibility impinges with peculiar force on the *Journal's* last words a few pages later, where H. F. concludes

> the Account of this calamitous Year . . . with a coarse but sincere Stanza of my own, which I plac'd at the End of my ordinary Memorandums, the same Year they were written:

> *A dreadful Plague in London was,*
> *In the Year Sixty Five,*
> *Which swept an Hundred Thousand Souls*
> *Away; yet I alive!* (248)

Working in tandem with the earlier editorial intervention, these last lines compactly accomplish a double action, simultaneously fusing and sundering reader and narrator. For the first and only time in the entire book, the published text corresponds exactly, in wording and arrangement, with the set of "Memorandums" we have not read: this "Stanza" concludes them both, and by its agency we are brought more closely into contact with the original manuscript and the "same," now distant, "Year" in which it was composed. At the same time, Defoe has undercut H. F.'s final utterance—or rather, redistributed its impact. The absence of a finite verb in the last, exultant exclamation allows our special knowledge to fill the void and double the application: H. F., "alive" when he wrote, is not so now. The condition that in 1665 distinguished him from "an Hundred Thousand Souls" now separates us from him. This relocation of H. F.'s solitary "I" effectively relocates the "you" whom he addressed and assured earlier in the anecdote of the waterman. The reader too is isolated, engaged in a dialogue that (like so many in the text) turns out to be a dialogue with the dead.

Throughout his fiction, Defoe orchestrates this temporal sundering, these mirrored separations, again and again. His narrators recount life-stories of complex isolation, of deep attractions inflected by great, untraversable divides: Crusoe "befriends" and rejoices in Friday, the archetypal Other, constructing the archetype all the while; Moll Flanders marries, recognizes, and rejects her brother; Roxana adores and annihilates her daughter. All these energetic autobiographers construe their texts, implicitly or explicitly, as a possible means of escape from their predicaments, as though their copious written renderings of lived time, urgently addressed to readers ("I assure you"), may at last make it possible (as Crusoe hopes in the case of his journal) for their "silent Lives" to find the full expression denied them in their vexed solitudes and troubled human encounters.

Defoe accords them at best an equivocal success; he enforces and indexes its uncertainty by calendrical designs of time. The *Journal* is one among many fictions in which he seals off his narrators and their narratives on the other side of the line that separates the present from the previous century: Crusoe's story unfolds there, as does the story of the Cavalier in *Memoirs of a Cavalier*, and of Moll Flanders: we learn on her last page that she has written her life story at the age of seventy in 1683; the book appears in 1722.

Roxana (1723) deals in a double time-scheme that by its patent artifice highlights the pattern of Defoe's temporal isolation effect. As has been often remarked, the details of Roxana's narrative simultaneously place her, at the height of her powers as a formidable woman and "Fortunate Mistress," during the reigns of *both* Charles II (1660–85) and George I (1714–27). To an alert early reader Roxana might seem at once a luminary of a vanished age (probably dead now, like Charles's "other" mistresses Nell Gwynne, who died in 1687, and Lady Castlemaine, who died in 1709) and a living contemporary. Here again, the temporal structure inculcates in the reader a local experience of the uncertainties and isolations narrated. Like many characters in the book (including Roxana's anguished daughter) we are prevented from readily identifying the woman by the most ordinary means: her dates and her name (which, like those of Defoe's other narrators—Moll, the Cavalier, H.F.—remains obscure). In the end, as reciprocal secrecy engulfs and alienates the principal characters—Roxana, her lifelong confidante Amy, and her desperate daughter—it encompasses the reader too, from whom, on the final page, Roxana withholds those details of her story for which she has awakened the sharpest desire and expectation: the particulars of her daughter's murder, and of the "dreadful Course of Calamities" that followed. Roxana's narrative, driven, voluble, confessional, falls abruptly back into the realm of "silent Life," of time untold. It promises full access, and then refuses it. In this respect *Roxana*'s final pages form a fitting conclusion to a novelistic career that had begun only four years earlier with Crusoe's "Journal," forever inaccessible behind its occlusive "Copy." Defoe's first fictive dealings in the structure of the calendar and form of the journal forecast a larger program of textual isolation that many novelists after him pursued. His narrators yearn for revelatory connection but, unable fully to experience or impart it, they implicate their readers as well as themselves in "one universal Act of Solitude."

At once inscribing diurnal form and writing against it, Defoe's journal narratives illuminate not only the temporality of his other fictions (where time form and text combine by slightly different means to index isolation), but also a recurrent feature of time in English novels throughout the eighteenth century—what I have already described as the temporal dimension of Barthes's "reality effect." [24] In his short, brilliantly suggestive essay of that title, Barthes begins by considering both spatial and temporal effects, supplying an example of each: Flaubert's description of a room in which "on an old piano, under a barometer, there was a pyramid of boxes and cartons"; and Michelet's account of Charlotte Corday in prison on the last night of her life, sitting for a portrait while awaiting her executioner, when "after an hour and a half, someone knocked softly at a little door behind her." Barthes's argument about such details, which seem to fulfill no function and complete no pattern specific to the texts in which they appear, is that they accomplish "what might be called the *referential illusion*. . . . [A]t the very moment when these details are supposed to denote reality directly, all that they do, tacitly, is signify it. . . . It is the category of the 'real,' and not its various contents, which is being signified" (16). "At the very moment," though, when he clinches this explanation by reinvoking his original examples, Barthes himself performs a tacit complication of their implicit categories: "Flaubert's barometer, Michelet's little door, say, in the last analysis, only this: *we are the real*" (16). Michelet's notation of time, his "hour and a half," has been displaced by a physical object, the "little door." Barthes has doubled the spatial examples and elided the temporal. Perhaps the temporal is more elusive to deal with: in what sense does it "stand in" for the "real"? I will not presume to determine the ontological differences between the door and the duration, but it may be possible to suggest how the paradigm of the journal and the notations of the calendar contribute to the new temporal realism of the novel in the eighteenth century. Most eighteenth-century novels represent their narrators as negotiating the dialectic of diurnal form in texts unprecedentedly thick with details and dates—as caught between an increasingly widespread cultural practice of representing successive days by copious particulars apparently free of the dictates of plot, and an awareness that such particulars may themselves prove problematic. In such texts, the notations of time do not merely stand in for the real (as in Barthes's argument); as in Defoe's fictions, and particularly in his unmade, remade "journals," they help to chart the narrative's navigation between real time and its layered representations. This navigation itself becomes a constant object of attention for both writer and reader, whether the navigation appears confident (as in *Tom Jones*) or agitated (as in *Tristram Shandy*). Barthes writes of an ineluctable, unspoken compromise in realistic fiction between the infinitely particularized reality and the inevitably selective representation. In the eighteenth-century novel, that compromise poses a problem endlessly vexed, openly discussed, repeatedly reworked. As a theoretical test case for recording "all occurrences and observations," the journal paradigm focused the problem, informed the discussion, and structured the reworkings.

As I suggested earlier, most novelists of the period, beginning with Defoe, exhibited a compound fascination with and resistance to diurnal form. At the same time, several major novelists display a deepening involvement over the course of their careers with the calendar as the template on which to shape and define their structures. Richardson's Pamela heads her letters by the day of the week and her journal by the number of days she has been confined, but the correspondents in *Clarissa* and *Sir Charles Grandison* supply more explicit notations for their epistles (day, date, and month, though not the number of the year). Fielding increasingly anchors his narratives in specific years: In *Tom Jones*, whose plot transpires primarily in 1745, certain formally gratuitous details of the kind that Barthes analyzes suggest that Fielding may be signifying not just the "real" in general but the actual and particular conditions (weather, time of moonrise) that occurred on a specific date.[25] His last novel, *Amelia*, set in 1733, displays a time scheme so elaborate, careful, and exact as to constitute "an achievement . . . unprecedented in the history of the novel."[26] As *Tristram Shandy* proceeds through its annual two-volume increments, Sterne plays increasingly on calendrical precision, at one point specifying the exact date of a chapter's inscription—a date not far removed from the passage's first print appearance.

By such devices, later novelists produced a time effect that in one respect reversed Defoe's: Richardson's readers could project his later novels onto the calendar of a recent year; many in Fielding's audience could recall what they were doing in the years of Amelia Booth's and Tom Jones's agitations; Sterne came close at times to the contemporaneity of the periodical (or at least of the annual). All, one way or another, fostered the specific, calendar-based sense of "simultaneity" that Benedict Anderson posits as one of the novel's distinguishing features.[27] But they cultivated a larger concurrency as well. In the eighteenth-century novel, the temporal reality effect involved a deep engagement with the secular calendar that was unprecedented in fiction. It rendered neither an object ("a barometer") nor a sensation (a "knock at the door") but an activity: the plotting of narratives and subjectivities within and against the grid of successive, dated days. This activity was real, and increasingly widespread: people read print narratives so plotted in newspapers, periodicals, and travel journals, and wrote them in memorandum books, diaries, and journal letters. Part of the novel's appeal to such readers lay in its capacity to show them, with a suppleness and variety no other mode could match, just how this new temporal and textual process worked.

BURNEY: FEMALE DIURNALITY UNMADE AND REMADE

Defoe's fictive treatment of journal-keeping tentatively genders the activity: Crusoe, H. F., and the Cavalier write diaries; Moll, Roxana, and his other women narrators do not. As a representation of who was actually writing what within his culture, this amounts to an unreality effect. Women as well as men wrote texts that they designated as "journals" and that they constructed at least in part along lines and for purposes that Defoe and his male diarists might well find familiar. Frances Burney, beginning such a text at the age of fifteen, affords a striking instance:

> *Poland Street, London, March 27th* [1768]
>
> To have some account of my thoughts, manners, acquaintance & actions . . . is the reason which induces me to keep a Journal: a Journal in which I must confess my *every* thought, must open my whole Heart! But a thing of th[is] kind ought to be addressed to somebody. . . . To whom, then, *must* I dedicate my wonderful surprising & interesting adventures? . . . my own hopes, fears, reflections & dislikes?—Nobody!
>
> To Nobody, then, will I write my Journal! since To Nobody can I be wholly unreserved—to Nobody can I reveal every thought, every wish of

my Heart, with the most unlimited confidence, the most unremitting sincerity to the end of my Life![28]

The strategy here centers on the pivot between the paragraphs. By energetic punning (which she will sustain a while longer), Burney converts her plight—having nobody to confide in—into a kind of privilege. In substance though not in tone, the passage displays certain affinities with Crusoe's account of his reasons for starting a journal. Despite dwelling in a heavily populated household on Poland Street, Burney, too, depicts herself as propelled by an ineluctable solitude to produce a text that perhaps "Nobody" will read. Like Crusoe, though more playfully, she remakes a circumstantial privation into a textual imperative.

Burney, though, writes her journal with (and from) a difference, one she tags when addressing her new-made audience towards the end of her witty preamble: "From this moment, then, my dear Girl—but why, permit me to ask, must a *female* be made Nobody?" (*EJL* 1.2). Burney's question strikingly reverses the gesture it interrogates. In addressing "Nobody" as "my dear Girl," Burney has technically "made Nobody a female," not the other way around. The question's reversal notably raises its stakes. Suddenly Burney asks not about the playful gendering of an arrant fiction, but about the annihilation of a living entity: a woman made into "Nobody." Much of the criticism on Burney begins from the question as Burney phrases it. I propose here to take up its temporal component as an element that operated throughout her writing life, ordering and disrupting both her diaries and her novels. In this preamble to her first journal, Burney devises "Nobody" as an ideal sponsor for a comprehensiveness ("*every* thought") and a continuity ("to the end of my Life!") that she apparently construes as critical *desiderata*, accessible nowhere else but in a private manuscript. These are precisely the satisfactions that Pepys contrived for himself throughout his journal, and that Boswell espoused in theory and pursued in practice. But for Burney and the women diarists among her contemporaries, familial, social, and cultural pressures rendered such satisfactions more elusive, enforcing lacunae of various kinds within their texts, and working against the kind of continuity that Burney in her preamble equates with a sustained sense of self. Within the agenda she there articulates, such lacunae amount to a dangerous negation: to leave time unrecorded is to abet the process by which a "*female* is made Nobody." In both her diaries and her novels Burney writes out of a deep strategic engagement with the problems and possibilities of eighteenth-century women's time.

Uncertainty as to how, or whether, the diary mode is "gendered" extends back to the world Burney was born into, and it conditioned her own writing throughout her life. Its workings are perhaps most fully documented and best seen in the milieu that ushered Burney from obscurity to eminence: the literary circle for whom Samuel Johnson served as oracle and Hester Thrale as (in Boswell's words) "lively hostess" and presiding sibyl. Boswell enacts a striking instance of the confusion about gender and journal-keeping at one point in the *Life*. While visiting the Thrales' house in Streatham, he, Johnson, Lord Trimlestown, and Thrale debate the merits of the *Memoirs* of Robert Sibbald, in which (according to Boswell's misrepresentation) that "celebrated Scottish antiquary" confessed that he had returned to Presbyterianism from Roman Catholicism because he had found religious fasting too rigorous a ritual:

> Mrs. Thrale. "I think you had as well let alone that publication. To discover such weakness exposes a man when he is gone." Johnson. "Nay, it is an honest picture of human nature. How often are the primary motives of our greatest actions as small as Sibbald's, for his reconversion." Mrs. Thrale. "But may they not as well be forgotten?" Johnson. "No, Madam, a man loves to review his own mind. That is the use of a diary, or journal." Lord Trimlestown. "True, Sir. As the ladies love to see themselves in a glass; so a man likes to see himself in his journal." Boswell. "And as a lady adjusts her dress before a mirror, a man adjusts his character by looking at his journal." I next year found the very same thought in Atterbury's *Funeral Sermon on Lady Cutts*; where, having mentioned her *Diary*, he says, "In this glass she every day dressed her mind." (*Life* 3.228)

The gendering here cuts both ways. Johnson, Trimlestown, and Boswell collaborate on an analogy that implicitly genders the journal as male, in keeping with larger cultural allotments: "mind" and "journal" are the province of "a man" (expressively individualized); "dress" and "mirror" are the province of "the ladies" (initially collectivized). No one registers the available complication that men too dress before mirrors and women too have minds and write journals. By writing up the conversation as a chain reaction of parallel structures, Boswell compounds the analogy's power of enclosure and containment; no melding of terms takes place across the sharply (syntactically) drawn boundary of the comparison. Yet such a melding is precisely what Atterbury effects in the retrospective addendum. The elements that Boswell construed as analogy, Atterbury conflates into metaphor in such a way as to acknowledge (as Boswell's analogy does not) that a "Lady" has in fact kept a "Diary," while gendering that textual activity in the opposite direction: in Atterbury's figure, the woman's writing becomes a mode of "dressing." In short, Boswell writes up the conversation as though oblivious to the possibility of female journal-keeping, then adds an afterword in which a woman serves as the paragraph's sole exemplar of the practice (Sibbald's book, which started the conversation, was autobiography rather than diary).

Other participants in the colloquy had shown themselves susceptible of a comparable confusion. In a letter to Henry Thrale from the midst of the Hebridean tour, Johnson preened himself on the copiousness of his journal letter, and couched the activity in a faintly Atterburyan metaphor: "I hope my mistress keeps all my very long letters, longer than I ever wrote before. I shall perhaps spin out one more before I [return home]" (*Letters* 2.100). The phrase "spin out" suggests that Johnson may momentarily conceive his textual task, addressed to a woman ("my mistress"), as fundamentally feminine in itself: the production and sustaining of a "very long" narrative thread. Yet in a letter to his "mistress" two weeks earlier, Johnson plainly posits journal writing as an activity available to both sexes. Immediately after likening Boswell to the " 'faithful Chronicler . . . Griffith,' " Johnson enjoins Thrale to keep a comparable account: "I hope, dearest Madam, you are equally careful to reposit proper memorials of all that happens to you and your family . . ." (*Letters* 2.95). Johnson's injunction for Thrale to be "equally careful" maps at least the possibility (and the "hope") that man and woman may write "memorials" in like abundance.[29]

Johnson's letters later became the focus of a mild divergence of judgment between Thrale and himself, grounded at least partly in their different genders. In her *Anecdotes of the Late Samuel Johnson* (1786), Thrale devoted a long passage to identifying those female friends of Johnson whose spoken opinions on literature he cites respectfully (without naming his sources) in his published criticism. In what amounts to an aside, Thrale voices an opinion of her own which Johnson never cited, in part because it elevated a private manuscript over the subsequent, published book: "The letters written in his journey [to the Hebrides], I used to tell him, were better than the printed book. . . ."[30] In the context of this highly gender-conscious paragraph on

the women who demonstrably affected Johnson's thinking, Thrale's statement implies that as a woman, she is able to judge the value of Johnson's
journal letters more justly than himself; here she comes near to gendering a
responsiveness to this mode of writing, though not the genre *per se*.[31] As a
practical matter, Boswell, Johnson, and Thrale know that within their culture, both men and women engage in serial self-recording, but they often
write and talk as though the practice might be—or is even assumed to be—
gendered one way or the other.

I want to try to reconcile the apparent discrepancy between these pre-
sumptions of sameness and figures of difference by linking it with an issue of
text and time of which self-chroniclers of both sexes were well aware. In
the eighteenth century, both men and women wrote up their days in texts
that they designated by the same names—"diaries," "journals," "journal
letters"—but that often defined and inhabited a different, gender-specific
temporality. The difference was not essential but circumstantial. That mode
of discretionary private time, lived and written at will, which underpins
Boswell's suggestion (in his essay on diaries) that "a *man* should not live
more than he can record" was in fact (as Boswell's complacent gendering
assumes) far more available to men of his rank—and Pepys's—than to
women of the same social stratum, who were constantly subject to the demands and interruptions of family and household management. In the bellman passage, Pepys writes his entry while his "wife and her maid" do the
washing; Boswell diarizes most copiously when traveling far from home—a
privilege that his wife never shares. Where Boswell and Pepys compose
"continuous serial" entries, recording every day in succession under its
date—a practice matched in many other male diaries composed during the
intervening century—the diaristic writings of their female contemporaries
are generally far more intermittent.

Thrale knew this distinction from her own experience with self-recording,
though she says nothing of it in Boswell's account of the conversation on
minds and mirrors, dress and diaries in March 1778. There, in contemplating Sibbald's self-revealing *Memoirs*, she raises questions not of time but of
publicity: "You had as well let alone that publication," she advises, and in
context her choice of noun itself seems charged. Boswell has been talking
not about the printed book but about the original manuscript, which he
possesses. Thrale, though, focuses not on the risks of inscription but on the
vulnerabilities of publication: "May not [Sibbald's weaknesses] as well be forgotten?" It is of course impossible to know all she said, much less thought,

during the exchange, in part because Boswell's report ensures that once she
has launched the conversation by arguing for silence and oblivion (with respect to Sibbald's foibles), she lapses into silence herself, forgotten by the
men as they elaborate their remarkably forgetful comparison of male diurnalists and female dressers.

At this juncture, though, Thrale was already recording her thoughts and
experiences in a text that by its temporality partly confirmed the elisions in
the men's analogy, and partly confounded them. For a year and a half (since
September 1776) she had been writing her *Thraliana*, whose title and genealogy concede a gendered difference in diaristic temporality and point to the
conditions that produce it. The ana is an intrinsically occasional form, a
record of observations, reflections, conversations and anecdotes composed
at moments when leisure and impulse converge. For Thrale such moments
arose irregularly and unpredictably; more often than not, her entries bear
no dates. She wrote over a period of thirty-three years, in a set of six blank
volumes her husband had given her as an anniversary present, each pre-
embossed with the word *Thraliana* on the cover: his surname (her married
name) melded with that of a genre of intermittence. The fusion was significant: over and over within the text itself, Thrale makes clear how randomly,
plentifully, and at times exasperatingly the predicaments of her children and
the peremptoriness of her husband punctuate her days, precluding the long
stretches of solitary time desirable for more systematic writing.

Like Boswell, Thrale pursued self-recording in many modes: she keeps a
Children's Book, a record of her progeny's process more calendrical than
Thraliana but even less continuous (with entries to mark birthdays and significant events); she writes travel journals (and publishes one travel book,
*Observations and Reflections Made in the Course of a Journey through France and
Italy* [1789], reworked from journals in the mode of Johnson's *Journey*); and
after Henry Thrale's death she even transforms the *Thraliana* itself, in its
later volumes, into a more diaristic, chronological account, couched in
highly sporadic dated entries, and mingled with the stuff of ana: undated
observations and anecdotes. But she never works in the time form characteristic of Pepys and Boswell: the continuous journal, temporally regular
and exact. She herself draws the distinction in a *Thraliana* entry from March
or April 1778 (so close in date to the Sibbald conversation that the two may
be causally connected): "Mr Boswell keeps a regular Literary Journal I believe of everything worth remarking; 'tis a good way, but Life is scarce long
enough to talk, & to write, and to live to rejoyce in what one has written—

at least I feel that I have begun too late." [32] Thrale's sense that she has started "too late" registers not a difference of age (she is thirty-seven, Boswell thirty-eight) but of situation. Thrale has something like Boswell's appetite for self-recording, but nothing like his opportunities. To the extent that the ana genre represents her own choice, it both aligns her with a European textual tradition that transcended gender and establishes her as an innovator in her own country. French authors, male and female, had been amassing and publishing anas for almost a century (Thrale prided herself on her collection of "20 of them in good Editions"). Embarking on her own text, she had (as her editor observes) "no real English precedent"; in her native language, she was an energetic pioneer.[33] As her musing on the counterexample of Boswell's "regular Literary Journal" suggests, though, the genre of the *Thraliana* was not entirely her choice: her husband, she writes in the first paragraph, devised that "pompous Title" for the blank books himself. Filling them over three decades in fits and starts, Thrale acknowledges that for her and for women similarly situated, the unmaking of the diurnal is less a textual choice (as it is for Crusoe and H. F. in their redacted journals, for Johnson in his *Journey*) than a fact of life. For them the dialectic of diurnal form is hardly an option: by circumstance, family obligation, and social pressure, they *must* write selectively and intermittently, leaving days and moments (however reluctantly) unrecorded.

Frances Burney, I want to show, contends with and critiques the fact of this unmaking, this gendered asymmetry in the diurnal dialectic, in both her private manuscripts and her published fictions, and at the end of her long life deepens her treatment of the problem by preparing her own diaries for publication, as no woman in Britain had done before. In the address to "Nobody" with which she commences her journal at the age of fifteen, she emphatically conceives the text as continuous and comprehensive, not intermittent: "a Journal in which I must confess my *every* thought" (*EJL* 1.1; italics Burney's). Apparently, the diary fell short of this goal from the first.[34] Without relinquishing the ideal of continuity, Burney writes up only certain days, for several reasons. First, she is engaged also with an alternate agenda of setting down her "wonderful, surprising & interesting adventures" (1.2), which she finds in scant supply: "Alas, alas! my poor Journal!—how dull, unentertaining, uninteresting thou art!—oh what would I give for some Adventure worthy reciting—for something which would surprise—astonish you!" (1.15). Second, she construes the writing itself as suspect within her household, something that must be held in check: "I make a kind of rule never to indulge myself in my two *most* favourite persuits[, r]eading & writing, in the morning—No, like a good Girl I give that up wholly, Accidental occasions & preventions excepted, to [needle] work, by which means my Reading & writing in the afternoon is a pleasure I am not blamed for, & does me no harm, as it does not take up the Time I ought to spend otherwise. I never pretend to be so superiour a Being as to be above having and indulging a *Hobby Horse*, & while I keep mine within due bounds & limits, Nobody, I flatter myself, would wish to deprive me of the poor Animal" (1.14−15). Those last clauses smack of wishful thinking, and of something more complex. The defensive tone of the whole passage suggests that Burney thinks somebody *may* "wish to deprive" her of her emphatically harmless "pleasure" (and she seems to suspect her own reassurance as a possibly hollow "flattery"). The presence of "Nobody" complicates matters further. From the journal's first page the term has done double duty, figuring both as a genuine absence and as an essential agent (best friend and confidante) whom Burney identifies with the journal itself. In fact this is the first instance in the extant text in which Burney appears to ignore the potential pun that she herself has so carefully fostered. It may, however, operate anyway, suggesting that within a household where "good Girl[s]" give themselves up "wholly" to needlework, and "Reading and writing" prompt thoughts of "blame" and "harm," the journal (figured as "Nobody") may somehow "wish to deprive" its author of itself, with the result that the author might "flatter herself" for having moved more firmly into line with familial precept.[35]

The pun proves prophetic a few days later, when the journal itself provides the "surprise" and "adventure" Burney has been searching for, by becoming an agent in its own (very physical) unmaking. Friday's entry breaks off abruptly: "I have a surprise to communicate to you, which is that [. . .]" (1.18). Burney explains the disruption in the next day's entry:

> Cabin. Saturday, July [30]
> And so I suppose you [i.e., "Nobody"] are staring at the torn paper, & unconnected sentences—I don't much wonder—I'll tell you how it happen'd. . . . You must know I always have the last sheet of my Journal in my pocket, & when I have wrote it half full—I Join it to the rest, & take another sheet—& so on. Now I happen'd unluckily, to take the last sheet out of my pocket with my Letter—& laid it on the piano forte, & there, negligent fool!—I left it. . . . Well, as ill fortune would have it, papa went into the Room—took my poor Journal—Read & pocketted it! Mama came

up to me & told me of it. O Dear! I was in a sad distress—I could not for the Life of me ask for it . . . (1.18 – 19)

Burney first takes stock of the material evidence of abruption (the "torn paper" and "unconnected sentences"), then details as never before her strategies of textual continuity in diction that pleonastically highlights the connective and the perpetual ("I *always* have the last sheet," "I Join [emphatically capitalized] it to the rest," "& *so on*"). The transfer of the sheet from her pocket to her father's breaks the continuity, which Burney seeks to restore the next night when she makes bold to ask for it back:

"[W]hat, Fanny, s^d he, kindly—are you in sad distress?"—I half laugh'd—
"well—I'll give it you, now I see you are in such distress——but take
care, my dear, of leaving your writings about the House again—Suppose
Any body else had found it—I declare I was going to Read it loud—
Here—take it—but if ever I find any more of your Journals, I vow I'll
stick them up in the market place!" . . .

    I was so frightened that I have not had the Heart to write since, till now,
I should not but that — — in short, but that I cannot help it!—As to the
paper, I destroyed it the moment I got it. (1.19)

Frightened, Burney both violates continuity and insists on it. The sheet that her father has "Read & pocketted" she immediately destroys, but she finds she "cannot help" inscribing still more sheets. The double gesture suggests a sacrifice: a propitiatory annihilation of a part in order to preserve (and precariously and compulsively enjoy) the whole.

    Charles Burney discourages the journals by exaggerating the perils of publicity. Appealing to his daughter's shyness (a trait already legendary in family lore), he argues, in effect, that her "writings" inevitably entail the risk of self-exposure at the hands of "Any body else"; even in the midst of his purported compassion—"I see you are in such distress"—he opts to aggravate the distress by proposing to read her papers "loud" or (more preposterously, and hence more pointedly) to "stick them up in the market place." The threat of publication, aural or material, produces its intended effect on Burney (it frightens her); it has also been the focus of much biographical and critical writing that construes this fear as an essential element in her career. But in a follow-up conversation a few days later with a family friend of her father's generation, Burney hears a different kind of argument for not keeping a journal. "I have been having a long conversation with Miss Young on journals. She has very seriously and earnestly advised me to give mine up—heigho-ho! Do you think I can bring myself to oblige her? . . . She says that it is the most dangerous employment young persons can have—it makes them often record things which ought *not* to be recorded, but instantly forgot. I told her, that as *my* Journal was *solely* for my own persual, nobody could in justice or even in sense, be angry or displeased at my writing any thing" (1.20–21). Burney's reply here returns to familiar ground: the question of who will read the journal, and even the hint, via "nobody," that the journal might somehow work against itself. Miss Young promptly picks up on the issue of privacy and, like Charles Burney (at whose request perhaps she is intervening), she develops from it the dangers of exposure in a long exchange.

Neither woman, though, appears to recognize how thoroughly Burney has shifted the terms of the debate away from those implicit in Young's original contention. There the peril of this "most dangerous employment" consists not in its potential publicity—that is, in its effect on the way others may view the diarist—but in its relentless continuity, which has consequences for the mind of the diarist herself. The practice, Young avers, makes the practitioner "record things which ought *not* to be recorded, but instantly forgot." This logic holds true even—or rather, especially—if as Burney insists "*my* Journal [is] *solely* for my own perusal," because her "perusal" will further reinforce the memory of those things that ought to be forgotten (and forgotten so "instantly" that Young cannot pause here to define or describe them).[36] Young's pronouncement comes strikingly close to the terms in which Burney has conceived her project, as "a Journal in which I *must* confess my *every* thought," a text she "cannot help" writing. In Burney's formulations as in Young's, the journal makes her write it.

That is Young's objection. "*Every* thought" is many thoughts too many, some of which, made durable as ink, will imperil the journal-keeper's character. Young here works a variation on the argument that underlay Pope's satire on the daily newspaper, and Defoe's take on travel writing: diurnal form writes into permanence particulars best left transitory (the gossip in "every little Town, Village and Hamlet"; the names of each inn visited and wine imbibed). Young, though, argues with a difference. The traditional redaction topos casts omission as a social and aesthetic choice: the journal writer has opted to leave things out in order to avoid burdening the reader with particulars of the wrong kind. In Young's argument, omission becomes a moral necessity, so compelling as to be comprehensive: the diaristic record ought not to be written at all.

As Burney records some days later, she and Young resolved their debate in a way that combined publicity and continuity. Burney lets Young hear a portion of the journal and Young permits the enterprise to go on: "Well, my Nobody, I *have* read part of my Journal to Miss Young—& what's more, let her chuse the Day herself. . . . I assure you I quite triumph!—prejudic'd as she was, she is pleasd to give it her sanction,—*if it is equally harmless every where*—nay, says she even approves of it" (2.23). The shape of Burney's triumph here—the achievement of sanctioned continuation by means of limited (here oral) publication—adumbrates the most important step in her diaristic career: her shift, five years later, from an intermittent journal addressed to "Nobody," to a long series (three decades' worth) of journal letters addressed to her favorite sister and confidant Susanna. The change in venue, from a text composed "*solely* for my own perusal" to one fashioned for the eyes of a close relation, considerably enhanced the continuity of the account. Burney dispatches her first packet of journal letters from the seaside resort of Teignmouth in the late summer of 1773, and the dated entries run in a closer series, with fewer interruptions, than in any narrative of the self that Burney had produced before; even where she skips a day or days, she usually recapitulates the events chronologically in the next entry by a series of what she calls "Daily Datings" (*EJL* 1.309).[37] Unlike private journals, journal letters received unequivocal family sanction. In Burney's home, the practice was gendered: all three sisters wrote abundantly to each other in this mode, while father and brother did not join in. Like the needlework that a "Good Girl" performed in order to afford pleasure to others, the journal letter constituted a social act, a "pleasure" she could pursue without the "blame" attached to the more solitary endeavors of "Reading & writing" for herself.

Burney's new method facilitated a real increase in calendrical continuity, but it fostered only an illusion of narrative comprehensiveness. In the Burney household (as in many others) the journal letter was deemed a quasi-communal property, belonging to (and often read aloud among) the family—and sometimes to a wider circle. In 1773, for example, Burney possessed the manuscript of her stepsister Maria Rishton's journal of a trip to Geneva. Upon returning from Teignmouth, she was alarmed to find that her mentor Samuel Crisp (a close friend of her father's), having borrowed and read the journal packet she had composed for Susanna, now wished her to send him Rishton's journal as well, so that he could forward both documents to his sister, who desired to savor firsthand the merits of texts that she had already heard much praised.[38] Towards the end of her conflicted reply to Crisp's letter, Burney refuses his request to release Rishton's manuscript ("I have—insuperable objections") and only reluctantly agrees to send her own:

> In regard to my own Tingmouth Nonsence . . . I would without fuss t[rust] it to [your sister and her family], though meerly as a proof of how re[adi]ly I would comply with any request they should honour me with, & that you should desire, *except* what concerns *other People*—though, in fact, no *Journal* can be Confined to the writer, but *must* contain anecdotes, &c of others.
> Now pray don't be angry. . . . (2.65–66)

Burney's present predicament doubly charges her phrasing. "No *Journal* can be confined to the writer" both because (as she explains) the text will inevitably represent others as well as the author, and because (as she is discovering) her milieu renders it virtually impossible to sequester the manuscript as private property. Burney here concedes that she has only half-fulfilled her principles "concern[ing] *other People*": she has successfully withheld Rishton's journal but forwarded her own, in whose text Rishton (a fellow traveler to Teignmouth) figures in a number of "anecdotes, &c," not all of them flattering. Amid this dense, encroaching network of other people (the subjects of the diarist's "anecdotes," the diarist's fellow journal writers, and the eager Crispian readers), Burney's initial agenda for "a Journal in which I must confess my *every* thought" becomes no more feasible than it was by Miss Young's strictures—and it is more effectively proscribed. A document subject to such varied scrutiny comes under considerable pressure to remain (in Young's phrase) "harmless every where," not only everywhere within its text, but everywhere it might be read. Burney's outburst to Crisp suggests that she finds the imperative to such harmlessness barely practicable.[39]

It is also starkly gendered. For Pepys and subsequent male diarists, the continuity and comprehensiveness of the account go hand in hand with its privacy; the more securely private the narrative, the more thorough it tends to be. For Burney these dimensions of writing are sundered: the less private her writing is, the more comprehensively she can write her time—and the more comfortably she can spend her time on writing. A few years after

Teignmouth, Burney contrived a way to turn this circumstance to new account. She managed to secure some household time for completing her first published novel, *Evelina*, in a kind of open secrecy (in plain view of her family) by pretending to her father (who knew nothing of the project) that she was composing journal letters to Susanna instead.[40]

In one respect she is telling the truth: she constructs the book primarily in the form of journal letters, addressed by the seventeen-year-old Evelina to her surrogate father Arthur Villars. The novel's structure corresponds exactly to the subterfuge that brings it into being, and its resonance with Burney's own diaristic history is conspicuous. Beginning with Evelina's first letter, Burney explores and insists upon the psychological efficacy of self-inscription in ways that seem calculated to confirm Miss Young's fears as to how journal writing operates on the youthful mind. Visiting friends in the country, Evelina writes for permission to accompany them to London.

> Well but, my dear Sir, I am desired to make a request to you. I hope you will not think me an incroacher; Lady Howard insists upon my writing! . . .
>
> . . . Ought I to form a wish that has not your sanction? Decide for me, therefore, without the least apprehension that I shall be uneasy, or discontented. . . .
>
> I believe I am bewitched! I made a resolution when I began, that I would not be urgent; but my pen—or rather my thoughts, will not suffer me to keep it—for I acknowledge, I must acknowledge, I cannot help wishing for your permission.
>
> I almost repent already that I have made this confession; pray forget that you have read it, if this journey is displeasing to you. But I will not write any longer; for the more I think of this affair the less indifferent to it I find myself.[41]

The "dangerous" links between writing and thinking that Miss Young sketched for Burney ten years earlier, Evelina restates and explicates as an act of discovery: in Evelina's self-corrective formulation, her "pen" is identified both as recording her "thoughts" and as directing them. As Young foretold, desire, when "recorded" rather than "instantly forgot," becomes real and self-perpetuating, transforming passivity ("I am desired to make a request") into activity ("I acknowledge, I must acknowledge . . ."), even though the writer seeks to mitigate the shift by confessing to compulsion: she "cannot help" it (Burney applied the same phrase to her journalizing). In Evelina's first letter it is the pen that "bewitches" and "incroaches";

by its intervention, the writer "form[s] a wish" despite her sense that she "ought" not to.

The letter maps out in miniature the trajectory of text and thought that Evelina will travel from the beginning to the end of the book, a process in which the more "I write" the more "I think" and the more "I find myself." She initially devises her journal letters as a means of remaining in contact with Villars's wisdom and submitting to his judgment ("Decide for me"). Over the course of the novel, though, the imperatives of the journal letter's time form carry her away. Her copious, continuous, headlong narrative outpaces Villars's prudent interventions, to the point where as a writer of ordinary (rather than journal) letters, he can barely keep up. Burney dramatizes this discrepancy several ways: by the pointed rubric—"*Evelina in continuation*"—that heads the heroine's letters and marks her textual dominion (she is the novel's sole continuous storyteller), by a tactical sequencing of letters, and by an adroit use of datelines. We often read Evelina's most recent letter, crammed with new developments, before we can take in Villars's considered (and chronologically earlier) response to her last; his advice is out of synch (Burney allows the continuation of Evelina's narrative to take precedence over straightforward, calendrical chronology).

As the novel progresses, the discrepancy becomes more pronounced. It culminates in the final episode, where Evelina chooses her husband and rejoices in his proposal despite having recently read (and at the time assented to) Villars's definitive but now outdated pronouncement on the subject: "You must quit him!—his sight is baneful to your repose, his society is death to your future tranquillity!" (309).[42] Yet despite this injunction, Evelina's announcement of his proposal and her response evinces confidence rather than alarm: "I cannot . . . apprehend that my frankness to [Lord Orville] will displease you. Perhaps the time is not very distant when your Evelina's choice may receive the sanction of her best friend's judgment and approbation,—which seems now all she has to wish" (355). The tone bespeaks Evelina's new assurance as to her own narrative efficacy: in telling her own love story over the preceding pages, she has given Villars ample reason to change his mind. The language of the passage reworks the links among key words that operated differently in her first letter to Villars. There, Evelina initially construed her own "wish" as following Villars's sanction, though by letter's end the intervention of the pen had begun to reverse that obedient, causal sequence. Here the unmaking is all but complete: Evelina's "wish" frankly precedes Villars's "sanction" and confidently solicits it (her "Perhaps" is predictive, not beseeching). Burney confirms this new autonomy by a final touch of timing. Villars does dispatch a letter of approbation, but Burney delays its transcription until after the final installment of Evelina's continuing journal letters, in which Evelina receives and responds to the letter before proceeding with her wedding. In narrative sequence, then, the text of Villars's permission follows the effect it is intended to cause. In the novel's plot Burney retains allegiance to patriarchal proprieties, but by her sequencing of text she tentatively trumps them.[43]

The timing within the novel notably conforms with the timing that produced it: like Evelina, Burney achieved her aims slightly ahead of paternal sanction. In her *Memoirs of Charles Burney* (1832) she recalls that when the manuscript was almost complete, she told her father of "her secret little work" (without specifying its title, or even its genre), and of her "odd inclination to see it in print."[44] Yet as Doody points out, Burney voiced this vague confession only after she "had lined up a publisher and made all her arrangements" (39)—and she postponed full disclosure until mid-1778, some six months after the novel had achieved enormous (and anonymous) success. For Burney as for Evelina, the action of the pen within the sanctioned structure of the journal letter made possible a rare escape from the familiar constraints of local "woman's time": under these conditions, a "Young Lady" can form and effectually fulfill a "wish" (or an "odd inclination") on her own, securing approbation after the fact (and on her own terms). Working in a world where a "Young Lady" can attain a certain narrative continuity only by incurring a certain degree of publicity (through the quasi-communal property of the journal letter), Burney contrives to push both elements of the equation to extremes, turning constraint into advantage: she produces her most copious and continuous narrative yet (a full six months in Evelina's life) in a venue far more public than anything her journal-exchanging family circle could provide or project for her. In effect she makes good on the threat her father leveled when he grasped one of the pages from her journal to "Nobody" and vowed to "stick them up in the marketplace." By appropriating it, she neutralizes it, commuting his aggression into her own volition, and so brings off another reversal within her own deployment of time and text. Her journal to "Nobody" was necessarily intermittent. *Evelina*, a journal letter to "everybody," proves not merely "harmless" (in Miss Young's negative injunction) but eminent "every where"; it exults in attaining the quality that eluded Burney in her solitary journal, and that her famous novel repeatedly names: continuation.[45]

In her later novels, Burney achieves continuity by other means. Though she went on writing journal letters for decades after *Evelina*, she never structured another fiction in that form. Beginning with *Cecilia* (1782), she opted instead for an omniscient narrative, more plastic in its temporality and its points of view, unconstrained by a linear chronology of closely clustered dates, and not limited to the self-narration of voices within the novel. By writing this way, Burney was partly following a shift in novelistic fashion away from the epistolary, but the shift acquires particular meaning in the context of her own career. She renounces "impersonation" (the author disguised as, or concealed behind, her characters) and asserts a more overt authorial control. This authority was figured also in the externals of the new text, such as their title pages: where *Evelina* was published in emphatic anonymity, the remaining three novels announced themselves, in a cumulative litany over the series, as having been written by "The Author of *Evelina*" (". . . and *Cecilia* and *Camilla*"), for a readership well acquainted with her name and fame. The books embodied authority also by sheer corporeality: *Evelina*, produced in secrecy, had been comparatively short; at five volumes each, *Cecilia*, *Camilla*, and *The Wanderer* weighed in (after *Clarissa*) among the longest fictions produced by any author in Burney's century.[46]

I want to argue, though, that in the later novels, despite Burney's shift in narrative mode, the temporal template of her diaries, though deeply submerged, remains still present, still encoded. The kind of continuation that she achieves within these protracted texts (and which drew much comment during her career and after) derives in large measure from temporalities first worked out in her diaries as problems and solutions of women's time.

The first signs of the journal's persistent presence in the novels' temporality appear in connection with *Cecilia*, in a debate that developed not around Burney's techniques of continuation, but about her choice of conclusion. Upon coming to the end of *Cecilia*, several male readers—Edmund Burke and Samuel Crisp the most formidable among them—expressed dissatisfaction with the novel's unconventional ending, in which the virtuous protagonist marries her beloved but loses her fortune and, "finding that of the few who had any happiness there were none without some misery," she resolves (in the book's closing words) to bear "partial evil with chearfullest resignation." Burke found these results too mixed and too long in coming, as Burney tells Susanna:

The masquerade he thought too long, and that something might be spared from Harrel's grand assembly . . . and he wished the conclusion either more happy or more miserable: "for in a work of imagination," said he, "there is no medium."

I was not easy enough to answer him, or I have much, though perhaps not good for much, to say in defence of following life and nature as much in the conclusion as in the progress of a tale; and when is life and nature completely happy or miserable?[47]

Crisp had leveled similar objections when the book was still in manuscript, and in response Burney supplied a little more of the answer she is here "not easy enough" to voice to Burke:

> With respect . . . to the great point of Cecilia's fortune, I have much to urge in my own defence, only now I can spare no time. . . . I think the book, in its present conclusion, somewhat original, for the hero and heroine are neither plunged in the depths of misery, nor exalted to un*human* happiness. Is not such a middle state more natural, more according to real life, and less resembling every other book of fiction? . . .
>
> You find, my dear daddy, I am prepared to fight a good battle here; . . . if I am made to give up this point, my whole plan is rendered abortive, and the last page of any novel in Mr. Noble's circulating library may serve for the last page of mine, since a marriage, a reconciliation, and some sudden expedient for great riches, concludes them all alike. (*DL* 2.136–37, Burney's emphases)

In both instances Burney's framing of the argument enacts its substance: she "has much to urge" but "no time" or "ease" for saying it, and so implies that her stipulations remain in a "middle state," energetically launched but as yet unconcluded (she is "*prepared* to fight a good battle"). Burney's argument centers (like Crisp's and Burke's) on her choice of a "medium" between happiness and misery, but in her wording, this question of affect verges on becoming an argument about temporal form: the tale's truest ending, she avers to Susanna, will resemble its progress. By this logic, the narrative will persuasively "follow life and nature" in proportion as its conclusion accords with a sense of the "continuation" that had served as *Evelina*'s watchword—which is to say, the less it resembles the novels "in Mr. Noble's circulating library" and the more it resembles the journal letter in which Burney voices her unspoken and unfinished reply to Edmund Burke.

The language in which Burney constructs a reality effect points away from a novelistic temporality and towards a diaristic one.

In *Camilla*, as Edward and Lillian Bloom observe, the ending is pro forma, as conventional as anything Mr. Noble put on offer, but with that novel the argument about Burney's form began in earnest. Male critics began to work up an accusation against the novelist that had hardened into received wisdom by early in the next century: its gist was that in her later fictions, the ending and the progress, the conclusion and the continuation, had become inextricably confused. Burney, the charge went, involved her protagonists in difficulties so mild and so easily dissolved that the novel might plausibly end at any time by an act of will on the part of the heroine; instead they advanced endlessly, through repetitious successions of similar difficulties (*Camilla*'s plot delivers the young woman to the brink of madness and death, but turns on what critics deemed an overscrupulous reluctance to reveal to her beloved an embarrassing debt). This delaying tactic was seen to infuse not only her structure but her style: in her later publications (the *Memoirs* as well as the novels) her periodic sentences grew longer and more intricate, in some cases postponing syntactic closure for more than a hundred words (Johnson's influence was suspected and deplored; in the nineteenth century this point too had become a commonplace).

Many critics interpreted these temporal flaws in the text as manifestations of fundamental faults in the protagonists, unrecognized and uncorrected by their creator. Shortly after Burney's death, a critic in the *Athenaeum* summed up an argument that had increasingly adhered to her in life: "In rising from a perusal of Miss Burney's novels, one cannot avoid a perception of the groundlessness of the difficulties into which her heroines are plunged,—of how much of their embarrassments arises from a weak alarm, . . . a yielding to paltry motives, and a want of power to break through the lace-like meshes of the filmy nets which accident . . . [has] cast around them."[49] Three decades earlier, in a review of *The Wanderer*, William Hazlitt had reckoned up the structural consequences of such fictive behavior: "The reader is led every moment to expect a denouement, and is as constantly disappointed on some trifling pretext. The whole artifice of her fable consists in coming to no conclusion."[50] Hazlitt's accusation, often quoted, has been variously answered by Burney's defenders in the past decade; again, I want to concentrate on its temporal component, and to suggest its intuitive but undiscerning accuracy. Hazlitt dismisses a principal of structure that Burney herself, in her journal letter to Susanna, proposed as intention: that the "progress" and the "conclusion," if rendered less distinguishable from each other, might produce a new kind of novel. There is this crucial difference: what Hazlitt dubs "the artifice of her fable," Burney singles out as a chief source of the "real." This "progressive" dimension of reality was what her journals and journal letters (much longer in the aggregate than her novelistic output) had devoted themselves to depicting (though not always successfully); and it is this reality of time that Burney seeks to render in her interruptive, ongoing, repetitive novels. Hazlitt mistakes for compulsion what Burney articulates as choice: he accuses her in effect of succeeding too well.

In one respect, Burney is translating into fiction a temporality common to the journals of both men and women. The scholar and novelist Thomas Mallon, who has read more diaries from more periods than most, once summarized his findings this way: "Diarists worry a lot."[51] Burney's later novels dramatize worry as the engine of plot. To a degree unusual even in fiction, worry becomes not a background hum to the actions of actual life (as in Mallon's formulation), but a determinant of action—and of inaction (as Burney's critics complained). The consequence of this worry that most bothered her critics was temporal—the delays made the novel too long. That temporality, though, corresponded precisely to the structure of worry that Burney documents in her diaries as arising out of the gendered arrangements by which social obligations, impinging on women's time, forestall their writing. Early in her diaries, she lamented the condition outright:

> O how I hate this vile custom which obliges us to make slaves of ourselves!
> to sell the most precious property we boast, our Time; —& to sacrifice it
> to every prattling impertinent who chuses to demand it! . . .
>
> For why should we not be permitted to be masters of our time?
> . . . I feel myself in no excellent mood—I will walk out & give my
> spirits another *turn*, & then resume my Pen. (*EJL* 1.72—73)

Throughout her journals, and with increasing acerbity in her later novels, Burney records the process by which that "precious property" is subverted and misappropriated: a relentless, repetitive cycle of interruptions, intermittencies, and discontinuities (*Evelina*'s mode unmade) that can only be represented by corresponding abruptions, resumptions, and repetitions in the narrative. Burney's novelistic time resembles no other in the works of her contemporaries: it deals less in the internal symmetries of plotting and more in the seeming chaos, contingency, and repetition of the private diary as her culture permitted her and contemporaries like Thrale to practice it. Her critics perceive such structures as miscalculation, but the texts themselves suggest rather a strategy by which to represent the problems entailed in a woman's attempt to assert possession of her self in both the forms of living and the forms of writing that late eighteenth-century culture makes available to her—to trump intrusion and interruption, and to attain continuation, and thus to reclaim the "precious property" of her "Time" and to "resume" her "Pen."

In her last novel, *The Wanderer* (1814), Burney offers her most extreme account of what the subtitle labels "Female Difficulties"—difficulties figured, in the protagonist Juliet Granville, as the convergence of an inexorable solitude, an indeterminate identity, and an ineluctable dependency. In the final paragraph, Burney harks back to the beginnings of the novel form and of the diary within the novel: she describes her heroine, and by extension her novel, as a "female Robinson Crusoe." [52]

The adjective measures difference within affinity. Crusoe, writing his journal on his island, embodies in the perspective of Burney's novel a particular masculine privilege, albeit one taken to a painful extreme. *All* his time is his own, to dispose and record as he will; if there is no one with whom to partake it, there is also no one to appropriate or violate it. Juliet Granville finds that *no* time is her own: whenever she enters a room in search of a moment's solitude, she finds there a new figure, usually a new antagonist. Burney contrives such surprises so often that this motif becomes the novel's chief source of significant repetition. A compact instance will suggest the recurrent narrative syntax of these moments: touring Arundel Castle, Juliet Granville seeks to escape her present companions, but finds herself propelled into a more intense encounter:

> Believing herself alone, and in a place of which the stillness suited her
> desire of solitude and concealment, she had already shut the door before
> she saw her mistake. What, then, was her astonishment, what her emotion,
> when she discerned, seated, and examining a part of the hangings, at the
> further end of the gallery, the gentle form of Lady Aurora Granville! (551)

Burney sets the culmination of this motif at Stonehenge, where Juliet, again "glad to breathe a few minutes alone," soon finds herself approached by a particularly unexpected and unwanted intruder: "Starting, and in dread of some new horrour, Juliet looked at [Riley] aghast; while clapping his hands, and turbently approaching her, he exclaimed, 'Yes! here she is, *in propria persona!*'" (769–70). Burney's coinage of the term "turbently," which is suggestive of the Latin *turba* or "crowd," encapsulates the problem that often besets her protagonists, who find their *propria persona* inaccessible to themselves because so crowded out and impinged upon by others seeking to lay a claim on it.

The Wanderer, then, posits a condition of the self in time that in one respect transcends gender and in another imposes a particular burden on women. The language in which Burney explains her striking construct of a "female Robinson Crusoe" closely echoes Crusoe's own analysis, in his retrospective *Reflections*, of the "universal Act of Solitude" that encompasses both men and women. Like Crusoe, Burney argues, Juliet Granville was "a being who had been cast upon herself . . . , as unaided and unprotected, though in the midst of the world, as that imaginary hero in his uninhabited island . . ." (873). Burney echoes Defoe echoing Addison, who also posited self-containment "in the midst of the world." But if, as those two males insist, all mortals live in an essential solitude all the time, then, *The Wanderer* argues, society places women in a particular, uninhabitable bind. For them, whether they are alone or in families, solitude may be (as for all humankind) unavoidable, but it is also *unattainable*: they must, like men, inhabit it, but they cannot, like men (like Crusoe) easily make use of it to discover or construct a self. The special "Difficulties" of the female self in time that first figure in the intermittent pages of Burney's early journals find fullest expression in her final novel.

Yet Burney has already orchestrated a more comfortable affinity with Crusoe, at the beginning of the book's final chapter. Virtually all the tangles of the plot have been straightened: having recovered her name, her fortune, her standing, and her family, Juliet finds a moment of satisfactory solitude at the sea's edge,

> in the beautiful verdant recess, between two rocks, overlooking the vast ocean, with which she had already been so much charmed.
>
> No sooner, at this favourite spot, was Juliet alone, than, according to her wonted custom, she vented the fulness of her heart in pious acknowledgements. (859–60)

The passage evokes Crusoe's accounts of himself at the height of his prosperity, when, sheltered also by a rock-formed recess, and awakened to pious gratitude, he can take pleasure in the place and in his self-sufficiency. In *The Wanderer* the moment is brief (Juliet is awaiting her newfound sister, but her beloved will approach before the end of the paragraph to propose marriage) but in the novel's terms it is complete: Juliet finds the privacy she sought, and finishes her acknowledgments before she must resume conversation; for the first time, she suffers no interruption. The passage may also possess a geographical resonance. Burney sets the scene at Teignmouth, the site from which she herself had dispatched her first journal letter to Susanna some fifty years before. *The Wanderer*'s last pages, setting a female Crusoe on the Teignmouth coast, hark back to autobiographical as well as literary-historical beginnings: Burney makes her protagonist whole at the place where she herself had discovered the precarious capacity to write continuous time—where like Crusoe she could begin "to keep a Journal of every Day's Employment."

E p i l o g u e

In the last literary action of her long life, Burney remade—and unmade—
the text of her days one final time: she edited her own papers for posterity.
The process occupied more than two decades (1817–1838), and involved
all manner of revision, from subjecting the texts both to intermittent aug-
mentations (clarifications, annotations, and new explanatory interpolations)
and to more drastic diminutions: Burney obliterated passages by pen, by
scissors, and by fire, and often took pains to conceal the fact of excision. Her
sense of who might read the resultant texts fluctuated often over the decades. She imagined her journals and journal letters primarily as a manuscript legacy for her only child, but she remained mindful too of the possibility of publication. Her son's death without heir in 1837 (when Burney was
eighty-four) brought the second possibility further forward, apparently with
an attendant increase in anxiety and ambivalence. A year later Burney's
younger sister Charlotte Broome wrote her pleading with her to make a
decision: "perhaps, you could Seal [the papers] up, & recollect some worthy
minded beloved friend with a good taste for literature—& write on the
direction to be delivered to that friend as a Bequest—adding, your own
positive direction—that they *may* be published—or *never* be published—"
(*JL* 1.xlii). As the designated friend and recipient of her bequest, Burney
chose her sister's daughter, Charlotte Barrett, but in the two years that remained before her death in 1840 she never delivered the "*positive* direction"
her sister sought. She left both the papers and the decision to Barrett, who
had long helped her with revision and was now to take up the role of literary
executor. When Barrett published the first volumes of Burney's *Diary and*

Letters in 1842, the occasion marked the first print appearance of a woman's private journal.

In preparing and conveying her diary (however equivocally) to the press, Burney both participated in a recent print tradition and effectually reinvented it. By the 1830s, the publication of private diaries was a fairly familiar practice, but it centered on texts recovered from two centuries before. The now-canonical exemplars, against which all new texts (including Burney's) were automatically judged, were William Bray's edition of Evelyn's diary, published in 1818, and Richard, Lord Braybrooke's edition of Pepys's (1825). In a review of the Pepys volumes, Sir Walter Scott devoted a long paragraph to the question of editorial excision, which bears on the effect of Burney's later publication:

> Lord Braybrooke informs us, that as Mr. Pepys was "in the habit of recording the most trifling actions of his life, it became absolutely necessary to curtail the MS. materially, and, in many instances, to condense the matter, but the greatest care has been taken to preserve the original meaning." It would be unreasonable to find fault with this freedom, nor are we disposed to suspect that it has, in any respect, been misused. On the contrary, judging from the peculiar character of Pepys, so uniformly sustained through the whole diary, we feel perfect conviction that the pruning knife has been exercised with that utmost caution necessary for preserving the shape and appearance of the tree in its original state. It may, besides, be accounted very superfluous to wish for a larger share of Mr. Pepys's private thoughts and confidences, than are to be found in the space of some five or six hundred pages of royal quarto. But when will antiquarian eyes be entirely satisfied with seeing? The idea of a work being imperfect, from whatever cause, the restless suspicion that something has been kept back, which would have rendered the whole more piquant, though perhaps less instructive, will always, in spite of us, haunt the curious indagator after the minute curiosities of literature.
>
>> That cruel something unpossessed
>> Corrodes and leavens all the rest.
>
> But we will push these observations no further at present, than just to observe that where contemporary documents are published for the use of the antiquary or historian, we think the editor will, generally speaking, best attain his purpose by giving a literal transcript of the papers in his hands;

whatever falls short of this, diminishes, to a certain degree, our confidence in the genuine character of his materials—it is giving us not the actual speech of the orator, but the substance of what was spoken. When there exists no moral reason for suppression of particular passages, we are not fond of abridgments or castrations—especially in cases like the present, where, after all, the matter communicated is not always so interesting as the peculiar mode in which it is told. Nay, even when decency or delicacy may appear on the one hand to demand omissions, it comes to be, on the other, a matter of very serious consideration in how far such demands can be complied with, without actual injustice to the characters handled by the author, the self-supplied key to whose own character and dispositions is thus mutilated and impaired.[1]

I quote this passage at length because length is both the substance of Scott's argument (he wants more of Pepys's words) and a measure of his problem. At one point the reviewer proposes to cut his own musings short ("we will push these observations no further"), only to belie the promise by extending the argument as long after as before. Dilation here indexes ambivalence, and even anxiety: Braybrooke's quasi-paradoxical claim "to condense the matter" but to "preserve the original meaning" elicits from Scott first agreement (he abets it by the simile of the tree, pruned back to its "original state"), then dissent (the editor's choice shakes "our confidence in the genuine character of his materials"). Scott turns his own line of argument in both directions: the "uniformity" of Pepys's character excuses curtailing (because the text is in every place essentially alike), but the "peculiar mode" of telling that derives from that character is so "interesting" as to require full preservation. The dialectic of diurnal form, and the uncertainties of redaction, are if anything more pronounced than in the previous century. What matters most for a reckoning of Burney's editorial policy is the grounds on which Scott resolves the question. He opts away from excision in favor of full transcription by referring the entire problem to the insatiable appetite of "antiquarian eyes": the text should be whole because it is old.[2]

Seventeen years later, the early readers of Burney's newly published *Diary and Letters* were struck first of all by the antiquity of the author and the text. In a sympathetic review that did much to resurrect her reputation, Thomas Macaulay began by remembering the widespread surprise and temporal disorientation with which, three years earlier, readers had taken in the news of her death at the age of eighty-eight: "[T]here were thousands, we believe, who felt a singular emotion when they learned that she was no longer among us. The news of her death carried the minds of men back at one leap, clear over two generations, to the time when her first literary triumphs were won . . . Frances Burney was at the height of fame and popularity before Cowper had published his first volume, . . . before Pitt had taken his seat in the House of Commons. . . . She lived to be a classic. Time set on her fame, before she went hence, that seal which is seldom set except on the fame of the departed." [3] Macaulay points to the peculiar status of the text at hand within the still young tradition of published journals: given the precedent of the travel journal, Burney was not the first diarist to edit her own text for publication, but her very longevity made her the first such editor whose production would hold immediate interest for "antiquarian eyes": "leap[ing] over generations," her work on her own text was in this respect partly comparable to Braybrooke's work on Pepys's and Bray's work on Evelyn's.

This circumstance imbues Burney's editorial excisions with a peculiar power deriving from a kind of double authority, as both author and antiquary. In two ways Burney reverses the process by which, when she began to write her journal, authority impinged on her and structured her time, unmaking continuity and enforcing occasionality. At that point, Charles Burney had implied his disapproval of the private diary by threatening to revoke the privacy: "if ever I find any more of your Journals, I vow I'll stick them up in the market place!" As I suggested earlier, Burney partly neutralized this threat by appropriating it—by placing *Evelina* on the market. More than half a century later she does so more directly, by preparing for possible publication that very manuscript whose appearance incensed her father. Burney's excisions have often been read as a last instance of her fearfulness and prudery, but within the long complex history of her writing life they seem to me rather to constitute a final assertion of autonomy and authorial power. The diary's lacunae—the unwritten days, the unavoidable discontinuities— were originally a function of interruption by others. Only by going partly public (in the form of the journal letter) could Burney achieve some measure of temporal continuity. Now, going public for the last time, she makes her own lacunae, sculpting the writing of time as she could not originally sculpt the time of writing. Her triumph tells, oddly enough, in the degree to which she has created difficulties for her most recent editors, who seek to recover from her mutilated manuscripts the kind of completeness Scott valued. Introducing her edition of the later journals, Joyce Hemlow takes stock of the challenges set up by an author/editor so careful to conceal her own interventions as to disguise (for example) "a truncated four-page letter . . . as a genuine original of two pages" (*JL* 1.xxxix).[4] A few pages into his edition of the *Early Diaries and Letters*, Lars E. Troide concedes a correlative defeat: just after the famous preamble to "Nobody," he remarks that "At this point perhaps two months of the journal have been cut away and destroyed." Even painstaking investigation, then, cannot quite determine which omissions of days were imposed upon Burney (because she could find no convenient time to write) and which she has effected by her own choice (because decades later she decided to tear the pages out).

If Scott's tentative strictures on Braybrooke's edition of Pepys point the way towards late twentieth-century editions like Hemlow's and Troide's, which seek to reproduce as much text as possible for a readership that wants it all, then Barrett's edition of Burney's *Diary* itself represents an important step in the sequence. It caters implicitly to an audience whose desire for at least the illusion of textual completeness had apparently increased considerably over the years since Braybrooke sought his reader's approval by the judicious deployment of a "pruning knife."[5] Barrett had been privy to the whole project of excision, occlusion, and annotation, and extended it beyond her aunt's death by eliminating from the published *Diary and Letters* perhaps half of the text that had survived Burney's own revisions. In the preface to the *Diary*, though, Barrett keeps these emendations all but silent, emphasizing instead the integrity, authenticity, and (by implication) the completeness of the text to follow. "It cannot be derogatory to [Burney's] beloved memory," Barrett insists,

> to make known her inmost thoughts, *as far as she has left them recorded*; while it might be unjust to withhold the lessons conveyed incidentally. . . .
>
> . . . [S]he herself arranged these Journals and Papers with the most scrupulous care; affixing to them such explanations as would make them intelligible to her successors—avowing a hope that some instruction might be derived from them—and finally, in her last hours, consigning them to the editor, with full permission to publish *whatever might be judged desirable* for that purpose, and with no negative injunction, except one, which has been scrupulously obeyed, viz.: that *whatever might be effaced or omitted*, nothing should in anywise be altered or added to her records. (*DL* xxi–xxii)

Where Bray and Braybrooke highlighted the editorial obligation to abridge, Barrett points instead to an act of preservation. These pages, she implies, represent the "Journals and Papers" as Burney "arranged," amplified, and "consigned" them, with "full permission to publish"; the adjective becomes an implicit attribute of the texts themselves, and Barrett does little to correct that impression. She does not mention, for example, that her aunt cut and burned many "Papers" too; she hints at the possibility of excision only in her use of the non-committal phrase "whatever," which leaves open the possibility that she has "omitted and effaced" nothing at all. Even Burney's one "negative injunction" does not proscribe the publication of some too-private portion of the text (as would be expected), but instead forbids the addition of alien matter, thus reinforcing rather than disrupting the impression of textual integrity. By such rhetoric Barrett mutes the redaction topos (so pronounced in Bray and Braybrooke) almost to inaudibility; she encourages her readers to believe that the text represents the minutiae of Burney's life "as far as she has left them recorded."

Barrett's representation is plainly calculated to appeal to a taste for time and text that had changed since the first publication of Evelyn and Pepys—though those volumes did much to prompt the shift. The calculation operated also on the new book's title page. Burney's *Diary and Letters* is not only the first private diary by a woman to find its way into print, it is also the first published non-fiction journal of any kind in the nineteenth century to give the word *Diary* pride of place in its title. Two decades earlier, Evelyn's and Pepys's prose had been marketed as *Memoirs*, with the word *Diary* subordinated somewhere in the long title: *Memoirs Illustrative of the Life and Writings of John Evelyn . . . Comprising his Diary . . . and a Selection of his Familiar Letters . . .* ; and (clearly in imitation), *Memoirs of Samuel Pepys . . . , Comprising his Diary . . . and a Selection of his Familiar Letters.* For more than a century, the first word in these titles had signaled an enterprise of judicious selection, illustrative of a larger body of fact and/or text (compare Sidney Bidulph's fictional *Memoirs . . . Extracted from her Journals*). The term *Diary*, by contrast, emphasizes diurnality and continuity, the succession of days enacted as text. It possesses some of this force even in Bray's and Braybrooke's titles, where *Selection* technically applies to the letters rather than the journals—though as I've noted both editors take pains to assure the reader that they have drastically culled the diaries as well. Even so, the journal text took up the bulk of both publications, constituted their greatest novelty, and generated the most comment and enthusiasm. Hence a discrepancy: the subordinate term identified the volumes' dominant attraction.

As a result, the word *Diary* gradually acquired a commercial cachet sufficient to sell books on its own, but until Barrett edited Burney, the term generally designated works not of fact but of fiction, some of them quite successful, including several satiric travel journals: Anna B. Jameson's *Diary of an Ennuyée* (1826), Catherine Gore's *Diary of a Désennuyée* (1836), Frederick Marryat's *Diary of a Blasé* (1836), and even an anonymous *Diary of a Little Dog* (1837). These authors accomplish what Defoe gestured towards a century earlier: a fiction structured wholly as a succession of dated, private entries. Plainly there was now a readership eager to absorb narratives produced under the explicit promise of diurnal continuity, tempered perhaps by the assumption that the authors of such patently comic concoctions would take upon themselves the redactive responsibility of a fictive Bray or Braybrooke, leaving out anything that their audience might find too minute or repetitious.

When Barrett takes the word *Diary* as her title's first term, she is at once falling in with a recent trend and critically rerouting it. She completes the title not with a fictional abstraction but with the proper name of a person widely known to have actually existed—and to have written fictions (another first: no *novelist's* diaries had appeared heretofore). Barrett thus becomes the first editor to displace the familiar selectivity of the *Memoir* with the implicit continuity of the *Diary* as the prose mode of most interest and value within the author's cluster of factual writings. Evelyn's and Pepys's editors soon followed suit: subsequent editions (Pepys in 1848, Evelyn in 1850) elevated *Diary* to the titles' leading term, and in the case of Pepys played out the implication by promising a text *Considerably Enlarged.*"

Barrett had herself enhanced the titular promise of diurnal continuity by another device—an epigraph from Edward Young's *Night-Thoughts* which adorned the title page of each volume: "The spirit walks of every day deceased." Addressed to the audience that Macaulay would soon conjure up and for whom Burney's recent death both recalled and definitively ended a distant epoch, Barrett's epigraph promises a specifically diurnal resurrection: the author and her age will arise temporally and textually whole. "Every day" is the structuring principle of the "regular journal" that Pepys implemented, Pope mocked, Johnson and Boswell aimed at—and that Thrale and Burney surrendered amid the relentlessly interruptive circumstances of gender and position that operated on their time and impinged on their timing. Prefacing her aunt's pages with Young's thought, Barrett casts Burney as the continuous diurnalist that her predicament as woman prevented her from becoming. She markets Burney's temporally various and intermittent accounts as though they were the work of another Pepys.

Scott, the antiquarian completist, had produced a comparable conflation of diarists in the closing lines of his review of Pepys seventeen years earlier. There he lamented that Pepys ended the diary too soon to record such major events later in the century as the Popish Plot, in which English "nobles and statesmen . . . sought vengeance on each other by mutual false accusation and general perjury." To measure the "great loss to posterity" effected by those "circumstances which induced Mr. Pepys to discontinue his diary," Scott in his last sentence invoked a phrase from Shakespeare which the print history of diurnal form had imbued with particular resonance: "considering how much of interest mingled even in that degrading contest [i.e., the Plot], considering how much talent was engaged on both sides, what a treasure would a record of its minute events have been if drawn up by 'such a faithful character as Griffiths!'" (314).

The line that Johnson applies to Boswell, Scott applies to Pepys, retaining even Johnson's expressive replacement of the original "honest" with the temporalized "faithful."[6] In doing so, Scott traces a textual lineage whose continuities would have been far clearer to him than to the writers he allusively links. I have tried both to limn and to extend it here. In the 165 years that separate Pepys's first entry from its first publication, diurnal form had come to function first as a private temporality in manuscript and then, concurrently, as a public tempo of print. As the eighteenth century advanced, various meldings of public and private diurnality came to constitute a spectrum of textual possibilities linking the two extremes—the manuscript journal letter, the redacted travel journal, the fictitious journal of a "silent Life," and all the journal-mindful, journal-resistant novels of solitary consciousness that followed from it. The influences and appropriations across the spectrum are complex, but acquire a certain unity from a common derivation, a common task of figuring the local cultural construction of time. Diurnal texts, whether public, private, or in between, draw their power and their appeal from their engagement with new structures of time, with *Tick, Tick, Tick* construed successively as private pleasure, scientific tool, social coordinate, and global dominion. What Scott treasures in Pepys (and by implication in Boswell) as the "record of . . . minute events" has much to do with the motion of the minute hand, exotic when Pepys writes, familiar and social when Boswell writes, and commonplace when Scott writes.

Lawrence Rosenwald has remarked that "Pepys is in some obvious way Boswell's natural father, but neither Boswell nor any other eighteenth-century diarist could ever have read him." [7] The way in which the kinship operates has remained elusive. It resides not in natural but in cultural time, in the new calibrations of chronometry as they operated on timepieces and in text. This common ground gives rise to intricate continuities: if Boswell's private diaries, for example, are inconceivable without the precedent of the *Spectator*, with its culturally powerful equation between diurnal accounting and the secret self, and if the *Spectator* is inconceivable without the temporalities that clocks first proposed and Pepys first narrated in the previous century, then Pepys's and Burney's printed diaries are inconceivable without Boswell, whose published *Tour* and *Life*, both pointedly and assertively grounded in journal time, prepared an audience (as did newspapers, *Spectators*, and novels) for the reading of actual diaries in the ensuing century. With their appearance, the line of development turns upon itself, and the first phase ends.

Notes

PREFACE

1. Even after the advent of the mechanical clock, a human bellringer remained indispensable for several reasons. A church might, for example, possess a clock whose mechanism was not strong enough to pull the bell itself; the bellman would read the time on the smaller clock and translate it manually to the larger bell. As tower clocks became more commonly mechanized so did the bellman himself; on many such clocks the hours were rung by an automaton (often elaborately wrought and decorated), the "Jack o' the clock." Still, human bellringers remained necessary for the tolling of those irregular signals the clock could not schedule: the passing bell, bells for private rites, etc. See Percival Price, *Bells and Man* (Oxford: Oxford University Press, 1983), 107–116 and 173–74.

2. Gerhard Dohrn–van Rossum made these remarks following an unpublished lecture, "Public Clocks and Modern Hours," delivered at the University of Chicago, 20 February 1991. His book, *History of the Hour: Clocks and Modern Temporal Orders*, trans. Thomas Dunlap (Chicago: University of Chicago Press, 1996), develops this observation by investigating the multiplicity of temporal orders (*Zeitordnungen*) at work in Europe from the thirteenth through the nineteenth centuries. Jacques Le Goff summarizes a similar argument by Maurice Halbwachs, to the effect that "there [are] as many collective notions of time in a society as there [are] separate groups" and that "the individual notion of time" is "no more than the internalized point of contact of the several collective notions." Le Goff, *Time, Work, and Culture in the Middle Ages*, trans. Arthur Goldhammer (Chicago: University of Chicago Press, 1980), 38; Halbwachs, "La mémoire collective et le temps," *Cahiers internationaux de sociologie*, 1947, 3–31.

CHAPTER ONE

1. E. P. Thompson, "Time, Work-Discipline, and Industrial Capitalism," in *Customs in Common: Studies in Traditional Popular Culture* (New York: The New Press, 1991), 352–403; quotation 354. Subsequent citations will appear parenthetically.

2. John Aubrey, *Brief Lives, chiefly of Contemporaries, set down by John Aubrey, between the Years 1669 & 1696*, 2 vols., ed. Andrew Clark (Oxford: Clarendon Press, 1898), 1.27–28. Quotations from *Brief Lives* will be cited parenthetically from this edition. The anecdote about Allen appears in MS. Aubr. 6, "written mostly in February 1679/80" (Clark 1.8).

"Minutes" was one of Aubrey's own terms for his manuscripts (see *Aubrey's Brief Lives*, ed. Oliver Lawson Dick [London: Penguin Classics, 1987], 92).

3. *The Winter's Tale*, ed. J. H. P. Pafford (London: Methuen, 1963), 1.2.43–44. Hermione's diction is perhaps prophetic at the outset of a play in which dramatic time will advance with conspicuous abruptness. Before this scene is over her husband will subject her to the shock, the harsh disharmony, of a jealousy so sudden as to constitute a permanent puzzle in the critical tradition. Later, the figure of Time incarnate will appear in order to explain the play's "swift passage" across a "wide gap" of sixteen years (4.1.4–6). The phrase "wide gap of time" returns in the play's penultimate line (5.3.154).

4. Thomas Fuller, *The Holy State and The Profane State* (1641), 1.8.21: "Though with the clock they have given the last stroke, yet they keep a jarring, muttering to themselves a good while after."

5. Robert Hooke, Trinity College MS. o.11a.1[15], f. E. Quoted in Michael Wright, "Robert Hooke's Longitude Timekeeper," in *Robert Hooke: New Studies*, ed. Michael Hunter and Simon Schaffer (Woodbridge, Suffolk: The Boydell Press, 1989, 63–118), 82. Wright transcribes the entire MS. as an appendix to the article. In the MS. the second "very" is crossed out. When quoting the passage within the article, Wright (curiously) gives the last word as "irregularly," at odds with his own transcription.

6. Hooke, Trinity MS., folios E and H (transcribed in Wright, "Longitude," 105, 107). Hooke's manuscript contains the only contemporary earwitness accounts I know of bearing directly on the sound of clockwork in the early and middle century. Context complicates their testimony. Internal evidence makes clear that Hooke composed this undated portion of the manuscript some time after 1660, probably, Wright argues, in 1665 (Wright, 80). So Hooke's pronouncement (quoted above) that he has "never yet heard a clock or watch" run evenly must, strictly speaking, include pendulum timekeepers as well as earlier types. Yet in passages like the one quoted here he appears to allow Huygens's invention a half-hearted exemption. The explanation lies in Hooke's motive for writing. He is here proposing that a spring regulator would constitute a significant improvement over the pendulum, especially in clocks and watches designed for travel. It comports with his argument to concede, on the one hand, that Huygens has wrought a genuine advancement and to insist on the other that he himself has devised a greater one. Hooke's (emblematically apt) oscillation between these positions at times becomes quite rapid, as in the full sentence excerpted above: "For though as to sense [Huygens's] Pendulum seems to vibrate in equall time, yet, that inequality [which] ariseth from any kind of inacuratenesse in the make of the clockwork or the vnequa[l] strength of the weight or Spring, is noe way remoued thoug[h] somewh^t lessened." The ambivalence manifest here ("though . . . yet . . . though") distills, over the course of the manuscript, into two kinds of pronouncement: (1) technically accurate claims (like the one here) that "inequalities" elsewhere in the clockwork prevent the pendulum from enforcing an audibly perfect regularity; (2) technically exaggerated claims (like the "never yet") downplaying the enormous improvement the pendulum had effected in making "equall time" available "to sense." Even this second kind of claim may not have seemed exaggerated from Hooke's idiosyncratic point of view (or hearing). He was remarkable for the acuity of his ear and his interest in the minutiae of sound. He "told me," Pepys records, "that having come to a certain Number of Vibracions proper to make any tone, he is able to tell how many strokes a fly makes with her wings (those flies that hum in their flying) by the note that it answers to in Musique during their flying. That, I suppose, is a little too much raffined. . . ." *The Diary of Samuel Pepys*, ed. Robert Latham and William Matthews. 11 vols. (Berkeley: University of California Press, 1970–1983), 7.239. See also Hooke's remarks on these

experiments in *Micrographia* [London, 1665], 172–74). Such an ear would likely perceive "inequalities" inaudible to ordinary listeners.

7. Aubrey, who describes himself repeatedly as "maggotie-headed," of course forgets things often. But he usually remembers that he forgets, and inserts the auto-imperative memorandum *quaere* to prompt a search for the missing information.

It is, of course, remotely possible that he is historically "accurate" in his onomatopoeia, and that listeners described clocks as ticking before the advent of the pendulum. But the nearly forty-year gap between the last recorded "jar" (see n. 3) and the first recorded "tick" suggests the change in language really did arise from the change in clocks. It is noteworthy too that Hooke, in his manuscript composed some seven years after the innovation of the pendulum, uses no onomatopoeia for the clock sound (he calls it the "beating"). *Tick, Tick, Tick* may not yet have been in circulation.

8. Frank Kermode, *The Sense of an Ending: Studies in the Theory of Fiction* (Oxford: Oxford University Press, 1966), 44–45. Subsequent citations will appear parenthetically.

9. The wording (quoted in the previous paragraph) by which Kermode introduces the topic closely echoes Fraisse's, which reads in translation, "Let us take a very simple case: the sound of a clock. I perceive a 'tick-tock,' then it is gone and another 'tick-tock' takes its place." Paul Fraisse, *The Psychology of Time*, trans. Jennifer Leith (New York: Harper and Row, 1963), 72.

10. An anecdote in *Dawks's News Letter* confirms the currency, familiarity, and (perhaps) exclusivity of the wording two decades after Aubrey. In it a drunken man accidentally drops his watch on the bed; his wife, hearing the "tick, tick, tick . . . told her Husband that Death was come for one or both of them." An apothecary is summoned, who "having information of the matter beforehand, sought for the Watch privately, and by conveying away tick, tick, tick, cured them both" (*Dawks's News Letter*, no. 330, 28 July 1698). The apparently long prevalence of *Tick, Tick, Tick* in English is the more striking because other European languages *did* incorporate a *tick-tock* pairing by the end of the century (Fr. *tic-tac* 1690, Ger. *tick-tack* 1700). In English, *tick-tack* appears first in the sixteenth century as an onomatopoeia for gunfire; the first clock-application cited by the *OED* is 1840.

11. For an account of London's rapid rise, see Carlo Cipolla, *Clocks and Culture 1300–1700* (New York: W. W. Norton, 1977), 65–69.

12. In a crowded field, these are the salient book-length studies: Carlo M. Cipolla, *Clocks and Culture 1300–1700* (see n. 11); Le Goff, *Time, Work, and Culture* (see Preface, n. 2); David S. Landes, *Revolution in Time: Clocks and the Making of the Modern World* (Cambridge: Belknap Press, 1983); Michael Young, *The Metronomic Society: Natural Rhythms and Human Timetables* (Cambridge: Harvard University Press, 1988); Dohrn–van Rossum, *History of the Hour* (see Preface, n. 2). Two classic articles on clocks and culture, to which virtually all subsequent work refers, are Lewis Mumford, "The Monastery and the Clock," in *Technics and Civilization* (New York: Harcourt, Brace and World, 1934) and Thompson, "Time, Work-Discipline, and Industrial Capitalism" (see n. 1).

13. Broader versions of these topics have, of course, produced more print. The capacious topic "time in literature" has prompted one study with that title—Hans Meyerhoff's *Time in Literature* (Berkeley: University of California Press, 1960)—and barely numerable books and articles on the treatment of time in the works of particular authors (those relevant to the authors in this study will be cited as occasion arises).

On the narrower subject of time*keeping* and literature, Samuel L. Macey has produced three books in which both clocks and texts figure prominently: *Clocks and the Cosmos: Time in Western Life and Thought* (Hamden: Archon Books, 1980); *Patriarchs of Time: Dualism in Saturn-*

Cronus, Father Time, The Watchmaker God, and Father Christmas (Athens: University of Georgia Press, 1987); and *The Dynamics of Progress: Time, Method, and Measure* (Athens: University of Georgia Press, 1989). As the titles suggest, Macey approaches his field as a surveyor of large tracts: each rather short volume surveys either several centuries, or several millennia. Macey quotes abundant passages from literature that bear explicit witness to the effects of clocks on culture, but he cannot pause to scrutinize. His books serve better as resources than as studies and indeed his work has culminated in the publication of a more systematic and useful resource, *Time: A Bibliographic Guide* (New York: Garland, 1991), which lists "some six thousand" of the "approximately 180,000 time-related articles" (xvi) and "95,000" time-related books (xviii) that have appeared since the start of the century. But Macey specializes also in eighteenth-century literature, and has produced an article on "Clocks and Chronology in the Eighteenth-Century Novel," *Eighteenth-Century Life* 7.2 (January 1982): 96–104, as well as notes on the workings of time in specific novels: "The Linear and Circular Time Schemes in Sterne's *Tristram Shandy*," *Notes and Queries*, n.s. 36.4 (December 1989), 477–79; "The Time Schemes in *Moll Flanders*," *Notes and Queries*, n.s., 16.9 (September 1969), 336–37. Paul K. Alkon provides more sustained and substantial accounts of time in eighteenth-century narrative and culture in several important articles and books, among them "Boswellian Time," *Studies in Burke and His Time* 14 (1973): 239–56; *Defoe and Fictional Time* (Athens: University of Georgia Press, 1979); and *Origins of Futuristic Fiction* (Athens: University of Georgia Press, 1987). Alkon is less engaged with clocks than with "larger" processes and practices of timekeeping: with the calendar in his excellent article "Changing the Calendar," *Eighteenth-Century Life* 7.2 (1982): 1–18; with chronology in "Johnson and Chronology," in *Greene Centennial Studies*, ed. Paul J. Korshin and Robert R. Allen (Charlottesville: University Press of Virginia, 1984): 143–71. He pays little attention to the way time forms (in chronometry or in narrative) contribute to self-reckoning and -recording.

Within the populous and busy field of "time and literature" there exists a subset of period studies, books devoted to the workings of time in the literature of a particular epoch: for the Middle Ages there is Richard Lock, *Aspects of Time in Medieval Literature* (New York: Garland, 1985); for the Renaissance, Ricardo J. Quinones, *The Renaissance Discovery of Time* (Cambridge: Harvard University Press, 1972), and Achsah Guibbory, *The Map of Time: Seventeenth-Century English Literature and Ideas of Pattern in History* (Urbana: University of Illinois Press, 1986); for the twentieth century there is Ricardo J. Quinones, *Mapping Literary Modernism: Time and Development* (Princeton: Princeton University Press, 1985); N. Katherine Hayles, *Chaos Bound: Orderly Disorder in Contemporary Literature and Science* (Ithaca: Cornell University Press, 1990); and Elizabeth Deeds Ermarth, *Sequel to History: Postmodernism and the Crisis of Representational Time* (Princeton: Princeton University Press, 1990); Carol Jacobs, *Telling Time: Levi-Strauss, Ford, Lessing, Benjamin, de Man, Wordsworth, Rilke* (Baltimore: Johns Hopkins University Press, 1993). No study of comparable scope exists for the late seventeenth and eighteenth centuries.

14. Walter Benjamin, "Theses on the Philosophy of History," in *Illuminations*, ed. Hannah Arendt, trans. Harry Zohn (New York: Schocken Books, 1969), 253–64; quotation 261, 263.

15. Gérard Genette, *Narrative Discourse: An Essay in Method*, trans. Jane E. Lewin (Ithaca: Cornell University Press, 1980), 230, n. 44. Here Genette insists on "an appreciable difference" between epistolary writing and the diary: "the difference is the existence of a receiver (even a mute one), and his traces in the text." But such "receivers" exist for diaries, too: Boswell and Burney often write (and often dispatch) their entries to audiences they know well (his friends, her sisters); such recipients leave "traces in the text" even though they are

never (as they might be in a letter) explicitly "addressed" in the second person; Evelyn inscribes his *Kalendarium* for his known and imagined progeny; Pepys identifies no specific audience either in his writing or his actions, but clearly depends on one in a sense; its requirements and lineaments shape the prose (in the extent, for example, to which he "fills in" his narrative with background he knows well, but to which a future reader may not otherwise have access) and even the book's design (its print-like legibility, its formalities of arrangement). Genette overestimates the "appreciable difference" in audience, and underestimates the role and power of "receivers" in diaristic self-performance.

16. Paul Ricoeur, *Time and Narrative*, trans. Kathleen McLaughlin and David Pellauer, 3 vols. (Chicago: University of Chicago Press, 1984–88), 1.30.

17. In fact, Virginia Woolf, one of Ricoeur's two exemplars of "deep temporality" in fiction (and, of course, a prolific diarist herself), saw and described in the journals of Pepys, Boswell, and Burney temporal practices and strategies parallel to those Ricoeur singles out for scrutiny in her own work. See "Papers on Pepys" in *The Essays of Virginia Woolf*, ed. Andrew McNeillie (New York: Harcourt, Brace, Jovanovich, 1986), volume 2, 233–38; "The Genius of Boswell" in *Essays*, volume 1 (1986), 249–55; and "Dr. Burney's Evening Party" in *The Second Common Reader*, ed. Andrew McNeillie (New York: Harcourt, Brace, Jovanovich, 1986), 108–25.

18. Hayden White, *The Content of the Form: Narrative Discourse and Historical Representation* (Baltimore: Johns Hopkins University Press, 1987), 9, 5–6. Subsequent citations will appear parenthetically.

19. Lawrence Rosenwald has provided the fullest articulation of the question and the most compelling proposals for answers in the "Prolegomena" to his *Emerson and the Art of the Diary* (New York: Oxford University Press, 1988), 3–28. To summarize too succinctly, he finds his solution in the multiple connections between the diary's text and the cultural contexts: the deeper the "diarist's *modus operandi*" is set "within the larger patterns of . . . the diarist's culture"—including those of secrecy, production, distribution, collateral diaristic and literary practices, and the "local language for the play of chance and control"—the more tools the critic will possess for making both historic and aesthetic sense of the particular diary in hand (26–28). Though I focus here on a "local language"—that of measured time—that Rosenwald does not specifically mention (though he briefly and indirectly explores it [15]), and on texts from a century and a nation different from those he studies, I owe his work an intellectual debt greater than mere citation can cover.

20. William Matthews, *British Diaries: An Annotated Bibliography of British Diaries Written between 1492 and 1942* (Berkeley: University of California Press, 1950), vii.

21. Among several works organized this way the most notable are Robert A. Fothergill's pioneering *Private Chronicles: A Study of English Diaries* (London: Oxford University Press, 1974), Thomas Mallon's popular survey *A Book of One's Own: People and Their Diaries* (New York: Ticknor and Fields, 1984), and Harriet Blodgett's *Centuries of Female Days: English-women's Private Diaries* (New Brunswick: Rutgers University Press, 1988). Fothergill groups his diarists by features of form ("Style, Tone, and Self-Projection," "Ego and Ideal," "Forms of Serial Autobiography"); Mallon by the character and purpose of the diary ("Travelers," "Creators," "Apologists," "Prisoners"); Blodgett by subject matter ("Marriage and Motherhood," "Daughterhood," "Diaries of the Great War"). Many anthologies—a very substantial subset of all published diary literature—are of course organized along similar lines. They include *A Treasury of the World's Great Diaries*, ed. Philip Dunaway and Mel Evans (Garden City: Doubleday, 1957), which contains sections titled "In Youth Is the Beginning," "The Many Chambers of the Heart," and "The Questing Mind"; *Revelations: Diaries of*

Women, ed. Mary Jane Moffat and Charlotte Painter (New York: Vintage, 1975), which contains sections on "Love," Work," and "Power"; *The Pleasures of Diaries: Four Centuries of Private Writing*, ed. Ronald Blythe (New York: Pantheon Books, 1989), which includes "The Diarist and the Difficult Marriage" and "The Sick Diarist"; and the more scholarly collection edited by Ralph Houlbrooke, *English Family Life 1567–1716: An Anthology from Diaries* (Oxford: Basil Blackwell, 1988), which includes sections on "Courtship and Marriage," "Childhood," and "Parents' Old Age and Deaths."

22. Examples include Arthur Ponsonby, *English Diaries* (London: Methuen, 1923) and *More English Diaries* (London: Methuen, 1927), which were for a long time the most influential books on the subject, and Judy Simons, *Diaries and Journals of Literary Women from Fanny Burney to Virginia Woolf* (Iowa City: University of Iowa Press, 1990).

23. The most comprehensive reference for these is Cheryl Cline, *Women's Diaries, Journals, and Letters: An Annotated Bibliography* (New York: Garland, 1989).

24. The impulse towards the introductory survey persists also in studies of European diaries: Michele Leleu, *Les Journaux intimes* (Paris: Presses Universitaires de France, 1952); Gustav René Hocke, *Das Europaeische Tagebuch* (Wiesbaden: Limes, 1963); Alain Girard, *Les Journaux intimes* (Paris: Presses Universitaires de France, 1963); Peter Boerner, *Tagebuch* (Stuttgart: Metzger, 1969); V. Del Litto, ed., *Le Journal intime et ses formes litteraires: Actes du Colloque de septembre 1975* (Geneva: Droz, 1978). Rosenwald remarks of this list: "As the titles suggest, all these books start from scratch, taking up the fundamental problems from the beginning; none of them except Girard's pursues a specific historical investigation, and neither these books nor any other offers a comprehensive literary study of any major European diarist" (*Emerson*, 3–4, n. 1).

25. That is perhaps why new anthologies are so numerous. Harriet Blodgett's recent work encapsulates the trend. Among the most useful features of her survey, *Centuries of Female Days*, are its plentiful excerpts from and bibliographical listings of previously obscure women's diaries. Her next book, an anthology of passages from some of these diaries (arranged in categories like those that shape her earlier volume), seems to follow naturally, as the less "mediated" (and in certain ways more useful) complement to her critical study. Harriet Blodgett, *Capacious Hold-All: An Anthology of Englishwomen's Diary Writings* (Charlottesville: University of Virginia Press, 1991).

26. In a limited way the process began before the advent of cultural studies, because the diary, recognized as a mode of autobiography, occasionally received attention in books on that extensive and various genre. In such analyses, Boswell in particular (whose journals were being freshly discovered and published during these decades) will appear, often sandwiched between Bunyan on the one side and a Romantic—Rousseau, Wordsworth, or De Quincey—on the other. Among the studies of autobiography that include Boswell's diaries are John N. Morris's *Versions of the Self: Studies in English Autobiography from John Bunyan to John Stuart Mill* (New York: Basic Books, 1966), Elizabeth Bruss's *Autobiographical Acts: The Changing Situation of a Literary Genre* (Baltimore: Johns Hopkins University Press, 1976), and A. O. J. Cockshut's *The Art of Autobiography in Nineteenth- and Twentieth-Century England* (New Haven: Yale University Press, 1984). The design proves in practice both illuminating and dangerous: the diary usually figures as the lone instance or "odd one out" among writers more conspicuously continuous with each other (Bunyan and Rousseau, for example, shaped their works for publication and saw them through the press; they share, too, a conscious Augustinianism). The critic, to justify the diarist's inclusion, emphasizes the diary's similarity with the other texts rather than its difference: commonality of "autobiographical" purpose occludes peculiarities of diaristic form and rhythm. The *London Journal*, with its markedly

novelistic and neatly Freudian feel—its shapely playing-out, for example, of a choice among surrogate fathers—has proven particularly suited to such assimilation; it lends itself to being (mis)read as polished autobiography rather than as diary. And even such limited reckoning of diarists as autobiographers has until recently been rare: many critics of autobiography exclude the diary altogether. Some, like Donald A. Stauffer, do so explicitly: "The diary has scant claim to consideration, for its makes no pretense to artistic structure" (*The Art of English Biography Before 1700* [Cambridge: Harvard University Press, 1930, 55]). Some shun the diary implicitly, like William C. Spengemann, whose very eclectic book studies, as "poetic autobiographies," *David Copperfield* and *The Scarlet Letter*, but examines no diaries (*The Forms of Autobiography: Episodes in the History of the Literary Genre* [New Haven: Yale University Press, 1980]). Cockshut works out a patronizing compromise: he includes Boswell's diary (and Byron's) in an opening chapter he calls "The Half-Way House"—half-way, that is, to the work of "the true autobiographers who answer . . . the question: 'How did I become what I am?'" (*Art of Autobiography* 16).

27. Patricia Meyer Spacks, *Imagining a Self: Autobiography and Novel in Eighteenth-Century England* (Cambridge: Harvard University Press, 1976), and Felicity A. Nussbaum, *The Autobiographical Subject: Gender and Ideology in Eighteenth-Century England* (Baltimore: Johns Hopkins University Press, 1989). Subsequent citations will appear parenthetically.

28. George Poulet, *Studies in Human Time*, trans. Elliott Coleman (Baltimore: Johns Hopkins University Press, 1956). Subsequent citations will appear parenthetically.

29. Poulet's impressionism shows itself most forcefully in the sentence fragments with which he often finishes and begins sections, as though the vision of time he names and describes can be rendered most truthfully without the distracting temporality of predication. Of Mallarmé's time: "A longing for non-creation" (34). Of Molière's: "A precarious, spasmodic duration, always under the menace of an instantaneous explosion; a duration essentially tragic" (102).

30. At one point Nussbaum touches, in three sentences, on a possible linkage in the eighteenth century between the journal and the clock (87), but she does not pursue the connection.

31. The omission is the more curious because Nussbaum in her early pages invokes Pepys's complex diaristic method—his retrospective self-revision, for example—as a paradigm for the unsuspected complexity of serial autobiography. But nowhere does she examine or even quote the particular writing this paradigm produces.

Even when Nussbaum does take up secular narratives, her choice of texts suggests and supports an argumentative bias. She deals, for example, with Thrale and not with Burney (who unlike her older friend carved out for herself a full-fledged career as professional author), and with Thrale's "Family Book"—the work that casts her explicitly as mother—more than with *Thraliana*—that work wherein she plays many different roles, including the important one of renegade, defying friends, mentors, and family to marry and emigrate with an "unsuitable" but loved musician. By omitting any mention of this central episode in Thrale's life and private writing, Nussbaum suppresses important evidence in a chapter purportedly balanced as to the ways Thrale both obeys and challenges cultural norms.

32. I take the phrases in quotation marks from (respectively) the subtitle of Landes's study and the title of Young's (see n. 12).

33. Michel Foucault, *Discipline and Punish: The Birth of the Prison*, trans. Alan Sheridan (New York: Pantheon Books, 1977); subsequent citations will appear parenthetically. The original French title is *Surveiller et Punir*, but Foucault suggested the English variant, "which relates closely to the book's structure" ("Translator's Note," ix); indeed the word "Disci-

pline," in both French and English versions, heads the book's pivotal section (pp. 135 – 230), in which Foucault examines the strategies and consequences of that phenomenon, and concerns himself most closely with the institutional "methodizing" of time.

34. This *voilà* effect appears everywhere in the narrative; for example, when Foucault demonstrates the late eighteenth-century triumph of "panopticism" (at both the start and the conclusion of the chapter bearing that name) by contrasting it with customary civic preparations against the plague in the seventeenth century: "The plague-stricken town, the panoptic establishment—the differences are important. They mark, at a distance of a century and a half, the transformation of the disciplinary programme" (205). Again, the effect of the procedure is to assert the importance of the intervening period (that same "century and a half" whose temporalities I propose to explore) while at the same time eliding its "internal" narrative, as either untellable or unnecessary for understanding. And the procedure becomes so pervasive that it often seems not merely to frame the argument (a necessary function) but to constitute it.

35. Nigel Thrift, "Owners' Time and Own Time: The Making of a Capitalist Time Consciousness, 1300 – 1880," in *Space and Time in Geography: Essays Dedicated to Torsten Hägerstrand*, Lund Studies in Geography, Series B, Human Geography, no. 48 (CWK Gleerup: Royal University of Lund Department of Geography, 1981), 56 – 84; quotation 62.

36. J. Paul Hunter, *Before Novels: The Cultural Contexts of Eighteenth Century English Fiction* (New York: W. W. Norton, 1990), xiii. Subsequent citations will appear parenthetically. Hunter describes this situation, "well past now" (xiv), in greater detail on the surrounding pages. See also Patricia B. Craddock's strictures on the title and underlying conception of Marshall Brown's *Preromanticism* (Stanford: Stanford University Press, 1991) in "Recent Studies in Restoration and Eighteenth-Century Literature," *Studies in English Literature* 32.3 (summer 1992): 571 – 606; quotation 572 – 73.

37. The actual metronome appears in the early nineteenth century (1814), at just that juncture when Foucault, Thompson, Young, and others see the "metronomic society" beginning to move in definitive synchrony.

38. In his last writings and interviews, Foucault made clear that through his work on the history of sexuality, he himself had become interested in the ways private documents complicated his earlier models of social discipline. See ch. 3, n. 20, for further discussion of Foucault's later work.

39. Benedict Anderson, *Imagined Communities: Reflections on the Origin and Spread of Nationalism*, revised edition (London: Verso, 1991), 24. Subsequent citations will appear parenthetically.

40. Fothergill remarks that Johnson "is important [to the history of diaries] not so much as a diarist in himself, but as the cause that diary-writing should be in other men." *Private Chronicles*, 25.

41. Raymond Williams, *Marxism and Literature* (Oxford: Oxford University Press, 1977), 132 – 33. Subsequent citations will appear parenthetically.

42. Rosenwald, *Emerson*, 3.

43. Michael G. Ketcham, *Transparent Designs: Reading, Performance, and Form in the Spectator Papers* (Athens: University of Georgia Press, 1985).

44. Among the rare exceptions to this rule Robert Fothergill's *Private Chronicles* offers by far the most discerning investigation into the diaristic handling of those elements central to New Criticism: manner, style, tone, form. Fothergill's predecessors and contemporaries devote much energy to showing that diary-keeping can be an "art." New Criticism virtually demanded such demonstration *a priori*, but severely limited its usefulness by universalizing

the key term and ignoring the local contexts in which an "art" might be fruitfully defined and grounded (see, for example, the very dilatory dissertation by Clifford Johnson, Jr., *Samuel Pepys and the Diarist's Art*, University of Virginia, 1970). Rosenwald, defining and restoring these contexts in the "Prolegomena" of his *Emerson and the Art of the Diary*, both solves the problem and makes unprecedentedly scrupulous sense of the title's closing phrase.

45. This procedure prevails in virtually all the studies cited in n. 13, but most strikingly (and, I think, most detrimentally) in those by Macey and Quinones.

CHAPTER TWO

1. *The Diary of Samuel Pepys*, ed. Robert Latham and William Matthews. 11 vols. (Berkeley: University of California Press, 1970–1983), 1.1.60; 1.3. Subsequent citations will appear parenthetically, with date of diary entry first, followed by volume and page number, as above.

2. Two books have drawn on Pepys as the central witness to cultural phenomena: Helen McAfee, *Pepys on the Restoration Stage* (New York: Benjamin Blom, 1916), and Marjorie Hope Nicolson, *Pepys's Diary and the New Science* (Charlottesville: University of Virginia Press, 1965). Among the most eminent "appreciations" are: Walter Scott's essay on the newly published diary in *Quarterly Review*, 33.66 (1826), 290–314; Robert Louis Stevenson, "Samuel Pepys," in *Familiar Studies of Men and Books* (New York: Scribner's, 1895), 243–71; J. R. Tanner, *Mr. Pepys: An Introduction to the Diary Together with a Sketch of his Later Life* (London: G. Bell, 1925); Virginia Woolf, "Papers on Pepys" (see ch. 1, n. 17); V. S. Pritchett, "The Great Snail," in *The Tale Bearers* (New York: Random House, 1980), 137–42. The few scholarly studies that treat Pepys as topic rather than cite him as witness have focused on his sexuality: E. Pearlman, "Pepys and Lady Castlemaine," *Restoration* 7:2 (1983), 43–53; Francis Barker, *The Tremulous Private Body: Essays on Subjection* (London: Methuen, 1984); John H. O'Neill, "Samuel Pepys: The War of Will and Pleasure," *Restoration* 19:2 (1995), 88–94; James Grantham Turner, "Pepys and the Private Parts of Monarchy," in *Culture and Society in the Stuart Restoration*, ed. Gerald MacLean (Cambridge: Cambridge University Press, 1995), 95–111.

3. Rosenwald, *Emerson*, 15, n. 22.

4. At least as far as we know: many early diaries have been lost, many have not been catalogued, and many have not been printed. I base the pronouncement on a survey of the pre-1660 diaries listed and described in the three major catalogues of the genre: Matthews, *British Diaries*; Cline, *Women's Diaries, Journals, and Letters*; and Élisabeth Bourcier, *Les Journaux privés en Angleterre de 1600 à 1660* (Paris: Publications de la Sorbonne, 1976). Robert Latham, Matthews's partner in the diary's definitive edition, sums up the contrast between Pepys and contemporary diarists in this way: "No other diarist of [Pepys's] day attempted anything so comprehensive. . . . None of Pepys's contemporaries, as far as we know, attempted a diary in the all-inclusive Pepysian sense and on the Pepysian scale." *The Shorter Pepys*, ed. Robert Latham (Berkeley: University of California Press, 1985), xxxv.

5. This is partly, of course, a matter of scale; atomic clocks can tell durations as small as a nine-billionth of a second (Landes, *Revolution* 8). But around 1660 this change of scale amounts virtually to a change in kind: the new clocks were the first to make the *progress* of time visible by the motion of the hands (hour hands alone move too slowly for the casual eye to catch).

6. For the fullest history of bellringing in seventeenth-century England, see David Cressy, *Bonfires and Bells: National Memory and the Protestant Calendar in Elizabethan and Stuart England* (Berkeley: University of California Press, 1989), 68–80. Broader histories include

Price, *Bells and Man*; George Tyack, *A Book About Bells* (London: Andrews, 1898); J. J. Raven, *The Bells of England* (London: Methuen, 1906); and H. B. Walters, *Church Bells of England* (London: Oxford University Press, 1912).

7. Hugh Latimer remarked that "if all the bells in England should be rung together at a certain hour, I think there would be almost no place but some bells might be heard there." *Sermons by Hugh Latimer*, ed. George Elwes Corrie (Cambridge, 1844), 498; quoted in Cressy, *Bonfires*, 69.

8. And vice versa. That is, bells originally designed to dictate actions—particularly prayer—persisted past their initial purpose to function as time markers in the encroaching system of abstract chronometry. This second function, Dohrn–van Rossum shows, accounts for the Reformation's failure to eliminate the ringing of the canonical hours, "particularly in small towns and villages" where a fuller twelve- or twenty-four-hour system of clock bells was not yet in place. "Countless pertinent texts reveal that many of the long-familiar [religious] bell signals had become practically indispensable time signals." Dohrn–van Rossum cites one such text, an ecclesiastical statute for Wolfenbüttel (1564), which mingles reproach and concession in order to shift the bells' use and meaning: "Since the highly praised Virgin Mary does not wish to have such an honor [as the popish ringing is designed to prompt] . . . and since this is also against the word of God, the people are to be instructed accordingly. The striking of the bell itself, however, . . . can be kept to indicate to the people morning, midday, and evening hour. . . ." Dohrn–van Rossum, *History of the Hour*, trans. Thomas Dunlap (Chicago: University of Chicago Press), 212–13.

9. Price, *Bells and Man*, 111–12.

10. Price points out that the Reformation, at various stages, tried unsuccessfully to limit or eliminate the practice: "Ringing the passing bell was forbidden by enactments of both the Lutheran and English churches, but it was impossible to stamp it out; the trust that its sound aided the soul of the dying had been too firmly established. . . . The Anglicans approved of funeral bells, except during the Commonwealth, when the religious lawfulness of this ringing was questioned" (*Bells and Man* 130). The fullest account of the tradition is to be found in Walters, *Church Bells*, 152–64.

11. John Donne, *Devotions upon Emergent Occasions*, ed. Anthony Raspa (New York: Oxford University Press, 1987), 91, 89. Subsequent citations will appear parenthetically.

12. Before the Reformation, the personification of bells and the ascription to them of a superhuman "voice" and affect were made explicit two ways: in the practice of baptizing the bells before they were used, and in the Latin mottoes inscribed on them. Some examples: *Vivos Voco*; *Est Mea Cunctorum Vox Daemoniorum*; and (for the sequence of death bells) *Fleo Mortua*; *Defunctos Ploro*; *Funera Plango*. The Reformation, of course, proscribed bell baptism and inscriptions proclaiming magic powers. Price, *Bells and Man*, 128, 133; see also Walters, *Church Bells*, 315–49.

13. The attempt to transcend clock time is reinforced throughout the *Devotions* by Donne's repeated references to the Old Testament story of Hezekiah, king of Judea, who when mortally ill prays for recovery. God grants the prayer, and signals His assent by a metaphorically apt distortion of earthly time. He causes the sun to go backwards, by "ten degrees," in "the sun dial of Ahaz" (Isaiah 38.1–8). The medieval and Renaissance iconography of the tale displays what Kate Gartner Frost describes as "a complex involvement with the developing technology of time measurement" (112). Since the artists tend to depict the dial of Ahaz by whatever chronometric instrument is most familiar or impressive to them— sundial, waterclock, or hour glass—the tradition offers a rich pictorial resource for the

history of horology. The iconography of Hezekiah gradually overlaps with that of Temperance, who instead of turning the time backwards, adjusts the timepiece (now a figure "of the Christian life") so that it runs right. Frost points out that "the iconography of the Hezekiah story is . . . deeply embedded in Donne's *Devotions*" and reads the motif exhaustively in order to develop from it a numerological reading of the text. Frost, *Holy Delight: Typology, Numerology, and Autobiography in Donne's* Devotions Upon Emergent Occasions (Princeton: Princeton University Press, 1990), 28–35, 44–52, 112–25. For the interplay between the iconographic tradition and the history of horology see Lynn White, Jr., "The Iconography of *Temperantia* and the Virtuousness of Technology," in *Action and Conviction in Early Modern Europe*, ed. Theodore Rabb and Jerrald Seigel (Princeton: Princeton University Press, 1969), 197–219.

14. For a fuller explication of Donne's title phrase, emphasizing overtones of falling and rising, death and resurrection, see Debora Shuger, "The Title of Donne's *Devotions*," *English Language Notes* 22.4 (June 1985), 39–40.

15. Richard Strier argues persuasively that Donne writes not merely to depict these effects but to defend their causes. The discourse on the death bells "is explicitly polemical," a crucial element in a larger argument for the importance of " 'outward meanes for assisting' devotion" which Donne is waging against both Catholics (who accuse the Anglican church of dispensing with such means) and Puritans (who urge dispensing with such means). The section on the bells is calculated not simply to assert their power to prompt devotion, but also to defend the practice against the Puritans who oppose it: to endorse, in other words, the role of the church in deliberately creating "occasions" for its congregation to "lay hold of." "We cannot," Donne writes, "O my God, take in too many helps for religious duties." See "Donne and the Politics of Devotion" in *Religion, Literature, and Politics in Post-Reformation England 1540–1688*, ed. Donna Hamilton and Richard Strier (Cambridge: Cambridge University Press, 1996), 93–114.

16. The two meanings are of similar date. The *OED* finds a first instance of the fractional denotation in 1377, of the momentary in 1390.

17. R. C. Bald, *John Donne: A Life* (New York: Oxford University Press, 1970), 450–52; Clara Lander, "A Dangerous Sickness which turned to a Spotted Fever," *Studies in English Literature 1500–1900*, 11 (1971): 89–108; Kate Gartner Frost, "John Donne's *Devotions*: An Early Record of Epidemic Typhus," *Journal of the History of Medicine and Allied Sciences* 21 (1976): 421–30, and *Holy Delight* ix.

18. Bald, *Donne*, 450; Frost, "Early Record," 427; Lander, "Dangerous Sickness," 89.

19. Lander and Frost both argue for the book as case study. Bald, Frost, and Lander each arrives at a different reckoning of the time by relying on different medical testimony (from both the seventeenth and the twentieth centuries) as to the exact nature and duration of the disease (Bald identifies a slightly different mode of the disease). The absence of time cues forces them to rely on external (and various) evidence.

20. St. Augustine, *Confessions*, trans. R. S. Pine-Coffin (New York: Penguin, 1961), 276.

21. Hall's treatise on *The Arte of Divine Meditation* appeared in 1606, a collection of his *Occasional Meditations* in 1633. Modern editions of both texts appear in Frank Livingston Huntley, *Bishop Joseph Hall and Protestant Meditation in Seventeenth-Century England* (Binghamton, New York: Center for Medieval & Early Renaissance Studies, 1981); page citations will be from this edition and will appear parenthetically. Of Hall's relationship with Donne, Huntley points out that the two were fellow recipients of Sir Robert Drury's largesse and were "partners" in the "literary exercise" of commemorating his daughter Elizabeth:

Donne's two *Anniversaries* (1611 and 1612), for each of which Hall wrote introductory verses. "They must have been well acquainted with each other's work" (Huntley 55).

22. Robert Boyle, *Occasional Reflections upon Several Subjects, whereto is Premised a Discourse about Such Kind of Thoughts*. 2 vols. (London: Henry Herringman, 1665). Subsequent citations will appear parenthetically. For a study of the method and cultural impact of the *Reflections*, see Hunter, *Before Novels*, 201–208. Hunter estimates that the vogue for occasional meditation lasted "at least through the 1680s, perhaps well into the eighteenth century" (384, n. 22).

23. Boyle 1.214. Donne and Boyle attend to different kinds of signals, one of occasion, the other of (mis)measure, and the differences index larger distinctions—between the preoccupations of cathedral dean and Royal Society virtuoso, and perhaps too between their horological and historical moments: Boyle writes during or after the interregnum, when the "emptying" of occasion bells accelerated and the proportion of pure time signals increased accordingly. It is all the more remarkable, then, that Boyle, like Donne, should seize upon instances in which the sound eludes chronicity.

24. The same holds true for sundials, which long remained in one sense the most exact timekeepers: watches and clocks were set by them well into the eighteenth century, and in more sophisticated variants they remained the arbiter of shipboard "local" time for reckonings of the longitude. But they were also unpredictable and intermittent; their efficacy was hostage to clouds and night. When Joseph Hall, in the second of his 140 meditations, reflects "Upon the Sight of a Dial," he focuses on its intermittent quality: "If the sun did not shine upon this dial, nobody would look at it; in a cloudy day it stands like a useless post, unheeded, unregarded" (124). This intermittent operation becomes, here at the book's beginning, a figure and an explanation for the timing of "occasional meditation," in which the writer serves as the dial's gnomon, or pointer: "Give Thou me light," Hall prays, "I shall give others information" (124). When Boyle examines a mariner's handheld dial, he ignores its timekeeping properties completely; instead, he builds one of the book's longest meditations by moralizing and theologizing the compass needle by which the waterman orients the instrument. Boyle echoes Hall more closely in his introductory "Discourse Touching Occasional Meditations," where he too compares the process to the working of a sundial: as astronomers can make the sun, "at so immense a Distance, by the Shadow of a little Gnomon, fitly plac'd, give us an exact account of all the Journeys he performs in the Zodiack" so we, in our occasional meditations, can "make, not the Stars onely, but all the Creatures of Nature, and the various occurrences that can fall under our notice, conspire to inrich us with Instructions . . ." (1.19–20). Again, Boyle's description of the dial de-emphasizes the temporal in favor of the celestial; the gnomon here tracks heavenly motions rather than sublunary time. In extemporal meditation, even the pointers of chronometry point away from numbers towards something (to take the Latin literally) "out of time."

25. George Swinnock, *The Christian Mans Calling, Third part, Directing a Christian to perform his duty* (London, 1665), 451; quoted in Hunter, *Before Novels*, 203.

26. Samuel Richardson, *The History of Sir Charles Grandison*, ed. Jocelyn Harris (Oxford: Oxford University Press, 1986), 4.

27. Already at this juncture Pepys has made it fairly clear that he doesn't write every day. In the previous day's entry, for Sunday, January 15, he records spending part of the evening "mak[ing] an end of this week's notes in this book" (1.15.60; 1.18).

28. Pepys apparently does not yet possess one. The next and last time he writes "to the moment" in this way it will also be to register the sound of a clock bell: "And then was

much troubled my wife was not come, it being ten a-clock just now striking as I write this last line" (1.15.61; 2.14).

29. The bellman participates in the common, occasional temporality of the criers, whose voices in effect announce to the hearer that "this moment, of my maximum 'volume,' is your specific opportunity to buy my wares." Hall meditates "Upon the Hearing of the Street-cries in London": "What a noise do these poor souls make in proclaiming their commodities! . . . and yet . . . it is but poor stuff that they set out with so much ostentation. I do not hear any of the rich merchants talk of what bags he hath in his chests or what treasures of rich wares in his storehouse" (139).

30. Price, *Bells and Man*, 135.

31. In a letter to Sir Robert Ker, Donne makes clear that he worked on the *Devotions* during his convalescence, after the crisis of the illness had passed (Frost, "Early Record," 430).

32. Lawrence Alan Rosenwald, "Cotton Mather as Diarist," *Prospects* 8 (1983), 134.

33. John Fuller, introduction to *The Journal or Diary of a Thankful Christian*, by John Beadle (London: Thomas Parkhurst, 1656), b1v. Subsequent citations will appear parenthetically.

34. This absence of self-reproach characterizes all the Puritan diarists discussed below: Samuel Ward, Richard Rogers, Margaret Hoby, and Ralph Josselin.

35. *Two Elizabethan Puritan Diaries by Richard Rogers and Samuel Ward*, ed. M. M. Knappen (Chicago: American Society of Church History, 1933), 107. Subsequent citations from both Rogers's and Ward's journals will appear parenthetically.

36. *The Diary of Lady Margaret Hoby 1599 – 1605*, ed. Dorothy M. Meads (Boston: Houghton Mifflin, 1930), 108. Subsequent citations will appear parenthetically.

37. Leopold Damrosch, *God's Plot and Man's Stories: Studies in the Fictional Imagination from Milton to Fielding* (Chicago: University of Chicago Press, 1985), 59 – 60.

38. *An Astrological Diary of the Seventeenth Century: Samuel Jeake of Rye, 1652 – 1699*, ed. Michael Hunter and Annabel Gregory (Oxford: Clarendon Press, 1988), 101. Subsequent citations will appear parenthetically. Horoscopic diagram from Samuel Jeake's diary, courtesy of William Andrews Clark Memorial Library, University of California, Los Angeles.

39. *Elias Ashmole (1617 – 1692)*, ed. C. H. Josten, 5 vols. (Oxford: Clarendon Press, 1966), 2.637. Subsequent citations will appear parenthetically.

40. Bernard Capp, *English Almanacs, 1500-1800: Astrology and the Popular Press* (Ithaca: Cornell University Press, 1979), 23. Subsequent citations will appear parenthetically. Capp cites Cyprian Blagden, "The Distribution of Almanacs in the Second Half of the Seventeenth Century," *Studies in Bibliography* 10 (1958), 11. For other studies of the subject, see Eustace F. Bosanquet, "English Seventeenth-Century Almanacks," *The Library* series 4, 10:4 (March 1930), 361 – 97; Bosanquet, *English Printed Almanacks and Prognostications* (London: Printed for the Bibliographical Society at the Chiswick Press, 1917), vii; and Marcellus Laroon, *The Criers and Hawkers of London*, ed. Sean Shesgreen (Stanford: Stanford University Press, 1990), 150.

41. *The Private Diary of Dr. John Dee*, ed. James O. Halliwell (London: Printed for the Camden Society, 1842), vii, 39.

42. Frank H. Stubbings, "A Cambridge Pocket-Diary, 1587 – 1592," *Transactions of the Cambridge Bibliographical Society* 5.3 (1971), 192.

43. The substantial volumes of Wood's *Life and Times* are filled out from his other autobiographical writings, which are often copious, but rarely continuous from day to day.

44. *Endymion*, 1663, quoted in Capp, *English Almanacs*, 62.

45. See *Paciolo on Accounting*, ed. R. Gene Brown and Kenneth S. Johnston (New York: McGraw-Hill, 1963), 45–63; and A. C. Littleton, *Accounting Evolution to 1900* (New York: Russell and Russell, 1966), 22–122.

46. *The Diary of Sir Henry Slingsby of Scriven, Bart.*, ed. Daniel Parsons (London: Longman, 1836), 54. Subsequent citations will appear parenthetically.

47. *The Complete Essays of Montaigne*, trans. Donald M. Frame (Stanford: Stanford University Press, 1958), 166.

48. Slingsby does append a further page about work on his estate; he died in 1658 without further extending his diary.

49. Daniel Defoe, *Robinson Crusoe*, ed. Michael Shinagel, 2nd edition (New York: W. W. Norton, 1994), 49. Subsequent citations will appear parenthetically.

50. Alan Macfarlane, *The Family Life of Ralph Josselin* (New York: W. W. Norton, 1970), 33.

51. *The Diary of Ralph Josselin, 1616–1683*, ed. Alan Macfarlane (London: Oxford University Press, 1976), 248.

52. *The Diary of Robert Hooke, M.A., M.D., F.R.S. (1672–1680)*, ed. Henry W. Robinson and Walter Adams (London: Taylor and Francis, 1935), 81.

53. *The Diary of Bulstrode Whitelocke, 1605–1675*, ed. Ruth Spalding (Oxford: Oxford University Press, 1990), 719.

54. *The Diary of John Evelyn*, ed. E. S. de Beer (Oxford: Clarendon Press, 1955), 2.200–201. Subsequent references will appear parenthetically.

55. Other days' notes work differently. All involve narrative and monetary elements, but the variety of formats in which Pepys distributes these elements is striking, as though he had no fixed method for making up the notes.

56. Pepys often omits a detailed narrative of business because those particulars (like his expenditures) were on record elsewhere. Extraordinary business (like extraordinary expense) does get detailed here. But even ordinary business (like ordinary dining) gets at least a mention, in accord with the paradigm of fullness.

57. John Price, *The Mystery and Method of His Majesty's Happy Restauration Laid Open to Publick View* (London: James Vade, 1680), 75. Quoted in J. G. Muddiman, *The King's Journalist 1659–1689* (London: Bodley Head, 1923), 94.

58. There is an interesting parallel in a late seventeenth-century epistolary practice, to which Pepys adhered assiduously: the letter both began and ended with the same phrase of respectful address (for example, "Reverend Sir"), inscribed in a large distinctive script, in the same position relative to the left margin, at the head and bottom of the page; the framing thus constituted the entire content as belonging to the recipient.

59. John Evelyn, Prefatory letter to *The State of France* (1652), in *The Miscellaneous Writings of John Evelyn*, ed. William Upcott, 1825 (London: Henry Colburn), 41–52; quotation 46.

CHAPTER THREE

1. *Further Correspondence of Samuel Pepys, 1662–1679*, ed. J. R. Tanner (London: G. Bell and Sons, 1929), 49.

2. Cedric Jagger, *The Artistry of the English Watch* (London: David and Charles, 1988), 42.

3. Derek Howse, *Greenwich Time and the Discovery of the Longitude* (Oxford: Oxford University Press, 1980), 9. Subsequent citations will appear parenthetically.

4. "A Narrative concerning the Success of Pendulum-Watches at Sea for the Longitudes," *Philosophical Transactions*, 1.1 (6 March 1664/5), 13–15.

5. Thomas Birch, *The History of the Royal Society of London for Improving of Natural Knowledge*, 4 vols. (London, 1756–57), 2.21. Subsequent citations will appear parenthetically.

6. "This day was left at my house a very neat Silver watch, by one Briggs, a Scrivener and Sollicitor; at which I was angry with my wife for receiving, or at least for opening the box wherein it was, and so far witnessing our receipt of it as to give the messenger 5s for bringing it. But it can't be helped, and I will endeavour to do the man a kindness—he being a friend of my uncle Wights." (4.17.65; 6.83) The twenty-six day gap between this initial reception of the gift and the enthusiastic coach ride (May 13) is accounted for by apparent technical trouble. Pepys brings the piece to a watchmaker who "put[s] it in order" and estimates its price, as cited above. This was not the first time Pepys experienced the precarious "order" of available watches: he remarks at the end of the coach-ride entry that "I remember . . . I had one and found it a trouble, and resolved to carry one no more about me while I lived."

7. Cecil Clutton and George Daniels, *Watches: A Complete History of the Technical and Decorative Development of the Watch*, third edition (London: Sotheby Parke Bernet, 1979), 85.

8. Clutton and Daniels, *Watches*, 85.

9. For the early history of pockets see Vanda Foster, *Bags and Purses* (London: B. T. Batsford, 1982), 9–10.

10. Rachel Doggett, ed., *Time: The Greatest Innovator* (Washington, D. C.: Folger Shakespeare Library, 1986), 65.

11. Clutton and Daniels, *Watches*, 85.

12. Joella G. Yoder, *Unrolling Time: Christiaan Huygens and the Mathematization of Nature* (Cambridge: Cambridge University Press, 1988), 154. Subsequent citations will appear parenthetically.

13. Thomas Shelton, *A Tutor to Tachygraphy or Short-Writing* (1642) and *Tachygraphy* (1647), ed. William Matthews (Los Angeles: Augustan Reprint Society, 1970), A3r. Subsequent citations from the facsimile of Shelton's texts and from Matthews's introduction will appear parenthetically.

14. Matthews, "Introduction" to Pepys's *Diary*, 1.lxi–lxii.

15. A striking instance of this mixed secrecy receives discerning scrutiny from James Grantham Turner in his essay on "Pepys and the Private Parts of Monarchy" (see ch. 2, n. 2), 95–98.

16. Evelyn's diary offers an instructive comparison: the narrative, addressed to his own descendants, is temporally intermittent partly because it confines itself by and large to presentation of a public self—the words, deeds, and thoughts he reports have mostly been witnessed by others before he writes.

17. *Charles II's Escape from Worcester: A Collection of Narratives Assembled by Samuel Pepys*, ed. William Matthews (Berkeley: University of California Press, 1966).

18. Young, *The Metronomic Society*, 257, 293–94.

19. For a critique of the limitations inherent in Foucault's method of extrapolating a model of subjectivity from the specific circumstances of the eighteenth-century prison, see Nancy Fraser, "Michel Foucault: A 'Young Conservative'?" in her *Unruly Practices: Power, Discourse and Gender in Contemporary Social Theory* (Minneapolis: University of Minnesota Press, 1989), 45–47.

20. Robert Latham, ed., *Catalogue of the Pepys Library at Magdalene College, Cambridge*, 7 vols. (London: D. S. Brewer/Rowman & Littlefield, 1978–). Pepys's sea journal collection is detailed in volume 5, part 2: *Modern Manuscripts*, ed. C. S. Knighton (1981). For

Pepys's interest in and acquisition of Holmes's documents of the voyage (PL2698), see Richard Ollard, *Man of War: Sir Robert Holmes and the Restoration Navy* (London: Hodder and Stoughton, 1969), 199.

21. *A Descriptive Catalogue of the Naval Manuscripts in the Pepysian Library at Magdalene College, Cambridge*, 4 vols., ed. J. R. Tanner (London: Naval Records Society, 1909), 3.345–46; Arthur Bryant, *Samuel Pepys: Saviour of the Navy* (London: Panther, 1967), 153; J. R. Tanner, *Samuel Pepys and the Royal Navy* (Cambridge: Cambridge University Press, 1920), 12. Tanner later observes that "it is extraordinary that a man should have written the *Diary*, but it is much more extraordinary that the man who wrote the *Diary* should also have been the 'right hand of the navy' " (16). Foucault's paradigm makes this doubling seem less extraordinary.

22. Foucault's late work suggests that he may have been growing interested in the manuscript book of the self as a device for attaining comparative opacity and a certain measure of autonomy. In Foucault's final work, *The History of Sexuality*, the confessional supplants the Panopticon as the controlling figure for explaining the construction of subjectivity, and Foucault comes closer to investigating the role of private documents in self-creation. Had he lived longer he might have come closer still. In an interview a year before his death Foucault speaks of a work in progress, to be titled *Le souci de soi*, related to his *History* but separate from it ("On the Genealogy of Ethics," in Hubert L. Dreyfus and Paul Rabinow, eds., *Michel Foucault: Beyond Structuralism and Hermeneutics* [Chicago: University of Chicago Press, 1983], 229–64). In this book he plans to examine the practice, "in the Greco-Roman culture, starting from about the third century B. C.," of the *hypomnemata*, a "copybook, a notebook," into which "one entered quotations, fragments of works, examples, and actions to which one had been witness or of which one had read the account. . . . [The *hypomnemata*] constituted a material memory of things read, heard, or thought." Foucault accords to the practitioners of this kind of writing a high degree of autonomy: "This work on the self . . . is not imposed on the individual . . . but is a choice about existence made by the individual. People decide for themselves whether or not to care for themselves" (243–46). The book's purpose, he suggests, will be to point up the contrast between the ancient "care of the self" and the more coercive Christian model of the confessional.

Foucault did not live to write the book. He transposed its intended title to the third volume of the *History*, in which he uses material from the *hypomnemata* but does not investigate the practice itself. It remains an open question what Foucault might have made of a practice like Pepys's, which finds in the genre of the journal a form long recognized as a venue for Christian confession, and converts it (back?) into a repository of "material memory," governed by time rather than piety: a quest for fullness of narrative record rather than of absolution or of grace.

23. *Private Correspondence and Miscellaneous Papers of Samuel Pepys, 1679–1703*, ed. J. R. Tanner (London: G. Bell and Sons, 1903), 2.312.

24. Richard Ollard, *Pepys: A Biography* (New York: Athenaeum, 1984), 340.

CHAPTER FOUR

1. James Sutherland, *The Restoration Newspaper and Its Development* (Cambridge: Cambridge University Press, 1986), 31. Subsequent citations will appear parenthetically.

2. The first *Spectator* bore an imprint identical to that which the *Courant* had instituted at the bottom of its page beginning a week before: "*LONDON*, Printed by *Sam. Buckley*, at the *Dolphin* in *Little Britain*; and Sold by *A[nne] Baldwin* in *Warwick-Lane*." As a result, "the new paper might almost seem to its readers a literary supplement to the old-established

newspaper." Joseph Addison and Richard Steele, *The Spectator*, 5 vols., ed. Donald F. Bond (Oxford: Oxford University Press, 1965), 1.xxi−xxii.

3. John Gay, *The Present State of Wit, in a Letter to a Friend in the Country*, ed. Donald F. Bond (Los Angeles: Augustan Reprint Society, 1947), ser. 1, no. 3, 6.

4. Alexander Pope, *Pastoral Poetry and an Essay on Criticism*, ed. E. Audra and Aubrey Williams, vol. 1 of *The Twickenham Edition of the Poems of Alexander Pope*, ed. John Butt et al. (New Haven: Yale University Press, 1961), 239−40.

5. *The Works of John Suckling: The Plays*, ed. L. A. Beaurline (Oxford: Clarendon Press, 1971), 95. A. S. West and J. C. Collins have identified the echo of Suckling in Pope's *Essay* (*Pastoral Poetry*, 239, n. 9). David Landes discusses some of the implications of both passages in *Revolution in Time*, 88 and 131.

6. Landes, *Revolution*, 131.

7. *M. Misson's Memoirs and Observations in His Travels over England with some Account of Scotland and Ireland*, trans. John Ozell (London: A. Bell et al., 1719), 36−37.

8. That the watch was by now at once a familiar and an exclusive form of property is suggested by a small but significant alteration that Ozell effects in his translation of Misson's *Mémoires*. Misson had originally written "tout le monde a des montres" (*Mémoires et observations faites par un voyageur en Angleterre* [The Hague: Henri van Bulderen, 1698], 239). Ozell's modification—"*almost* every Body"—doubtless better reflects the real distribution of watches in London even two decades after Misson's visit: widespread among the prosperous, but hardly universal. Pope's use of the word "our," like Suckling's in a different context, suggests that everybody who is anybody owns one.

9. Rhyme and meter contribute to the mix: the sight rhyme "None/own" pulls slightly apart; the second line's prosody, more even than the first's, suggests agreement even as the line's substance maps divergence.

10. Anderson, *Imagined Communities*, 32−36. Jürgen Habermas, *The Structural Transformation of the Public Sphere: An Inquiry into a Category of Bourgeois Society*, trans. Thomas Burger and Frederick Lawrence (Cambridge: MIT Press, 1991), 42. Subsequent citations to both books will appear parenthetically.

11. His discussion is a little vague about the date as well: he is primarily describing the reading practices surrounding later newspapers, but he lets this account stand in for the entire history of the genre.

12. Addison and Steele, *Spectator*, 1.2. Subsequent citations will appear parenthetically, with the paper's number given first: (*S* 1; 1.2).

13. Richmond P. Bond examines the similarities in *The Tatler: The Making of a Literary Journal* (Cambridge: Harvard University Press, 1971), 23−25.

14. At the rate of "perhaps 4,000" copies of each paper, the *Spectator* matched or exceeded the rival papers in the quantity sold of any one number and it produced at least twice as many numbers per week as any paper other than the *Courant*. See Donald F. Bond, "The First Printing of the *Spectator*," *Modern Philology*, 47 (1950), 164−77, and *Spectator*, 1.xxvii−xxix, lxxxiii.

15. Joseph Collet, *Private Letter Books of Joseph Collet*, ed. by H. H. Dodwell (1933), 100; quoted by Bond in *Spectator*, 1.xcv.

16. Joseph Frank, *The Beginnings of the English Newspaper, 1620−1660* (Cambridge: Harvard University Press, 1961), 7−8.

17. Nonetheless it earned its title. "In addition to being the most competent newspaper of the 1640's, *A Perfect Diurnall* was the most regular." Frank, *Beginnings*, 67. Many dailies followed; Frank indexes eighteen (365−66) as well as three papers entitled "A Diary" or "Diarie."

18. Frank provides the details (*Beginnings* 56 – 57). Even Sunday could for a time pretend to a paper of its own. Stanley Morison claims that the Royalist paper *Aulicus* "was published on Sundays, doubtless for the purpose of registering its protest against the puritan sabbatarianising of that day." Morison, *The English Newspaper: Some Account of the Physical Development of Journals Printed in London between 1622 and the Present Day* (Cambridge: Cambridge University Press, 1932), 24. Frank, though, conjectures that the paper, "despite its Sunday dateline probably came out in London on Monday" (*Beginnings* 56).

19. This facet of the *Athenian Mercury* is well examined in Hunter's *Before Novels*, 12 – 16 and 99 – 106, and in Kathryn Shevelow's chapter "Readers as Writers: The Female Subject in the *Athenian Mercury*" in *Women and Print Culture: The Construction of Femininity in the Early Periodical* (London: Routledge, 1989), 58 – 92.

20. Muddiman went on to create the new government organ *The Oxford* (later *London*) *Gazette* in November 1665, but his print career ended a few months later through political infighting. His prosperity in manuscript, though, as "chief official supplier of written news" lasted until his death in 1689 (J. G. Muddiman, *The King's Journalist 1659 – 1689* [London: Bodley Head, 1923], 193). At Muddiman's death the Tory John Dyer (1653?–1713) succeeded him as "the best-known and most influential" writer of newsletters in England. See Henry L. Snyder, "Newsletters in England, 1689 – 1715: with Special Reference to John Dyer—a Byway in the History of England" in *Newsletters to Newspapers: Eighteenth-Century Journalism*, ed. Donovan H. Bond and W. Reynolds McLeod (Morgantown: School of Journalism, West Virginia University, 1977), 3 – 19.

21. For a full account of Dawks and his script type, see Stanley Morison, *Ichabod Dawks and His News-Letter with an Account of the Dawks Family of Booksellers and Stationers 1635 – 1731* (Cambridge: Cambridge University Press, 1931).

22. Quoted in Morison, *Dawks*, 25.

23. Morison, *English Newspaper*, 48, 47.

24. Richard Steele and Joseph Addison, *The Tatler*, 3 vols., ed. Donald F. Bond (Oxford: Clarendon Press, 1987), 2.471. Subsequent citations will appear parenthetically, giving the paper's number first: (*T* 178; 2.471).

25. Quoted by Frank Staff in *The Penny Post 1680 – 1918* (London: Lutterworth Press, 1964), 168.

26. When Steele wrote, the innovation was freshly controversial. The Post Office had just suppressed Charles Povey, the inventor of this private scheme, but they adapted his use of bellmen, expanded the program to provincial towns, and kept it in use in London until 1846. The pillar-box eventually took over their function as collectors. An invention of Anthony Trollope's, it debuted in Jersey in 1853, in London in 1855. Howard Robinson, *The British Post Office: A History* (Princeton: Princeton University Press, 1948), 88 – 89, 333 – 34.

27. For the *Tatler's* relation with the *Gazette* and other newspapers as precedents, sources, and rivals, see R. P. Bond, *The Tatler*, 44 – 70 and 220 – 23, and Robert Waller Achurch, "Richard Steele, Gazetteer and Bickerstaff" in *Studies in the Early English Periodical*, ed. Richmond P. Bond (Chapel Hill: University of North Carolina Press, 1957), 49 – 72. For possible influences on the *Tatler* among earlier literary periodicals see Walter Graham, *English Literary Periodicals* (New York: Thomas Nelson, 1930), 19 – 64; and Charles A. Knight, "Bibliography and the Shape of the Literary Periodical in the Early Eighteenth Century," *Library* 8, 6th series (1986): 242 – 46.

28. Bickerstaff makes ironic use of his transformation in "his" Dedication to Arthur Maywaring at the opening of the *Tatler's* first collected volume: "I could not, I confess, long

keep up the Opinion of the Town, that these Lucubrations were written by the same Hand with the first Works which were published under my Name . . ." (*T* 1.8).

29. Kathryn Shevelow reads this passage as a "back-handed compliment to women" in *Women and Print Culture*, 93. But Steele has been evenhandedly "back-handed" to his male readers as well, whom he has just depicted as "of strong Zeal and weak Intellects." Bickerstaff is mocking—and identifying with—both genders in his self-declared commitment to talk.

30. *The Lover* No. 23 ⟨17 April 1714⟩, in *Richard Steele's Periodical Journalism 1714 – 16*, ed. Rae Blanchard (Oxford: Clarendon Press, 1959), 86; quoted in R. P. Bond, *The Tatler*, 233, n. 4. The letter, signed "Charles Lasie" (a name that had appeared in other Steele periodicals), may have been an "inside job" by one of Steele's assistants or contributors; Blanchard does not think it was written by Steele himself (280).

31. The news reports not only filled space; they drew an audience. In his dedication of the first volume of the collected *Tatler*, Steele recalls that at the paper's start "the Additions or the ordinary Occurrences of common Journals of News brought in a Multitude of . . . Readers" (*T* 1.8).

32. Steele had decided in any case to reduce Bickerstaff's news supply severely; the *Gazette* had just switched from a Monday-Thursday schedule to one that exactly matched the *Tatler's*, and even Steele could not provide fresh, distinct intelligence for both papers on the same days. This shift in circumstance helped foster in the *Tatler* the independence of breaking news that Addison as Bickerstaff had argued for. See R. P. Bond, *The Tatler*, 49 – 54.

33. Juvenal, *Satires*, 1.85 – 86. Unless otherwise noted, translations of *Tatler* and *Spectator* mottoes will be those used in Bond's editions. In many cases Bond draws his translations from the Loeb Classical Library; in others he quotes eighteenth-century sources, here Thomas Percy's annotation for *The Tatler, with Illustrations and Notes, Historical, Biographical, and Critical*, ed. John Nichols (London, 1786).

34. The *Spectator*, a periodical of identical length, explicitly makes this estimate of its reading time early on (*S* 10; 1.21).

35. Imagery of metamorphosis clustered thick around the last *Tatler*s and early *Spectator*s. Gay, speculating as to the real motivations behind the *Tatler's* demise, shrewdly saves for the emphatic final possibility a reason that Steele had scarcely hinted at: ". . . most People judg'd the true cause to be, either that he was quite spent, and wanted matter to continue his undertaking any longer. . . . Or lastly, that he had a Mind to vary his Shape, and appear again in some new Light" (*Present State* 3).

This last surmise responds astutely to a subtle open-endedness in Steele's tight-lipped proclamation of closure: though he has "nothing more to say under the Character of Isaac Bickerstaff," he may find more to say under another character altogether. In advancing the surmise, Gay enjoyed the advantage of fresh hindsight: by the date on which he publishes these remarks (May 1711) Addison and Steele's new paper had already been appearing for two months, and at whose hands, Gay thinks he knows.

36. Horace, *Satires, Epistles, and Ars Poetica*, trans. H. Rushton Fairclough. Loeb Classical Library (London: W. Heinemann, 1929), 2.463.

37. The resemblance to Mr. Spectator goes even deeper. Pepys's words apply ambiguously to two "courses," that of ending the diary and that of descending into blindness. The equivocation suggests a link: sightlessness will subdue him to silence. Mr. Spectator operates from a parallel premise. As his sobriquet announces, his eyes supply him with those essential "Discoveries" that will fill his "Sheets." For him too, then, blindness would

enforce a silence and a kind of death; it would deprive him of the faculty from which he draws his name and whole identity.

38. The identification that Addison and Steele cultivate between the *Spectator* and its female audience, and the intimations of androgyny in the *eidolon*, complicate without in the least overturning Shevelow's reading of "the more programmatic construction of female nature" which the paper performs in the many numbers it devotes to women's narratives, predicaments, and proper conduct. If anything, the identification functions as medium for the didactic program, and the asserted "correspondence" between the sensibilities of the male author and his female readers underwrites that more palpable correspondence that Shevelow traces in the letters from women that the *Spectator* publishes. See Shevelow, *Women and Print Culture*, 93 – 145.

39. *Virgil*, trans. H. Rushton Fairclough, 2 vols., revised edition (Cambridge: Harvard University Press, 1965), 1.95.

40. The *Spectator* thus anticipates the trend John Bender traces, beginning with *Robinson Crusoe*, away from "liminal" notions of self-transformation—abrupt, definitive, even terminal—toward the "narrative" projects for reform inherent in the name and nature of the new "penitentiaries," where the misdoer could change his ways by a pattern of repeated self-examinations over time. See *Imagining the Penitentiary* (Chicago: University of Chicago Press, 1987), 43 – 61.

41. Two excellent essays on the *Spectator*'s representations of property and commerce are Charles A. Knight, "The *Spectator*'s Moral Economy," *Modern Philology* 91.2 (1993), 161 – 79, and Carole Fabricant, "The Aesthetics and Politics of Landscape in the Eighteenth Century" in *Studies in Eighteenth-Century British Art and Aesthetics*, ed. Ralph Cohen (Berkeley: University of California Press, 1985), 49 – 81.

42. John Locke, *An Essay Concerning Human Understanding*, ed. Peter H. Nidditch (Oxford: Clarendon Press, 1975), bk. 2, ch. 14, secs. 4 – 7.

43. Addison here first paraphrases, then quotes directly from, Locke's *Essay* (2.14.4).

44. I am indebted to Michael Ketcham's discussion of *Spectators* 93 and 94 in *Transparent Designs*, 90 – 91. By treating Locke's *Essay* as a recurrent point of reference throughout his study, Ketcham produces a rich account of the philosopher's influence on the form and substance of the *Spectator*.

45. Lorna Martens, *The Diary Novel* (Cambridge: Cambridge University Press, 1985), 67.

46. By other small touches within this essay, Addison elaborates the network of connections between male author and female reader, between the present paper and the larger project, and among the readership at large. First, in the paper's motto he makes more explicit than usual Mr. Spectator's aspiration to a kind of doubled gender status, calculated to speak for (even to incarnate) both the men and the women in his audience: *modo Vir, modo Faemina* [now man, now woman]. Drawn (appropriately) from Ovid's *Metamorphosis* (4.280), the phrase alludes to the (otherwise unrecorded) sex change of the mythological Sithon, king of Thrace. At the top of this *Spectator*, the words forecast the shift from the Citizen's journal a week ago to Clarinda's here, and advertise Mr. Spectator's capacity not merely to advise but to become his readers, male and female (as, in an analogous operation, Addison has impersonated both the man and the woman by producing the self-evident fictions of the two journals). Addison further links the present paper with the *Spectator*'s whole program by looking back, in his closing advice to Clarinda, at "one of the Morals of my First Paper" (185); technically he refers to the earlier paper on the Citizen's journal (*S* 317), but the wording reaches further back to the initial paper (*S* 1) in which Mr. Spectator first established the program of writing in which he now involves Clarinda (the original folio sheet's plural—

"my first Paper*s*"—enhances this retrospective sense). Finally, Addison coordinates his community of readers by means of the calendar (on Anderson's model) with remarkable nuance in this number. Clarinda absorbs the citizen's journal and the *Spectator*'s advice on the Tuesday that they appear (her first entry reads "TUESDAY *Night*. Could not go to Sleep till one in the Morning for Thinking of my Journal" [182]); she writes through Saturday, finishing in time to post the journal so that Mr. Spectator receives it Monday and prints it Tuesday. The fiction takes place in real time carefully spelled out; readers on Tuesday can compare their week with hers.

47. "Voyeuristic Dreams: Mr. Spectator and the Power of Spectacle," *The Eighteenth Century: Theory and Interpretation* 36.1 (1995): 2–23. Subsequent citations will appear parenthetically.

48. *London Journal*, ed. Frederick A. Pottle (New York: McGraw-Hill, 1950), 76.

CHAPTER FIVE

1. Daniel Defoe, *A Tour Thro' the Whole Island of Great Britain*, 3 vols. (London: G. Strahan, 1724–1727), 3.3–4. Subsequent citations will appear parenthetically.

2. *A Plat for Mariners: Or, the Seaman's Preacher* (London, 1672), A3, quoted in J. Paul Hunter, *The Reluctant Pilgrim: Defoe's Emblematic Method and Quest for Form in Robinson Crusoe* (Baltimore: Johns Hopkins University Press, 1966), 83.

3. Letter to Giuseppe Baretti, 10 June 1761. *Letters of Samuel Johnson*, 5 vols., ed. Bruce Redford (Princeton: Princeton University Press, 1992–94), 1.200.

4. Paul Fussell uses lending-library records to help establish "that throughout the eighteenth century the travel book was one of the primary genres." "Patrick Brydone: The Eighteenth-Century Traveler as Representative Man," in *Literature as a Mode of Travel: Five Essays and a Postscript*, ed. Warner G. Rice (New York: New York Public Library, 1963), 53–67; quotation 54.

5. The fullest account of the cultural and scientific impact of the longitude problem is Howse's *Greenwich Time and the Discovery of the Longitude* (see ch. 3, n. 3), to which I am indebted for many of the facts in the following discussion.

6. Joseph Addison, Richard Steele, et al., *The Guardian*, ed. John Calhoun Stephens (Lexington: University Press of Kentucky, 1982), 371–72.

7. A detailed account of the Scriblerian response to the longitude competition appears in Marjorie Nicolson and G. S. Rousseau, *"This Long Disease My Life": Alexander Pope and the Sciences* (Princeton: Princeton University Press, 1968), 166–87.

8. Letter from John Arbuthnot to Jonathan Swift, 17 July 1714. *The Correspondence of Jonathan Swift*, ed. Harold Williams, 5 vols. (Oxford: Clarendon Press, 1963), 2.70. Quoted (from an earlier, modernized edition of Swift's correspondence) in James M. Osborn, " 'That on Whiston' by John Gay," *Papers of the Bibliographic Society of America* 56 (1962), 73–78; quotation 74.

9. Claude J. Rawson, "Parnell on Whiston," *Papers of the Bibliographic Society of America* 57 (1963), 91–92.

10. *Gentleman's Magazine* 22 (1752), 359; cited in Albert J. Kuhn, "Dr. Johnson, Zachariah Williams, and the Eighteenth-Century Search for the Longitude," *Modern Philology* 82.1 (August 1984), 40–53; quotation 40.

11. Howse, *Greenwich Time*, 71

12. Such accuracy was not long confined to navigators. "In the last quarter of the eighteenth century," writes David Landes, "the British turned the marine chronometer into an object of industrial manufacture and commercial use," partly by refining the technology and

partly by miniaturizing it so that it could operate within the confines of the pocket watch (*Revolution in Time* 171). The new technology was carried over from the maritime to the domestic market by some of Harrison's rivals for the longitude prize, most notably John Arnold, who in the 1770s produced the first precision pocket watch, capable of tracking seconds in lockstep over a period of years. The technological advances achieved during the third quarter of the eighteenth century governed the working of watches into the twentieth. Clutton and Daniels parse out the intricately intertwined developments in navigational and domestic horology in *Watches*, 44 – 66. See also Anthony G. Randall, *The Time Museum Catalogue of Chronometers* (Rockford, IL: The Time Museum, 1991), 2 – 33.

13. The two preeminent French innovators in navigational chronometry were Pierre Le Roy and Ferdinand Berthoud, neither of whose instruments, tested in the 1760s and 1770s, performed as consistently as Harrison's H4. Through the inventions of the horologist Abraham Louis Breguet (1747 – 1823), France subsequently attained a long ascendancy in horological innovation, but Britain continued to dominate the international market through the end of the century, annually producing nearly half the timekeepers sold in Europe (about 150,000 – 200,000 watches in 1797, for example). See Randall, *Chronometers*, 16 – 31, 77 – 82, 96 – 111, and 226 – 27.

14. The initial steps towards making Greenwich the center for time measurement occurred in the 1760s with the first publication of Nevil Maskelyne's annual *Nautical Almanac*, designed to assist navigators in the "lunar-distance" (i.e., astronomical) reckoning of the longitude; created at the Royal Observatory, the new periodical reckoned Greenwich as the prime meridian, and did much to globalize that reckoning. As Howse observes, "a very high proportion of the world's deep-sea navigators" began to use the *Almanac* at its first appearance, and so "map and chart publishers the world over began to provide longitude graduations based on Greenwich" (*Greenwich Time* 66, 67). The establishment of Greenwich as the reference point for standardized time as well as calibrated space began in 1848, with Great Britain's adoption of Greenwich Mean Time; by 1978 "all countries" except Guyana and Chatham Island "were keeping time within an even hour or half-hour of Greenwich" (Howse, 155).

15. Mary Louise Pratt, *Imperial Eyes: Travel Writing and Transculturation* (London: Routledge, 1992), 5, 31. Subsequent citations will appear parenthetically.

16. My positing the longitude as such a pattern may seem at odds with Pratt's account, which associates "planetary consciousness" with the shift "toward interior, as opposed to maritime, exploration" (9) and with the emergent science of natural history, in which "the planet's life forms were to be drawn out of the tangled threads of their life surroundings" and placed within a Eurocentric paradigm. Still, the longitude quest meshes well with Pratt's schema. She acknowledges that "planetary consciousness" originates in two earlier "totalizing or planetary projects"—the expeditions and narratives of global circumnavigation, and the "mapping of the world's coastlines"—which for three hundred years "had been construing the planet above all in navigational terms" (29). Harrison's chronometry brings this project to one kind of culmination by delivering its chief desideratum at the same time that natural history initiates (in Pratt's account) a third "totalizing project" with a new mode of operation. In fact, the projects overlap historically to a greater extent than Pratt acknowledges. In James Cook's first exploratory voyage to the South Seas, for example, the naturalist Joseph Banks assiduously gathers specimens of flora and fauna. In Cook's second voyage, his navigators use Harrison's marine chronometer to "map the South Atlantic and South Pacific Ocean regions, establishing accurately the positions of numerous islands, and charting part of Tasmania, the east coast of Australia, and the islands of New Zealand, which he discov-

ered" (Randall, *Chronometers*, 28). The naturalist advances Pratt's second "totalizing project"; then the navigator advances her first. The commingling of the projects persists in the person of Banks himself: as president of the Royal Society, he became deeply interested in questions of horology, championing the chronometers of John Arnold over those of all rivals. See Landes, *Revolution in Time*, 176 – 79.

17. Martens, *Diary Novel*, 65. Martens's insistence on the "present tense" as a criterion for reckoning the degree of actual immediacy in a particular entry somewhat distorts both her descriptions of individual journals and her pronouncements on diaries in general. She claims, for example, that the sea journals from this second stage "consist of present-tense entries that were evidently written from day to day." As the entries quoted in the next paragraph show, the writers of sea journals dealt (like Pepys) in a running mix of tenses: present, perfect, simple past. The evidence that the entries were composed soon after the experience they narrate depends not on verb tense but on the time limits of manifest knowledge. Such immediacy is readily fabricated; what is new in 1712 is that the writers of sea journals find it *worth* fabricating.

18. Woodes Rogers, *A Cruising Voyage Round the World* (London: A. Bell, 1712), 103.

19. William Dampier, *A New Voyage Round the World*, 4th edition (London: James Knapton, 1699), A3r. Subsequent citations will appear parenthetically.

20. Edward Cooke, *A Voyage to the South Sea, and around the World* (London: Lintot et al., 1712), A1r.

21. Daniel Defoe, *The Compleat English Gentleman*, ed. Karl D. Bülbring (London: David Nutt, 1890), 225 – 26. Pratt quotes and comments discerningly on part of this passage, but without attending to the temporal implications of the sea journals Defoe cites (15, 30, 36).

22. Jonathan Swift, *Gulliver's Travels*, ed. Herbert Davis (Oxford: Basil Blackwell, 1959), 35.

23. *The Ladies Diary: or the Womens Almanack, for the Year of our Lord, 1706* (London: J. Wilde, 1706), A4v.

24. Bernard Capp, *English Almanacs*, 244 – 46.

25. On Dodsley's memorandum books see Ralph Straus, *Robert Dodsley: Poet, Publisher, and Playwright* (London: John Lane, 1910), 274 – 75 and 336 – 37; and Alvin Kernan, *Printing Technology, Letters and Samuel Johnson* (Princeton: Princeton University Press, 1987), 65.

26. *Daily Post*, 3 August 1722. Quoted in Sutherland, *Restoration Newspaper*, 129.

27. Pope points out that the papers' problems in this regard have recently been aggravated, "since the great Fountain of News, I mean the War, is very near being dried up" (4.92). Satirical essays on the predicament of news writers in peacetime had by now become virtually a sub-genre, providing the satirists with a ready topos for registering the new insatiability of both press and readers for copy to fill the daily page. For an originary instance see Addison's *Tatler* 18, already discussed in ch. 4 above.

28. Brian Lake, *British Newspapers: A History and Guide for Collectors* (London: Sheppard Press, 1984), 45 – 59; and R. S. Crane and F. B. Kaye, *A Census of British Newspapers and Periodicals, 1620 – 1800* (Chapel Hill: University of North Carolina Press, 1927). The number of dailies fluctuated upward throughout the century; the increase was not as steady as this list suggests.

29. In *British Diaries*, William Matthews lists 320 diarists for the seventeenth century. For the eighteenth, he identifies 680, about two-thirds of whom begin their journals in the century's second half. The trend in diary-keeping is of course far more elusive to track than that in daily newspapers, thanks to the variables of preservation and location. More recent texts are probably more likely to be found. Still, this variable is offset by others (for example, the

preservation of many Puritan diaries in the Williams library) and Matthews's numbers almost certainly correspond (however roughly) to a real increase over the period. Among the Pepysian diurnalists committed to a narrative of each successive day were William Ryder, Thomas Turner, John Wesley and many of his followers, as well as (for long stretches of his journals) James Boswell.

30. *The Poems of Jonathan Swift*, ed. Harold Williams, 2nd edition, 3 vols. (Oxford: Clarendon Press, 1958), 2.444–53.

31. Jonathan Swift, *Journal to Stella*, ed. Harold Williams, 2 vols. (Oxford: Clarendon Press, 1948), 35, 8–9. Subsequent citations will appear parenthetically. "MD" stands for "my dears" (Esther Johnson and Dingley), "Presto" stands for Swift himself, and "PMD" refers to all three together.

32. Swift, as it happens, is preoccupied with bellmen, too; in the *Journal to Stella* he refers repeatedly to their approach (1.11, 35, 343; 2.472, 537, 607). He values the bellman, though, not as a momentarily private timekeeper but as a social emissary, the first link in the postal chain that connects him with Dublin and Esther Johnson (he also frets frequently about the inefficiency of the delivery system). The small parallel to Pepys underlines the basic difference. Pepys in the diary is concerned with modes of appropriation; Swift in the journal letter is concerned with strategies of transmission. See Helen O'Brien Molitor, "Swift's Bellmen in *The Journal to Stella*," *American Notes and Queries*, 24.3 and 4 (November-December, 1985), 40–41, and "Jonathan Swift and the Post Office: 1710–1713," *Eighteenth-Century Life* 13 (November 1989): 70–78.

33. Jonathan Swift, *Miscellaneous and Autobiographical Pieces*, ed. Herbert Davis (Oxford: Basil Blackwell, 1962), 203–5.

34. Michael Rosenblum, "The World Promiscuously Described: Minute Particulars and Thresholds of Narration in the Eighteenth Century," a talk presented to the Samuel Johnson Society of the Central Region, Ann Arbor, April 1992. I am grateful to Professor Rosenblum for permission to quote from a typescript of his talk.

35. Irvin Ehrenpreis, *Swift: The Man, His Works, and the Age*, 3 vols. (Cambridge: Harvard University Press, 1967), 2.653.

36. The satiric strategy inverts that of the "Epistle Dedicatory, to His Royal Highness Prince Posterity" in *A Tale of a Tub*, where Swift feels obliged to *remind* Prince Posterity that such hacks as Dryden once existed.

37. Swift does this not only in the "Journal of a Modern Lady," but also in "Description of a Morning," "Description of a City Shower," and in the nearly innumerable long lists of material objects that become one of his trademark gestures (cf., for example, Gulliver's catalogue of European weaponry: "I gave [my Houyhnhnm host] a description of Cannons, Culverins, Muskets, Carabines, Pistols, Bullets, Powder, Swords, Bayonets . . ." (*Gulliver's Travels*, 247).

38. Even on the question of publishing ordinary (non-journal) letters, which were more selective because less date-driven, Swift was far more hesitant than Pope. Ehrenpreis details the complications (and Swift's resistances) that attended the publication of the Swift-Pope correspondence (*Swift*, 3.883–98).

39. Patrick Brydone, *A Tour Through Sicily and Malta. In a Series of Letters to William Beckford*, 2nd edition, 2 vols. (London: Strahan and Cadell, 1774), 1.A3r. Subsequent citations will appear parenthetically.

40. Jonas Hanway, *A Journal of Eight Days Journey from Portsmouth to Kingston upon Thames*, 2nd edition, 2 vols. (London: H. Woodfall, 1757), 1.2–3. Subsequent citations will appear parenthetically.

41. The *OED* cites Hanway's *Journal* as the earliest appearance of the term "journal letter." Hanway uses the term in the peroration of his prefatory letters, as the name of a genre whose merits he has demonstrated by both argument and literary context: "You see I have begun my *journal letters*, with the solemnity of a *dedication*, and the length of a *preface* . . ." (15). Hanway's use of italics resembles Cooke's use of small caps which I discussed earlier: the typeface links the genre new to print ("journal" for Cooke, "journal letter" for Hanway) with matter more familiar (e.g., "description" and "account" for Cooke, "preface" and "dedication" for Hanway).

Seventeen years earlier, Richardson's Pamela attempts to describe her journal letters in a phrase that suggests that a familiar term for the form had yet to be developed: "At last I end my Journal-wise letters as I may call them." *Pamela: or, Virtue Rewarded*, 6th edition, 4 vols. (London: S. Richardson, 1742), 3.415.

42. Henry Fielding, *Jonathan Wild* and *The Journal of a Voyage to Lisbon*, ed. Douglas Brooks-Davies (London: Dent, 1932), 183, 187. Subsequent citations will appear parenthetically.

43. Fielding is here reworking a narrative and temporal contract that he originally and emphatically hammered out in *Tom Jones*, where the objects of critique are not the personal diary but the copious, unselective "history" and (by way of simile) the daily newspaper; the method of mockery is the now familiar stagecoach trope: Other writer's histories "do, in reality, very much resemble a News-paper, which consists of just the same Number of Words, whether there be any News in it or not. They may, likewise, be compared to a Stage-Coach, which performs constantly the same Course empty as well as full. The writer, indeed, seems to think himself obliged to keep even Pace with time, whose Amanuensis he is. . . . Now it is our Purpose in the ensuing Pages, to pursue a contrary method. . . . We shall not be afraid of a Chasm in our History; but shall hasten on to Matters of Consequence, and leave [unimportant] periods of time totally unobserved." *The History of Tom Jones, A Foundling*, ed. Fredson Bowers. 2 vols. (Oxford: Clarendon Press, 1975), 1.75–76.

44. Samuel Paterson, *Another Traveller!* (1767–69). Quoted in Charles L. Batten, Jr., *Pleasurable Instruction: Form and Convention in Eighteenth-Century Travel Literature* (Berkeley: University of California Press, 1978), 41.

45. Samuel Sharp, *Letters from Italy, Describing the Customs and Manners of that Country. . . ,* 3rd edition (London: Henry and Cave, 1767), A2r. Subsequent citations will appear parenthetically.

46. Joseph Baretti, *A Journey from London to Genoa, through England, Portugal, Spain and France*, 4 vols. (London: T. Davies and L. Davis, 1770), 1.vi.

47. Batten, *Pleasurable Instruction*, 79–81.

CHAPTER SIX

1. *The Letters of Samuel Johnson*, ed. Bruce Redford, 5 vols. (Princeton: Princeton University Press, 1992–4), 2.95. Subsequent citations will appear parenthetically.

2. In the introduction to his edition of the *Journey*, J. D. Fleeman notes that the published *Journey* offers little internal evidence that Johnson necessarily wrote with his journal letters at hand. Differences between the texts suggest "that the letters themselves were collateral descendants [with the *Journey*] from the notebooks [i.e., Johnson's "book of remarks"] rather than intermediate sources for the eventual narrative manuscript of the *Journey*." *A Journey to the Western Islands of Scotland*, ed. J. D. Fleeman (Oxford: Clarendon Press, 1985), xxxviii. On the other hand, Pat Rogers tries (inconclusively, I think) to demonstrate close affinities between the *Journey* and the letters in his *Johnson and Boswell: The Transit of Caledonia* (Oxford: Clarendon Press, 1995), 108–38.

3. *Boswell's Life of Johnson*, ed. G. B. Hill, rev. L. F. Powell, 6 vols. (Oxford: Clarendon Press, 1934–50), 2.117. Subsequent references to the *Life* will be to this edition, and will appear parenthetically.

4. *Diaries, Prayers, and Annals*, ed. E. L. McAdam, Jr., with Donald and Mary Hyde. Vol. 1 in *The Yale Edition of the Works of Samuel Johnson* (New Haven: Yale University Press, 1958), 50, 71, 303. All subsequent citations from the *Diaries* will appear parenthetically.

5. J. G. A. Pocock, *Virtue, Commerce, and History* (Cambridge: Cambridge University Press, 1985), 98, 112. Subsequent citations will appear parenthetically.

6. J. G. A. Pocock, *The Machiavellian Moment* (Princeton: Princeton University Press, 1975), 461. On Defoe and Addison, see *Moment*, 451–61, and *Virtue*, 113–16.

7. Samuel Johnson, *The Rambler*, ed. W. J. Bate and Albrecht B. Strauss, vols. 3–5 of *The Yale Edition of the Works of Samuel Johnson* (New Haven: Yale University Press, 1969), 3.25. Subsequent citations will appear parenthetically, giving the paper's number first: (*R5*; 3.25).

8. Or rather, the differences in prose style embody the temporal differences. In Johnson's intricate periods and parallel structures, the sentences enact from their beginnings a keen, operative awareness of their "futures": they forecast the syntax and shapes by which they will resolve. In Addison's "middle style," which Johnson praises so famously in *Lives of the Poets*, the much higher proportion of parataxis enacts attention to the present clause, independent of syntactical futurity. Even Johnson's praise displays a tincture of un-Addisonian syntactic suspense: "Whoever wishes to attain an English style, familiar but not coarse, and elegant but not ostentatious, must give his days and nights to the volumes of Addison." *Lives of the English Poets*, ed. G. Birkbeck Hill, 3 vols. (Oxford: Clarendon Press, 1895), 2.150. Subsequent citations will appear parenthetically.

9. See, for example, *Idler* 43 and *Adventurer* 120.

10. Samuel Johnson, *An Account of an Attempt to Ascertain the Longitude at Sea, by an Exact Theory of the Variation of the Magnetical Needle* (London: R. Dodsley, 1755), 2–4. Subsequent citations will appear parenthetically.

11. Bruce Redford, "Samuel Johnson and Mrs. Thrale: The 'Little Language' of the Public Moralist," in *The Converse of the Pen* (Chicago: University of Chicago Press, 1986), 206–43 and particularly 208–9.

12. *A Journal of a Tour to the Hebrides with Samuel Johnson LL.D.*, vol. 5 of *Boswell's Life of Johnson*, ed. G. Birkbeck Hill, rev. L. F. Powell (Oxford: Clarendon Press, 1950), 109–10. Subsequent references to the published *Journal* will be from this edition and will appear parenthetically.

13. *The Idler and The Adventurer*, ed. W. J. Bate, J. M. Bullitt, and L. F. Powell. Vol. 2 of *The Yale Edition of the Works of Samuel Johnson*, ed. Herman W. Liebert et al. (New Haven: Yale University Press, 1958–), 2.299. Subsequent citations will appear parenthetically.

14. Johnson gave Hanway's *Journal* a negative review in the *Literary Magazine*, 2.13 (1757). Hanway replied by charging that Johnson had read the journal prematurely, in the private edition published for friends; the letters, he reiterates, "were not written to be printed." Johnson retorted: "I concluded . . . that, though not *written* to be *printed*, they were *printed* to be *read*." *The Works of Samuel Johnson, LL.D.*, 9 vols. (Oxford: Talboys and Wheeler, 1825), 6.32. Johnson's initial review appears on 6.20–31, his reply to Hanway on 6.32–37. Boswell observes that this is the only instance in Johnson's career as reviewer in which he responded to an offended author (*Life* 1.313–14).

15. *A Journey to the Western Islands of Scotland*, ed. J. D. Fleeman, 1. Subsequent citations from the *Journey* will be from this edition and will appear parenthetically.

16. Kathryn Temple, "Johnson and Macpherson: Cultural Authority and the Construc-

tion of Literary Property," *Yale Journal of Law & the Humanities* 5 (1993), 355–87; Katie Trumpener, "The End of an Auld Sang: Oral Tradition and Literary History" in *Bardic Nationalism, British Imperialism, and the 'English Novel,' 1760–1830* (Princeton: Princeton University Press, forthcoming). For other important political analyses of Johnson's and Boswell's tour, see Deidre Lynch, " 'Beating the Track of the Alphabet': Samuel Johnson, Tourism, and the ABCs of Modern Authority," *ELH* 57.2 (1990), 357–405; and Gordon Turnbull, " 'Generous Attachment': The Politics of Biography in the *Tour to the Hebrides*," in *Dr. Samuel Johnson and James Boswell*, ed. Harold Bloom (New York: Chelsea House, 1986), 227–38.

17. James Boswell, *The Hypochondriack*, No. 66, in *Boswell's Column*, ed. Margery Bailey (London: William Kimber, 1951), 332.

18. Shortly after arriving in London, for example, Boswell writes up particulars designed to reproach Johnston for not coming to bid good-bye to him when he left Scotland: "I dreamt that Johnston did not care for me. That he came to see me set off on a long journey, and that he seemed dissipated and tired, and left me before I got away." *Boswell's London Journal 1762–3*, ed. Frederick A. Pottle (New York: McGraw-Hill, 1950), 49. Subsequent citations will appear parenthetically.

19. Some examples: During a period of depression, Boswell writes up his despondency and then recoils: "I am vexed at such a distempered suggestion's being inserted in my journal, which I wished to contain a consistent picture of a young fellow eagerly pushing through life. . . . Let me consider that the hero of a romance or novel must not go uniformly along in bliss, but the story must be chequered with bad fortune. Aeneas met with many disasters in his voyage to Italy, and must not Boswell have his rubs?" (205–6). At another point, he visits David Garrick, who prophesies, "you will be a very great man. And when you are so, remember the year 1763. . . ." Boswell comments, "What he meant by my being a great man I can understand" (161).

20. The instance most often remarked is his ecstatic account of his first night with his lover Louisa, composed on the day when he has discerned the symptoms of a venereal disease caught in that encounter. See *London Journal*, 13, n. 4.

21. For a discussion of the hybrid's subsequent influence (notably on the prolific travel writer Arthur Young), see Batten's *Pleasurable Instruction*, 33–34.

22. *Boswell on the Grand Tour: Italy, Corsica, and France, 1765–1766*, ed. Frank Brady and Frederick A. Pottle (New York: McGraw-Hill, 1955), 154. Subsequent citations will appear parenthetically.

23. One surviving particular in the *Journal* angered Johnson. Without his permission, Boswell had included in his published narrative Johnson's comment in which the journal imperative mingles with the fear of "disappointing" insatiable "expectations." Johnson's irritation both fulfilled and inverted the paragraph's forecast: he deemed that Boswell's selective, tactical redaction of his *Journal* had not been selective (or tactful) enough.

24. *Boswell: The Applause of the Jury, 1782–1785*, ed. Irma S. Lustig and Frederick A. Pottle (New York: McGraw-Hill, 1981), 272, n. 3. Subsequent citations will appear parenthetically.

25. Quoted by Fleeman, *Journey*, 157, n. 7. The MS. of Boswell's "Remarks" is now in the Hyde Collection; a facsimile is included in Robert Borthwick Adams, *The R. B. Adams Library*, 3 vols. (Oxford: Oxford University Press, 1959), 2.45 ff.

26. Quoted by Fleeman, *Journey*, 247, n. 137

27. *Letters of James Boswell*, ed. Chauncey Brewster Tinker, 2 vols. (Oxford: Clarendon Press, 1935–50), 1.212, 222. E. Matthew Goyette cites these letters and discusses their significance as clues to the development of the *Tour*; see his "Boswell's Changing Conceptions

of his *Journal of a Tour to the Hebrides,*" *PBSA* 73 (1979): 305–14. I am indebted to his fine article for many of the facts on which I draw in this discussion.

28. James Boswell, *Boswell: The Ominous Years, 1774–1776,* ed. Charles Ryskamp and Frederick A. Pottle (New York: McGraw-Hill, 1963), 102. Subsequent citations will appear parenthetically.

29. It is difficult to date the leaves precisely; Frederick Pottle argues for the later date in his edition (with Charles H. Bennett) of the original manuscript of Boswell's *Journal of a Tour to the Hebrides* (New York: McGraw-Hill, 1961), xx–xxi, 411–12; subsequent citations from Boswell's manuscript will be from this edition and will appear (as *Hebrides*) parenthetically. Goyette argues for the earlier date, but admits that the evidence does not make for absolute certainty (311).

30. Quoted by Pottle in his edition of the manuscript journal, *Hebrides* 411–12.

31. John Wolcot, "A Poetic and Congratulatory Epistle to James Boswell, Esq. on his Journal of a Tour to the Hebrides with the celebrated Doctor Johnson" in *The Works of Peter Pindar,* 3 vols. (London: John Walker, 1794), 1.356.

32. Walter James, *A Defence of Mr. Boswell's Journal, in a Letter to the Author of the Remarks Signed Verax* (London, 1785), 3–4.

33. William Shakespeare, *King Henry VIII,* ed. R. A. Foakes (London: Methuen, 1957), 4.2.69–72.

CHAPTER SEVEN

1. Virginia Woolf, *The Common Reader,* 1st series, ed. Andrew McNeillie (New York: Harvest/HBJ, 1984), 103. Subsequent citations will appear parenthetically. Macaulay's assertion appears in his review of Lucy Aikin's *Life and Writings of Joseph Addison* in the *Edinburgh Review,* July 1843, reprinted in *Addison and Steele: The Critical Heritage,* ed. Edward A. Bloom and Lillian D. Bloom (London: Routledge and Kegan Paul, 1980), 409–42.

2. Mikhail Bakhtin, *The Dialogic Imagination,* ed. Michael Holquist, trans. Caryl Emerson and Michael Holquist (Austin: University of Texas Press, 1981), 355, 321. Subsequent citations will appear parenthetically.

3. This holds true too for the original Russian term *byt* ("being"), for which *everyday life* is the translators' equivalent.

4. These included Clarinda's journal "reproduced" in the *Spectator* (no. 323) and two parodic pamphlets purporting to have been written by Swift: *An Hue and Cry after Dr. S——t* (London, 1714) and *Dr. S——t's Real Diary* (London, 1715). See Lorna Martens's "Bibliography of Diary Fiction" in *The Diary Novel,* 274–81.

5. Paul Alkon, *Defoe and Fictional Time* (Athens: University of Georgia Press, 1979), 163. The assumption derives from two groundbreaking studies of Defoe's debt to spiritual autobiography: J. Paul Hunter's *The Reluctant Pilgrim,* and G. A. Starr, *Defoe and Spiritual Autobiography* (Princeton: Princeton University Press, 1965). It is striking, though, that while Hunter and Starr devote whole sections to the Puritan diary as one of a cluster of traditions underlying *Crusoe,* neither critic explicitly claims the direct causal relation with Crusoe's journal that Alkon and others subsequently assume.

6. Hunter, *Reluctant Pilgrim,* 85. Further considerations of the centrality (and persistent re-enactment) of the conversion experience in Puritan autobiography appear in Baird Tipson, "The Routinized Piety of Thomas Shepard's Diary," *Early American Literature* 13 (1978): 64–80; and Bruce Tucker, "Joseph Sewall's Diary and the Rhythm of Puritan Spirituality," *Early American Literature* 22 (1987): 3–18.

7. See Dewey Ganzel, "Chronology in *Robinson Crusoe,*" *Philological Quarterly* 40.4 (Oc-

tober 1961): 495–512; Homer O. Brown, "The Displaced Self in the Novels of Daniel Defoe," *ELH* 38.4 (December 1971): 562–90; Paul Goetsch, "The First Day on the Island: *Robinson Crusoe* and the Problem of Coherence," in *Modes of Narrative*, ed. Reingard M. Nischik and Barbara Korte (Würzburg: Königshausen und Neumann, 1990), 191–202.

8. Damrosch, *God's Plot and Man's Stories*, 194.

9. Thompson, "Time, Work-Discipline," 357, 358.

10. G. M., *The Inrichment of the Weald of Kent*, 10th edition (1660). Cited in Thompson, 359, n. 2.

11. Michel de Certeau, *The Practice of Everyday Life*, trans. Steven Randall (Berkeley: University of California Press, 1988), 136. Subsequent citations will appear parenthetically.

12. Richard Braverman, too, reads this passage as pivotal: "The history of Crusoe's island . . . only properly dates from the beginning of the journal, which marks the actual moment of creation, or ordering, on the island." "Crusoe's Legacy," *Studies in the Novel*, 18.1 (Spring 1986):1–26, 14.

13. Crusoe runs out of ink in 1660 (a year into his journal). His first chance at revision would come in 1688, with his rescue from the island. Those who read the book when it first appeared in 1719 might well assume a more recent revision (Crusoe, born in 1632, would now be eighty-seven).

14. Oddly enough, these illness entries begot the first notable tradition in diary fiction after the *Spectator's*, a small trickle of texts in which a solitary shipwrecked diarist writes the slow process of his own starvation; in one case the diary enacts death by ending, Sterne- and Joyce-like, in the middle of a sentence. See *An Authentic Relation of the Many Hardships and Sufferings of a Dutch Sailor* (London: George Faulkner, 1728) and *The Just Vengeance of Heaven Exemplify'd in a Journal Lately Found by Captain Mawson* (London, 1730).

15. Hunter, *Reluctant Pilgrim*, 148–55.

16. The premise that Defoe always sought to fabricate seamlessly persuasive fictions that his readers would take as simple fact underlies, in different ways, the researches of Arthur Secord's *Studies in the Narrative Method of Defoe* (Urbana: University of Illinois Press, 1924) and *Robert Drury's Journal and Other Studies* (Urbana: University of Illinois Press, 1961); and Lennard Davis's "Defoe: Lies as Truth," in *Factual Fictions* (New York: Columbia University Press, 1983), 154–73. David Blewett pays close attention to those features of Defoe's writing that may have signaled fiction rather than truth to his initial audience in *Defoe's Art of Fiction* (Toronto: University of Toronto Press, 1979).

17. See, for example, Pat Rogers, *Robinson Crusoe* (London: George Allen and Unwin, 1979), 118: "As for the journal, . . . its most conspicuous feature is its strict redundance."

18. The strongest concentration of such observations occurs in the chapter on "Tempo" in Alkon's *Defoe and Fictional Time* (207–25).

19. Daniel Defoe, *A Journal of the Plague Year*, ed. Louis Landa (London: Oxford University Press, 1969), 1. Subsequent citations will appear parenthetically.

20. H. F.'s injunction that his private meditations remain private conjures up the possibility of a second stage of redaction, performed by an external editor working on the text. Defoe explicitly realizes this possibility only once in the text, as I discuss below (pp. 242–43).

21. Daniel Defoe, *Serious Reflections during the Life and Surprising Adventures of Robinson Crusoe* (London, 1720), 1.2. Subsequent citations will appear parenthetically.

22. *Spectator* 69; 1.292. As it happens, this is one of the few specific numbers of the *Spectator* for which Defoe's reading is explicitly documented: he spends an entire number of the *Review* responding to it (*A Review of the State of the British Nation* 8.30 [2 June 1711]).

23. Rogers, *Robinson Crusoe*, 107.

308   Notes to pp. 245 – 53

24. Roland Barthes, "The Reality Effect," in *French Literary Theory Today*, ed. Tzvetan Todorov, trans. R. Carter (Cambridge: Cambridge University Press, 1982), 11 – 17.

25. Henry Fielding, *The History of Tom Jones, a Foundling*, ed. Fredson Bowers, introduction and commentary by Martin C. Battestin, 2 vols. (Oxford: Clarendon Press, 1975), 1.xxxvi–xxxviii, and 368, n. 1.

26. Martin C. Battestin, appendix on "The Time-Scheme of *Amelia*" in his edition of Henry Fielding's *Amelia* (Oxford: Clarendon Press, 1983), 539.

27. Nonetheless, such timing did not undo the "isolation effect" that Defoe had pioneered. Sterne, for example, simply turns the temporal arrow of isolation in the opposite direction: Tristram devotes nearly all his narrative energies to reconstituting—at length and with a particularity that surpasses any known diary—the distant days and lives of friends and relations now dead: mother, father, Yorick, Uncle Toby. In a sense he reads them as we read H. F. In fact Defoe accomplishes a comparable gesture, couched as tacit autobiography rather than obvious fiction, in the many narratives he sets in the mid-seventeenth century. Like Tristram he returns repeatedly to the world of his vanished forebears. The character and possibly the history of H. F. is probably based, for example, on his father's brother Henry Foe. To that extent at least, H. F. is Defoe's "Uncle Toby," and Defoe the most Shandean novelist of the century besides Sterne himself.

28. *The Early Journals and Letters of Fanny Burney*, ed. Lars E. Troide. 3 vols. (Kingston: McGill-Queen's University Press, 1988 –), 1.1 – 2. Subsequent citations to the *EJL* will appear parenthetically.

29. Johnson double genders journal-keeping in the same way later in his correspondence with Thrale. Two years after the tour, in a period when Johnson was again writing often to Thrale, she apparently suggested that her pleasure in his constant letters would surpass his own. Johnson disagreed: "Do you keep my letters? Never surely was I such a writer before [i.e., of short, closely consecutive letters]. I am not of your opinion that I shall not like to read them hereafter" (*Letters* 2.260). Johnson immediately proceeds to urge Thrale to be "such a writer" too—but of a journal rather than a letter: "Why you should suppose yourself not desirous hereafter to read the history of your own mind I do not see." The diction here echoes that in which he admitted to Boswell that he "never could persevere" in journal-keeping ("The great thing to be recorded . . . is the state of your own mind") and anticipates the phrasing in which he will gender journal-keeping ("a man loves to review his own mind") in the conversation with Boswell, Thrale, and Trimlestown.

30. *Johnsonian Miscellanies*, ed. G. Birkbeck Hill, 2 vols. (Oxford: Clarendon Press, 1897), 1.258.

31. Thrale would soon incorporate these manuscripts into a "printed book" of her own—her edition of *Letters to and from the Late Samuel Johnson* (1788); in the passage from the *Anecdotes*, she is crying wares that she will soon sell.

32. Hester Thrale Piozzi, *Thraliana*, ed. Katherine Balderston, 2nd edition, 2 vols. (Oxford: Clarendon Press, 1951), 1.257. Felicity Nussbaum quotes this passage at the start of her chapter on Thrale in *The Autobiographical Subject* (201), slightly misrepresenting it as a comment on "Boswell's method to live no more than he could record" (a method Boswell articulated in the *Hypochondriack* five years after Thrale wrote the entry).

33. *Thraliana* 1.467, xi. Thrale's collection of French *Anas* eventually increased to 31 (467, n. 3).

34. I say "apparently" because the journal's first two months are unavailable for scrutiny, having been (in Troide's words) "cut away and destroyed" (*EJL* 1.2). I discuss their disappearance later in this chapter.

35. For the most thorough investigations of the ways in which family pressures impinged on Burney's writing, see Margaret Anne Doody, *Frances Burney: The Life in the Works* (New Brunswick: Rutgers University Press, 1988); Julia Epstein, *The Iron Pen: Frances Burney and the Politics of Women's Writing* (Bristol: Bristol Classical Press, 1989); and Catherine Gallagher, *Nobody's Story: The Vanishing Acts of Women Writers in the Marketplace 1670–1820* (Berkeley: University of California Press, 1994), 203–56.

36. The permanence of the record is of course a precondition for the kind of publicity with which Burney's father and friend both threaten her—there must be written sheets to be "read" or "marketed"—but in Young's opening argument such publication is at best a secondary (and unmentioned) effect; the primary danger is permanence itself.

37. Like Pepys's diary, Burney's journal letters to Susanna were the product (often considerably delayed) of an even more continuous textual practice, which she explained in one of them: "I shall now begin a new pacquet [of journal letters] from my Pocket Book memorandums, which are minutely faithful, and which I set down every morning from the events . . . of the preceding Day." Diary MS. 3.2177, 10–12 August 1786. Quoted in Joyce Hemlow et. al., eds., *Journals and Letters, 1791–1840*, 12 vols. (Oxford: Oxford University Press, 1972–84), 1.xxxii, n. 1. Citations to the *JL* will appear parenthetically.

38. The language in which Crisp had earlier reiterated his request for Burney's Teignmouth journal deserves quoting, for it indicates both his peremptoriness and her resistance: "Now Fan, I do by no means allow of your reconsideration, & revocation of your Tingmouth Journal; on the contrary,—I demand it, & claim your promise . . ." (*EJL* 1.320). Crisp's diction in a later letter, when discussing the journal letters Burney writes to him, implies a similar tension between his desire and her resistance: "You Young Devil You, You know in your Conscience I devour greedily your Journalizing letters, & You once promis'd they would be *Weekly* Journals [i.e., more frequent than at present]; tho' now you fight off, both in your Declarations & your Practice—I desire You would reform both . . ." (*EJL* 2.108).

39. Margaret Doody observes that even in the journal letters to her cherished confidante Susanna, Burney's self-expression is still "somewhat censored" (*Burney* 177).

40. In her actual letters to Susanna (who was in on the secret of *Evelina*) Burney exulted in the stratagem: "Do you know I write to *you* every Evening, while the family play at Cards? The folks here often marvel at your ingratitude in sending me so few returns in kind" (*EJL* 2.221).

41. Frances Burney, *Evelina, or the History of a Young Lady's Entrance into the World*, ed. Edward A. Bloom (Oxford: Oxford University Press, 1968), 23–24. Subsequent citations will appear parenthetically.

42. Villars writes these words on September 28; Evelina reads them on October 1; she hears and delights in Lord Orville's proposal on October 6.

43. Burney compounds the effect by a further detail in Evelina's account to Villars of receiving his letter: "While we were engaged in a most delightful conversation, a servant brought me a letter, which he told me had, by some accident, been mislaid. Judge my feelings, when I saw, my dearest Sir, your revered handwriting!" (403). Evelina proceeds to expatiate on her reverence, but this "accident"—the only one that remains unexplained in a novel minutely attentive to textual transactions—has created a delay that gives the heroine even more time to act on her own and choose for herself. The delay is gratuitous within the novel's structure but congruent with its use of timing as an index of autonomy.

44. Madame D'Arblay, *Memoirs of Doctor Burney*, 3 vols. (London: Edward Moxon, 1832), 2.130. The language of anxiety in which the *Memoirs* couches this episode resonates remarkably with that of Evelina's first letter to Villars: Burney wondered, she writes, "whether it

were right to allow herself such an amusement . . . unknown to her father? She had never taken any step without the sanction of his permission" (2.130). *velina's* language is nearly identical: "Ought I to form a wish that has not your sanction?"

45. Within the trajectory of Burney's writing (already abundant at twenty-five) the publication of *Evelina* represents a counter-reversal. When Burney began her journal to "Nobody" at the age of fifteen she had already completed, and burned, a novel about Evelina's mother, *The History of Caroline Evelyn. Evelina*, then, represents a resumption of novel writing after almost ten years of diarizing. Burney's modulation among narrative genres displays a certain calendrical symmetry, unfolding in five-year stages: she burns the *History* and begins her journal to "Nobody" at the age of fifteen; she writes her first journal letter to Susanna at the age of twenty; she publishes *Evelina* at twenty-five, ten years after destroying the *History*. Certain biographical details suggest that Burney was not only alert to such symmetries, but in some instances actually managed them in such a way as to suggest that she was trying to make time itself a tool and an index of autonomy, of her authority over her own life. She burned her early manuscripts, for example, in a solitary ceremony on her fifteenth birthday. After the death of her sister Susanna on 6 January 1800, Burney kept the day as a solemn anniversary; she died on that date exactly four decades later, after a long illness. Her biographers surmise a determination on her part to fill out the calendrical pattern (Doody, *Burney*, 381; Hemlow, *The History of Fanny Burney* [Oxford: Oxford University Press, 1958]), 490.

46. Burney's increasing authority was embodied in other material ways as well. With her third novel, the relations for her among writing, privacy, and power shift once again: she composes *Camilla* in order to earn money for the family she has newly started as wife and mother, and she names the house built with that novel's proceeds "Camilla Cottage." Writing has by now become a primary household task, not equivocal, secret, or tucked into temporal interstices.

47. Frances Burney, *Diary and Letters of Madame D'Arblay*, ed. Charlotte Barrett (London: Henry Colburn, 1842–46), 2.195. Subsequent citations to *DL* will appear parenthetically.

48. *Camilla*, ed. Edward A. Bloom and Lillian D. Bloom (Oxford: Oxford University Press, 1983), xvii.

49. Anonymous review of the *Diary and Letters of Madame D'Arblay, Vol. 3, Athenaeum* 756 (23 April 1842): 355.

50. William Hazlitt, review of *The Wanderer: or, Female Difficulties, Edinburgh Review* 24.48 (February 1815), 337.

51. Mallon, author of *A Book of One's Own: People and Their Diaries* (New York: Ticknor and Fields, 1984), made this remark in an interview with Susan Stamberg on National Public Radio's *All Things Considered*, November 19, 1984.

52. Frances Burney, *The Wanderer*, ed. Margaret Doody (Oxford: Oxford World Classics, 1991), 873. Subsequent citations will appear parenthetically.

EPILOGUE

1. Sir Walter Scott, review of *Memoirs of Samuel Pepys*, ed. Richard, Lord Braybrook (1825), *The Quarterly Review*, 33.66 (1826): 290–314; quotation 297–98.

2. Of course Scott wrote from extensive antiquarian experience, not only with the Border ballads by which he made his reputation (in *Minstrelsy of the Scottish Border*) but also as an editor of seventeenth-century diaries: in 1806 he had produced the *Original Memoirs written during the Great Civil War* by Henry Slingsby and Captain Hodgson, and in 1806 a new edition

of Defoe's *Memoirs of Captain Carleton* (which Scott believed to be the authentic work of Carleton himself).

3. *Edinburgh Review*, 75 (1843), reprinted in T. Babington Macaulay, *Critical and Miscellaneous Essays* (New York: Appleton, 1865), 5.13–67; quotation 13–14.

4. Hemlow's introduction to the *Journals and Letters* (1.xxix–lix) provides the fullest account available of Burney's editorial practices, as well as those of Charlotte Barrett and subsequent editors.

5. Braybrooke's subsequent career as Pepys's editor registers the trajectory of this trend, and possibly the pressures of Scott's particular critique. In the preface to his third edition (1848) Braybrooke announces that he has expanded the diary text in deference to a conviction widespread among his readership that he had previously "used the pruning-knife with too much freedom" (Scott's metaphor two decades earlier had apparently struck and stuck). The demand for further expansion persisted throughout the nineteenth century and into the twentieth; Robert Latham details its history and its results in the introduction to his and Matthews's edition, 1.lxxviii–xcvi.

6. By changing Shakespeare's "chronicler" to "character," Scott adds a substitution of his own, which resonates with his argument about Pepys (that his character is what makes the chronicle valuable) as Johnson's error resonates with his point about Boswell (that his "faithfulness" makes the record full).

7. Rosenwald, *Emerson*, 18.

Index